Arthritis Sourcebook

Basic Consumer Health Information about Specific Forms of Arthritis ~~and Related Disorders, Including~~
Rheumatoid Ar ...
gia Rheumati ...
pathies, Juven ...
Ankylosing Sp ...
Medical, Surgi ...
and Including ...
and Stress ...

Edited by Alla... 2. $78.

Burns Sourcebook

Basic Information about Various Types of Burns and Scalds, Including Flame, Heat, Electrical, Chemical, and Sun; Along with Short- and Long-Term Treat- ...ction, *Plastic Surgery,* ...rst Aid

...es. 1999. 0-7808-0204-

616.8
BRA
Brain disorders sourcebook

1st Edition

...*pes, Symptoms, Diag-* ...*s, Including Statistics* ...*dwide and the Risks* ...*gens and Activities*

...s. 1990. 1-55888-888-8.

Back & N... Sourcebo...

Basic Informa... *Spinal Cord a*... *practic Treatm*... *and Rehabilit*... *Back Trouble*...

Edited by Kare... 0. $78.

"The strength... **mat. Recomm**...
— *Reference*...

...ge. **Useful for patients,** ...als, **and librarians."** ...*o Reference Books, '96*

...l **professional in mind.** ...interested **in patient** ...der adding the *Cancer* ...his **compact collection** ...avaluable **tool for help-** ...es **and friends to take** ...e **many difficulties of**

...*Quarterly, Winter '91*

...echnical reader ... an ...eral **reader trying to** ...ancer."
...*e Books Annual, '91*

Blood & ... Disorde...

Basic Inform... *Anemias, Le*... *tory Disorde*... *mia, Sickle-*... *philia, Von W*... *Along with a*... *Blood Supply*... *Further Help*...

Edited by Kar... 1998. 0-7808-...

...ature **and very com-** ...**for both the general** ...." — *Choice, Oct '90*

...ook,

...Forms and Stages of *...mary and Secondary* *...ervous, Lymphatic,* *...ointestinal Systems,* *...l and Demographic* *...rategies for Coping*

...pages. 1996. 0-7808-

Brain Di...

Basic Consur... *Epilepsy, Am*... *Gehrig's Disea*... *Cerebral Pals*... *More; Along*... *Rehabilitation Options, Coping Strategies, Reports on Current Research Initiatives, a Glossary, and Resource Listings for Additional Help and Information*

Edited by Karen Bellenir. 600 pages. 1999. 0-7808-0229-2. $78.

...rce **for patients with** ...ir **families. The dia-**logue **is simple, direct, and comprehensive. Highly recommended for patients and families to aid in their understanding of cancer and its treatment."**
— *Booklist Health Sciences Supplement, Oct '97*

"The amount of factual and useful information is extensive. The writing is very clear, geared to general readers. Recommended for all levels." — *Choice, Jan '97*

Continues next page

DATE DUE

Cancer Sourcebook, 3rd Edition

Basic Information about Major Forms and Stages of Cancer, Featuring Facts about Primary and Secondary Tumors of the Respiratory, Nervous, Lymphatic, Circulatory, Skeletal, and Gastrointestinal Systems, and Specific Organs, Statistical and Demographic Data, Treatment Options, and Strategies for Coping

Edited by Edward J. Prucha. 800 pages. 1999. 0-7808-0227-6. $78.

Cancer Sourcebook for Women

Basic Information about Specific Forms of Cancer That Affect Women, Featuring Facts about Breast Cancer, Cervical Cancer, Ovarian Cancer, Cancer of the Uterus and Uterine Sarcoma, Cancer of the Vagina, and Cancer of the Vulva; Statistical and Demographic Data; Treatments, Self-Help Management Suggestions, and Current Research Initiatives

Edited by Allan R. Cook and Peter D. Dresser. 524 pages. 1996. 0-7808-0076-1. $78.

". . . written in easily understandable, non-technical language. Recommended for public libraries or hospital and academic libraries that collect patient education or consumer health materials."
— *Medical Reference Services Quarterly, Spring '97*

"Would be of value in a consumer health library. . . . written with the health care consumer in mind. Medical jargon is at a minimum, and medical terms are explained in clear, understandable sentences."
— *Bulletin of the MLA, Oct '96*

"The availability under one cover of all these pertinent publications, grouped under cohesive headings, makes this certainly a most useful sourcebook."
— *Choice, Jun '96*

"Presents a comprehensive knowledge base for general readers. Men and women both benefit from the gold mine of information nestled between the two covers of this book. Recommended."
— *Academic Library Book Review, Summer '96*

"This timely book is highly recommended for consumer health and patient education collections in all libraries."
— *Library Journal, Apr '96*

Cancer Sourcebook for Women, 2nd Edition

Basic Information about Specific Forms of Cancer That Affect Women, Featuring Facts about Breast Cancer, Cervical Cancer, Ovarian Cancer, Cancer of the Uterus and Uterine Sarcoma, Cancer of the Vagina, and Cancer of the Vulva, Statistical and Demographic Data, Treatments, Self-Help Management Suggestions, and Current Research Initiatives

Edited by Edward J. Prucha. 600 pages. 1999. 0-7808-0226-8. $78.

Cardiovascular Diseases & Disorders Sourcebook

Basic Information about Cardiovascular Diseases and Disorders, Featuring Facts about the Cardiovascular System, Demographic and Statistical Data, Descriptions of Pharmacological and Surgical Interventions, Lifestyle Modifications, and a Special Section Focusing on Heart Disorders in Children

Edited by Karen Bellenir and Peter D. Dresser. 683 pages. 1995. 0-7808-0032-X. $78.

". . . comprehensive format provides an extensive overview on this subject."
— *Choice, Jun '96*

". . . an easily understood, complete, up-to-date resource. This well executed public health tool will make valuable information available to those that need it most, patients and their families. The typeface, sturdy non-reflective paper, and library binding add a feel of quality found wanting in other publications. Highly recommended for academic and general libraries. "
— *Academic Library Book Review, Summer '96*

Communication Disorders Sourcebook

Basic Information about Deafness and Hearing Loss, Speech and Language Disorders, Voice Disorders, Balance and Vestibular Disorders, and Disorders of Smell, Taste, and Touch

Edited by Linda M. Ross. 533 pages. 1996. 0-7808-0077-X. $78.

"This is skillfully edited and is a welcome resource for the layperson. It should be found in every public and medical library."
— *Booklist Health Sciences Supplement, Oct '97*

Congenital Disorders Sourcebook

Basic Information about Disorders Acquired during Gestation, Including Spina Bifida, Hydrocephalus, Cerebral Palsy, Heart Defects, Craniofacial Abnormalities, Fetal Alcohol Syndrome, and More, Along with Current Treatment Options and Statistical Data

Edited by Karen Bellenir. 607 pages. 1997. 0-7808-0205-5. $78.

"Recommended reference source." — *Booklist, Oct '97*

Consumer Issues in Health Care Sourcebook

Basic Information about Health Care Fundamentals and Related Consumer Issues, Including Exams and Screening Tests, Physician Specialties, Choosing a Doctor, Using Prescription and Over-the-Counter Medications Safely, Avoiding Health Scams, Managing Common Health Risks in the Home, Care Options for Chronically or Terminally Ill Patients, and a List of Resources for Obtaining Help and Further Information

Edited by Karen Bellenir. 592 pages. 1998. 0-7808-0221-7. $78.

Continues in back end sheets

Health Reference Series

First Edition

Brain Disorders SOURCEBOOK

Basic Consumer Health Information about Strokes, Epilepsy, Amyotrophic Lateral Sclerosis (ALS/Lou Gehrig's Disease), Parkinson's Disease, Brain Tumors, Cerebral Palsy, Headache, Tourette Syndrome, and More; Along with Statistical Data, Treatment and Rehabilitation Options, Coping Strategies, Reports on Current Research Initiatives, a Glossary, and Resource Listings for Additional Help and Information

Edited by
Karen Bellenir

Omnigraphics, Inc.

Penobscot Building / Detroit, MI 48226

Bibliographic Note

Because this page cannot legibly accommodate all the copyright notices, the Bibliographic Note portion of the Preface constitutes an extension of the copyright notice.

Beginning with books published in 1999, each volume of the *Health Reference Series* on a new topic will be individually titled and called a "First Edition." Subsequent updates will carry sequential edition numbers. To help avoid confusion and to provide maximum flexibility in our ability to respond to informational needs, the practice of consecutively numbering each volume will be discontinued.

Edited by Karen Bellenir

Health Reference Series

Karen Bellenir, *Series Editor*
Peter D. Dresser, *Managing Editor*
Joan Margeson, *Research Associate*
Dawn Matthews, *Verification Assistant*
Margaret Mary Missar, *Research Coordinator*
Jenifer Swanson, *Research Associate*

Omnigraphics, Inc.

Matthew P. Barbour, *Vice President, Operations*
Laurie Lanzen Harris, *Vice President, Editorial Director*
Peter E. Ruffner, *Vice President, Administration*
James A. Sellgren, *Executive Vice President, Operations and Finance*
Jane J. Steele, *Marketing Consultant*

Frederick G. Ruffner, Jr., Publisher

Library of Congress Cataloging-in-Publication Data

Brain disorders sourcebook ; basic consumer health information about strokes, epilepsy, amyotrophic lateral sclerosis (ALS/Lou Gehrig's disease) Parkinson's disease, brain tumors, cerebral palsy, headache, Tourette syndrome, and more ; along with statistical data, treatment and rehabilitation options, coping strategies, reports on current initiatives, a glossary, and resource listings for additional help and information / edited by Karen Bellenir.
    p. cm. — (Health reference series)
    Includes bibliographical references and index.
    ISBN 0-7808-0229-2 (alk. paper)
    1. Brain — Diseases Popular works. I. Belenir, Karen. II. Series ; Health reference series (Unnumbered)
RC386.B726   1999   99-15539
616.8 — dc21   CIP

∞

This book is printed on acid-free paper meeting the ANSI Z39.48 Standard. The infinity symbol that appears above indicates that the paper in this book meets that standard.

Printed in the United States

Table of Contents

Part III: Seizure Disorders

Part IV: Amyotrophic Lateral Sclerosis (ALS)/Lou Gehrig's Disease

Part V: Parkinson's Disease

Part VI: Other Brain Disorders

Part VII: Additional Help and Information

Preface

About This Book

The brain controls everything the human body does. It enables people to perform such voluntary activities as walking and talking. It regulates automatic processes like breathing and digesting food. It is responsible for emotions, thoughts, and memory. When diseases or disorders strike the brain, the results can be devastating. For example:

- Strokes, also called "brain attacks," are the most common cause of adult disability in the United States. In addition, stroke ranks as the third leading killer, behind heart disease and cancer. An estimated half million Americans suffer strokes each year.

- Epilepsy, a group of more than 40 different conditions that cause seizures, affects 2.5 million Americans. It can have profound social and medical consequences.

- Cerebral palsy, a disorder that disrupts the brain's ability to adequately control movement and posture, afflicts more than 500,000 Americans.

- Chronic headaches, perhaps the most ubiquitous of all brain disorders, plague an estimated 45 million Americans. For at least half of these people, the problem is severe and sometimes disabling. It can also be costly: headache sufferers make over 8 million visits a year to doctors' offices. Migraine victims alone lose over 157 million workdays because of headache pain.

This *Sourcebook* provides basic consumer information about the complex issues surrounding brain disorders. Using documents written for lay audiences, it explains the causes and treatments for such disorders as stroke, epilepsy, amyotrophic lateral sclerosis (ALS/Lou Gehrig's disease), Parkinson's disease, benign and malignant brain tumors, cerebral palsy, headaches, Tourette syndrome, and more. Readers will learn to recognize symptoms, understand diagnostic tests, and become acquainted with various treatment options and coping strategies. A glossary helps define the terminology used by health-care providers. A directory of organizational resources with up-to-date contact information, including websites and E-mail addresses, and a list of other reading material provide sources of additional help and information.

Two other volumes of the *Health Reference Series* contain information closely related to the topics in this book. Readers seeking more detailed information on traumatic brain injury will find an in-depth treatment in *Head Trauma Sourcebook*. People looking for information about Alzheimer's disease and other dementias, including multi-infarct dementia, AIDS-related dementia, alcoholic dementia, Huntington's disease, Binswanger's disease, metachromatic leukodystrophy, Pick's disease, corticobasal degeneration, delirium, and confusional states, will find information about warning signs, symptoms, treatments, and current research initiatives in *Alzheimer's Disease Sourcebook, Second Edition*.

How to Use This Book

This book is divided into parts and chapters. Parts focus on broad areas of interest. Chapters are devoted to single topics within a part.

Part I: The Human Brain includes an anatomical overview of the brain and its function. Individual chapters describe some common tests used to diagnose and monitor brain disorders. Information is also provided for patients and family members considering brain or brain tissue donation for research.

Part II: Stroke describes the differences between ischemic strokes, which occur when a blood vessel in the brain or neck is blocked, and hemorrhagic strokes, which occur when a blood vessel bursts. It also presents the results of current research in stroke prevention and post-stroke rehabilitation.

Part III: Seizure Disorders presents information about epilepsy and other types of disorders characterized by seizures. It describes different types of seizures and their causes, first aid suggestions, newly developed drugs, and other treatment issues, including topics of concern for pregnant women with epilepsy.

Part IV: Amyotrophic Lateral Sclerosis (ALS)/Lou Gehrig's Disease provides information about the brain's ability to control voluntary movement, how it is diminished in ALS, and what treatment options are available for ALS patients.

Part V: Parkinson's Disease describes the portion of the brain called the substantia nigra and its role in the production of dopamine, a brain chemical necessary to produce smooth, purposeful muscle activity. Early warning signs of Parkinson's Disease are presented along with information about disease progression and management.

Part VI: Other Brain Disorders includes basic consumer information on such disorders as benign and malignant brain tumors, cerebral palsy, headache, narcolepsy, neurotrauma, Tourette syndrome, and tuberous sclerosis.

Part VII: Additional Help and Information includes a glossary, a directory of resources, and a list of additional reading for patients with brain disorders, caregivers, and family members.

Bibliographic Note

This volume contains documents and excerpts from publications issued by the following U.S. government agencies: Agency for Health Care Policy and Research (AHCPR); National Cancer Institute (NCI); National Center for Research Resources (NCRR); National Heart, Lung, and Blood Institute (NHLBI); National Institute of Neurological and Communicative Disorders and Stroke (NINDS); National Institutes of Health (NIH) Consensus Development Program; U.S. Department of Health and Human Services (DHHS); and the U.S. Food and Drug Administration (FDA).

In addition, this volume contains copyrighted documents from the following organizations: American Academy of Neurology; American Association of Neurological Surgeons; American Parkinson Disease Association; Amyotrophic Lateral Sclerosis Association (ALSA); Brain Tissue Resource Center at McLean Hospital (Boston); Brain Tumor Foundation of Canada; Family Caregiver Alliance; Springhouse Corporation; State University of New York at Buffalo; and Washington University at St. Louis/Comprehensive Epilepsy Program. Articles from the following journals are also included: *American Family Physician; Clinician Reviews; Drug Topics; Geriatrics;* and *On the Brain.*

Full citation information is provided on the first page of each chapter. Every effort has been made to secure all necessary rights to reprint the copyrighted material. If any omissions have been made, please contact Omnigraphics to make corrections for future editions.

Acknowledgements

In addition to the many organizations listed above that provided the material presented in this volume, special thanks are due to researchers Joan Margeson, Margaret Mary Missar, and Jenifer Swanson, permissions specialist Maria Franklin, verification assistant Dawn Matthews, indexer Edward J. Prucha, and document engineer Bruce Bellenir.

Note from the Editor

This book is part of Omnigraphics' *Health Reference Series.* The series provides basic consumer health information about a broad range of medical concerns. It is not intended to serve as a tool for diagnosing illness, in prescribing treatments, or as a substitute for the physician/patient relationship. All persons concerned about medical symptoms or the possibility of disease are encouraged to seek professional care from an appropriate health care provider.

Our Advisory Board

The *Health Reference Series* is reviewed by an Advisory Board comprised of librarians from public, academic, and medical libraries. We would like to thank the following board members for providing guidance to the development of this series:

Nancy Bulgarelli
William Beaumont Hospital Library, Royal Oak, MI

Karen Morgan
Mardigian Library, University of Michigan, Dearborn, MI

Rosemary Orlando
St. Clair Shores Public Library, St. Clair Shores, MI

Health Reference Series *Update Policy*

The inaugural book in the *Health Reference Series* was the first edition of *Cancer Sourcebook* published in 1992. Since then, the *Series* has been enthusiastically received by librarians and in the medical community. In order to maintain the standard of providing high-quality health information for the lay person, the editorial staff at Omnigraphics felt it was necessary to implement a policy of updating volumes when warranted.

Medical researchers have been making tremendous strides, and the challenge to stay current with the most recent advances is one our editors take seriously. Each decision to update a volume will be made on an individual basis. Some of the considerations will include how much new information is available and the feedback we receive from people who use the books. If there's a topic you would like to see added to the update list, or an area of medical concern you feel has not been adequately addressed, please write to:

Editor
Health Reference Series
Omnigraphics, Inc.
2500 Penobscot Bldg.
Detroit, MI 48226

The commitment to providing on-going coverage of important medical developments has also led to some technical changes in the *Health Reference Series*. Beginning with books published in 1999, each volume on a new topic will be individually titled and called a "First Edition." Subsequent updates will carry sequential edition numbers. To help avoid confusion and to provide maximum flexibility in our ability to respond to informational needs, the practice of consecutively numbering each volume will be discontinued.

Part One

The Human Brain

Chapter 1

Anatomy of the Brain

Introduction

The brain serves many important functions. It gives meaning to things that happen in the world surrounding us.

We have five senses: sight, smell, hearing, touch, and taste. Through these senses, our brain receives messages, often many at one time. It puts together the messages in a way that has meaning for us, and can store that information in our memory. For example: An oven burner has been left on. By accident we touch the burner. Our brain receives a message from skin sensors on our hand. Instead of leaving our hand on the burner, our brain gives meaning to the signal and tells us to quickly remove our hand from the burner. Heat has been felt. If we were to leave our hand on the burner, pain and injury would result. As adults, we may have had a childhood memory of touching something hot that resulted in pain or watching someone else who has done so. Our brain uses that memory in a time of need and guides our actions and reactions in a harmful situation.

With the use of our senses: sight, smell, touch, taste, and hearing, the brain receives many messages at one time. It can select those which are most important. Our brain controls our thoughts, memory and speech, the movements of our arms and legs and the function of

Excerpted from *Brain Tumor Patient Resource Handbook, Adult Version, Third Edition,* ©1996 Brain Tumor Foundation of Canada, 650 Waterloo Street, Suite 100, London, Ontario N6B 2R4, (800) 265-5106, website: http://www.btfc.org; reprinted with permission.

many organs within our body. It also determines how we respond to stressful situations (i.e. writing of an exam, loss of a job, birth of a child, illness, etc.) by regulating our heart and breathing rate. The brain is an organized structure, divided into many parts that serve specific and important functions.

Understanding the Nervous System

The nervous system is commonly divided into the central nervous system and the peripheral nervous system. The central nervous system is made up of the brain, its cranial nerves, and the spinal cord. The peripheral nervous system is composed of the spinal nerves that branch from the spinal cord and the autonomous nervous system (divided into the sympathetic and parasympathetic nervous system). It controls our response to stressful situations.

For the purpose of this chapter, we will speak specifically about some of the functions and parts of the brain. This is not to say that the brain functions alone. The central and peripheral nervous systems play many interconnected and complex roles.

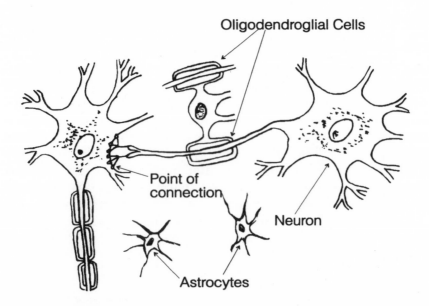

Figure 1.1. Brain Cells. Neurons are interconnected and send messages from one neuron to another.

A Microscopic View of the Brain

The brain is made up of two types of cells: neurons and neuroglia. The neuron is responsible for sending and receiving nerve impulses or signals. Try to picture electrical wiring in your home. An electrical circuit is made up of numerous wires connected in such a way that when a light switch is turned on, a light bulb will beam. A neuron that is excited will transmit its energy to neurons that are within its vicinity. Remember the sequence of events of drawing your hand away from a hot oven burner. A series of excited, interconnected neurons made you withdraw your hand.

The Meninges

The brain is found inside the bony covering called the cranium. The cranium protects the brain from injury. Together, the cranium and bones that protect our face are called the skull.

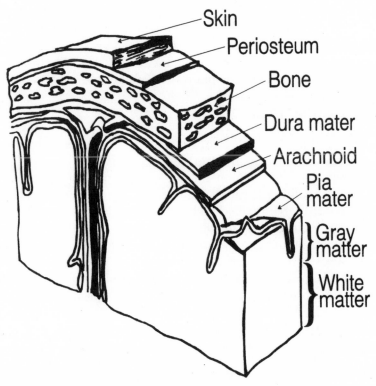

Figure 1.2. *Layers of the Meninges.*

Meninges are three layers of tissue that cover and protect the brain and spinal cord. From the outermost layer inward they are: the dura mater, arachnoid and pia mater.

In the brain, the dura mater is made up of two layers of whitish, inelastic (not stretchy) film or membrane. The outer layer is called the periosteum. An inner layer, the dura, lines the inside of the entire skull and creates little folds or compartments in which parts of the brain are neatly protected and secured. There are two special folds of the dura in the brain, the falx and the tentorium. The falx separates the right and left half of the brain and the tentorium separates the upper and lower parts of the brain.

The second layer of the meninges is the arachnoid. This membrane is thin and delicate and covers the entire brain. There is a space between the dura and the arachnoid membranes that is called the subdural space. The arachnoid is made up of delicate, elastic tissue and blood vessels of different sizes.

The layer of meninges closest to the surface of the brain is called the pia mater. The pia mater has many blood vessels that reach deep into the surface of the brain. The pia, which covers the entire surface of the brain, follows the folds of the brain. The major arteries supplying the brain provide the pia with its blood vessels. The space that separates the arachnoid and the pia is called the subarachnoid space. It is here where the cerebrospinal fluid (discussed next) will flow.

Cerebrospinal Fluid

Cerebrospinal fluid, also known as CSF, is found within the brain and surrounds the brain and the spinal cord. It is a clear, watery substance that helps to cushion the brain and spinal cord from injury. This fluid circulates through channels around the spinal cord and brain, constantly being absorbed and replenished. It is within hollow channels in the brain, called ventricles, where the fluid is produced. A specialized structure within each ventricle, called the choroid plexus, is responsible for the majority of CSF production. The brain normally maintains a balance between the amount of cerebrospinal fluid that is absorbed and the amount that is produced. Often, disruptions in the system occur.

The Ventricular System

The ventricular system is divided into four cavities called ventricles which are connected by a series of holes (called foramen) and tubes.

Two ventricles enclosed in the cerebral hemispheres are called the lateral ventricles (first and second). They each communicate with the third ventricle through a separate opening called the Foramen of Munro. The third ventricle is in the center of the brain and its walls are made up of the thalamus and hypothalamus.

The third ventricle connects with the fourth ventricle through a long tube called the Aqueduct of Sylvius. Cerebrospinal fluid flowing through the fourth ventricle gets around the brain and spinal cord by passing through another series of openings.

The condition "hydrocephalus" may occur when there is a blockage in the pathways through which the fluid normally travels. It may also arise from an overproduction of fluid or a difficulty in absorbing the fluid that is produced. Because the brain is enclosed within the bony skull, the extra fluid, trapped by blocked pathways, has no escape. This extra fluid within the brain will produce increased pressure symptoms: headaches, vomiting, drowsiness and in some cases, confusion.

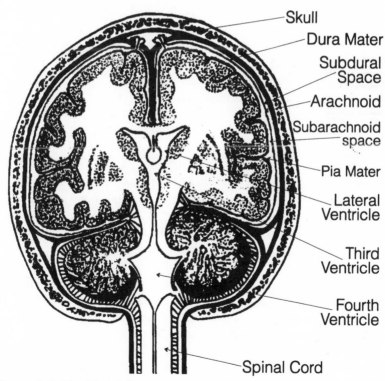

Figure 1.3. The Ventricles.

Structures of the Brain

Cerebrum

The cerebrum, which forms the bulk of the brain, may be divided into two major parts: the right and left cerebral hemispheres. The cerebrum is often a term used to describe the entire brain. There is a fissure or groove that separates the two hemispheres, called the great longitudinal fissure (the falx of the dura is here). The two sides of the brain are joined at the bottom by the corpus callosum. The corpus callosum connects the two halves of the brain and delivers messages from one half of the brain to the other. The surface of the cerebrum (brain) contains billions of neurons and glia that together form the cerebral cortex.

The (cerebral) cortex appears greyish brown in color and is called the "gray matter." The surface of the brain appears wrinkled. The cerebral cortex has small grooves (sulci), larger grooves (fissures), and bulges between the grooves called gyri. Scientists have specific names for the bulges and grooves on the surface of our brain. They serve as landmarks and are used to help isolate very specific regions of the brain. Decades of scientific research have revealed the specific functions of the various regions of the brain. Beneath the cerebral cortex or surface of the brain, connecting fibers between neurons form the "white matter" (appear white in color).

The cerebral hemispheres have several distinct fissures. By finding these landmarks on the surface of a brain, the brain can effectively be divided into pairs of "lobes." Lobes are simply broad regions of the brain. The cerebrum or brain may be divided into pairs of frontal, temporal, parietal, and occipital lobes. To state this in another way, each hemisphere has a frontal, temporal, parietal and occipital lobe (see Figure 1.4). Each lobe may be divided, once again, into areas that serve very specific functions. It must be remembered that each lobe of the brain does not function alone. There are very complex relationships between the lobes of the brain.

Messages within the brain are delivered in many ways. The signals are transported along routes called pathways. Any destruction of brain tissue can disrupt the communication between different parts of the brain. The result will be a loss of function such as speech, ability to read, or ability to follow simple spoken commands. Messages can travel from one bulge on the brain to another (gyri to gyri), from one lobe to another, from one side of the brain to the other, from one lobe of the brain to structures that are found deep in the brain, e.g.

8

thalamus or from the deep structures of the brain to another region in the central nervous system.

Researchers during neurosurgery have stimulated the surface of the brain with an electrode which delivered a very weak electrical shock. It has been found that specific regions of the motor and sensory regions, when electrically stimulated will cause movement or sensation to occur in a very specific part of the body. Touching one side of the brain sends the electrical signals to the other side of the body. If we touched the motor region on the right side of the brain, we would cause the opposite side or the left side of the body to move. Stimulating the left primary motor cortex would cause the right side of the body to move. The messages for movement and sensation will always cross to the other side of the brain and cause the opposite limb to move or feel a sensation. One side of the brain controls the opposite side of the body.

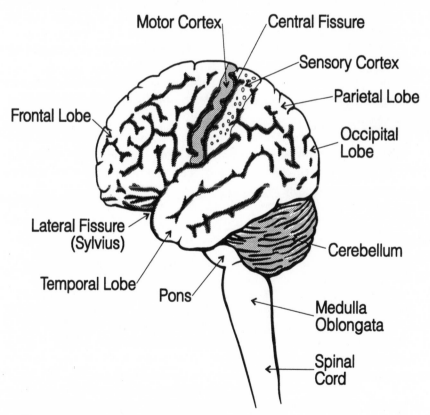

Figure 1.4. *The Lobes of the Brain.*

The following is a summary of the functions of parts of the brain and their location:

Frontal Lobes

The areas that produce movement of parts of the body are found in the primary motor cortex or precentral gyrus. These regions are found in the frontal lobes. The prefrontal cortex plays an important part in our memory, intelligence, concentration, temper, and personality. It helps us set goals, make plans, and judge our priorities.

The premotor cortex is a region found beside the primary motor cortex. It guides our eye and head movements and sense of orientation. Broca's area, important in language production, is found in the frontal lobe, usually on the left side.

Occipital Lobes

These lobes contain regions that contribute to our visual field or how our eyes see the world around us. They help us see light and objects and allow us to recognize and identify them. This region is called the visual cortex. The occipital lobe on the right interprets visual signals from your left visual space, while the left occipital lobe does the same for your right visual space. Damage to one occipital lobe may result in loss of vision in the opposite visual field.

Temporal Lobes

The primary auditory cortex helps us hear sounds and gives sounds their meaning, e.g. the bark of a dog. The temporal lobes are the primary region responsible for memory. It contains Wernicke's area (language and speech functions.)

Parietal Lobes

The parietal lobes interpret, simultaneously, sensory signals received from other areas of the brain such as our vision, hearing, motor, sensory, and memory. Together, memory and the new information that is received give meaning to objects. A furry object touching your skin, that purrs and appears to be your cat, will have a different meaning than a furry object that barks and you see to be a dog.

Hypothalamus

The hypothalamus is a small structure that contains nerve connections that send messages to the pituitary gland. The hypothalamus handles information that comes from the autonomic nervous system. It plays a role in controlling our behavior such as eating, sexual behavior, and sleeping, and regulates body temperature, emotions, secretion of hormones, and movement. The pituitary gland develops from an extension of the hypothalamus downwards and from a second component extending upward from the roof of the mouth. These two components form the pituitary gland which sits in a specialized boney container at the base of the skull called the pituitary fossa. It is involved in controlling a number of hormonal functions including thyroid functions, functions of the adrenal glands, growth and sexual maturation. The posterior part of the pituitary gland regulates the formation of urine.

Pineal Gland

The pineal gland is an outgrowth from the posterior or back portion of the third ventricle. In some mammals, it controls the response to darkness and light. In humans, it has some role in sexual maturation although the exact function of the pineal gland in humans is unclear.

Thalamus

The thalamus serves as a relay station for almost all information that comes and goes to the cortex. It plays a role in pain sensation, attention, and alertness.

Cerebellum

The cerebellum is located at the back of the brain beneath the occipital lobes. It is separated from the cerebrum by the tentorium (fold of dura). The cerebellum fine tunes our motor activity or movement, e.g. the fine movements of our fingers as they print a story or color a picture. It helps us maintain our posture, our sense of balance or equilibrium by controlling the tone of our muscles, and senses the position of our limbs. A tumor affecting the cerebellum may cause an individual to stagger and sway when he/she walks or has jerky movements of the arms and legs (a drunken appearance). An individual trying to reach an object may misjudge the distance and location of the object and fail to reach the object. The cerebellum is important in one's ability to perform rapid and repetitive actions such as playing a video game. In the cerebellum, right-sided abnormalities produce symptoms on the same side of the body.

Brain Stem

The brain stem is located in front of the cerebellum and may be considered as a "stem" or structure holding up the cerebrum. It consists of three structures: the midbrain, pons, and medulla oblongata. It serves as a relay station, passing messages back and forth between various parts of the body and cerebral cortex. Many simple or primitive functions that are essential for survival are located here.

The midbrain is an important center for ocular motion while the pons is involved with coordinating the eye and facial movements, facial sensation, hearing and balance.

The medulla oblongata controls our breathing, blood pressure, heart rhythms, and swallowing. These functions are important to our survival. Messages from the cortex to the spinal cord and nerves that branch from the spinal cord are sent through the pons and the brain stem. Destruction of these regions of the brain will cause "brain death." The heart can no longer beat on its own. Lungs cannot work on their own. Unable to breathe, oxygen will not be delivered to the brain. Brain cells, which require oxygen to survive, will die.

The reticular activating system is found in the midbrain, pons, medulla and part of the thalamus. It controls our level of wakefulness, the attention we pay to what happens in the world that surrounds us and our pattern of sleep.

Originating in the brain stem are ten of the twelve cranial nerves that control hearing, eye movement, facial sensations, taste, swallowing, and movement of the face, neck, shoulder, and tongue muscles. The cranial nerves for smell and vision originate in the cerebrum.

Limbic System

This system is involved in our emotions. Included in this system are the hypothalamus, part of the thalamus, amygdala (active in producing aggressive behavior) and hippocampus (plays a role in our ability to remember new information).

Language and Speech Functions

In general, the left hemisphere or side of the brain is responsible for language and speech. Because of this, it has been called the "dominant" hemisphere. The right hemisphere plays a large part in interpreting visual information and spatial processing. In about one third of individuals who are left-handed, speech function may be located on the right side of the brain. Left-handed individuals may need specialized testing to determine if their speech center is on the left or right side prior to any surgery in that area.

There is an area in the frontal lobe of the left hemisphere called Broca's area. It is beside the region that controls the movement of our facial muscles, tongue, jaw, and throat. If this area is destroyed, there is difficulty in producing the sounds of speech. One is unable to move the tongue or facial muscles in the appropriate way to make words. The individual can still read and understand spoken language but has difficulty in speaking and writing (i.e. forming letters and words, doesn't write within lines). This problem is called Broca's aphasia.

There is a region in the left temporal lobe called Wernicke's area. Damage to this area causes Wernicke's aphasia. Words are heard but are meaningless (receptive aphasia). An individual can make speech sounds. These sounds however have no meaning for the individual is unable to understand what is said by him or others.

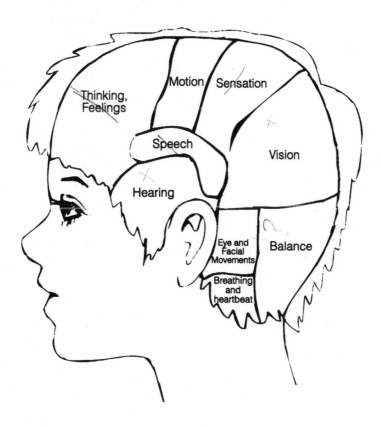

Figure 1.5. *Localization of Brain Functions.*

Many neuroscientists believe that the left hemisphere and perhaps other portions of the brain are important in language. An aphasia is simply a disturbance of language. Certain parts of the brain are responsible for specific functions in language production. There are many types of aphasias, each depending upon the brain area that is affected, and the role that area plays in language production.

Cranial Nerves

There are twelve pairs of nerves that come from the brain itself. These are called the cranial nerves. These nerves are responsible for some very specialized features and they have traditionally been both named and numbered.

- I: Olfactory—Smell
- II: Optic—Visual fields and ability to see
- III: Oculomotor—Eye movements; eyelid opening
- IV: Trochlear—Eye movements
- V: Trigeminal—Facial sensation
- VI: Abducens—Eye movements
- VII: Facial—Eyelid closing; facial expression; taste sensation
- VIII: Acoustic—Hearing; sense of balance
- IX: Glossopharyngeal—Taste sensation; swallowing
- X: Vagus—Swallowing; taste sensation
- XI: Accessory—Controls neck and shoulder muscles
- XII: Hypoglossal—Tongue movement

The Spinal Cord

The spinal cord is an extension of the brain. It is protected by a bony structure called the vertebral or spinal column. The spinal cord is covered with the same three membranes as the brain, called the meninges. There is a wide subarachnoid space that surrounds the spinal cord.

All the information going from the brain to the limbs travels through the spinal cord. This then allows for movement. The spinal cord is the first relay station for sensory information (what we fell in our arms and legs) on its way to consciousness in various centers of the brain.

Chapter 2

Electroencephalography (EEG)

What Is the EEG?

The EEG (electroencephalogram) displays the electrical activity of the brain. Nerve cells in the brain are constantly creating very small electrical signals, whether a patient is waking or sleeping. The EEG machine contains amplifiers which make these signals, or brainwaves, big enough so we can see them. The electrical signals are picked up by electrodes glued to the scalp, and travel to the amplifiers of the EEG machine and then are either written out on paper or saved on the hard drive of a computer and displayed on the computer's monitor. There are two electrodes plugged into each amplifier on the EEG machine. The amplifier looks at the two electrode signals coming into it and cancels out signals that are the same. So, the signal that you see on the paper or on the computer screen is actually the difference between the electrical activity picked up by two electrodes. The placement of the electrodes is important because the closer the electrodes are to each other the less differences in their brainwaves. Therefore, if the electrodes are too close, the EEG will look like a straight line instead of showing the brainwaves. This is why the technician measures the head of each patient. Measuring the electrode placements allows

---

This chapter combines text from "EEG Questions and Answers" by Seline Haines, R.EEG.T., Head EEG Technician at the Epilepsy Center at Barnes Hospital and a member of the professional advisory board of the Epilepsy Foundation of the St. Louis Region (EFS), reprinted with permission; and "Electroencephalography (Brain Monitoring)," used with permission from *Everything You Need to Know about Medical Tests*, © 1996 Springhouse Corporation.

the technician to have equal distances between all the electrodes to get clear and symmetrical brainwaves. The technician also has to constantly watch the EEG to make sure the electrodes are working properly and to eliminate any artifact or electrical interference that might occur.

Why Is This Test Done?

An electroencephalograph may be performed for the following reasons:

- To determine the presence and type of seizures

- To help diagnose brain abscesses and tumors

- To evaluate the brain's electrical activity in head injury, meningitis, encephalitis, mental retardation, and psychological disorders

- To confirm brain death.

What Should You Know Before the Test?

- Don't drink caffeine-containing coffee, tea, colas, or other beverages beforehand. Otherwise, you can follow your usual diet.

- Thoroughly wash and dry your hair to remove hair sprays, creams, or oils.

- Tell the doctor or nurse if you take any medications—especially drugs for seizures, anxiety, insomnia, or depression. You may have to stop taking any of these medications for a day or two before the test.

- If you're going to have a "sleep electroencephalograph," you'll need to stay awake the night before the test. Just before the test, a nurse will give you a sedative to help you sleep during the test.

- You'll be asked to sign a form that gives your permission to do the test. Read the form carefully and ask questions if any portion of it isn't clear.

What Happens during the Test?

- During the test, you relax in a reclining chair or lie on a bed, and electrodes are attached to your scalp with a special paste. The electrodes don't cause any electric shocks.

- Before the recording procedure begins, close your eyes, relax, and remain still. Don't talk.

- The recording may be stopped now and then to let you rest or reposition yourself.

- After the initial recording, you may be tested under various stress-producing conditions to elicit patterns not observable while you're resting. For example, you may be asked to breathe deeply and rapidly for 3 minutes, which may elicit brain wave patterns typical of seizures or other problems. Or a bright light may be shone at you.

What Happens after the Test?

- The nurse will remove the electrode paste from your hair.

- If you received a sedative before the test, you'll feel drowsy afterward.

- The nurse will tell you when you can take any medications that were suspended for the test.

Does the Test Have Risks?

An electroencephalograph can cause seizures in a person with a seizure disorder. If a seizure occurs, the doctor will treat it right away.

What Are the Normal Results?

An electroencephalograph records a portion of the brain's electrical activity as waves. Some of the waves are irregular, while others demonstrate frequent patterns. Among the basic waveforms are the alpha, beta, theta, and delta rhythms. Alpha waves occur at a frequency of 8 to 12 cycles per second in a regular rhythm. They're present only when you're awake and alert but your eyes are closed. Usually, they disappear with visual activity or mental concentration. Beta waves occur at a frequency of 13 to 30 cycles per second. They're generally associated with anxiety, depression, or the use of sedatives. Theta waves occur at a frequency of 4 to 7 cycles per second. They're most common in children and young adults. Delta waves occur at a frequency of 0.5 to 3.5 cycles per second. Normally, they occur only in young children and during sleep.

What Do Abnormal Results Mean?

Usually, about 100 pages of recording paper are evaluated, with particular attention paid to basic waveforms, symmetry of brain activity, brief bursts of energy, and responses to stimulation. In seizure disorders, the electroencephalograph pattern may identify the specific type of seizure. In absence seizures, the electroencephalograph shows spikes and waves at a frequency of 3 cycles per second. In generalized tonic-clonic or grand mal seizures, it usually shows multiple, high-voltage, spiked waves in both hemispheres of the brain. In complex partial seizures, the electroencephalograph usually shows spiked waves in the affected region. And in focal seizures, it usually shows localized, spiked discharges. In brain tumors or abscesses, the electroencephalograph may show slow waves (usually delta waves, but possibly beta waves). Generally, any condition that causes a diminishing level of consciousness alters the electroencephalograph pattern in proportion to the degree of consciousness lost. For example, if a person has meningitis or encephalitis, the electroencephalograph shows generalized, diffuse, and slow brain waves.

How Can the EEG Help in the Treatment of Seizures?

The EEG is still the leading test used to help diagnose seizures. Many people do not have a detectable brain lesion causing their seizures, and tests like the MRI and CT scan show normal brain structure. The EEG, however, can show abnormal electrical function of the brain even when these other tests are normal.

The EEG of persons with epilepsy can be divided into two categories, the interictal and ictal EEG. The interictal (routine) EEG is the EEG recording taken when the patient is not having seizures. Most patients with seizures will have at least one routine EEG. This test is done to look for interictal epiliptiform abnormalities, that is, abnormal activity that can occur in a patient with epilepsy in the absence of an actual seizure. Sometimes the patient is asked to attempt to go to sleep, or to hyperventilate, or a strobe light is flashed in his or her eyes to try to bring out these abnormalities. Finding these abnormalities confirms that the patient has seizures, and helps the doctor determine what type they are.

The ictal EEG is the EEG recording taken during an aura and/or a seizure. This is done when a patient's seizures fail to respond to treatment, and the doctor wants to confirm the diagnosis, or possibly determine if brain surgery can be used to treat the seizures. Usually, ictal EEG recordings need to be made during closed-circuit television monitoring in an Epilepsy Center. For these tests, the person is usually admitted to the hospital and has their EEG and their video recorded continuously to capture actual seizure events. In our center [Epilepsy Center at Barnes Hospital], it typically takes about 1 or 2 days to confirm a patient's seizure diagnosis, while it takes an average of 5 days in the hospital to evaluate a patient for epilepsy surgery.

What Does the EEG Tell the Doctor?

The most common interictal EEG abnormality in persons with epilepsy is a spike, which is a burst of electrical activity which stands out from the normal EEG patterns. These spikes can be confined to one area of the brain (focal), or can occur in several areas of the brain independently of each other (multifocal), or come simultaneously from wide areas of the brain (generalized). The pattern of interictal abnormalities can determine if the person has focal or generalized epilepsy. These types of epilepsy have different causes, and may respond to different drugs.

The ictal EEG abnormalities are a little more complicated. These abnormalities can show rhythmic activity but can also show other EEG patterns depending on whether the recording was done from scalp electrodes or from electrodes implanted on the brain itself. The ictal EEG of the person with generalized epilepsy will usually show widespread brain involvement from the onset of the seizure. The ictal EEG of the person with focal epilepsy will usually show the seizure starting from a specific brain area but it can then spread to involve other areas, or even the whole brain. These patterns can tell the doctor which part of the brain is causing the seizure and how much of the brain becomes involved during it.

Chapter 3

Magnetic Resonance Imaging (MRI)

MRI (which is the abbreviation for magnetic resonance imaging) produces computerized images of various sections of the brain and spine. These images are highly detailed. Unlike a CAT scan, which uses X-rays, an MRI scan uses magnetic fields and radio waves to produce images of the brain and spine. The magnetic fields and radio waves aren't noticed by the person undergoing the test, and no harmful effects have been reported.

Why Is This Test Done?

An MRI scan of the brain and spinal cord may be performed to diagnose brain and spinal tumors, tissue damage, or soft-tissue abnormalities.

What Should You Know Before the Test?

- This test takes up to 90 minutes to complete.

- Although MRI is painless and involves no exposure to radiation from the scanner, a radioactive contrast dye may be used. The contrast dye is injected, usually near the organ or tissue that is being observed.

Reprinted with permission from *Everything You Need to Know about Medical Tests*, ©1996 Springhouse Corporation.

- The opening for your head and body in most MRI scanners is small and deep. If you've ever experienced claustrophobia, you may need a sedative to help you relax before the test. Some of the newer MRI scanners, though, are transparent.

- During the test, you'll hear the scanner clicking, whirring, and thumping as it moves inside its housing.

- You'll be able to talk with the technician at all times during the test.

- You'll be asked to remove all metallic objects, including jewelry, hair pins, and watches. You'll also asked if you have any surgically implanted joints, pins, clips, valves, pumps, or pacemakers containing metal that could be attracted to the strong MRI magnet. If you do, you won't be able to undergo the test.

- You'll be asked to sign a consent form before the test takes place.

What Happens during the Test?

- You're asked to lie on a narrow bed, which then slides into the desired position inside the scanner.

- During the procedure you're asked to remain very still.

- The images that are generated are displayed on a monitor and recorded on film or magnetic tape for permanent storage; the radiologist may use the computer to manipulate and enhance the images.

What Happens after the Test?

- You may resume normal activity.

- If the test took a long time, you'll be watched for signs of lightheadedness or fainting when you sit or stand up.

Does the Test Have Risks?

- Because MRI works through the use of powerful magnets, it can't be performed on people with pacemakers, intracranial aneurysm clips, or other iron implants, or on a person with gunshot wounds to the head.

- Because of the strong magnetic field, metallic or computer-based equipment—for example, ventilators—can't be used in the MRI area.

What Are the Normal Results?

An MRI scan can distinctly show the brain and spine. Tissue color and shading vary, depending in part on the magnetic strength used and the amount of computer enhancement. MRI can detect nerve-related disorders, for example, multiple sclerosis (MS).

What Do Abnormal Results Mean?

MRI clearly shows changes that result when water accumulates in an organ or tissue. Examples include certain brain tumors and disorders such as cerebral edema, in which fluid accumulates in the brain.

Chapter 4

MRI Helps Pathfinders Chart the Mind

Since its introduction in the 1970's, magnetic resonance imaging (MRI) has become a staple diagnostic tool for many clinicians, allowing them to peer at the body's internal anatomy noninvasively and without the use of harmful radiation. Not content to look simply at the body's interior structure, scientists are now developing new MRI techniques that open a window on the body's functions. These researchers are essentially high-tech pathfinders, seeking new avenues to detect signs of thought and action and to analyze the structure of the brain and other organs. Already these investigations have uncovered novel diagnostic techniques for disorders like epilepsy and found unexpected evidence of cognitive activities in an enigmatic region of the brain.

MRI cartographers prize speed and power, and NCRR supports two of the three most powerful whole-body magnets for human MRI studies in the United States. Operating at more than 4 tesla, or about 80,000 times the magnetic field of the earth, these magnets at the University of Alabama at Birmingham (UAB) and the University of Minnesota in Minneapolis are producing dramatically detailed portraits of the body's inner anatomy and actions. At other NCRR-supported resources like the NIH In Vivo NMR Research Center in Bethesda, Maryland, scientists are working to develop techniques that will equip researchers around the country to conduct advanced studies using standard 1.5-tesla clinical instruments, which number more than 2,000 in the United States.

National Center for Research Resources, *NCRR Reporter*, July/August 1994.

MRI works because the nuclei of many atoms behave like tiny bar magnets when placed in a magnetic field. During a scan the patient lies inside a large magnet, which directs the tiny atomic magnets in blood and tissues to align and rotate at the same frequency. A radio pulse broadcast by the MRI machine then knocks the nuclei out of alignment and, as they return to their former orientations, or "relax," they emit a radio signal that is detected and analyzed by the MRI scanner. Atomic nuclei relax at different rates depending on the surrounding chemical environment. Computers translate the differing signals to construct precise images of the body's tissues. These images give clinicians valuable information about the body's status that helps them diagnose and treat disease.

One of the main advantages of powerful 4-tesla magnets is that they prompt aligned nuclei to rotate with greater vigor, which enhances the distinction between the nuclei of interest and background noise. These magnets thus amplify the signal-to-noise ratio, serving as a kind of magnifying glass for MRI mapmakers. Relative newcomers to the clinical arena, 4-tesla magnets have been used on humans for less than 4 years. Two years ago Minnesota's Dr. Michael Garwood surprised the MRI community when he used a 4-tesla magnet to produce the first high-resolution images of the human brain's anatomy, a feat that some believed impossible. That is because jostling aligned nuclei in stronger magnetic fields requires higher radio frequencies, which resist penetrating the body.

"The 4-T magnets give us a much more detailed picture of anatomy than is available at 1.5 T, which allows us to visualize anatomical features that we might not otherwise see," says Dr. Hoby Hetherington, director of 4-tesla studies at UAB's Center for NMR Research and Development. Center director Dr. Gerald Pohost and his colleagues have developed new MRI methods and instruments that enhance the contrast between the brain's gray and white matter and produce striking images of the basal ganglia and thalamus, common sites of small strokes. The scientists' ultimate goal is to improve diagnosis and treatment of neurological disorders like Alzheimer's disease and epilepsy.

When epilepsy does not respond to medication, surgeons sometimes remove the site of seizure focus, typically a patch of abnormal or damaged brain tissue that triggers convulsions. Prior to surgery the seizure focus is usually identified using intracranial electroencephalography (EEG), a risky procedure that requires doctors to place electrodes in the brain. In a study to be described at the August meeting of the Society of Magnetic Resonance, the Alabama researchers found that high-resolution spectroscopic MRI, a much safer procedure than intracranial EEG, can accurately pinpoint the seizure focus. In an evaluation of 9 epileptic patients and 10 healthy volunteers who served as controls, MRI showed that concentrations of N-acetyl aspartate, a compound produced by nerve cells, were abnormally low at the damaged sites. "The nine patients were identifiable immediately with MRI," says Dr. Hetherington.

"They subsequently went to surgery for resection, and the abnormal regions we identified were confirmed histologically and also by intracranial EEG. There was perfect correlation."

Other high-field studies of the brain combine MRI's power to pinpoint brain structures with newer techniques to detect brain activity. Dr. Kamil Ugurbil, director of the Center for Magnetic Resonance Research at the University of Minnesota, and his colleagues helped pioneer the application of blood oxygenation level-dependent (BOLD) functional imaging to studies of the human brain. BOLD imaging—now one of the hottest areas of MRI research—is possible because the oxygenated hemoglobin in oxygen-rich blood and the deoxygenated hemoglobin in oxygen-poor blood behave differently in a magnetic field. Like curtains on a lighted window, deoxyhemoglobin dampens the magnetic properties of neighboring nuclei and darkens the image. When clusters of stimulated nerve cells summon a flow of nutrient-rich oxygenated blood, the activated region "lights up" in a BOLD-based scan because deoxyhemoglobin concentrations become relatively low.

Initial brain activation experiments examined areas like the visual or motor cortex, already well-mapped using positron emission tomography (PET) and other techniques. Scientists are now setting their sights on more enigmatic brain territories. One of these lesser understood regions is the cerebellum, a rounded structure at the base of the brain known to control posture and coordinate movement.

In earlier PET studies scientists have found only weak evidence of cerebellar participation in higher thought processes, but these experiments did not have the sensitivity to distinguish between activation of the cerebellar cortex, which accepts input from surrounding brain regions, and output signals produced by the cerebellum, which indicate active involvement in cognition. "Whether the cerebellum is involved in cognitive tasks and in modifying behavior is a very controversial question," says Dr. Ugurbil.

Seeking an answer to this question Dr. Ugurbil teamed up with Minnesota's Dr. Seong-Gi Kim and Dr. Peter Strick of Syracuse University. The scientists looked first at the dentate nucleus, a tiny cluster of nerve cells that is nearly impossible to detect with other imaging techniques. The dentate nucleus is one of several output regions of the cerebellum. "We reasoned that if the cerebellum were participating in a cognitive task, and not simply accepting incoming information, then the output stage would be activated," says Dr. Ugurbil.

Volunteers solved a difficult pegboard puzzle inside the MRI scanner, and these images were compared with scans taken while the volunteers simply moved the pegs. Activated regions of the dentate nucleus were on average 3-4 times larger during puzzle solving than during simple movement tasks, "which was an entirely new finding," says Dr. Ugurbil. "It goes a long way toward demonstrating that the cerebellum is involved in cognitive processes."

While 4-tesla magnets offer unparalleled sensitivity for functional imaging, these instruments are not a requisite for pioneering MRI research. Indeed some of the first brain activation studies were conducted using conventional 1.5-tesla scanners. Dr. Chris Moonen, director of the NCRR-supported NIH In Vivo NMR Research Center, is developing rapid new techniques for collecting detailed functional images without the use of expensive high-field magnets and costly accessories. "One of our main goals is to invent and develop novel pulse sequences that enable anybody who has a conventional clinical instrument to do functional imaging," says Dr. Moonen.

In fact, the first three-dimensional functional map of the human brain with a conventional 1.5-T magnet and standard equipment resulted from teamwork between Dr. Moonen and his colleagues and the teams of Dr. Daniel Weinberger of the National Institute of Mental Health and Dr. Joe Frank of the Laboratory of Diagnostic Radiology Research. The key to their success lay in their use of a recently patented technique known as echo-shifted FLASH, invented and developed at NIH.

When choosing an MRI technique, researchers generally must sacrifice speed for sensitivity or vice versa. Ultrafast and sensitive MRI protocols like echo-planar imaging require high-performance hardware that can cost half a million dollars or more. But echo-shifted FLASH was designed to offer greater speed while maintaining sensitivity. Dr. Moonen and his colleagues were able to acquire a single three-dimensional data set in 20 seconds, and the image was sensitive enough to show activation of the visual cortex in response to flashing lights.

A newcomer to the MRI toolkit, echo-shifted FLASH is still used almost exclusively at NIH, "but instrument builders are working on expanding the implementation of these methods," says Dr. Moonen.

"We really hope to give people the edge when they are working with conventional MRI scanners. Not everyone has the luxury of using a 4-T imaging system."

Additional Reading

1. Kim, S.-G., Hendrich, K., Hu, X., et al., Potential pitfalls of functional MRI using conventional gradient-recalled echo techniques. *NMR in Biomedicine*, in press.

2. Hetherington, H. P., Pan, J. W., Ponder, S. L., et al., 2-D spectroscopic imaging of the human brain at 4.1T without field of view restriction. *Magnetic Resonance in Medicine*, in press.

3. Duyn, J. H., Mattay, V. S., Sexton, R. H., et al., 3-Dimensional functional imaging of human brain using echo-shifted FLASH MRI. *Magnetic Resonance in Medicine* 32:150-155,1994.

—by Victoria L Contie

This research is supported by the Biomedical Research Technology and the Biomedical Engineering and Instrumentation Programs of the National Center for Research Resources, the National Institute Of Neurological Disorders and Stroke, the National Institute of Mental Health, and the Epilepsy Foundation of America.

Chapter 5

Computed Tomography (CT)

Computed tomography is a diagnostic procedure in which cross-sectional pictures or "tomographic slices" of the body are made by x-ray. This technique may also be called a CT scan or CAT scan.

During the procedure, the patient lies very still on a table. The table passes through the x-ray machine, which is shaped like a doughnut with a large hole. The machine, which is linked to a computer, rotates around the patient, taking pictures of one thin slice of tissue after another. To obtain a clearer picture, the patient may be given a solution of contrast material to drink or get an injection into an arm vein before the CT is done. The length of the procedure depends on the size of the area to be x-rayed.

Images from these x-rays are then processed by the computer. The final image, called a "computed tomogram" or "CT slice," is displayed on a cathode-ray tube (CRT), a device similar to a television picture tube and screen. This image can be recorded permanently on film. In addition, a CT scan can be stored on magnetic tape or optical disk.

Computed tomography offers some advantages over other x-ray techniques in diagnosing disease, particularly because it clearly shows the shape and exact location of organs, soft tissues, and bones in any "slice" of the body. CT scans help doctors distinguish between a simple cyst and a solid tumor and, thus, evaluate abnormalities more accurately. CT scanning is more accurate than conventional x-ray in determining the stage (extent) of some types of cancer. Information about

Fact Sheet, National Cancer Institute (NCI). This fact sheet was reviewed on July 27, 1998.

31

the stage of the disease helps the doctor decide how to treat it. CT scanning is also used to plan radiation therapy or surgery. The scans help doctors target treatment to the cancer and protect healthy tissue.

Spiral CT scanners are one of the latest innovations. They use continuous scanning to generate cross-sectional slices and make a set of 3-dimensional images. Spiral CT has decreased the time it takes to produce tomographic pictures.

Some people may be concerned about the amount of radiation they receive during a CT scan. It is true that the radiation exposure from a CT scan is slightly higher than from a regular x-ray. However, not having the procedure can be more risky than having it. If cancer is suspected, patients must weigh the risks and benefits.

For More Information

Additional information about CT is available from:

Public Relations
Department of the American College of Radiology
1891 Preston White Drive
Reston, VA 20191
(703) 648-8900
Website: http://www.acr.org

Additional information about cancer is available from:

National Cancer Institute (NCI)
Cancer Information Service
Toll-free: 1-800-4-CANCER (1-800-422-6237)
TTY: 1-800-332-8615

NCI Online
Website: http://www.nci.nih.gov

CancerMail Service
To obtain a contents list, send e-mail to cancermail@icicc.nci.nih.gov with the word "help" in the body of the message.

CancerFax fax on demand service
Dial 301-402-5874 and listen to recorded instructions.

Chapter 6

Positron Emission Tomography (PET)

Viewing the Brain as It Works

Positron emission tomography (PET) is the first imaging technique that shows, in the living, awake human being, ongoing metabolic activity in various regions of the brain. PET's advantages spring from the knowledge that active nerve cells consume oxygen and glucose. In fact, the brain is one of the most metabolically active organs, consuming 80 percent of the glucose that the body uses. PET measures this activity in specific areas of the brain, detecting subtle increases or decreases in glucose use during tasks such as listening or remembering, or in persons who have brain disease. It is the unique ability to observe brain function that allows PET to reveal fundamental information about the healthy and diseased brain.

At the center of PET's unique abilities is a small family of radio isotopes that decay by emitting a subatomic particle called a positron. These positron-emitting isotopes, joined to harmless chemicals dispatched to the brain, have three properties that endow PET with its impressive imaging capabilities.

The isotopes all have very short half-lives, emitting half of their radioactivity between 2 and 110 minutes. Such rapid decay allows

This chapter includes excerpts from *Positron Emission Tomography*, National Institute of Neurological and Communicative Disorders and Stroke, NIH Pub. No. 84-2620, September 1984, and "Positron Emission Tomography (PET)," Center for Positron Emission Tomography (CPET), State University of New York at Buffalo, November 1998; reprinted with permission.

research patients to be studied after receiving a very low dose of a radioactively tagged chemical. Because the radioactivity dose to the subject is so low, PET can be used for serial studies in the same patient to follow the course of a disease. It can also be used safely to study healthy persons. This latter capability enables scientists to gather information on how the healthy brain works.

Positron-emitting isotopes produce a unique radioactivity event: an emitted positron shortly collides with its antimatter particle, an electron, producing mutual annihilation. The energy released takes the form of two photons which fly apart at approximately 180°. Thus, each positron decay sends a two-directional signal. These photons register virtually simultaneously on the opposite sides of a ring of detectors, each detector being geographically positioned to record the time and location of a positron annihilation. A specially programmed computer then picks up, stores, and correlates the information from many different annihilations and reconstructs from that data an image of a narrow sector of the brain.

But these favorable physical properties would mean nothing were it not for these isotopes' biochemical advantage: since each is a variant of an element that is intrinsically associated with the life process, the isotopes can be attached to compounds involved in the brain's metabolism.

Labeling Chemical Compounds

Many areas of inquiry have developed from the desire to follow where things go in the body, how they get there, how long they take to arrive or leave, and what happens to them on the way. The goal of this inquiry is to learn how the physiological and chemical processes in our bodies work. In the research phase, techniques are explored to gather the fundamental data on these processes. In the later clinical phase that knowledge is used to aid the physician in caring for the patient.

PET contributes to this inquiry by labeling chemical compounds we'd like to follow through the body with radioactive atoms that decay by emitting positrons. Labeling is a process of attaching some kind of identifying tag to the compound you want to follow which will later let you identify where the compound has gone. In PET the compounds that can be labeled are limited only by the imagination of the investigators and the physical half-life of the positron emitting label. One of the big advantages of PET is that the atoms which can be labeled (turned into positron emitters) are the same atoms which naturally comprise the organic molecules utilized in the body. These atoms include oxygen, carbon, and nitrogen to name a few. Since these atoms occur naturally in organic compounds, replacing the naturally occurring atoms in a compound with a labeled atom leaves you a compound that is chemically and biologically identical to the original (so it will behave in a manner identical to its unlabeled sibling) and that is traceable. In addition to naturally occurring compounds such as neurotransmitters, sugars, etc., it is also possible to label synthesized compounds (such as drugs) and follow them as well.

Tracers

A second important attribute of PET is that it can follow labeled compounds in trace quantities. This means that the labeled compounds can be introduced into the body without affecting the normal processes of the body. For example, labeling a pound of sugar and ingesting that sugar would be a good example of a non-trace quantity of labeled compound. At these quantities, blood chemistry would be altered (e.g. insulin produced in response to rising blood sugar levels). Often you want to follow the time course of a compound in the body by introducing trace quantities of a compound that will behave the same as the unlabeled compound without altering the ongoing physiological state of chemical processes of the body. PET is sensitive enough to detect trace amounts of labeled compound and so is well suited to this kind of investigation.

Steps in the PET Process

- production of positron emitting isotope in a cyclotron

- chemistry of labeling compound with positron emitter and preparing compound in a form suitable for administration in humans

- transport of labeled compound from chemistry group to camera group

- administration (injection) of tracer compound and data acquisition with PET camera

- processing of data from PET camera to extract information related to the tracer's kinetics in the body

- interpretation of results

Chapter 7

What You Should Know about Brain Donation

The Facts

Research over the past decade has shown that the study of human brain tissue is essential to increase our understanding of how the nervous system functions. Most recently, postmortem human brain research played a significant role in the development of a genetic test for Huntington's disease and a treatment for Parkinson's disease. Current reports indicate that a gene associated with one form of dystonia will soon be isolated, but only if more brain tissue is donated by individuals afflicted with this disease. Similarly, several neurochemical and anatomical studies focusing on other neurologic and psychiatric disorders are under way. Unfortunately, many are being delayed due to the scarcity of tissue donors.

The McLean Brain Tissue Resource Center (commonly referred to as The Brain Bank) was established in 1978 as a centralized resource for the collection and distribution of human brain specimens for research and diagnostic studies. Over the years, hundreds of scientists from the nation's top research and medical centers have requested tissue from The Brain Bank for their investigations. Since the majority of these studies can be carried out on a very small amount of tissue, each donated brain provides a large number of samples for many researchers.

"Give the Gift of Hope," The Brain Tissue Resource Center, McLean Hospital, 15 Mill Street, Belmont, MA 02178; reprinted with permission.

For comparative purposes brain tissue is needed from healthy individuals, as well as from those who died with a neurologic or psychiatric illness. There is also a critical need for relatives of people with genetically inherited disorders to donate their brains after death. When possible, a small portion of frozen tissue taken from each brain donated to The Brain Bank will be kept available to serve as a resource for future genetic (DNA) testing.

What You Should Know

Becoming a prospective tissue donor is easy. Any person, 18 years of age or older can simply complete a donor card. Then, do the most important thing of all—inform your family that you would like your brain donated to the McLean Brain Tissue Resource Center after death. Your next-of-kin must be available to verify your intent to donate at the time of your death.

- Even if a decision to donate was not made prior to death, family members can arrange for the donation of brain tissue after an individual's death.

- In all cases, the identity of each donor and potential donor will remain strictly confidential.

- After an autopsy is performed, only a donor's brain will be sent to The Brain Bank. The donor's body will not need to be transported.

- Brain donation does not interfere with an open casket or other traditional funeral arrangements.

- When appropriate, a diagnostic report will be sent to the family and health professionals involved with the case.

There are three major reasons why a brain generally becomes unsuitable for donation:
1. When a person dies while on a respirator.
2. When a person dies from a highly contagious disease.
3. When a person plans to make a whole body donation to a medical school.

The McLean Brain Bank is funded by government grants and private foundations. Usually, brain donation involves no cost to the family.

Occasionally, however, charges may be incurred with the local hospital or funeral director.

Remember

The McLean Brain Bank should be contacted as soon as a potential donor dies. Delay could result in the loss of the donation.

A donor card will help to identify you as a donor or donor family. Ultimately, however, your next of kin will be responsible for making sure your wishes are fulfilled. Please, discuss your plans with your family as soon as you have made a decision to donate.

With Your Help

- We can help researchers to develop more refined treatment and better prognoses for those now suffering with neurologic and psychiatric illnesses.

- We can provide hope for the millions of people who wonder, each day, when or if symptoms will soon appear.

- We can help to assure a healthier future for all of the unborn children who are at risk for inheriting a neurologic or psychiatric illness tomorrow.

For More Information

For more information or to receive a copy of a donor card, contact:

The Brain Tissue Resource Center
McLean Hospital
115 Mill Street
Belmont, MA 02178
(617) 855-2400 or 855-2000

Part Two

Stroke

Chapter 8

Stroke: An Overview

What Is a Stroke?

Strokes—also referred to as "Brain Attacks"—or cerebrovascular accidents (CVAs), are physical or mental impairments caused by damage to the brain. A common type of stroke is cerebral thrombosis, caused by a blockage of an artery in the brain. When blood flow to the brain is interrupted, vital supplies of oxygen and nutrients are cut-off and brain cells in the affected area begin to die almost immediately. When a blood clot forms elsewhere in the body and is carried to the brain, blocking a vessel and causing a stroke, it's called a cerebral embolism. (The heart is the most common source for emboli.) Both cerebral thrombosis and cerebral embolism are ischemic strokes. Hemorrhagic stroke occurs when blood vessels burst, causing bleeding within the brain or in the space surrounding the brain. Intracerebral hemorrhages and subarachnoid hemorrhages are both hemorrhagic strokes.

What Causes Stroke?

Causes of ischemic stroke include atherosclerosis (hardening of the arteries), emboli from the heart, inflammation of blood vessels, trauma

©1997 American Academy of Neurology, 1080 Montreal Avenue, St. Paul, MN 55116-2325, (612) 695-1940; reprinted with permission. Visit the American Academy of Neurology's on the Internet at www.aan.com. Illustrations and captions added from "National Survey of Stroke," National Institute of Neurological and Communicative Disorders and Stroke, NIH Pub. No. 83-2069.

to blood vessels, migraine, and drug use. Intracerebral hemorrhages can occur from uncontrolled hypertension, underlying malformations of blood vessels or unsuspected tumors. Subarachnoid hemorrhages

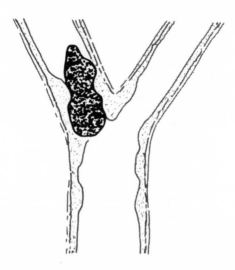

Figure 8.1. Thrombotic Infarction—A blood clot that develops at the site and causes the death of brain tissue.

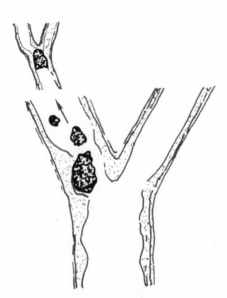

Figure 8.2. Embolic Infarction—A blood clot that breaks off from a more distant clot, moves to the site, and causes the death of brain tissue.

occur most frequently from rupture of an aneurysm (a weakened spot or blister in the wall of the blood vessel).

Who Gets a Stroke?

Approximately 550,000 Americans suffer strokes every year. Someone experiences a stroke every minute in the United States. While

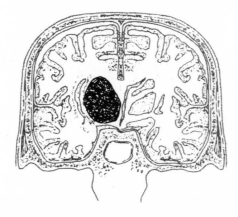

Figure 8.3. *Intracerebral Hemorrhage—Spontaneous bleeding from a brain blood vessel into brain tissue, creating a localized collection of blood (hematoma) that presses on the brain, destroying brain tissue.*

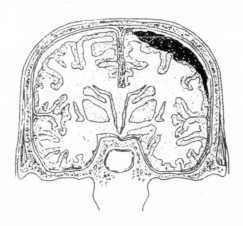

Figure 8.4. *Subarachnoid Hemorrhage—Spontaneous bleeding into space surrounding the brain, thus narrowing the brain blood vessels and reducing blood flow to a segment of the brain.*

the death rate for stroke has dropped significantly due to improvements in medical care and the control of high blood pressure, stroke is still our nation's third leading cause of death, killing 150,000 Americans each year. Stroke risk increases with age with at least two-thirds of all stroke victims 65 or older. However, middle-aged or young adults may also suffer stroke. Stroke is rare in children and infants. Young and middle-aged African Americans have a stroke incidence rate almost twice as high as whites, and are almost twice as likely to die from stroke.

Stroke is the number one cause of adult disability in the United States, with an estimated three million stroke survivors often living with impaired speech, movement, and swallowing abilities. Of the 400,000 Americans who survive stroke each year, 10 to 18 percent will have another stroke within one year, and approximately one-third of the survivors will have another stroke within five years. Stroke annually costs the United States $30 billion from hospital, physician and rehabilitation expenses.

What Are the Symptoms?

The most common stroke symptoms are numbness, weakness or paralysis of face, arm, leg (particularly on one side of the body); sudden decreased or blurred vision; difficulty speaking or understanding words; dizziness, loss of balance or coordination; sudden and intense headache; sudden nausea and fever, and loss of consciousness.

How Is It Treated?

Medical care should be sought immediately as stroke-related brain damage worsens the longer it goes untreated. A clot-busting medicine, t-PA, has been shown to improve outcome following a stroke, if given within 3 hours after onset. Other new drugs are being tested which may lessen the severity of brain damage when given immediately after stroke. Carotid endarterectomy (surgery performed to unclog the carotid artery), hospital care and rehabilitation therapy are all used to treat victims of stroke. Controlling risk factors such as high blood pressure, diabetes, smoking and alcohol abuse may prevent stroke. Aspirin, ticlopidine or anticoagulants can decrease the chance of further stroke. The level of recovery depends on the extent of brain damage, the patient's determination to get better, and the support of friends and family members.

Chapter 9

Stroke in Children

Description

Stroke occurs when brain cells are damaged due to decreased blood flow to the brain. Although stroke is a relatively frequent occurrence in adults, it is much less common in children. However, strokes can occur in children of all ages, from newborns to adolescents. There are 2 types of stroke, ischemic and hemorrhagic. An ischemic stroke is caused by a blockage of a blood vessel. A hemorrhagic stroke is caused by bleeding into the brain (also called intracerebral hemorrhage) or into the spaces surrounding the brain (also called subarachnoid hemorrhage). Hemorrhagic stroke in newborns is usually caused by a subarachnoid hemorrhage. The most common cause of stroke in children is congenital heart disease. Other causes include sickle cell anemia, intracranial infection, brain injury, vascular malformations, occlusive vascular disease, and some genetic diseases. Symptoms of stroke in children are similar to those in adults, with some significant differences. In children (especially those under 4 years of age) seizures are frequently present at the onset. Other symptoms include loss of expressive language, hemiplegia (paralysis on one side of the body), dysarthria (impairment of speech), convulsions, headache, and fever. The warning signs of stroke in children include sudden weakness on one side of the body and/or a sudden loss of speech. The sooner a stroke in a child is diagnosed the better the chance for recovery.

National Institute of Neurological Disorders and Stroke (NINDS), September 1997.

Treatment

Treatment of stroke in children is similar to treatment of stroke in adults. Immediate attention must be paid to any signs of increased cranial pressure and associated illnesses which may need to be treated. The child should be hospitalized and closely monitored. The underlying conditions which led to the stroke must be determined and managed to prevent recurrences. Rehabilitation including physical therapy should be initiated as the child recovers.

Prognosis

Although the prognosis for children with stroke is generally thought to be better than for adults—possibly due to the greater plasticity (flexibility) of the immature brain—some children may have a poor outcome. Children who experience seizures at onset tend to have a worse prognosis for intellectual development and a higher incidence of subsequent seizures than children who have no seizures. Depending on the underlying condition, some children have a residual deficit such as epilepsy, movement disorders, hyperactive behavior, hemiplegia, learning disabilities, or mental retardation. However, most children with residual hemiplegia will be able to walk.

Research and More Information

The NINDS supports a broad range of basic and clinical research aimed at finding better ways to prevent, diagnose, and treat stroke and ultimately restore functions lost as a result of stroke.

These articles, available from a medical library, may provide more in-depth information on stroke in children:

Allan, W, and Riviello, Jr., J. "Perinatal Cerebrovascular Disease in the Neonate." *Pediatric Neurology*, 39:4; 621-650 (August 1992).

Horwitz, S, and Wiznitzer, M. "Stroke in Childhood." In *Neurology in Clinical Practice: Principles of Diagnosis and Management*, Butterworth-Heinemann, Boston, pp. 979-982 (1991).

Pavlakis, S, Gould, R, and Zito, J. "Stroke in Children." *Advances in Pediatrics*, 38; 151-179 (1991).

Trescher, W. "Ischemic Stroke Syndromes in Childhood." *Pediatric Annals*, 21:6; 374-383 (June 1992).

Information may also be available from the following organizations:

National Stroke Association
96 Inverness Drive East, Suite 1
Englewood, CO 80112-5112
(303) 649-9299
(800) 787-6537

National Rehabilitation Information Center
8455 Colesville Road, Suite 935
Silver Spring, MD 20910-3319
(800) 346-2742

Institute for Health and Disability
University of Minnesota, Box 721
420 Delaware Street, SE
Minneapolis, MN 55455-0392
(612) 626-2825

National Institute on Deafness and Other Communication Disorders
Building 31, Room 3C35
Bethesda, MD 20892-2320
(301) 496-7243

Chapter 10

What You Should Know about Stroke Prevention

A stroke occurs when blood flow to the brain is blocked, either by narrowed blood vessels or blood clots or when there is bleeding in the brain. Deprived of nutrients, brain nerve cells begin to die within a few minutes. As a result, stroke can cause vision and sensory loss, problems with walking and talking, or difficulty in thinking clearly. In many cases, the effects of stroke are irreversible.

Some people are more at risk for stroke than others. Chronic health conditions such as high blood pressure and diabetes can increase your risk, as well as lifestyle choices such as smoking cigarettes, being overweight, or drinking excessively. Men, African Americans, and people with a family history of stroke have a higher risk as well. If you have already had a stroke or a transient ischemic attack (referred to as a TIA or "mini-stroke"), you are at highest risk. Warning signs include sudden unexplained numbness or tingling (especially on one side), slurred speech, blurred vision, stumbling, or clumsiness.

Preventing Stroke

Experts now believe that stroke is as preventable as heart attack. In addition to primary prevention tactics such as quitting smoking, drinking only in moderation, and exercising, there are medical interventions

What You Should Know About Stroke Prevention. Consumer brochure. Agency for Health Care Policy and Research (AHCPR), Rockville, MD. AHCPR Pub. No. 95-0090 (http://www.ahcpr.gov/consumer/strokcon.htm) Pub. No. 95-0090, September 1995.

51

that can decrease your risk of stroke if you are in a high-risk group. Recent studies, including those supported by the Agency for Health Care Policy and Research (AHCPR), show that if you have conditions known as atrial fibrillation or carotid artery disease, there are interventions that can dramatically lower your risk of stroke.

Atrial Fibrillation

If you have atrial fibrillation, the upper left chamber of your heart beats rapidly and unpredictably, making it hard for all the blood in the chamber to empty. The remaining blood tends to form clots that can travel to any part of your body. If they travel to the brain, these clots can cause a stroke. Treatment with anticoagulants (or blood-thinners) such as warfarin can prevent these clots from forming. Aspirin also is used to reduce the risk of stroke, but the most recent clinical studies have shown that warfarin is superior to aspirin in preventing stroke. Current studies show that treatment with warfarin can prevent over half of the 80,000 strokes that are caused annually by atrial fibrillation.

If you have atrial fibrillation, your health care provider may recommend that you take warfarin. If you do, you need to know:

- Warfarin may increase the risk of bleeding. Careful regular monitoring of blood levels and proper dosage should keep this risk in check. Your health care provider will tell you where to go for monitoring.

- When properly administered, warfarin prevents 20 strokes for every major bleeding complication caused by the medicine.

- Most bleeding incidents are preventable and treatable.

- Certain drugs can interfere with proper anticoagulation. Antibiotics and anticonvulsants (for example, phenobarbital and Tegretol) are examples of drugs that can cause problems. Talk to your physician or pharmacist for more complete information.

Carotid Artery Disease

The carotid arteries run through the neck and supply blood to the brain. When the walls of the carotid arteries are narrowed by fatty deposits known as plaque, small clots in the blood can cut off blood supply to the brain and cause a stroke. A surgical procedure known as a carotid endarterectomy clears arteries of plaque. If you have had a minor stroke or symptoms that suggest you are at high risk for a stroke, and there is evidence of severe blockage in your carotid arteries, your health care provider may suggest you consider carotid endarterectomy as a preventive procedure.

If you are considering this surgery, you should know:

- Certain tests may be required to confirm the diagnosis of carotid artery disease. With angiography, a dye is injected into the artery, followed by an x-ray to check for blockage. Magnetic resonance imaging (MRI) and ultrasonic scans also can test for blockage without entering the arteries.

- Carotid endarterectomy carries some risks. There can be complications if parts of the plaque break away during the procedure and block an artery to the brain or if artery incisions leak.

- Complication rates vary greatly by hospital and surgeon. Ask if your hospital monitors its complication rates for carotid endarterectomy and ask your surgeon how many times he or she has performed the procedure. Evidence shows that surgeons who have performed more procedures have higher success rates.

AHCPR Research

This information is based on research by the Stroke Prevention Patient Outcomes Research Team (PORT) headed by David B. Matchar, MD, of Duke University's Center for Health Policy Research and Education. PORTs are multidisciplinary research studies, sponsored by AHCPR, that are focused on common and costly clinical conditions. PORTs examine the outcomes of treatments provided to typical patients by typical practitioners in typical health care settings.

Like other AHCPR medical effectiveness research studies, PORTs address three core questions about available treatments:

- Are they effective?
- For which patients are they most effective?
- Are they cost-effective?

Printed copies of *What You Should Know About Stroke Prevention* are available by writing or calling:

AHCPR Publications Clearinghouse
P.O. Box 8547
Silver Spring, MD 20907
800-358-9295 (24 hours a day)

Recovering After a Stroke, the Consumer Version of a Clinical Practice Guideline, is available from the AHCPR Publications Clearinghouse (AHCPR Pub. No. 95-0664). The booklet is on the Internet at URL: http://text.nlm.nih.gov/ftrs/dbaccess/psrp

Fax copies of these materials are available by calling AHCPR InstantFAX at 301/594-2800 using a fax machine with a telephone handset.

Chapter 11

The Choice between Aspirin and Warfarin in Stroke Prevention

A new study outlines the criteria for identifying hundreds of thousands of Americans who have the most or least to gain from the use of anticoagulants such as warfarin to prevent stroke. The study identifies certain patients with a common type of irregular heartbeat called atrial fibrillation, and a low-risk for stroke who fare well by taking aspirin instead of warfarin to prevent stroke. Previous studies have shown that warfarin can cut by two-thirds the stroke risk in patients with atrial fibrillation who are at high risk for stroke. However, because treatment with aspirin carries a lower risk of bleeding and requires less medical monitoring than warfarin, doctors have been interested in identifying the specific group of patients who would do well on aspirin alone.

People with atrial fibrillation are six times more likely to have a stroke than people without, and account for as many as 80,000 strokes a year.

The findings are from Part III of a decade-long study called Stroke Prevention in Atrial Fibrillation (SPAF), designed to find the best way to reduce strokes in the 2 million Americans who have atrial fibrillation. This series of clinical trials is funded by the National Institute of Neurological Disorders and Stroke (NINDS). All of the SPAF studies look at preventive treatment with aspirin and warfarin, both of which lessen the tendency of blood to clot. The latest research appears in the April 22, 1998, issue of *The Journal of the American Medical*

NIH News Release, National Institutes of Neurological Disorders and Stroke (NINDS), April 21, 1998.

Association.[1] SPAF is coordinated by Robert G. Hart, M.D., and David G. Sherman, M.D., from the University of Texas Health Sciences Center at San Antonio.

"Stroke prevention research is absolutely vital. The number of strokes has risen so dramatically in recent years that we must find ways to stop strokes from happening in the first place," said Audrey Penn, M.D., Acting Director of the NINDS.

A group of 892 low-risk atrial fibrillation patients in the study took a daily dose of adult aspirin and were evaluated for an average of 2 years to see if they had a stroke or developed a systemic embolism, a clot causing sudden blockage of arterial blood supply to a limb or body organ (blood clots are the cause of 80 percent of all strokes). Investigators found that the rate of ischemic stroke or embolism among these patients was 2.2 percent a year, only slightly higher than the 1 percent rate experienced by the general population in this age range. However, for patients with hypertension, but none of the four other risk factors, the rate of strokes or embolism was significantly higher— 3.6 percent. The rate of disabling stroke, however, was low in both groups.

The researchers concluded that, while hypertension in atrial fibrillation patients is a significant predictor of stroke, it remains to be seen whether these patients should take aspirin or warfarin. The final treatment decision should be made between the physician and the patient after considering the individual's risk for stroke, benefits from treatment, and personal preferences.

Higher-risk patients, who have one or more specified risk factors, suffer strokes at a rate of 8 percent a year, and through previous SPAF studies have been shown to benefit greatly from treatment with warfarin.

The study estimates that for every 1,000 atrial fibrillation patients in the low risk category, about five ischemic strokes would be prevented among those taking aspirin and three major hemorrhages would occur. If these same patients were given warfarin instead of aspirin over a 1-year period, about 10 ischemic strokes would be prevented, but the treatment might cause 10 to 12 major hemorrhages.

"When someone is prescribed warfarin for stroke prevention, it often means a 20-year commitment to taking the drug, and the risk of bleeding goes up every year you're on it," said Dr. Sherman. "For this reason, we have been eager to find exactly which patients will do well on aspirin therapy and I think this study identifies them with certainty."

In people with atrial fibrillation, blood clots can form in the upper chambers of the heart. These clots can break loose, be pumped into the bloodstream, and carried to the brain where they can cause a stroke. Atrial fibrillation primarily affects people over the age of 60 and is diagnosed by electrocardiogram. While some people have no symptoms, most experience a sensation of rapid heart beats or skipped beats.

The SPAF trials, which started in 1987, have involved about 4,000 patient volunteers with atrial fibrillation at 25 medical centers in the United States and Canada. Results from SPAF I, reported in 1990, found an 80 percent reduction in stroke risk for persons with atrial fibrillation who receive treatment with aspirin or warfarin. The SPAF II study, reported in 1994, identified the 60 percent of people with atrial fibrillation for whom a daily adult aspirin provides adequate protection against stroke with minimal complications. This group consists of those younger than 75 and those older than 75 with no additional stroke risk factors such as high blood pressure or heart disease. SPAF III studied the remaining 40 percent of atrial fibrillation patients who had additional risk factors for stroke.

The NINDS, one of the National Institutes of Health located in Bethesda, Maryland, is the nation's leading supporter of research on the brain and nervous system and is a lead agency for the Congressionally designated Decade of the Brain.

Note

[1]Stroke Prevention in Atrial Fibrillation Investigators. "Prospective Identification of Patients with Nonvalvular Atrial Fibrillation at Low Risk of Stroke During Treatment with Aspirin: Stroke Prevention in Atrial Fibrillation III Study." *JAMA*, Vol. 279, No. 16, April 22/29, 1998, pp. 1273-1277.

Chapter 12

Carotid Endarterectomy: Questions and Answers

What Is a Carotid Endarterectomy?

A carotid endarterectomy is a surgical procedure in which a doctor removes fatty deposits from one of the two main arteries in the neck supplying blood to the brain. Carotid artery problems become more common as people age. The disease process that causes the buildup of fat and other material on the artery walls is called atherosclerosis, popularly known as "hardening of the arteries." The fatty deposit is called plaque; the narrowing of the artery is called stenosis. The degree of stenosis is usually expressed as a percentage of the normal diameter of the opening.

Why Is the Surgery Performed?

Carotid endarterectomies are performed to prevent stroke. Two large clinical trials supported by the National Institute of Neurological Disorders and Stroke (NINDS) have identified specific individuals for whom the surgery is highly beneficial when performed by surgeons and in institutions that can match the standards set in those studies. The surgery has been found highly beneficial for persons who have already had a stroke or experienced the warning signs of a stroke and have a severe stenosis of 70 percent to 99 percent. In this group, surgery reduces the estimated 2-year risk of stroke by more than 80 percent, from greater than 1 in 4 to less than 1 in 10.

National Institute of Neurological Disorders and Stroke (NINDS), 1994, 1998.

In a second trial, the procedure has also been found highly beneficial for persons who are symptom-free but have a severe stenosis of 60 percent to 99 percent. In this group, the surgery reduces the estimated 5-year risk of stroke by more than one-half, from about 1 in 10 to less than 1 in 20.

What Is a Stroke?

A stroke occurs when brain cells die because of decreased blood flow to the brain. In some cases, small pieces of plaque in the carotid artery may break loose and block an artery in the brain. The narrowed opening in the carotid artery can be a source of blood clots that travel to the brain, can trap blood clots from other areas of the body, or can become completely clogged.

What Are the Warning Signs and Symptoms of a Stroke?

Warning signs and symptoms of stroke include: sudden weakness or numbness of the face, arm, or leg; sudden dimness or loss of vision, particularly in one eye; sudden difficulty speaking or understanding speech; sudden severe headache with no known cause; and unexplained dizziness, unsteadiness, or sudden falls, especially with any of the other signs. Warning signs may last a few moments and then disappear. When they disappear within 24 hours or less, they are called a transient ischemic attacks (TIA).

How Important Is a Blockage as a Cause of Stroke?

A blockage of a blood vessel is the most frequent cause of stroke and is responsible for about 75 percent of the nearly 150,000 U.S. stroke deaths each year. Stroke ranks as the third leading killer in the United States after heart disease and cancer. There are 500,000 to 600,000 new strokes in the United States each year. As many as 3 million Americans have survived a stroke with more than 2 million of them sustaining some permanent disability. The overall cost of stroke to the nation is $30 billion a year.

How Many Carotid Endarterectomies Are Performed Each Year?

In 1992, the most recent year for which statistics are available from the National Hospital Discharge Survey, there were about 91,000 carotid endarterectomies performed in the United States. The procedure has a 40-year history. It was first described in the mid-1950s. It began to be used increasingly as a stroke prevention measure in the 1960s and 1970s. Its use peaked in the mid-1980s when more than 100,000 operations were performed each year. At that time, several authorities began to question the trend and the risk-benefit ratio for some groups, and the use of the procedure dropped precipitously. The NINDS-supported North American Symptomatic Carotid Endarterectomy Trial (NASCET) and the NINDS-supported Asymptomatic Carotid Atherosclerosis Study (ACAS) were launched in the mid-1980s to identify the specific groups of people with carotid artery disease who would clearly benefit from the procedure.

How Much Does a Carotid Endarterectomy Cost?

The total average cost for the diagnostic tests, surgical procedure, hospitalization, and follow-up care is about $15,000.

How Risky Is the Surgery?

The degree of risk varies with the hospital, the surgeon, and the underlying disease conditions.

How Is Carotid Artery Disease Diagnosed?

In most cases, the disease can be detected during a normal checkup with a physician. Some of the tests a physician can use or order include history and physical exam, Doppler ultrasound imaging, oculoplethysmography (OPG), computed tomography (CT), arteriography and digital subtraction angiography (DSA), magnetic resonance angiography (MRA). Frequently these procedures are carried out in a stepwise fashion: from a doctor's evaluation of signs and symptoms to ultrasound, with arteriography, DSA or MRA reserved for difficult diagnoses.

- *History and physical exam.* A doctor will ask about symptoms of a stroke such as numbness or muscle weakness, speech or vision difficulties, or lightheadedness. Using a stethoscope, a doctor may hear a rushing sound, called a bruit (pronounced "brew-ee"), in the carotid artery. Unfortunately, dangerous levels of disease sometimes fail to make a sound, and some blockages with a low risk can make a sound.

• *Doppler ultrasound imaging.* This is a painless, noninvasive test in which sound waves above the range of human hearing are sent into the neck. Echoes bounce off the moving blood and the tissue in the artery and can be formed into an image. Ultrasound is fast, risk-free, relatively inexpensive, and painless. Unfortunately, there is a small possibility of error in an ultrasound study. A stenosis with a high level of risk will occasionally be incorrectly reported as a low-risk finding. Conversely, a stenosis with a low level of risk will sometimes be reported as a high level of risk. In carefully calibrated ultrasound laboratories, ultrasound studies can be up to 95 percent accurate and offer visualization of the anatomy, evaluation of the blood flow rate and turbulence, and characterization of the plaque. Performing an ultrasound study requires a great deal of skill which is not always available.

• *Oculoplethysmography (OPG).* This procedure measures the pulsation of the arteries in the back of the eye. It is used as an indirect check for blockages in the carotid arteries.

• *Computed tomography (CT).* This test produces a series of cross-sectional X-rays of the head and brain. It cannot detect carotid artery disease but may be ordered by a doctor to investigate other possible causes of symptoms. The test is also called a CAT scan, for computer assisted tomography.

• *Arteriography and digital subtraction angiography (DSA).* Arteriography is an X-ray of the carotid artery taken when a special dye is injected into another artery in the leg or arm. A burning sensation may be felt when the dye is injected. DSA is also an X-ray study of the carotid artery. It is similar to arteriography except that less dye is used. A person having a DSA must remain still during the test. These invasive procedures are more expensive and carry their own small risk of causing a stroke.

• *Magnetic resonance angiography (MRA).* This is a very new imaging technique that is more accurate than ultrasound yet avoids the risks associated with X-rays and dye injection. An MRA is a type of magnetic resonance image that uses special software to create an image of the arteries in the brain. A magnetic resonance image uses harmless but powerful magnetic fields to create a highly detailed image of the body's tissues.

What Is "Best Medical Therapy" for Stroke Prevention?

The mainstay of stroke prevention is risk factor management: smoking cessation, treatment of high blood pressure and heart disease, and control of blood sugar levels among persons with diabetes. Additionally, physicians may prescribe aspirin, warfarin, or ticlopidine.

Chapter 13

Asymptomatic Carotid Atherosclerosis Study

Officials at the National Institute of Neurological Disorders and Stroke (NINDS) announced that surgery can prevent stroke in carefully selected individuals who have no outward sign of disease but are at risk for stroke from a severe narrowing of a major artery in the neck. The NINDS brought to an early conclusion a 7-year clinical trial investigating the effectiveness of a surgical procedure, called carotid endarterectomy, in reducing stroke in these individuals.

The trial, called the Asymptomatic Carotid Atherosclerosis Study (ACAS), found that surgery to remove fatty deposits from one of the main arteries in the neck supplying blood to the brain lowered the 5-year risk of stroke by about one-half, from greater than 1 in 10 to less than 1 in 20.

"This finding will be of vital interest for individuals who are at risk of stroke and who may already know that their carotid arteries are partially blocked," said NINDS Director Zach W. Hall, Ph.D. "During the last 48 hours the NINDS has taken steps to inform the medical community of these important results so that they might be better able to evaluate and advise patients on the risks and benefits of surgical treatment to prevent stroke."

As part of the $20 million trial, investigators at 39 sites in the United States and Canada studied 1,662 men and women between the ages of 40 and 79 years with a 60 percent or greater narrowing of

"Asymptomatic Carotid Atherosclerosis Study—Lay Language Summary," National Institutes of Neurological Disorders and Stroke (NINDS), 1994, 1998.

the carotid artery but no stroke-like symptoms attributable to the blockage. The study was carried out under the direction of James F. Toole, M.D., Director of The Stroke Center and Professor of Neurology at the Bowman Gray School of Medicine, Wake Forest University in Winston-Salem, North Carolina. The University of North Carolina School of Public Health at Chapel Hill served as the coordinating center on the study. In 1992, about 91,000 Americans had a carotid endarterectomy. Clinical trials in both North America and Europe have established that this surgery is highly beneficial for people who have had a stroke or stroke-like symptoms and a demonstrated blockage of 70 percent or more. However, the trials have left open questions as to the effectiveness of surgery in patients with less severe blockage as well as those with blockage and no symptoms of an impending stroke.

In this multi-center trial, investigators provided all patients with the best available medical care, including one adult aspirin daily and aggressive management of modifiable risk factors, such as counseling to help them stop smoking and treatment for high blood pressure, high cholesterol, and diabetes when indicated. Among the individuals in the study, 64 percent had high blood pressure, 26 percent had a history of cigarette smoking, 23 percent had diabetes, 21 percent had a previous heart attack, and 25 percent had a previous mild stroke or TIA unrelated to the carotid artery involved in the study.

In addition to best medical care, 828 randomly chosen patients also underwent surgery by a neurosurgeon or vascular surgeon who had demonstrated a complication rate of less than 3 percent for symptom-free patients based on an audit of their last 50 consecutive carotid endarterectomies.

"When surgery is performed to the standards set in this study, its long-term benefits clearly outweigh any short-term risks," said Michael D. Walker, M.D., director of the NINDS Division of Stroke and Trauma which oversaw the trial. "Appropriate use of this technique has the potential for preventing many thousands of strokes every year."

Dr. Toole and his colleagues showed that the surgical groups had a substantially lower risk of stroke (4.8 percent over a 5-year period) as compared with those who were managed medically (10.6 percent). Surgery conferred a relative risk reduction of 55 percent. Men in the surgical group had a 69 percent relative risk reduction, and women had a 16 percent relative risk reduction. According to the investigators, the reasons for this difference are unknown and will require additional study.

Scientists involved with this study point to the standards that were set to measure the blockage and caution against unfounded mass screening efforts. In order to be eligible for this study, patients had to have a 60 percent or greater blockage as determined by ultrasound and, in some cases, more extensive tests, and confirmed by arteriogram prior to surgery.

"This study highlights the fact that ultrasound alone may not be sufficient to select patients who can maximally benefit from carotid endarterectomy unless it is done in carefully calibrated ultrasound laboratories and confirmed by more extensive tests prior to surgery," said Dr. Walker.

Additional information about carotid endarterectomy can be obtained from the National Institute of Neurological Disorders and Stroke (NINDS). NINDS's website is located at www.ninds.nih.gov.

Chapter 14

Emergency Treatment for Stroke

Introduction

Each year about 700,000 Americans suffer a stroke. Of these strokes, approximately 80 percent are ischemic, caused by a blood clot that reduces blood flow to the brain. The remaining 20 percent are hemorrhagic strokes, caused by bleeding into the brain. Stroke is the number one cause of adult disability in the United States, costing the nation more than $40 billion a year, and is the third leading cause of death in the country after heart disease and cancer, killing about 150,000 Americans each year.

T-PA Is Effective for Acute Ischemic Stroke

A five-year clinical trial has shown that treatment with the clot-dissolving drug t-PA (tissue plasminogen activator) is an effective emergency treatment for acute ischemic stroke despite some risk from bleeding. The trial found that carefully selected stroke patients who received t-PA treatment within 3 hours of their initial stroke symptoms were at least 30 percent more likely than untreated patients to recover from their stroke with little or no disability after three months. The nationwide study of more than 600 stroke patients was organized and funded by the National Institute of Neurological Disorders and

This chapter includes text from "NIH Announces Emergency Treatment for Stroke," National Institute of Neurological Disorders and Stroke (NINDS), 1995, 1998; and NIH New Release "New Stroke Treatment Likely to Decrease Health Care Costs and Increase Quality of Life," NINDS, April 1998.

Stroke (NINDS). Results appear in the December 14, 1995, issue of *The New England Journal of Medicine*.[1]

"Stroke, which leaves millions of adults disabled, is one of the most devastating and costly health problems that we face," said Zach W. Hall, Ph.D., director of the NINDS. "The positive result of this trial should be encouraging to all Americans at risk of stroke who hope to live to a healthy, independent old age. A notable feature of this study is that its quality sets a very high standard for future clinical trials."

In the two-part NINDS trial conducted at nine centers across the country, 624 patients received either intravenous t-PA or a placebo within 3 hours of the initial symptoms of a stroke. Before treatment could start, a medical team performed a CT scan to be sure the stroke was not caused by bleeding, administered a variety of blood tests, and obtained informed consent. Part 1 of the trial was designed to look for marked improvement in the patients' conditions 24 hours after treatment and, secondarily, to examine efficacy of the treatment at 3 months. Part 2 was designed to confirm the long-term benefit of the drug. In both parts, there was a dramatic 3-month improvement in those who received t-PA. The investigators demonstrated that the number of patients with complete or almost complete recovery was increased by 30 percent or more as measured by four different medical outcome scales. For every 100 patients receiving t-PA, at least 11 more had an excellent recovery as measured by the four scales. A powerful statistical approach, the global test statistic, combined information from all four outcome scales in order to compare the odds of an excellent outcome between treatments. The overall odds in favor of the t-PA treated group were 1.7 times greater than the placebo group.

The drug t-PA works by dissolving the blood clots that block brain arteries and cause over 80 percent of all strokes. Although it has been proven effective in the treatment of heart attack, t-PA's potential as a treatment for stroke has been unclear because of an increased risk of brain hemorrhage. In the NINDS trial, bleeding into the brain within 36 hours of treatment worsened strokes in 6.4 percent of those patients who received t-PA compared to 0.6 percent of those who received placebo. Overall, however, there were greater numbers of stroke survivors who were able to live normal lives in the t-PA treated group, leading the investigators to conclude that the use of t-PA for stroke is beneficial. Furthermore, the NINDS trial showed lower levels of brain hemorrhage than previously published stroke trials involving clot-dissolving drugs.

According to the investigators, timing is a critical factor. Over the past 12 years basic and clinical scientists have been working to discover the window of opportunity for emergency treatment of stroke. Based on research in animal models and clinical observations, the NINDS t-PA clinical investigators designed their highly coordinated emergency treatment program to work within the narrow time window of 3 hours.

"One of the keys to the success of this study was treating stroke as the true emergency that it is. The concept that stroke is every bit as serious as heart attack is one that physicians must recognize in order for this new treatment to have widespread benefit," said Thomas Brott, M.D., clinical investigator at the University of Cincinnati Medical Center in Ohio, the study site that treated the most patients.

Because of the risks involved, investigators urge physicians to take a cautious approach before introducing the use of this new stroke treatment. "It would be a mistake for physicians with limited experience in treating stroke to rush in and begin treatment with t-PA," said Patrick D. Lyden, M.D., clinical investigator at the University of California at San Diego School of Medicine. "Starting t-PA treatment more than three hours after stroke could easily result in a much higher rate of bleeding into the brain." He also emphasized that t-PA should be given only after a complete evaluation of the patient including a careful examination of a brain CT scan.

The investigators agree that substantial efforts by the health care community will be necessary before t-PA can be used on a widespread basis. These efforts include intensive public education about the signs of stroke and the importance of immediate treatment; the organization and training of medical personnel to evaluate and treat stroke patients; as well as planning for the rapid transport of patients to treatment centers through emergency medical services.

"This is a major breakthrough that will forever change the way stroke is treated. After years of discouraging results, the positive results of this trial will lead to renewed efforts to make even more progress in treating and preventing the devastating consequences of stroke," said John R. Marler, M.D., NINDS neurologist and project officer for the trial.

Principal investigators participating in the trial were: Thomas Brott, M.D., University of Cincinnati Medical Center, OH; Patrick D. Lyden, M.D., University of California, San Diego; James C. Grotta, M.D., University of Texas Medical Center, Houston; Thomas Kwiatkowski, M.D., Long Island Jewish Medical Center, New Hyde Park, NY; Steven R. Levine, M.D., Henry Ford Hospital, Detroit, MI; Michael R. Frankel, M.D., Emory University, Atlanta, GA; E. Clarke Haley, Jr., M.D., University of Virginia Medical Center,

Charlottesville; Michael Meyer, M.D., University of Tennessee Medical Center, Knoxville and Memphis. Barbara C. Tilley, Ph.D., headed the Coordinating Center at Henry Ford Health Science Center, Detroit, MI. K.M.A. Welch, M.D., Henry Ford Health Science Center, Detroit, MI, was the medical monitor and chairman of the steering committee. John R. Marler, M.D., was the NINDS project officer for the trial.

New Stroke Treatment Likely to Decrease Health Care Costs and Increase Quality of Life

Results from a new study show a greater than 90 percent probability that treating acute ischemic stroke patients with the clot-busting drug t-PA could result in a substantial net cost savings to the health care system. These savings are based on the fact that t-PA-treated stroke patients leave the hospital sooner and require less rehabilitation and nursing after discharge than do patients who do not receive t-PA. The study also showed that t-PA-treated stroke patients, because of their decreased disability, can expect to have an improved quality of life. These results, published in the April 1998 issue of *Neurology*, were reported by Susan Fagan, Pharm. D., Associate Professor of Pharmacy Practice at Wayne State University and Henry Ford Hospital. This study was sponsored by the National Institute of Neurological Disorders and Stroke (NINDS).[2]

Dr. Fagan estimated the costs per 1,000 patients eligible for treatment with t-PA compared with the costs per 1,000 stroke patients not treated with t-PA. The study used data from the NINDS t-PA Stroke Trial,[1] in which the average length of a hospital stay was shorter in t-PA-treated patients, 10.9 days, than in patients not treated with t-PA, 12.4 days. T-PA-treated patients were more frequently discharged to their home than to inpatient rehabilitation centers or nursing homes.

The cost of t-PA treatment increases hospital costs for patients when they are first admitted. However, because t-PA shortens hospital stays and decreases long-term disabilities, there is a net savings. For 1,000 t-PA patients, the researchers estimate an initial increase in hospital costs of $1.7 million, but an eventual savings of $4.8 million in nursing home care costs and $1.3 million in rehabilitation costs. The overall impact is a net decrease of more than $4 million in health care costs for every 1,000 patients treated.

"Considering that there are tens of thousands of stroke patients who could be eligible for t-PA, we are talking about a potential cost savings in excess of $100 million per year," said Michael D. Walker, M.D., Director of the Division of Stroke, Trauma, and Neurodegenerative Disorders at the NINDS.

"The use of t-PA for eligible patients with acute ischemic stroke appears to be a 'win-win' situation, with improved patient outcomes accompanied by a net cost savings to the health care system," said Dr. Fagan.

The NINDS t-PA Stroke Trial, which included more than 600 carefully selected stroke patients and was completed in December 1995, found that those treated with t-PA within the critical 3-hour time window of their initial stroke symptoms were at least 30 percent more likely than untreated patients to recover from their stroke with little or no disability.

"The good news about this study is the benefit it delivers both to the patient and the health care system in terms of long-term quality of life and realized cost savings," said Michael D. Walker, MD, Director of the Division of Stroke, Trauma and Neurodegenerative Disorders at the National Institute of Neurological Disorders and Stroke.

For More Information

The NINDS is the nation's principal supporter of research on the brain and nervous system and a lead agency for the Congressionally designated Decade of the Brain. The Institute supports and conducts a broad program of basic and clinical neurological investigations and is part of the National Institutes of Health, located in Bethesda, MD. For more information contact NINDS Office of Scientific and Health Reports, (301) 496-5751 or visit the NINDS website at www.ninds. nih.gov.

Notes

[1] The National Institute of Neurological Disorders and Stroke t-PA Stroke Study Group. "Tissue Plasminogen Activator for Acute Ischemic Stroke." *The New England Journal of Medicine*, Vol. 333, No. 24, December 15, 1995, pp. 1581-1587.

[2] Fagan, S.C.; Morgenstern, L.B.; Petitta, A.; Ward, R.E.; Tilley, B.C.; Marler, J.R.; Levine, S.R.; Broderick, J.P.; Kwiatkowski, T.G.; Frankel, M.; Brott, T.G.; Walker, M.D.; and the NINDS rt-PA Stroke Study Group. "Cost-effectiveness of Tissue Plasminogen Activator for Acute Ischemic Stroke." *Neurology*, Vol. 50, No. 4, April 1, 1998, p. 883.

Chapter 15

Recovering After a Stroke

What Is a Stroke?

A stroke is a type of brain injury. Symptoms depend on the part of the brain that is affected. People who survive a stroke often have weakness on one side of the body or trouble with moving, talking, or thinking.

Most strokes are ischemic (is-KEE-mic) strokes. These are caused by reduced blood flow to the brain when blood vessels are blocked by a clot or become too narrow for blood to get through. Brain cells in the area die from lack of oxygen. In another type of stroke, called hemorrhagic (hem-or-AJ-ic) stroke, the blood vessel isn't blocked; it bursts, and blood leaks into the brain, causing damage.

Strokes are more common in older people. Almost three-fourths of all strokes occur in people 65 years of age or over. However, a person of any age can have a stroke.

A person may also have a transient ischemic attack (TIA). This has the same symptoms as a stroke, but only lasts for a few hours or a day and does not cause permanent brain damage. A TIA is not a stroke but it is an important warning signal. The person needs treatment to help prevent an actual stroke in the future.

Recovering After a Stroke: Patient and Family Guide, Consumer Version, Clinical Practice Guidelines Number 16, Agency for Health Care Policy and Research (AHCPR), AHCPR Publication No. 95-0664, May 1995.

Purpose of This Chapter

This chapter is about stroke rehabilitation. Its goal is to help the person who has had a stroke achieve the best possible recovery. Its purpose is to help people who have had strokes and their families get the most out of rehabilitation.

Note that this text sometimes uses the terms "stroke survivor" and "person" instead of "patient' to refer to someone who has had a stroke. This is because people who have had a stroke are patients for only a short time, first in the acute care hospital and then perhaps in a rehabilitation program. For the rest of their lives, they are people who happen to have had a stroke. The text also uses the word "family" to include those people who are closest to the stroke survivor, whether or not they are relatives.

Rehabilitation works best when stroke survivors and their families work together as a team. For this reason, both stroke survivors and family members are encouraged to read all parts of the text.

Recovering from Stroke

The process of recovering from a stroke usually includes treatment, spontaneous recovery, rehabilitation, and the return to community living. Because stroke survivors often have complex rehabilitation needs, progress and recovery are different for each person.

Treatment for stroke begins in a hospital with "acute care." This first step includes helping the patient survive, preventing another stroke, and taking care of any other medical problems.

Spontaneous recovery happens naturally to most people. Soon after the stroke, some abilities that have been lost usually start to come back. This process is quickest during the first few weeks, but it sometimes continues for a long time.

Rehabilitation is another part of treatment. It helps the person keep abilities and gain back lost abilities to become more independent. It usually begins while the patient is still in acute care. For many patients, it continues afterward, either as a formal rehabilitation program or as individual rehabilitation services. Many decisions about rehabilitation are made by the patient, family, and hospital staff before discharge from acute care.

The last stage in stroke recovery begins with the person's return to community living after acute care or rehabilitation. This stage can last for a lifetime as the stroke survivor and family learn to live with the effects of the stroke. This may include doing common tasks in new ways or making up for damage to or limits of one part of the body by greater activity of another. For example, a stroke survivor can wear shoes with velcro closures instead of laces or may learn to write with the opposite hand.

How Stroke Affects People

Effects on the Body, Mind, and Feelings

Each stroke is different depending on the part of the brain injured, how bad the injury is, and the person's general health. Some of the effects of stroke are:

- **Weakness (hemiparesis—hem-ee-par-EE-sis) or paralysis (hemiplegia—hem-ee-PLEE-ja) on one side of the body.** This may affect the whole side or just the arm or the leg. The weakness or paralysis is on the side of the body opposite the side of the brain injured by the stroke. For example, if the stroke injured the left side of the brain, the weakness or paralysis will be on the right side of the body.

- **Problems with balance or coordination.** These can make it hard for the person to sit, stand, or walk, even if muscles are strong enough.

- **Problems using language (aphasia and dysarthria).** A person with aphasia (a-FAY-zha) may have trouble understanding speech or writing. Or, the person may understand but may not be able to think of the words to speak or write. A person with dysarthria (dis-AR-three-a) knows the right words but has trouble saying them clearly.

- **Being unaware of or ignoring things on one side of the body (bodily neglect or inattention).** Often, the person will not turn to look toward the weaker side or even eat food from the half of the plate on that side.

- **Pain, numbness, or odd sensations.** These can make it hard for the person to relax and feel comfortable.

- **Problems with memory, thinking, attention, or learning (cognitive problems).** A person may have trouble with many mental activities or just a few. For example, the person may have trouble following directions, may get confused if something

77

in a room is moved, or may not be able to keep track of the date or time.

- **Being unaware of the effects of the stroke.** The person may show poor judgment by trying to do things that are unsafe as a result of the stroke.

- **Trouble swallowing (dysphagia—dis-FAY-ja).** This can make it hard for the person to get enough food. Also, care must sometimes be taken to prevent the person from breathing in food (aspiration—as-per-AY-shun) while trying to swallow it.

- **Problems with bowel or bladder control.** These problems can be helped with the use of portable urinals, bedpans, and other toileting devices.

- **Getting tired very quickly.** Becoming tired very quickly may limit the person's participation and performance in a rehabilitation program.

- **Sudden bursts of emotion, such as laughing, crying, or anger.** These emotions may indicate that the person needs help, understanding, and support in adjusting to the effects of the stroke.

- **Depression.** This is common in people who have had strokes. It can begin soon after the stroke or many weeks later, and family members often notice it first.

Depression After Stroke

It is normal for a stroke survivor to feel sad over the problems caused by stroke. However, some people experience a major depressive disorder, which should be diagnosed and treated as soon as possible. A person with a major depressive disorder has a number of symptoms nearly every day, all day, for at least 2 weeks. These always include at least one of the following:

- Feeling sad, blue, or down in the dumps.
- Loss of interest in things that the person used to enjoy.

A person may also have other physical or psychological symptoms, including:

- Feeling slowed down or restless and unable to sit still.
- Feeling worthless or guilty.

- Increase or decrease in appetite or weight.
- Problems concentrating, thinking, remembering, or making decisions.
- Trouble sleeping or sleeping too much.
- Loss of energy or feeling tired all of the time.
- Headaches.
- Other aches and pains.
- Digestive problems.
- Sexual problems.
- Feeling pessimistic or hopeless.
- Being anxious or worried.
- Thoughts of death or suicide.

If a stroke survivor has symptoms of depression, **especially thoughts of death or suicide**, professional help is needed right away. Once the depression is properly treated, these thoughts will go away. Depression can be treated with medication, psychotherapy, or both. If it is not treated, it can cause needless suffering and also makes it harder to recover from the stroke.

Disabilities after Stroke

A "disability" is difficulty doing something that is a normal part of daily life. People who have had a stroke may have trouble with many activities that were easy before, such as walking, talking, and taking care of "activities of daily living" (ADLs). These include basic tasks such as bathing, dressing, eating, and using the toilet, as well as more complex tasks called "instrumental activities of daily living" (IADLs), such as housekeeping, using the telephone, driving, and writing checks.

Some disabilities are obvious right after the stroke. Others may not be noticed until the person is back home and is trying to do something for the first time since the stroke.

What Happens during Acute Care

The main purposes of acute care are to:

- Make sure the patient's condition is caused by a stroke and not by some other medical problem.

- Determine the type and location of the stroke and how serious it is.

79

- Prevent or treat complications such as bowel or bladder problems or pressure ulcers (bed sores).

- Prevent another stroke.

- Encourage the patient to move and perform self-care tasks, such as eating and getting out of bed, as early as medically possible. This is the first step in rehabilitation.

Before acute care ends, the patient and family with the hospital staff decide what the next step will be. For many patients, the next step will be to continue rehabilitation.

Preventing Another Stroke

People who have had a stroke have an increased risk of another stroke, especially during the first year after the original stroke. The risk of another stroke goes up with older age, high blood pressure (hypertension), high cholesterol, diabetes, obesity, having had a transient ischemic attack (TIA), heart disease, cigarette smoking, heavy alcohol use, and drug abuse. While some risk factors for stroke (such as age) cannot be changed, the risk factors for the others can be reduced through use of medicines or changes in lifestyle.

Patients and families should ask for guidance from their doctor or nurse about preventing another stroke. They need to work together to make healthy changes in the patient's lifestyle. Patients and families should also learn the warning signs of a TIA (such as weakness on one side of the body and slurred speech) and see a doctor immediately if these happen.

Deciding about Rehabilitation

Some people do not need rehabilitation after a stroke because the stroke was mild or they have fully recovered. Others may be too disabled to participate. However, many patients can be helped by rehabilitation. Hospital staff will help the patient and family decide about rehabilitation and choose the right services or program.

Types of Rehabilitation Programs

There are several kinds of rehabilitation programs:

- **Hospital programs.** These programs can be provided by special rehabilitation hospitals or by rehabilitation units in acute care hospitals. Complete rehabilitation services are available. The patient stays in the hospital during rehabilitation. An organized team of specially trained professionals provides the therapy. Hospital programs are usually more intense than other programs and require more effort from the patient.

- **Nursing facility (nursing home) programs.** As in hospital programs, the person stays at the facility during rehabilitation. Nursing facility programs are very different from each other, so it is important to get specific information about each one. Some provide a complete range of rehabilitation services; others provide only limited services.

- **Outpatient programs.** Outpatient programs allow a patient who lives at home to get a full range of services by visiting a hospital outpatient department, outpatient rehabilitation facility, or day hospital program.

- **Home-based programs.** The patient can live at home and receive rehabilitation services from visiting professionals. An important advantage of home programs is that patients learn skills in the same place where they will use them.

Individual Rehabilitation Services

Many stroke survivors do not need a complete range of rehabilitation services. Instead, they may need an individual type of service, such as regular physical therapy or speech therapy. These services are available from outpatient and home care programs.

Paying for Rehabilitation

Medicare and many health insurance policies will help pay for rehabilitation. Medicare is the Federal health insurance program for Americans 65 years of age or over and for certain Americans with disabilities. It has two parts: hospital insurance (known as Part A) and supplementary medical insurance (known as Part B). Part A helps pay for home health care, hospice care, inpatient hospital care, and inpatient care in a skilled nursing facility. Part B helps pay for doctors' services, outpatient hospital services, durable medical equipment, and a number of other medical services and supplies not covered by Part A. Social Security Administration offices across the country take applications for Medicare and provide general information about the program.

In some cases, Medicare will help pay for outpatient services from a Medicare-participating comprehensive outpatient rehabilitation facility. Covered services include physicians' services; physical, speech, occupational, and respiratory therapies; counseling; and other related services. A stroke survivor must be referred by a physician who certifies that skilled rehabilitation services are needed.

Medicaid is a Federal program that is operated by the States, and each State decides who is eligible and the scope of health services offered. Medicaid provides health care coverage for some low-income people who cannot afford it. This includes people who are eligible because they are older, blind, or disabled, or certain people in families with dependent children.

These programs have certain restrictions and limitations, and coverage may stop as soon as the patient stops making progress. Therefore, it is important for patients and families to find out exactly what their insurance will cover. The hospital's social service department can answer questions about insurance coverage and can help with financial planning.

Choosing a Rehabilitation Program

The doctor and other hospital staff will provide information and advice about rehabilitation programs, but the patient and family make the final choice. Hospital staff know the patient's disabilities and medical condition. They should also be familiar with the rehabilitation programs in the community and should be able to answer questions about them. The patient and family may have a preference about whether the patient lives at home or at a rehabilitation facility. They may have reasons for preferring one program over another. Their concerns are important and should be discussed with hospital staff.

Things to Consider When Choosing a Rehabilitation Program

- Does the program provide the services the patient needs?

- Does it match the patient's abilities or is it too demanding or not demanding enough?

- What kind of standing does it have in the community for the quality of the program?

- Is it certified and does its staff have good credentials?

- Is it located where family members can easily visit?

- Does it actively involve the patient and family members in rehabilitation decisions?

- Does it encourage family members to participate in some rehabilitation sessions and practice with the patient?

- How well are its costs covered by insurance or Medicare?

- If it is an outpatient or home program, is there someone living at home who can provide care?

- If it is an outpatient program, is transportation available?

A person may start rehabilitation in one program and later transfer to another. For example, some patients who get tired quickly may start out in a less intense rehabilitation program. After they build up their strength, they are able to transfer to a more intense program.

When Rehabilitation Is Not Recommended

Some families and patients may be disappointed if the doctor does not recommend rehabilitation. However, a person may be unconscious or too disabled to benefit. For example, a person who is unable to learn may be better helped by maintenance care at home or in a nursing facility. A person who is, at first, too weak for rehabilitation may benefit from a gradual recovery period at home or in a nursing facility. This person can consider rehabilitation at a later time. It is important to remember that:

- Hospital staff are responsible for helping plan the best way to care for the patient after discharge from acute care. They can also provide or arrange for needed social services and family education.

- This is not the only chance to participate in rehabilitation. People who are too disabled at first may recover enough to enter rehabilitation later.

What Happens during Rehabilitation

In hospital or nursing facility rehabilitation programs, the patient may spend several hours a day in activities such as physical therapy, occupational therapy, speech therapy, recreational therapy, group

activities, and patient and family education. It is important to maintain skills that help recovery. Part of the time is spent relearning skills
(such as walking and speaking) that the person had before the stroke.
Part of it is spent learning new ways to do things that can no longer
be done the old way (for example, using one hand for tasks that usually need both hands).

Setting Rehabilitation Goals

The goals of rehabilitation depend on the effects of the stroke, what
the patient was able to do before the stroke, and the patient's wishes.
Working together, goals are set by the patient, family, and rehabilitation program staff. Sometimes, a person may need to repeat steps
in striving to reach goals.

If goals are too high, the patient will not be able to reach them. If
they are too low, the patient may not get all the services that would
help. If they do not match the patient's interests, the patient may not
want to work at them. Therefore, it is important for goals to be realistic. To help achieve realistic goals, the patient and family should tell
program staff about things that the patient wants to be able to do.

Rehabilitation Goals

- Being able to walk, at least with a walker or cane, is a realistic
  goal for most stroke survivors.

- Being able to take care of oneself with some special equipment
  is a realistic goal for most.

- Being able to drive a car is a realistic goal for some.

- Having a job can be a realistic goal for some people who were
  working before the stroke. For some, the old job may not be possible but another job or a volunteer activity may be.

Reaching treatment goals does not mean the end of recovery. It just
means that the stroke survivor and family are ready to continue recovery on their own.

Rehabilitation Specialists

Because every stroke is different, treatment will be different for
each person. Rehabilitation is provided by several types of specially
trained professionals. A person may work with any or all of these:

- **Physician.** All patients in stroke rehabilitation have a physician in charge of their care. Several kinds of doctors with rehabilitation experience may have this role. These include family physicians and internists (primary care doctors), geriatricians (specialists in working with older patients), neurologists (specialists in the brain and nervous system), and physiatrists (specialists in physical medicine and rehabilitation).

- **Rehabilitation nurse.** Rehabilitation nurses specialize in nursing care for people with disabilities. They provide direct care, educate patients and families, and help the doctor to coordinate care.

- **Physical therapist.** Physical therapists evaluate and treat problems with moving, balance, and coordination. They provide training and exercises to improve walking, getting in and out of a bed or chair, and moving around without losing balance. They teach family members how to help with exercises for the patient and how to help the patient move or walk, if needed.

- **Occupational therapist.** Occupational therapists provide exercises and practice to help patients do things they could do before the stroke such as eating, bathing, dressing, writing, or cooking. The old way of doing an activity sometimes is no longer possible, so the therapist teaches a new technique.

- **Speech-language pathologist.** Speech-language pathologists help patients get back language skills and learn other ways to communicate. Teaching families how to improve communication is very important. Speech-language pathologists also work with patients who have swallowing problems (dysphagia).

- **Social worker.** Social workers help patients and families make decisions about rehabilitation and plan the return to the home or a new living place. They help the family answer questions about insurance and other financial issues and can arrange for a variety of support services. They may also provide or arrange for patient and family counseling to help cope with any emotional problems.

- **Psychologist.** Psychologists are concerned with the mental and emotional health of patients. They use interviews and tests to identify and understand problems. They may also treat thinking or memory problems or may provide advice to other professionals about patients with these problems.

85

- **Therapeutic recreation specialist.** These therapists help patients return to activities that they enjoyed before the stroke such as playing cards, gardening, bowling, or community activities. Recreational therapy helps the rehabilitation process and encourages the patient to practice skills.

- **Other professionals.** Other professionals may also help with the patient's treatment. An orthotist may make special braces to support weak ankles and feet. A urologist may help with bladder problems. Other physician specialists may help with medical or emotional problems. Dietitians make sure that the patient has a healthy diet during rehabilitation. They also educate the family about proper diet after the patient leaves the program. Vocational counselors may help patients go back to work or school.

Rehabilitation Team

In many programs, a special rehabilitation team with a team leader is organized for each patient. The patient, family, and rehabilitation professionals are all members. The team has regular meetings to discuss the progress of treatment. Using a team approach often helps everyone work together to meet goals.

Getting the Most Out of Rehabilitation

What the Patient Can Do

If you are a stroke survivor in rehabilitation, keep in mind that you are the most important person in your treatment. You should have a major say in decisions about your care. This is hard for many stroke patients. You may sometimes feel tempted to sit back and let the program staff take charge. If you need extra time to think or have trouble talking, you may find that others are going ahead and making decisions without waiting. Try not to let this happen.

- Make sure others understand that you want to help make decisions about your care.

- Bring your questions and concerns to program staff.

- State your wishes and opinions on matters that affect you.

- Speak up if you feel that anyone is "talking down" to you; or, if people start talking about you as if you are not there.

- Remember that you have the right to see your medical records.

To be a partner in your care, you need to be well informed about your treatment and how well you are doing. It may help to record important information about your treatment and progress and write down any questions you have.

If you have speech problems, making your wishes known is hard. The speech-language pathologist can help you to communicate with other staff members, and family members may also help to communicate your ideas and needs.

Most patients find that rehabilitation is hard work. They need to maintain abilities at the same time they are working to regain abilities. It is normal to feel tired and discouraged at times because things that used to be easy before the stroke are now difficult. The important thing is to notice the progress you make and take pride in each achievement.

How the Family Can Help

If you are a family member of a stroke survivor, here are some things you can do:

- Support the patient's efforts to participate in rehabilitation decisions.

- Visit and talk with the patient. You can relax together while playing cards, watching television, listening to the radio, or playing a board game.

- If the patient has trouble communicating (aphasia), ask the speech-language pathologist how you can help.

- Participate in education offered for stroke survivors and their families. Learn as much as you can and how you can help.

- Ask to attend some of the rehabilitation sessions. This is a good way to learn how rehabilitation works and how to help.

- Encourage and help the patient to practice skills learned in rehabilitation.

- Make sure that the program staff suggests activities that fit the patient's needs and interests. Find out what the patient can do alone, what the patient can do with help, and what the patient can't do. Then avoid doing things for the patient that the patient is able to do. Each time the patient does them, his or her ability and confidence will grow.

- Take care of yourself by eating well, getting enough rest, and taking time to do things that you enjoy.

To gain more control over the rehabilitation process, keep important information where you can find it. One suggestion is to keep a notebook with the patient. Some things to include are:

- Rehabilitation goals

- The name, phone number, and job of each person on the program staff who works with the patient

- Schedule of rehabilitation activities

- Treatment instructions

- The patient's goals or planned activities for the week

- Other things accomplished during each day (include small steps in reaching goals)

- Questions and concerns to talk about with the program staff.

Discharge Planning

Discharge planning begins early during rehabilitation. It involves the patient, family, and rehabilitation staff. The purpose of discharge planning is to help maintain the benefits of rehabilitation after the patient has been discharged from the program. Patients are usually discharged from rehabilitation soon after their goals have been reached.

Some of the things discharge planning can include are to:

- Make sure that the stroke survivor has a safe place to live after discharge.

- Decide what care, assistance, or special equipment will be needed.

- Arrange for more rehabilitation services or for other services in the home (such as visits by a home health aide).

- Choose the health care provider who will monitor the person's health and medical needs.

- Determine the caregivers who will work as a partner with the patient to provide daily care and assistance at home, and teach them the skills they will need.

- Help the stroke survivor explore employment opportunities, volunteer activities, and driving a car (if able and interested).

- Discuss any sexual concerns the stroke survivor or husband/wife may have. Many people who have had strokes enjoy active sex lives.

Preparing a Living Place

Many stroke survivors can return to their own homes after rehabilitation. Others need to live in a place with professional staff such as a nursing home or assisted living facility. An assisted living facility can provide residential living with a full range of services and staff. The choice usually depends on the person's needs for care and whether caregivers are available in the home. The stroke survivor needs a living place that supports continuing recovery.

It is important to choose a living place that is safe. If the person needs a new place to live, a social worker can help find the best place.

During discharge planning, program staff will ask about the home and may also visit it. They may suggest changes to make it safer. These might include changing rooms around so that a stroke survivor can stay on one floor, moving scatter rugs or small pieces of furniture that could cause falls, and putting grab bars and seats in tubs and showers.

It is a good idea for the stroke survivor to go home for a trial visit before discharge. This will help identify problems that need to be discussed or corrected before the patient returns.

Deciding about Special Equipment

Even after rehabilitation, some stroke survivors have trouble walking, balancing, or performing certain activities of daily living. Special equipment can sometimes help. Here are some examples:

- **Cane.** Many people who have had strokes use a cane when walking. For people with balancing problems, special canes with three or four "feet" are available.

89

- **Walker.** A walker provides more support than a cane. Several designs are available for people who can only use one hand and for different problems with walking or balance.

- **Ankle-foot orthotic devices (braces).** Braces help a person to walk by keeping the ankle and foot in the correct position and providing support for the knee.

- **Wheelchair.** Some people will need a wheelchair. Wheelchairs come in many different designs. They can be customized to fit the user's needs and abilities. Find out which features are most important for the stroke survivor.

- **Aids for bathing, dressing, and eating.** Some of these are safety devices such as grab bars and nonskid tub and floor mats. Others make it easier to do things with one hand. Examples are velcro fasteners on clothes and placemats that won't slide on the table.

- **Communication aids.** These range from small computers to homemade communication boards. The stroke survivor, family, and rehabilitation program staff should decide together what special equipment is needed. Program staff can help in making the best choices. Medicare or health insurance will often help pay for the equipment.

Preparing Caregivers

Caregivers who help stroke survivors at home are usually family members such as a husband or wife or an adult son or daughter. They may also be friends or even professional home health aides. Usually, one person is the main caregiver, while others help from time to time. An important part of discharge planning is to make sure that caregivers understand the safety, physical, and emotional needs of the stroke survivor, and that they will be available to provide needed care.

Since every stroke is different, people have different needs for help from caregivers. Here are some of the things caregivers may do:

- Keep notes on discharge plans and instructions and ask about anything that is not clear.

- Help to make sure that the stroke survivor takes all prescribed medicines and follows suggestions from program staff about diet, exercise, rest, and other health practices.

- Encourage and help the person to practice skills learned in rehabilitation.

- Help the person solve problems and discover new ways to do things.

- Help the person with activities performed before the stroke. These could include using tools, buttoning a shirt, household tasks, and leisure or social activities.

- Help with personal care, if the person cannot manage alone.

- Help with communication, if the person has speech problems. Include the stroke survivor in conversations even when the person cannot actively participate.

- Arrange for needed community services.

- Stand up for the rights of the stroke survivor.

If you expect to be a caregiver, think carefully about this role ahead of time. Are you prepared to work with the patient on stroke recovery? Talk it over with other people who will share the caregiving job with you. What are the stroke survivor's needs? Who can best help meet each of them? Who will be the main caregiver? Does caregiving need to be scheduled around the caregivers' jobs or other activities? There is time during discharge planning to talk with program staff about caregiving and to develop a workable plan.

Going Home

Adjusting to the Change

Going home to the old home or a new one is a big adjustment. For the stroke survivor, it may be hard to transfer the skills learned during rehabilitation to a new location. Also, more problems caused by the stroke may appear as the person tries to go back to old activities. During this time, the stroke survivor and family learn how the stroke will affect daily life and can make the necessary adjustments.

These adjustments are a physical and emotional challenge for the main caregiver as well as the stroke survivor. The caregiver has many new responsibilities and may not have time for some favorite activities. The caregiver needs support, understanding, and some time to rest. Caregiving that falls too heavily on one person can be very stressful.

91

Even when family members and friends are nearby and willing to help, conflicts over caregiving can cause stress.

Tips for Reducing Stress

The following tips for reducing stress are for both caregivers and stroke survivors.

- Take stroke recovery and caregiving one day at a time and be hopeful.

- Remember that adjusting to the effects of stroke takes time. Appreciate each small gain as you discover better ways of doing things.

- Caregiving is learned. Expect that knowledge and skills will grow with experience.

- Experiment. Until you find what works for you, try new ways of doing activities of daily living, communicating with each other, scheduling the day, and organizing your social life.

- Plan for "breaks" so that you are not together all the time. This is a good way for family and friends to help on occasion. You can also plan activities that get both of you out of the house.

- Ask family members and friends to help in specific ways and commit to certain times to help. This gives others a chance to help in useful ways.

- Read about the experiences of other people in similar situations. Your public library has life stories by people who have had a stroke as well as books for caregivers.

- Join or start a support group for stroke survivors or caregivers. You can work on problems together and develop new friendships.

- Be kind to each other. If you sometimes feel irritated, this is natural and you don't need to blame yourself. But don't "take it out" on the other person. It often helps to talk about these feelings with a friend, rehabilitation professional, or support group.

- Plan and enjoy new experiences and don't look back. Avoid comparing life as it is now with how it was before the stroke.

Follow-up Appointments

After a stroke survivor returns to the community, regular follow-up appointments are usually scheduled with the doctor and sometimes with rehabilitation professionals. The purpose of follow-up is to check on the stroke survivor's medical condition and ability to use the skills learned in rehabilitation. It is also important to check on how well the stroke survivor and family are adjusting. The stroke survivor and caregiver can be prepared for these visits with a list of questions or concerns.

Where to Get Help

Many kinds of help are available for people who have had strokes and their families and caregivers. Some of the most important are:

- **Information about stroke.** A good place to start is with the books and pamphlets available from national organizations that provide information on this subject. Many of their materials are available free of charge. A list of some organizations is located at the end of this chapter. Additional resources can be found in the Chapter titled "Organizational Resources for Patients with Brain Disorders" near the end of this book.

- **Local stroke clubs or other support groups.** These are groups where stroke survivors and family members can share their experiences, help each other solve problems, and expand their social lives.

- **Home health services.** These are available from the Visiting Nurses Association (VNA), public health departments, hospital home care departments, and private home health agencies. Services may include nursing care, rehabilitation therapies, personal care (for example, help with bathing or dressing), respite care (staying with the stroke survivor so that the caregiver can take a vacation or short break), homemaker services, and other kinds of help.

- **Meals on Wheels.** Hot meals are delivered to the homes of people who cannot easily shop and cook.

- **Adult day care.** People who cannot be completely independent sometimes spend the day at an adult day care center. There they get meals, participate in social activities, and may also get some health care and rehabilitation services.

93

- **Friendly Visitor (or other companion services).** A paid or volunteer companion makes regular visits or phone calls to a person with disabilities.

- **Transportation services.** Most public transportation systems have buses that a person in a wheelchair can board. Some organizations and communities provide vans to take wheelchair users and others on errands such as shopping or doctor's visits.

Many communities have service organizations that can help. Some free services may be available or fees may be on a "sliding scale" based on income. It takes some work to find out what services and payment arrangements are available. A good way to start is to ask the social workers in the hospital or rehabilitation program where the stroke survivor was treated. Also, talk to the local United Way or places of worship. Another good place to look is the Yellow Pages of the telephone book, under "Health Services," "Home Health Care," "Senior Citizen Services," or "Social Service Organizations." Just asking friends may turn up useful information. The more you ask, the more you will learn.

Additional Resources

ACTION
1100 Vermont Avenue, NW
Washington, DC 20525
(202) 606-4855 (call for telephone number of regional office)
Sponsors older American volunteer programs.

Administration on Aging
330 Independence Avenue, SW
Washington, DC 20201
(800) 677-1116 (call for list of community services for older Americans in your area)

AHA Stroke Connection (formerly the Courage Stroke Network)
American Heart Association
7272 Greenville Avenue
Dallas, TX 75231
(800) 553-6321 (or check telephone book for local AHA office)
Provides prevention, diagnosis, treatment, and rehabilitation information to stroke survivors and their families.

American Dietetic Association/National Center for Nutrition and Dietetics

216 West Jackson Boulevard
Chicago, IL 60606
(800) 366-1655 (Consumer Nutrition Hotline)
Consumers may speak to a registered dietitian for answers to nutrition questions, or obtain a referral to a local registered dietitian.

American Self-Help Clearinghouse

St. Clares-Riverside Medical Center
Denville, NJ 07834
(201) 625-7101 (call for name and telephone number of State or local clearinghouse)
Provides information and assistance on local self-help groups.

National Aphasia Association

P.O. Box 1887 Murray Hill Station
New York, NY 10156
(800) 922-4622
Provides information on the partial or total loss of the ability to speak or comprehend speech, resulting from stroke or other causes.

National Easter Seal Society

230 West Monroe Street, Suite 1800
Chicago, IL 60606
(312) 726-6200 (or check telephone book for local Easter Seal Society)
Provides information and services to help people with disabilities.

National Stroke Association

8480 East Orchard Road, Suite 1000
Englewood, CO 80111
(303) 771-1700
(800) STROKES (787-6537)
Serves as an information referral clearinghouse on stroke. Offers guidance on forming stroke support groups and clubs.

Rosalynn Carter Institute

Georgia Southwestern College
600 Simmons Street
Americus, GA 31709

Provides information on caregiving. Reading lists, video products, and other caregiver resources are available by writing to the address listed above.

Stroke Clubs International
805 12ᵗʰ Street
Galveston, TX 77550
(409) 762-1022 (call for the name of a stroke club located in your area)
Maintains list of over 800 stroke clubs throughout the United States.

The Well Spouse Foundation
P.O. Box 801
New York, NY 10023
(212) 724-7209
(800) 838-0879
Provides support for the husbands, wives, and partners of people who are chronically ill or disabled.

Medicare Information

Consumer Information Center
Department 59
Pueblo, CO 81009
By writing to this address, you can receive a free copy of *The Medicare Handbook* (updated and published annually). This handbook provides information about Medicare benefits, health insurance to supplement Medicare, and limits to Medicare coverage. It is also available in Spanish.

For Further Information

Information in this booklet is based on *Post-Stroke Rehabilitation, Clinical Practice Guideline, Number 16*. It was developed by a non-Federal panel sponsored by the Agency for Health Care Policy and Research (AHCPR), an agency of the Public Health Service. Other guidelines on common health problems are available, and more are being developed.

Four other patient guides are available from AHCPR that may be of interest to stroke survivors and their caregivers:

- *Preventing Pressure Ulcers: Patient Guide* gives detailed information about how to prevent pressure sores (AHCPR Publication No. 92-0048).

- *Treating Pressure Sores: Patient Guide* gives detailed information about treating pressure sores (AHCPR Publication No. 95-0654).

- *Urinary Incontinence in Adults: Patient Guide* describes why people lose urine when they don't want to and how that can be treated (AHCPR Publication No. 92-0040).

- *Depression Is a Treatable Illness: Patient Guide* discusses major depressive disorder, which most often can be successfully treated with the help of a health professional (AHCPR Publication No. 93-0053).

For more information about these and other guidelines, or to get more copies of this booklet, call toll-free: 800-358-9295 or write to:

Agency for Health Care Policy and Research
Publications Clearinghouse
P.O. Box 8547
Silver Spring, MD 20907

Chapter 16

New Success against Stroke

Rusty Van Sickle considers herself one of the lucky ones.

A victim of two massive strokes in 1993, one of which left her in a three-week coma, the Florida resident has, in her words, "come back." She's at the point where, with some accommodations, she can hold down a job in her field of social work.

"I can drive now," says Van Sickle, 43. "I cook and do home chores. I do many of the things I used to do." But, she adds, hinting at the long road she's had to recovery, "I've had to relearn all of them."

She has lingering effects such as a lack of visual sharpness and skewed spatial judgment. Paralysis on the left side of her body and damage to her brain's balance center keep her confined to a wheelchair most of the time.

But she keeps a positive outlook and admits that her stroke was "not really that bad when you compare it with what others have been through."

Stroke ranks as the third leading killer in the United States, behind heart disease and cancer. More than a half million Americans have a stroke each year, according to the National Institute of Neurological Disorders and Stroke (NINDS). Following a 25-year decline, stroke deaths are now on an upswing. Figures from the American Heart Association show that 158,061 Americans died of stroke in 1995, the latest year for which statistics are available—a 10 percent jump over the 143,769 deaths in 1992.

FDA Consumer, March/April 1998.

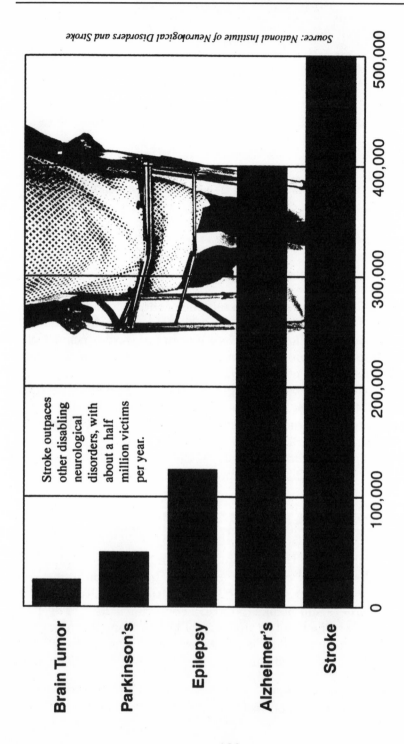

Source: *National Institute of Neurological Disorders and Stroke*

Stroke outpaces other disabling neurological disorders, with about a half million victims per year.

Figure 16.1. New Cases of Neurological Conditions

Some professionals have explanations. "The increase in stroke deaths is linked to the aging of the population and may also be the result of a decrease in the detection and treatment of high blood pressure," says Russell Luepker, M.D., director of epidemiology at the University of Minnesota. He adds that high blood pressure is one of the primary risk factors for stroke, and that about one-third of the Americans who have it are unaware.

Stroke also is the most common cause of adult disability. "Millions of people are challenged by the devastating aftermath of stroke," says Jan Breslow, M.D., president of the American Heart Association, adding that up to one-third of stroke survivors need help caring for themselves, 20 percent need help walking, and 70 percent are not able to perform the same job tasks they did before the stroke.

Amid these grim statistics, however, hope is emerging that the devastating effects of stroke can be lessened, possibly reversed, in many cases. Activase (alteplase), a genetically engineered version of the body's own tissue plasminogen activator (t-PA) that can dissolve clots, was approved by the Food and Drug Administration in 1996 for treating the most common type of stroke. It had been approved earlier for treating heart attacks. In clinical trials, Activase boosted recovery odds significantly in selected stroke patients treated within the first three hours of the onset of symptoms.

FDA also has approved the anticoagulant drug Coumadin (warfarin) for treating patients at high risk of having a stroke, such as those with a heart valve defect or who have suffered a heart attack. Doctors also prescribe low-dose aspirin to their patients who have had previous heart attacks or strokes because studies have shown that aspirin can prevent repeat heart attacks and strokes in these patients. Aspirin is an "antiplatelet" that can prevent the "clumping" of blood platelets that creates clots and triggers heart attacks and strokes. Last November, FDA approved another antiplatelet drug for treating stroke, Plavix (clopidogrel), and for several years, doctors have prescribed the drug Ticlid (ticlopidine hydrochloride), also approved as an antiplatelet.

Several drug treatments, including one designed to stop the rapid death of brain cells following a stroke, are in clinical trials now. Also under study is a spring-like device used to prop open blood vessels after blockages are removed, a therapy that may reduce the chance of stroke.

Medical professionals emphasize that there are at least five risk factors that, when treated, can decrease the possibility of stroke. Knowing stroke's warning signs and seeking emergency help immediately if they appear can reduce the risk of death or disability significantly. See "Control Stroke Risk Factors" and "Heed Stroke's Warning Signs" below.

What Is a Stroke?

Sometimes called a "brain attack," a stroke occurs when blood circulation to the brain fails. This cuts off oxygen and can kill brain cells, affecting neurological functions such as speech, vision, coordination, and thought.

Strokes fall into two broad categories: those caused by blood-flow blockage and those caused by bleeding. An *ischemic stroke*, which occurs when a blood vessel in the brain or neck is blocked, is the most common stroke, responsible for about 80 percent of cases. Such blockages may form within a blood vessel of the brain or neck (thrombosis), may migrate to the brain or neck as a clot from another part of the body (embolism), or may result from severe narrowing of an artery in or leading to the brain (stenosis).

Less common is *hemorrhagic stroke*, in which a blood vessel bursts, causing bleeding into the brain or in the spaces surrounding the brain.

Stroke is an equal threat to men and women. It occurs in all age groups and races, though African Americans suffer more severe strokes and have a death rate nearly double that of whites. Scientists have identified a "stroke belt" in the Southeastern states, especially in the coastal plain areas of the Carolinas and Georgia. A study in the May 1997 issue of the journal *Stroke* showed that stroke deaths in this Southern region are more than double those of the nation overall in ages 35 to 54. For ages 55 to 74, deaths in the belt are 1.7 times greater. Why? "It could be a wide range of things," says George Howard, professor of epidemiology at Bowman Gray School of Medicine in Winston-Salem, N.C., and lead author of the *Stroke* study. He says possible factors include the region's lifestyle choices such as smoking more or eating more fat and salt.

Though most strokes occur in adults over 40, children also have strokes, though these are typically caused by underlying conditions such as congenital heart disease or sickle cell anemia.

Sometimes young adults between 20 and 40 fall victim. Bill McGarry was a 22-year-old engineer in 1977 when a stroke plunged him into a three-month coma on advanced life-support machines. More than 20 years later, he still has paralysis, blindness, and nagging problems such as greatly reduced mathematical and analytical abilities. Speech therapy allowed him to regain control of his vocal cords. In 1989, he received a master of education degree from the University of New Orleans and began working as a career counselor in 1990. He now lives independently in his own home in Austin, Texas.

The key to this kind of recovery, he says, is to stay focused on getting better and to not lose faith when rehabilitation reaches a plateau. Support from family and friends also is crucial. "Improvement is almost glacial at times," he says. "But it adds up ... a step here and a second there and eventually you can walk across the room or down to the corner."

Turning the Tide

While strokes like McGarry's continue to cause devastating effects, new treatments now offer the potential for reversing or lessening stroke effects. The conclusion of a December 1996 symposium sponsored by NINDS that brought together experts from medical centers nationwide was that stroke is always a medical emergency. To survive or recover from it requires immediate care and effective responses from everyone in the "chain of care": medical technicians, emergency departments, and doctors. Public education also is crucial so stroke victims and those around them will recognize stroke symptoms and seek help quickly.

Before 1995, the medical community viewed stroke mainly as an "unfortunate medical problem requiring only supportive care and monitoring," writes Paul E. Pepe, M.D., of Pittsburgh's Allegheny General Hospital, in an overview of the NINDS symposium. Unless a patient had passed out or was having trouble breathing, the case often was not handled urgently.

Now the stroke-care landscape is changing—albeit slowly—as more emergency rooms adopt policies of treating appropriate stroke patients with the bioengineered clot-dissolving drug Activase. In a dramatic five-year clinical trial sponsored by the National Institutes of Health and concluded in 1995, 624 patients received either intravenous Activase or a placebo within three hours of stroke symptoms' onset. The result was that 11 percent more of the Activase-treated patients had few or no signs of disability compared to the placebo group.

"One of the keys to the success of [the NIH study] was treating stroke as the true emergency that it is," says Thomas Brott, M.D., clinical investigator at the University of Cincinnati Medical Center, one of the study sites. "The concept that stroke is every bit as serious as heart attack is one that physicians must recognize in order for this new treatment to have widespread benefit."

Activase is indicated only for treating ischemic strokes. So before the drug is used, medical professionals must rule out hemorrhagic stroke by various tests, including a computerized axial tomography

(CT) scan, which can indicate hemorrhages through sectional views of the brain.

Despite Activase's promise, it has been slow to catch on as a stroke treatment. In a November 1997 American Heart Association conference, researchers presented findings estimating that of 200,000 stroke patients who might have benefited from the drug, only 6,000 received it. Though some of these patients reached the emergency room too late to get the drug, others were not treated because emergency personnel were not trained or prepared to administer it, the researchers say.

Another drug, Coumadin (warfarin), can cut in half the 80,000 strokes that occur each year due to the rapid and erratic heartbeat condition called atrial fibrillation. But it too is underused, according to a study by the Agency for Health Care Policy and Research (AHCPR). Atrial fibrillation makes people more prone to form blood clots in the heart that can lodge in the brain and cause strokes. Though Coumadin can thin blood and keep clots from forming, only a quarter of atrial fibrillation patients undergo the therapy. AHCPR researchers say 50 to 75 percent of all atrial fibrillation patients over 60 should receive this blood-thinning therapy.

AHCPR also has reported on carotid endarterectomy, a surgical procedure that removes fatty plaque from the arteries that carry blood from the heart to the brain. Because carotid artery blockage is a major cause of stroke, the surgery can be beneficial and cost-effective for patients with stroke-related symptoms and a high-degree of blockage. But AHCPR stresses that surgery benefits diminish when applied to patients without symptoms but with known blockages. Identifying blockages in asymptomatic patients can involve expensive and invasive diagnostic methods such as angiography, which carries its own risk of stroke and other complications. For that reason, AHCPR does not advocate large-scale screening of asymptomatic people.

Though stroke occurrence overall is on a slight upswing, there's reason to be hopeful. Medical professionals say it is unlikely that stroke will ever be eliminated completely. But medical weapons such as Activase and Coumadin hold promise to at least help curb the disorder's destructive path.

Control Stroke Risk Factors

The National Institute of Neurological Disorders and Stroke has identified five *treatable* risk factors associated with stroke. Agency officials emphasize that having a risk factor doesn't mean you'll have a stroke. And not having a risk factor doesn't mean you'll avoid a stroke. But your likelihood of having a stroke grows as the number and severity of risk factors increase. Risk factors that can be controlled by medical treatment include:

- **High blood pressure.** This is by far the most important risk factor. Have your blood pressure checked by a qualified professional, and if it is high, seek medical attention to bring it into the normal range. Some over-the-counter (OTC) drugs may cause high blood pressure. For example, phenylpropanolamine (PPA), a widely used ingredient in OTC cough, cold, and weight-loss drugs, is under review because of concerns that the compound, especially in doses beyond those recommended, may elevate blood pressure and increase the risk of stroke. The Nonprescription Drug Manufacturers Association, at FDA's request, is sponsoring a study of PPA in OTC drugs and its possible relationship to an increased risk of stroke.

- **Cigarette smoking.** Studies have linked smoking to the buildup of fatty substances in the carotid artery, the main neck artery supplying blood to the brain. Blockage of this artery is the main cause of strokes in Americans. Nicotine in cigarettes can raise blood pressure, and smoke can make blood thicker and more likely to clot.

- **Heart disease.** Disorders such as coronary artery disease, valve defects, irregular heartbeat, and enlargement of one of the heart's chambers can create clots that may break loose and cause a stroke. Regular physicals will pinpoint treatable problems.

- **History of stroke.** If you experience a "mini-stroke," or transient ischemic attack (TIA), with symptoms that quickly subside, seek emergency help. If you have had a stroke, consult with your doctor about what you can do to avoid a second stroke.

- **Diabetes.** This causes destructive changes in blood vessels throughout the body, including the brain. If blood glucose levels are high at the time of a stroke, brain damage is usually more severe than when glucose is well controlled. Treating diabetes can delay complications that increase stroke risk. (See "Diabetes Demands a Triad of Treatments" in the May-June 1997 *FDA Consumer*.)

Heed Stroke's Warning Signs

From the onset of stroke symptoms, time is precious. Getting emergency help within three hours can mean the difference between severe brain damage and full or partial recovery.

If you have any of the following warning signs, call, or have someone call, 911 immediately:

- sudden weakness or numbness in the face, arm or leg
- sudden dimness or loss of vision, particularly in one eye
- sudden difficulty speaking or understanding, speech
- sudden severe headache with no known cause
- unexplained dizziness, unsteadiness, or sudden falls, especially in conjunction with the other warning signs.

Occasionally, strokes cause double vision, drowsiness, nausea or vomiting. Also, because warning signs sometimes may last only a few minutes and disappear, it may be tempting to ignore them. But these "mini-strokes," or transient ischemic attacks (TIAs), could be your body's warning of a future full-blown stroke. So even if the symptoms go away quickly, seek medical help right away.

For More Information

These organizations have information on stroke prevention, treatment and rehabilitation.

American Heart Association
7272 Greenville Ave.
Dallas, TX 75231
1-800-242-8721
http://www.americanheart.org/

Agency for Health Care Policy and Research
Box 8547
Silver Spring, MD 20907
1-800-358-9295
http://www.ahcpr.gov/

National Institute of Neurological Disorders and Stroke
Office of Science and Health Reports
P.O. Box 5801
Bethesda, MD 20824

1-800-352-9424
http://www.ninds.nih.gov/

National Rehabilitation Information Center
8455 Colesville Road, Suite 935
Silver Spring, MD 20910-3319
1-800-346-2742
http://www.cais.net/naric/

National Stroke Association
96 Inverness Drive, E., Suite One
Englewood, CO 80112-5112
1-800-787-6537
http://www.stroke.org/

In addition, these Websites have information on how to start or join a stroke support group in your area:

Stroke Support and Information
http://members.aol.com/scmmlm/main.htm

Stroke Connection Support Group
http://www.amhrt.org/Heart_and_Stroke_A_Z_Guide/strokecl.html

—by John Henkel

John Henkel is a staff writer for *FDA Consumer*.

Part Three

Seizure Disorders

Chapter 17

Epilepsy: What You Should Know

What Is Epilepsy?

Epilepsy is a family of more than 40 neurological conditions that share a common symptom—seizures. It affects about 2.5 million Americans and can result from head injury, infection, fever, brain tumors, or other trauma that damages the brain.

Normally, brain cells communicate with each other through electrical impulses that work together to control the body's movements and keep the body's organs functioning properly. When thousands to millions of electrical impulses occur at the same time producing abnormal brain electrical activity, the result can be a seizure. The part of the brain where the abnormal electrical activity occurs determines the type of seizure.

There are over thirty types of seizures, some more severe than others. Some people have seizures that last a short time and cause them to stare off into space, giving the appearance that the per on is simply daydreaming. Others may experience a more dramatic seizure (tonic-clonic seizure) where the person loses consciousness and the entire body stiffens and then twitches or jerks uncontrollably.

People of all ages, races, and in all walks of life can develop epilepsy. It affects about one in 100 people. It is not contagious, and it is not a mental illness. Most forms of epilepsy are not inherited, but it may run in some families.

While there is, as yet, no cure for epilepsy, today's treatment options can control most cases. In fact, many people with epilepsy lead normal lives and have no symptoms between seizures. The aim of treatment is to stop the seizures.

What Are the Symptoms?

The doctor diagnoses epilepsy after a person has had multiple seizures. The frequency and type of seizure varies from person to person. Some people have more than one type.

The medical community classifies epileptic seizures into two major categories: partial and generalized. The form a seizure takes depends on the part of the brain in which it occurs and on how widely and rapidly it fans out from its point of origin.

Partial Seizures

If the abnormal electrical activity involves one area of the brain, the seizure is partial. The person may not lose consciousness, but can experience a range of symptoms: sudden jerky movements of one part of the body, such as an arm or leg; sudden fear; facial movements; disturbances or hallucinations of vision, hearing, or smell; nausea, vomiting, or stomach discomfort.

Some types of partial seizures (called complex partial seizures) may cause the person to have a change of consciousness. They may be dazed and confused, unaware of where they are or what they are doing. They may wander around randomly, mumble, and behave in unusual ways. They may exhibit chewing or repetitive arm and hand movements. Moreover, people with this type of seizure will not remember what they have experienced.

Generalized Seizures

When the entire brain is involved, the seizure is generalized. Like partial seizures, there are many different symptoms, body movements, and activities. Some people stare off into space, while others may have a full convulsion with the complete loss of consciousness and jerking movements of limbs (tonic-clonic seizures).

Just before having seizures, some people experience an aura, which is a sensation or warning of a coming seizure. Some people feel a sense of tension or anxiety, may hear a musical sound, sense an odor or taste, or experience some other change in sensation. Often this aura gives the person time to get to a safe place to avoid injury.

112

How Is Epilepsy Diagnosed?

Because there is no test to diagnose epilepsy, a doctor must rely mainly on interpreting the patient's medical and family history. Thus, it is important that the doctor have experience with and treat people with neurological disorders such as a neurologist. When the patient describes what he or she experienced and someone who witnessed the seizures describes what he saw, the doctor can often determine what kind of seizure the patient experienced and treat it.

The doctor asks about the patient's past medical history, the mother's pregnancy, and the family's medical history. The doctor will do general physical and neurological examinations to look for the underlying cause of the seizure.

The doctor usually orders an electroencephalogram (EEG) test, a painless recording of the patient's brain waves. The EEG, however, may appear normal even if the patient has epilepsy. Another painless test—a magnetic resonance imaging study or MRI—may reveal scar tissue or a structural abnormality within the brain, helping the doctor to make a diagnosis of epilepsy.

What Causes Epilepsy?

There is no single cause of epilepsy, and in 70% of cases, no known cause is ever found.

Some of the known causes of epilepsy are:

- Injury to the brain before, during, or after birth
- Infections that damage the brain
- Toxic substances that affect the brain
- Injury and lack of oxygen to the brain
- Disturbance in blood circulation to the brain (stroke and other vascular problems)
- Metabolism or nutrition imbalance
- Tumors of the brain
- Hereditary disease affecting the brain
- High fever
- Other degenerative diseases

Treatments

Most major epileptic seizures (generalized or tonic-clonic) last only a minute or two and demand little of the bystander. All that is necessary is to let the seizure run its course and to ensure that the person is in no physical danger and can breathe.

However, a person who experiences repeated seizures and does not recover consciousness between attacks should get immediate medical attention. This type of repeated seizure is called status epilepticus. This is life threatening, and could also cause brain damage.

First Aid

The goal of first aid is to keep the person safe:

- Keep calm, help the person to the floor, and loosen clothing around the neck

- Remove sharp or hot objects that could injure

- Turn the person on one side so saliva can flow out of the mouth

- Place a cushion such as a folded coat under the head

- Do NOT put anything into the person's mouth

- After the seizure, allow the person to rest or sleep if necessary

- Some people will be confused or weak after a seizure. They may need help getting home

- Contact the parent or guardian if a child had the seizure

People often wonder whether they should call an ambulance when someone has a seizure. If you know the person has epilepsy, an ambulance is probably unnecessary unless the seizure continues for more than five minutes. If you don't know, or if the person is pregnant, diabetic, or seems otherwise ill, play it safe and call for help.

The most common treatment of epilepsy is daily use of anti-convulsant drugs, which allow many people with epilepsy to enjoy a healthy life and continue normal activities. The drugs, prescribed alone or in combination, are adjusted over time until the best combination is found for each person. Many people with epilepsy must take their anti-convulsant drugs for the rest of their lives to prevent further seizures. However, the doctor may advise a slow withdrawal of the drug if a person has had no seizures for several years.

Those for whom anti-convulsant drugs fail to control the seizures, surgery to remove injured brain tissue may be possible. A thorough evaluation including the recording of a seizure with EEG, video, and neuropsychological testing is performed to determine surgical candidacy. Other surgical techniques are being developed that offer new hope to people with uncontrollable epilepsy.

Epilepsy treatment should include discussions about the physical (e.g., side-effects), social, and emotional problems that can accompany the disorder. These discussions should involve family and individual counseling and education. In addition, information about epilepsy should be shared with schools, employers, and friends. Women with epilepsy should seek medical counseling prior to and during pregnancy.

State regulations mandate that persons who suffer altered consciousness due to a seizure abstain from driving a motor vehicle for a specific period thereafter. The period varies from state to state.

Progress through Research

Epilepsy research has focused on finding the cause of epilepsy and on understanding ways to accurately diagnose and treat it. Researchers continue to study the chemical and electrical changes that occur within the brain cells. Clinical trials of new drugs are constantly underway, and new surgical procedures are being developed.

Among the new drugs being introduced are some that inhibit or change the brain cell activity that causes seizures. These are new strategies for seizure control and mean that doctors will be able to offer new choices to prevent previously difficult to control seizures.

In addition to developing new drugs, researchers are taking a fresh look at some of the ideas that have been part of epilepsy treatment for many years. It is important that patients talk with their neurologist if they wish to pursue these lines of treatment. For example, the ketogenic diet, high in fat and low in carbohydrates and protein, creates a condition in the body known as "ketosis," that has been helpful in controlling seizures, particularly in children. Researchers are looking at the exact mechanism of action of the ketogenic diet to shed new light on the biochemical mechanisms of epilepsy.

Surgeons have found that implanting a small device in the body that gives off electronic signals to the brain can stop seizures. This treatment has been especially promising for those with uncontrollable epilepsy.

Please contact the AAN Education and Research Foundation to contribute to the fight against epilepsy and other neurological disorders. Only through continued research can we hope for more treatments and a cure. Call (612) 695-2712.

For More Information

American Academy of Neurology
1080 Montreal Avenue
St. Paul, MN 55116-2325
(612) 695-1940
(612) 695-2791 fax
Website: http://www.aan.com

Epilepsy Foundation of America
4351 Garden City Drive
Landover, MD 20785
(800) EFA-1000
(301) 459-3700
(301) 577-2684 fax
E-mail: postmaster@efa.org
Website: http://www.efa.org

Chapter 18

Epilepsy in Pregnancy

Epilepsy and Pregnancy—What You Should Know

This information provides a general overview on epilepsy and pregnancy and may not apply to everyone. Talk to your family doctor to find out if this information applies to you and to get more information on this subject.

What Are the Risks to Me If I Become Pregnant

Women with epilepsy who become pregnant have a higher risk for complications that women who don't have epilepsy. These complications include the possibility that your seizures will occur more often. The seizures can cause you to fall and have a serious injury. Also, when you are pregnant, your body processes your seizure medicines differently. This can lead to medicine levels that are too high (which can cause problems with medicine side effects) or too low (which can make you have more seizures). Every woman who has epilepsy and becomes pregnant will react differently, so your doctor will watch your risks closely.

What Are the Risks to My Baby?

More than 90 percent of women with epilepsy give birth to normal, healthy babies. Babies who are born to mothers with epilepsy

"Epilepsy in Pregnancy," by James A. Rochester and Jeffrey T. Kirchner, *American Family Physician*, October 15, 1997, © 1997 American Academy of Family Physicians, Kansas City, MO; reprinted with permission.

117

have a higher risk of being stillborn. There is also more risk for problems such as bleeding, premature birth and delays in development and growth, as well as the possibility of birth defects due to the medication you take. However, the risks if you don't take your medicine are much higher for your baby, and include physical injury, developmental delay and even death from your seizures. You child would also have a slightly greater chance of developing seizures as he or she grows older.

What Can I do to Help Protect Myself and My Baby?

It's very important that you take your seizure medicine as directed by your doctor. If you haven't had any seizures for two years or more, your doctor may wish to try and slowly stop your seizure medicine. It's also very important for you to take vitamin supplements and folic acid (a B vitamin), which can help prevent certain kinds of birth defects. Taking these vitamins before you get pregnant will give you the most benefit. Tell your doctor about any history in your family (or in the family of the baby's father) of brain or spinal defects. This is very important. Eating a healthy diet, getting enough sleep, and exercising regularly are other things you can do to have a safe and healthy pregnancy and baby.

What Can I Expect When I'm Pregnant?

During your pregnancy, you will visit your doctor often. Your doctor will test your blood to be sure that you're getting enough seizure medicine. Don't be surprised if many changes are made in the dose of your medicine during your pregnancy. This is very common. Your doctor may also want you to have several ultrasounds (sonograms) during your pregnancy. You may even have an amniocentesis. In this procedure, a small amount of fluid is removed from your uterus. This fluid gives your doctor some information about the health of your unborn child. Your doctor can explain this test to you in greater detail if you need to have one.

Epilepsy and Pregnancy—More Information about Associated Risks

Epilepsy is the most commonly encountered major neurologic complication of pregnancy. The prevalence of epilepsy in the general population is about 0.6 to 1 percent; about 0.5 percent of all pregnancies occur in women with epilepsy.[1] There are a number of maternal and fetal problems that should be considered. Unfortunately, a limited number of clinical studies exist on which to base management decisions and, often, opinions regarding management of epilepsy in pregnancy are conflicting.

Problems Associated with Epilepsy in Pregnancy

Changes in Drug Metabolism

One of the normal physiologic changes that occurs in pregnancy is a large increase in circulating serum proteins. Because most antiepileptic drugs are highly protein-bound, there may be a decrease in free or active blood levels of these drugs as more of the drug is bound.[2] This is primarily true in the first trimester, but as the pregnancy progresses, the free or unbound fraction of the drug will increase. Consequently, a free, rather than total, serum drug level should be obtained in pregnant patients. For instance, in a patient with a phenobarbital level of 12 mg per L, the free level may only be 4 or 5 mg per L, which is below the normal therapeutic threshold. In one study,[2] 38 percent of patients required dosing changes during pregnancy to control seizures.

The normal increase in extracellular fluid may also cause fluctuations in antiepileptic drug levels. Other factors that may suppress drug levels are delayed gastric emptying and hyperemesis, especially in the first trimester. Ideally, serum drug levels should be monitored monthly, as it is often necessary to adjust the drug dosage. Serum drug levels should also be checked at the onset of labor.

Increase in Seizure Frequency

For reasons that are not completely clear, approximately 30 to 50 percent of women with epilepsy who become pregnant will experience an increased rate of seizures.[3] Contributing factors likely include noncompliance with medications, hyperventilation, dilutional hypocalcemia and hyponatremia, emotional stress, and sleep deprivation.[4] An attempt to address these last two issues should be made at every prenatal visit.

The ultimate concern of seizure during pregnancy is usually not the seizure itself but the potential for blunt abdominal trauma secondary to patient falls or motor vehicle accidents. Placental abruption has been noted to occur in 1 to 5 percent of minor blunt traumas and 20 to 50 percent of major blunt traumas in pregnancy.[5] Premature rupture of the membranes is another serious complication of trauma.

This complication is associated with infection, preterm labor and fetal death. According to the literature, an increased rate of spontaneous miscarriage has been reported, as well as an increased risk of fetal malformations, if the mother has seizures during the first trimester.[6] This increase in risk is probably related to transient fetal hypoxia and acidosis secondary to altered uteroplacental circulation.

Decrease in Fetal Viability

The rates of stillbirth, neonatal death and perinatal death are three times greater in infants born to women with epilepsy.[3] These infants are also more likely to have lower Apgar scores. A 1986 study[7] demonstrated that infant mortality rates among infants born to women with epilepsy remained above those of control subjects from birth well into the first year of life. The reasons for this were not determined.

Increased Risk of Fetal Bleeding

Antiepileptic drugs, particularly phenytoin (Dilantin), primidone (Mysoline) and phenobarbital, are known to inhibit transport of vitamin K across the placenta.[4] This results in a decrease in fetal vitamin K-dependent clotting factors (II, VII, IX, X) and an increased risk of fetal hemorrhage, especially in the first 24 hours after birth. These infants may require additional vitamin K (in addition to the routine 1 mg usually given after birth) and fresh frozen plasma to correct the coagulopathy. Most authorities recommend that vitamin K be given to women with epilepsy during the last two months of pregnancy, although the efficacy of this supplementation has not been definitively proven.[4]

Decrease in Fetal Growth

Infants of mothers with epilepsy are more likely to be small for gestational age. Approximately 7 to 10 percent of these infants will meet the criteria for low birth weight (less than 2,500 g [5 lb, 8 oz]). In addition, infants of mothers with epilepsy have a 4 to 11 percent risk of prematurity.[8]

Decrease in Childhood Intelligence

Several studies have attempted to describe the effect of maternal epilepsy on intellectual development of the child. One investigation[9] found that 35 percent of children who were exposed to antiepileptic medication *in utero* required special education, compared with 8 percent of children who were not exposed. This study did not control for parental intelligence or socioeconomic status. A 1982 Finnish study[10] followed 23 infants of epileptic mothers to the age of four years. Researchers found that 48 percent of these infants were diagnosed as having a learning disability based on standardized psychometric testing.

A later study[11] prospectively followed children of epileptic mothers and found that 23 percent of the children had specific cognitive dysfunction, compared with 7 percent of the control subjects. The latter findings were not associated with antiepileptic drug exposure but seemed to be related to simple partial seizures, seizures during pregnancy, and low levels of parental education. Collectively, the evidence is not strong that epilepsy itself is a significant risk factor for decreased childhood intelligence.

Problems Associated with Antiepileptic Drugs

Five antiepileptic medications have been used and/or studied in pregnant patients. These include phenytoin, valproic acid (Depakene), carbamazepine (Tegretol), phenobarbital, and primidone. All of these drugs cross the placenta; individually, they have been implicated in congenital malformations, including craniofacial abnormalities, cardiac defects, and neural tube defects. Data from several studies performed in the 1970s and 1980s form the basis of most of what is known about the teratogenic effects of antiepileptic drugs. However, many of these studies did not control for paternal genetic factors, environmental factors, drug dosing and combination therapy.

The mechanisms by which a specific antiepileptic drug acts to cause teratogenicity is still poorly understood. One theory is that phenytoin, carbamazepine, and phenobarbital are metabolized through the hepatic arene oxide pathway. This leads to high levels of epoxide intermediaries, which may be teratogenic.[4] This would also explain the similarity of anomalies that occur in children who have been exposed to antiepileptic drugs *in utero*. A recent review[12] of currently available data estimated the absolute risk of major malformations in infants exposed to antiepileptic drugs to be about 7 to 10 percent, compared with 5 percent in the general population. Currently, little information is available regarding the teratogenic potential of the new antiepileptic drugs felbamate (Felbatol), gabapentin (Neurontin), and lamotrigine (Lamictal).

Phenytoin

The fetal hydantoin syndrome was first reported in the literature in 1973; seven children with hypoplasia and irregular ossification of the distal phalanges were described.[13] In a series reported two years later,[14] the syndrome was formally named and described as including epicanthal folds, wide prominent lips, hypertelorism, upturned nasal tip, a flat nasal bridge, digital distal hypoplasia, intrauterine growth restriction, and mental retardation. This series included only five children, four of whom were also concurrently exposed to phenobarbital. No study to date has verified all of these findings. A more recent study[15] examined 82 children exposed to phenytoin *in utero* and found that a statistically insignificant number had digital hypoplasia and hypertelorism.

Phenobarbital

A 1976 Swedish study[16] noted prenatal and postnatal growth deficiency along with developmental delay in children with *in utero* exposure to phenobarbital. These findings were similar to those in children with fetal alcohol syndrome and fetal hydantoin syndrome, making the existence of a new syndrome suspect. A high correlation between maternal ingestion of phenobarbital and congenital heart defects has also been noted.[17] A 1995 report[18] found that prenatal exposure to phenobarbital resulted in negative long-term effects on verbal IQ scores for as many as 30 years postexposure. The authors of this study concluded that phenobarbital should be used with "increased caution" in pregnancy.

Phenobarbital has also been associated with withdrawal symptoms such as hyperexcitability, irritability, and regurgitation in exposed infants. Onset of such symptoms usually occurs at the seventh day of life, and symptoms may persist for two to six weeks.

Valproic Acid

At least one study[19] has demonstrated several physical deformities presumptively due to *in utero* exposure to valproic acid. The findings in this cohort of seven children included a flat nasal bridge; upturned nasal tip; inferior epicanthal folds; a shallow philtrum; thin vermilion border; long, thin, overlapping fingers, and hyperconvex nails. Two other studies[20,21] found an increased rate of perinatal distress (43 percent), low Apgar scores (28 percent), microcephaly, and postnatal growth deficiency in children with *in utero* exposure to this drug.

A more recent study[22] found no perinatal distress and complete resolution of microcephaly and growth deficiency by five years of age. A 1.5 percent increase in the risk of neural tube defects, specifically spine bifida aperta, may occur when valproic acid is taken in the first trimester.[23,24] It is also believed that this drug may enhance the teratogenicity of other anticonvulsants.

Carbamazepine

A single study[25] has been published that associates carbamazepine with multiple congenital abnormalities.[25] These include a short nose, long philtrum, upslanting palpebral fissures, distal digital hypoplasia, and microcephaly. There was also some concern of developmental delay. However, this diagnosis was based on one standard deviation from the mean (as opposed to two), which is not statistically significant. One study[26] determined that *in utero* exposure to this drug carries a 1 percent risk of spine bifida.

Primidone

Primidone, which is metabolized to phenobarbital, has been reported in two studies to result in a severe embryopathy.[27,28] This includes hirsute foreheads, thick nasal roots, anteverted nostrils, long philtrums, straight and thin upper lips, and distal digital hypoplasia. These children were also found to be small for gestational age and at increased risk for psychomotor retardation and cardiac abnormalities. In addition, primidone has reportedly resulted in a neonatal withdrawal syndrome, as well as vitamin K-dependent coagulopathy.

Management Recommendations

Preconception Counseling

It is imperative that women with epilepsy who are contemplating pregnancy should understand the risks to themselves and the fetus after conception (Table 18.1). These risks include a 30 to 50 percent increase in the frequency of seizures with the risk for resultant physical harm to the mother and infant. There is a 200 to 300 percent increase in the risk of stillbirth, prematurity, and developmental delay. The risk of neonatal hemorrhage (7 percent), dysmorphism (7 to 10 percent) and major malformations (4 to 6 percent) should also be discussed.[3] Women should also be warned that the risk of the child later developing epilepsy is 2 to 3 percent, which is five times that of the general population.[4] The risk is increased further if the maternal onset of seizures was before the age of 18 years. The same risk is not apparent if the father has epilepsy.

Ideally, if the patient has been seizure-free for two years, an attempt at drug withdrawal before conception should be strongly considered. An assessment of the patient's living, driving, and work situation should be made. The withdrawal is usually done gradually over a one- to three-month period, and patients should be told that the chance of relapse is up to 50 percent. Most recurrences will manifest during the first six months after withdrawal.[29] If medication is necessary, monotherapy is ideal and the lowest therapeutic dose should be given.

Table 18.1. Guidelines for Counseling Women with Epilepsy Who Are Planning Pregnancy

The risk of major malformations, minor anomalies and dysmorphic features is two- to threefold higher in infants born to women who take antiepileptic drugs while they are pregnant than the risk in infants born to women who do not take these drugs.

A possibility exists that some of this risk is caused by a genetic predisposition for birth defects inherent in certain families. Maternal and paternal family medical histories should be reviewed for birth defects.

The potential for prenatal diagnosis with ultrasound and/or amniocentesis for major malformations should be discussed with the parents.

Effects of tonic-clonic seizures may be deleterious to the fetus, may injure the mother, and can result in miscarriage.

The preconception diet should contain adequate amounts of folate.

If the patient is seizure-free for at least two years, withdrawal of the antiepileptic drug should be considered.

If antiepileptic drug therapy is necessary, a switch to monotherapy should be made if possible.

Adapted with permission from Delgado-Escueta AV, Janz D. Consensus guidelines: preconception counseling, management, and care of the pregnant women with epilepsy. Neurology 1992;42(4 Suppl 5):149-60. Reproduced with permission from Advanstar Communications Inc. as reprinted from Neurology® 1992, Vol. 42, Suppl. 5, pp. 149-60.Neurology® is a registered trademark of the American Academy of Neurology.

Pregnancy Management

Managing the pregnant patient with epilepsy presents a formidable challenge to the clinician for many of the reasons noted previously. Some basic management principles include the administration of folic acid (4 mg per day) and multivitamins, which have been shown to decrease the risk of major malformations, especially neural tube defects. The higher dose of folic acid is recommended because all of the antiepileptic drugs interfere with folate metabolism. Vitamin K at a dose of 10 mg per day should be given during the last one to two months of gestation to prevent neonatal hemorrhage, especially if the mother is taking phenytoin or phenobarbital. If the patient is seen

Table 18.2. Guidelines for Using Antiepileptic Drugs during Pregnancy

Use a first-choice antiepileptic drug for seizure type and epilepsy syndrome.

Use the antiepileptic drug as monotherapy and at the lowest dose possible that protects against tonic-clonic seizures.

Monitor plasma antiepileptic drug levels monthly and, if possible, obtain free or unbound levels.

Avoid polytherapy, especially combinations of valproate (Depakene), phenobarbital and carbamazepine (Tegretol).

Avoid valproate and carbamazepine when there is a family history of neural tube defects.

Begin folate supplementation (4 mg per day) in the preconception period.

When using valproate, avoid high plasma levels and divide the dose over three to four administrations per day.

Adapted with permission from Delgado-Escueta AV, Janz D. Consensus guidelines: preconception counseling, management, and care of the pregnant women with epilepsy. Neurology 1992;42(4 Suppl 5):149-60. Reproduced with permission from Advanstar Communications Inc. as reprinted from Neurology® 1992, Vol. 42, Suppl. 5, pp. 149-60.Neurology® is a registered trademark of the American Academy of Neurology.

early in pregnancy, she should not be withdrawn from medications because of the high risk for inducing status epilepticus.[3] Monthly monitoring of free serum antiepileptic drug levels should be performed with adjustment to the lowest dose that adequately controls seizures. The serum drug levels should be drawn immediately before the next dose is due (to assess trough level).

Consideration should be given to offering the mother serum alpha-fetoprotein and ultrasonography at 16 weeks of gestation to evaluate for neural tube defects.[30] An alternative is amniocentesis, particularly if the patient is taking valproate or carbamazepine. An comprehensive ultrasound may be performed at 18 to 22 weeks to further evaluate for congenital malformations. A fetal echocardiogram at 20 to 22 weeks should also be considered in light of the association of antiepileptic drugs with cardiac anomalies. Paternal attitudes towards prenatal diagnostic testing should always be discussed.

Intrapartum plans for the administration of anticonvulsants should be made. A short-acting benzodiazepine, such as diazepam (Valium), given intravenously is usually recommended if oral therapy is not tolerated or is impossible to administer during the second or third stages of labor. Benzodiazepines may be problematic in that they can result in fetal and maternal respiratory depression. An alternative is to give phenytoin intravenously or phenobarbital intramuscularly. Clotting studies should be performed on cord blood, and 1 mg of vitamin K should be given to the infant. Nurses and physicians caring for these infants should be alerted to the possibility of hemorrhage and apprised of antiepileptic drug withdrawal signs and symptoms. Table 18.2 summarizes the guidelines for using antiepileptic drugs during pregnancy.

Final Comment

A recently published consensus opinion that reviewed the data on epilepsy and pregnancy concluded that the disease of epilepsy itself as well as the use of anticonvulsant medications present inherent risks to the fetus.[30] These risks include malformation, hemorrhage, and delays in growth and development. The cumulative risk of these problems in this population is believed to be two to three times that of the general population. The authors stated that all antiepileptic drugs are associated with an increased risk of adverse outcomes and, with the exception of valproic acid (because of its greater association with spine bifida), no single antiepileptic drug offers any particular hazard versus another in pregnancy.

On a positive note, the majority of women with epilepsy (90 percent) will have uneventful pregnancies, uncomplicated deliveries, and healthy babies. For the remaining 10 percent, the possibility of adverse outcomes will be decreased by appropriate management with attention to serum antiepileptic drug levels, prophylaxis for neonatal hemorrhage, previous planning for the treatment of intrapartum seizures, and close observation of the infant.

References

1. Martin PJ, Millac PA. Pregnancy, epilepsy, management and outcome: a 10-year perspective. *Seizure* 1993;2:277-80.

2. Yerby MS, Friel PN, McCormick K. Antiepileptic drug disposition during pregnancy. *Neurology* 1992;42(4 Suppl 5):12-6.

3. Yerby MS. Epilepsy and pregnancy. New issues for an old disorder. *Neurol Clin* 1993;11:777-86.

4. Samuels P. Neurologic disorders. In: Gabbe SG Niebyl JR, Simpson JL, Annas GJ, eds. *Obstetrics: normal and problem pregnancies. 3d ed.* New York: Churchill-Livingstone, 1996:1135-54.

5. Pearlman MD, Tintinalli JE, Lorenz RP. Blunt trauma during pregnancy. *N Eng J Med* 1990;323:1609-13.

6. Lindhout D, Omtzigt JC, Cornel MC. Spectrum of neural-tube defects in 34 infants prenatally exposed to antiepileptic drugs. *Neurology* 1992;42(4 Suppl 5):111-8.

7. Beaussart-Deaye J, Bastin N, Demarcq C. *Epilepsies and reproduction. Vol. 2.* Grine Lille, France: Nord Epilepsy Research and Information Group, 1986;72.

8. Yerby M, Koepsell T, Daling J. Pregnancy complications and outcomes in a cohort of women with epilepsy. *Epilepsia* 1985;26:631-5.

9. Beck-Managetta G, *et al.* Malformations and minor anomalies in children of epileptic mothers: Preliminary results of the prospective Helsinki study. In: Janz D, Dam M, Richens A, eds. *Epilepsy, pregnancy, and the child.* New York: Raven 1982;317-23.

10. Hill RM, Vernaiud WM, Retting GM, *et al*. Relationship of antiepileptic drug exposure of the infant and developmental potential. In: Janz D, Dam M, Richens A, eds. *Epilepsy, pregnancy, and the child*. New York: Raven, 1982.

11. Gaily E, Kantola-Sorsa E, Granstrom ML. Specific cognitive dysfunction in children with epileptic mothers. *Dev Med Child Neurol* 1990;32:403-14.

12. Lindhout D, Omtzigt JG. Teratogenic effects of antiepileptic drugs: implications for the management of epilepsy in women of childbearing age. *Epilepsia* 1994;35(Suppl 4):S19-28.

13. Loughnan PM, Gold H, Vance JC. Phenytoin teratogenicity in man. *Lancet* 1973;1(794):70-2.

14. Hanson JW, Smith DW. The fetal hydantoin syndrome. *J Pediatr* 1975;87:285-90.

15. Gaily E, Granstrom ML, Hiilesmaa V, Bardy A. Minor anomalies in offspring of epileptic mothers. *J Pediatr* 1988;112:520-9.

16. Seip M. Growth retardation, dysmorphic facies and minor malformations following massive exposure to phenobarbitone *in utero*. *Acta Paediatr Scand* 1976;65:617-21.

17. Dravet C, Julian C, Legras C, Magaudda A, Guerrini R, Genton P, *et al*. Epilepsy, antiepileptic drugs, and malformations in children of women with epilepsy: a French prospective cohort study. *Neurology* 1992 42(4 Suppl 5):75-82.

18. Reinisch JM, Sanders SA, Mortensen EL, Rubin DB. *In utero* exposure to phenobarbital and intelligence deficits in adult men. *JAMA* 1995;274;1518-25.

19. DiLiberti JH, Farndon PA, Dennis NR, Curry CJ. The fetal valproate syndrome. *Am J Med Genet* 1984;19:473-81.

20. Ardinger HH, Atkin JF, Blackston RD, Elsas LJ, Clarren SK, Livingstone S, *et al*. Verification of the fetal valproate syndrome phenotype. *Am J Med Genet* 1988;29:171-85.

21. Jager-Roman E, Deichl A, Jakob S, Hartmann AM, Koch S, Rahng D, *et al*. Fetal growth, major malformations, and minor anomalies in infants born to women receiving valproic acid. *J Pediatr* 1986;108: 997-1004.

22. Gaily EK, Granstrom ML, Hiilesmaa VK, Bardy AH. Head circumference in children of epileptic mothers: contributions of drug exposure and genetic background. *Epilepsy Res* 1990;5:217-22.

23. Lindhout D, Schmidt D. *In utero* exposure to valproate and neural tube defects. *Lancet* 1986;1 (8494):1392-3.

24. Robert E, Guibaud P Maternal valproic acid and congenital neural tube defects [Letter]. *Lancet* 1982;2 (8304):937.

25. Jones KL, Lacro RV, Johnson KA, Adams J. Pattern of malformations in the children of women treated with carbamazepine during pregnancy. *N Engl J Med* 1989;320:1661-6.

26. Rosa FW. Spina bifida in infants of women treated with carbamazepine during pregnancy. *N Engl J Med* 1991;324:674-7.

27. Rudd NL, Freedom RM. A possible primidone embryopathy. *J Pediatr* 1979 94:835-7.

28. Gustavson EE, Chen H. Goldenhar syndrome, anterior encephalocele, and aquaductal stenosis following fetal primidone exposure. *Teratology* 1985;32:13-7.

29. Shuster EA. Epilepsy in women. *Mayo Clin Proc* 1996;71:991-9.

30. Delgado-Escueta AV, Janz D. Consensus guidelines: preconception counseling, management, and care of the pregnant women with epilepsy. *Neurology* 1992; 42(4 Suppl 5):149-60.

—by Jeffrey T. Kirchner and James A. Rochester

Jeffrey T. Kirchner, D.O. is associate director of the Family Practice Residency Program at the Lancaster (PA) General Hospital. A graduate of the Philadelphia College of Osteopathic Medicine, Dr. Kirchner completed a rotating internship at the Osteopathic Medical Center of Philadelphia and a residency in Family Practice at Abington (PA) Memorial Hospital.

James A. Rochester, M.D. is currently a third-year resident in Family Practice at Lancaster General Hospital. Dr. Rochester earned a medical degree from Temple University School of Medicine in Philadelphia.

Chapter 19

New Generation of Epilepsy Drugs

Short Circuit: New Epilepsy Drugs

In the early 1900s, a young German physician faced a dilemma: He lived above a ward filled with noisy epileptics. Unable to get any sleep, the doctor began dosing the epileptic patients with a new hypnotic. Not only did the patients fall asleep, but, as the doctor was astonished to find, they were seizure-free in the morning. The name of the drug was phenobarbital.

Thus began the modern age of epileptic therapy. Phenobarbital was followed into the marketplace by phenytoin (Dilantin, Parke-Davis) 30 years later. Then came a rapid succession of antiseizure products—from the notoriously toxic trimethadione (Tridione, Abbott Laboratories) in 1943 to the suximides of the 1950s. In 1963, researchers tinkering with the chlorpromazine molecule came up with carbamazepine (Tegretol, Ciba-Geigy). And that same year, lab workers discovered that a common solvent imparted coumarin with anticonvulsant activity. The solvent was called valproic acid (Depakene, Abbott).

This chapter contains text from two articles: "Short Circuit: New Epilepsy Drugs Convulsing Treatment of Seizure Disorders," by Jim Morelli, *Drug Topics*, July 7, 1997, © 1997 Medical Economics Publishing, Montvale, NJ, reprinted with permission; and "Newer Antiepileptic Drugs: Gabapentin, Lamotrigine, Felbamate, Topiramate and Fosphenytoin," by William J. Curry, M.D. and David L. Kulling, M.D., *American Family Physician*, February 1, 1998, © 1998 American Academy of Family Physicians, Kansas City, MO; reprinted with permission.

131

Those products represented the first wave of antiseizure medications, and now the second wave is upon us. Within the past couple of years, three new epilepsy drugs entered the market: gabapentin (Neurontin, Parke-Davis), lamotrigine (Lamictal, Glaxo Wellcome), and topiramate (Topamax, Ortho McNeil). In a few months, two more will likely be approved. And, under development for introduction further down the road are half a dozen new compounds, including a drug related to phencyclidine and an extract from a toxic marine snail.

What has caused this sudden renaissance in epilepsy drugs? In a word, knowledge. "The neurotransmitters in epilepsy have been worked out, particularly GABA and glutamate," said Steven Schachter, M.D., director of clinical research at Boston's Beth Israel Hospital. Yesterday's products, while effective, didn't always hit the mark when it came to clinical practice. Most of the new products work more precisely by enhancing the effect of GABA, a calming neurotransmitter, or inhibiting glutamate—an excitatory chemical, he said.

Lamotrigine, for example, works by inhibiting the release of two excitatory compounds—glutamate and aspartate. "It's a very good drug for certain types of seizure patients," said Kimford Meidor, M.D., of the Medical College of Georgia in Augusta. "What's interesting is lamotrigine has a psychotropic effect—kind of a 'positive' quality-of-life effect. There's some controversy over it, but I think it's real." Gabapentin sales more than doubled last year, according to Jeff Baum of Warner-Lambert/Parke-Davis. In fact, the new antiseizure medication almost knocked Parke-Davis' king from its throne: Baum reports sales of phenytoin grew to $277 million last year; gabapentin's sales grew to $231 million. Barring reports of a catastrophic side effect, gabapentin sales will likely continue to soar, thanks in part to the drug's usefulness in the elderly, one of the fastest-growing segments of the epilepsy population. Gabapentin, an amino acid, doesn't interact with other drugs.

Topiramate, discovered by scientists at the National Institutes of Health, also enhances GABA activity. Meidor said topiramate is an effective anticonvulsant that sometimes works when others fail.

But in one area, each of the new drugs has fallen short. All three carry significant central nervous system side effects. About 30% of patients taking lamotrigine or topiramate, for example, will complain of dizziness. A sizable number of gabapentin users suffer feelings of irritability and impatience, and, worse, they gain weight—on average, about 16 lbs.

By far, the most severe side effect discovered so far with the new drugs is the tendency for lamotrigine to cause severe, potentially fatal skin rashes, especially in children. The incidence of these reactions is shockingly high, according to Larry Sasich, Pharm.D., of the Health Research Group in Washington, D.C., with reports from clinical trials suggesting one in 50 children and one in 1,000 adults could be affected. Accordingly, the Food & Drug Administration recently approved new labeling for the drug, which reiterates that the product shouldn't be used in children under 16 years of age.

As many as 1.5% of patients taking topiramate may develop kidney stones. This unusual side effect occurs because topiramate is a weak carbonic anhydrase inhibitor. Patients taking topiramate should drink lots of water to flush excess citric acid from the system.

Ironically, just as a flood of new medications has made it to market, clinicians are prying some epileptics off their drugs. "There are people with certain types of epilepsy who will typically grow out of the seizures," said Thomas Henry, M.D., director of the Emory Epilepsy Center in Atlanta. "But even with lifelong epilepsy, there are people who don't have lifelong problems."

Henry said that four patient groups are eligible for therapy cessation:

- Patients misdiagnosed in the first place
- Children who grow out of early-life seizure disorders
- Lifelong epileptics who don't seem to be having any seizures
- Epileptics whose seizure disorder was caused by something identifiable and correctable—metabolic disorder, for example.

However, not every patient eligible to be weaned off medication remains seizure-free once the drugs are removed. A recent study from Sweden found that over six years' time, about 40% of a group of children taken off medication, relapsed. The study found the strongest predictor of relapse was the age at which the child first had a seizure. The later in life it occurred, the more likely relapse would occur.

With no guarantee of a seizure-free life, some epileptics refuse to give up their drugs. "If one has been seizure-free for one to four years, you might consider it," said Meidor. "But some patients who have been seizure-free for 20 years won't let me touch their medications."

And with no test to determine who might relapse, Schachter said doctors are often learning about failures "the hard way."

Of course, there is a permanent solution for some epileptics—and it sounds like something out of the dark ages: surgery to remove part of the brain. "Surgery for many individuals can be the most effective treatment," Henry said, especially if an isolated, identifiable part of the brain is the locus of trouble. However, surgery usually isn't considered until drugs have been tried, he added.

And what's the effect of losing part of the brain? "Many with uncontrolled seizures already have so much damage that loss of an area of the brain would not result in a problem," Henry said. In fact, many return to work, happier than they've been in years.

—by Jim Morelli

Trained as a pharmacist, the author now writes full-time in the Atlanta area.

Newer Antiepileptic Drugs

Newer antiepileptic drugs may control seizures more effectively, but their significant potential for serious side effects requires a thorough knowledge of the drugs and careful consideration of the risks and benefits.

Gabapentin

Gabapentin (Neurontin) has been approved as adjunctive therapy in adults with partial seizures with or without secondary generalization (Table 19.1). A gamma-aminobutyric acid (GABA) analog, gabapentin does not interact with GABA receptors. Its mechanism of action is unknown.

Gabapentin is well absorbed orally, circulates mostly unbound in the plasma and is excreted unchanged in the kidneys without appreciable metabolism in the body. Oral bioavailability is approximately 60 percent and is not affected by food. The half-life is five to seven hours and is related to the creatinine clearance. Therefore, excretion is decreased in patients with renal impairment and decreased cardiac function, and in elderly patients.[1] Gabapentin can be removed from the system through hemodialysis.

In clinical studies,[2] gabapentin was found to be effective in adults with refractory partial seizures and was also effective in preventing the progression of partial seizures to generalized tonic-clonic seizures. Because gabapentin has no known pharmacokinetic interactions with any other antiepileptic drugs, it is useful in patients taking other antiepileptic medication.

The only known contraindication to gabapentin is hypersensitivity to the drug. As with any antiepileptic drug, withdrawal should be gradual, performed over a minimum of one week to minimize the risk of withdrawal seizures and status epilepticus. Side effects include somnolence, fatigue, ataxia, dizziness, gastrointestinal upset, dyspnea and a sense of well-being.[3] Patients should be counseled that these effects could impair driving and the ability to safely operate complex machinery. Use of alcohol can magnify these effects.

Gabapentin has shown no effect on phenytoin (Dilantin), carbamazepine (Tegretol), valproic acid (Depakene) and phenobarbital levels (Table 19.2). No clinically important interaction has been demonstrated with oral contraceptives. However, when taken concurrently with antacids, the bioavailability of gabapentin is reduced by 20 percent. We recommend allowing two hours to elapse after using antacids and before taking gabapentin. Gabapentin may also cause a urine dipstick test to show a false-positive result for protein.

High doses of gabapentin have caused pancreatic acinar cell carcinoma in laboratory rats; however, in humans, pancreatic carcinoma is usually ductal in origin.[4] Increased rates of pancreatic tumor occurrence have not been reported in patients using gabapentin, although data to date are limited.

Overdoses of 15 times the usual daily dose have resulted in diplopia, slurred speech, drowsiness, lethargy and diarrhea. In all reports of overdose, the patients recovered with supportive care. If necessary, overdose can be treated with hemodialysis.

Gabapentin has been shown to be toxic to the fetus in laboratory rats and is, thus, considered a category C medication during pregnancy. It should be used during pregnancy only if the potential benefit justifies the potential risks. It is not known whether gabapentin is excreted into breast milk.

Gabapentin has been found to be useful in the treatment of neuropathic pain. It is effective in decreasing intractable pain at antiepileptic dosages with minimal side effects and minimal drug interactions,[5] although it currently is not officially indicated for this use.

The usual dosage is 900 to 1,800 mg daily, divided into three doses. Dosing should begin with 300 mg daily and increase by an additional 300 mg every one to three days.[1] Dosages up to 3,600 mg have been given. The dosage should be adjusted according to creatinine clearance.

Gabapentin is available in 100-mg, 300-mg and 400-mg capsules[3] (Table 19.1). The average cost of 30 days of treatment at the lowest recommended dosage is approximately $88.[6]

Gabapentin may be used as adjunctive therapy in adults with poorly controlled partial seizures. In the future, gabapentin may become

Table 19.1. Comparison of Newer Anticonvulsant Drugs, continued on next page.

Gabapentin (Neurontin)

Indication:	Adjunctive therapy for partial seizures with or without secondary generalization
Age:	12 years and older
Dosing Range:	Begin with 300 mg daily; increase to 900 to 1,800 mg daily given every 6 to 8 hours
Availability:	100-mg, 300-mg and 400-mg capsules
Side Effects:	Somnolence, fatigue, ataxia, dizziness, gastrointestinal upset, dyspnea

Lamotrigine (Lamictal)

Indication:	Adjunctive therapy for partial seizures with or without secondary generalization
Age:	16 years and older
Dosing Range:	Begin with 50 mg daily; increase to 300 to 500 mg daily given every 12 hours for concomitant use with valproic acid (Depakene): begin with 25 mg every other day; increase to 150 mg daily given every 12 hours
Availability:	25-mg, 100-mg, 150-mg and 200-mg scored tablets
Side Effects:	Rash, including life-threatening rashes, dizziness, ataxia, blurred vision, nausea

Felbamate (Felbatol), continued on next page

Indication:	Adjunctive therapy or monotherapy in adults when seizures are so severe as to warrant use despite risk of aplastic anemia or hepatic failure; in children with Lennox-Gastaut syndrome when seizures are not controlled
Age:	14 years or older for adults; 2 to 14 years for children

Table 19.1. Comparison of Newer Anticonvulsant Drugs, continued from previous page.

Felbamate (Felbatol), continued from previous page

Dosing Range:	Adults: begin with 1,200 mg daily given every 6 to 8 hours; Children: 15 to 45 mg per kg per day given every 6 to 8 hours
Availability:	400-mg and 600 mg scored tablets; 600 mg per 5-mL suspension
Side Effects:	Anorexia, vomiting, insomnia, somnolence, aplastic anemia, hepatoxicity

Topiramate (Topamax)

Indication:	Adjunctive therapy for partial onset of seizures
Age:	16 years or older
Dosing Range:	Begin with 50 mg daily; increase to 50 to 400 mg daily given every 12 hours
Availability:	25-mg, 100-mg, and 200-mg caplets
Side effects:	Dizziness, somnolence, ataxia, confusion, fatigue, paresthesias, speech difficulties, diplopia, impaired concentration and nausea

Fosphenytoin (Cerebyx)

Indication:	Status epilepticus; parenteral maintenance of phenytoin levels; parenteral treatment and/or prevention of seizures
Dosing Range:	For status epilepticus: 22.5 to 30 mg per kg IV*; For nonemergent therapy: 15 to 30 mg per kg IV* or IM**, followed by 6 to 12 mg per kg IV* or IM** for maintenance therapy
Availability:	2-mL vials (150 mg); 10-mL vials (750 mg)

*IV = intravenously
** IM = intramuscularly.

Table 19.2. Effects of Newer Anticonvulsants on Drug Levels of Standard Anticonvulsants

Standard Anticonvulsants
  Effects of Newer Anticonvulsants

Phenytoin (Dilantin)
  Gabapentin (Neurontin): No effect
  Lamotrigine (Lamictal): No effect
  Felbamate (Felbatol): Increased 25%
  Topiramate (Topamax): No effect or increased 25%
  Fosphenytoin (Cerebyx): No effect

Valproic acid (Depakene)
  Gabapentin (Neurontin): No effect
  Lamotrigine (Lamictal): Decreased 25%
  Felbamate (Felbatol): Increased 40%
  Topiramate (Topamax): Decreased 11%
  Fosphenytoin (Cerebyx): No effect

Carbamazepine (Tegretol)
  Gabapentin (Neurontin): No effect
  Lamotrigine (Lamictal): No effect
  Felbamate (Felbatol): Decreased 30%
  Topiramate (Topamax): No effect
  Fosphenytoin (Cerebyx): No effect

Carbamazepine epoxide
  Gabapentin (Neurontin): No effect
  Lamotrigine (Lamictal): No effect
  Felbamate (Felbatol): Increased 55%
  Topiramate (Topamax): No effect
  Fosphenytoin (Cerebyx): No effect

Phenobarbital
  Gabapentin (Neurontin): No effect
  Lamotrigine (Lamictal): No effect
  Felbamate (Felbatol): No data
  Topiramate (Topamax): No effect
  Fosphenytoin (Cerebyx): No effect

first-line therapy in patients with newly diagnosed epilepsy. At present, it has not been approved by the US. Food and Drug Administration for use in children. Gabapentin is easy to use and has relatively mild side effects. Lack of drug-drug interactions make it an attractive therapy.

Lamotrigine

Lamotrigine (Lamictal) is included in the phenyltriazine class. It is used as adjunctive therapy or monotherapy in adults with partial seizures with or without secondary generalization. The mechanism of action is unknown. Lamotrigine has been shown to act at voltage-sensitive sodium channels, stabilizing neural membranes and inhibiting the release of excitatory neural transmitters.[2]

Lamotrigine is well absorbed orally, with up to 98 percent bioavailability. Absorption is not affected by food. Approximately 55 percent of the drug is protein bound; therefore, clinical interaction with other protein-bound drugs is unlikely. Ninety percent of the drug undergoes glucuronic acid conjugation in the liver, with the conjugate and the remaining 10 percent of unmetabolized drug excreted in the urine.[7] Clearance is markedly increased by the co-administration of other antiepileptic drugs that induce hepatic enzymes. These include carbamazepine (Tegretol), phenobarbital, phenytoin (Dilantin) and primidone (Mysoline). The half-life of lamotrigine may be reduced by about 50 percent with concomitant use of one or more of these medications (Tables 19.2 and 19.3). However, when combined with valproic acid, its elimination is decreased, and its half-life may be more than doubled.

Lamotrigine does not impair cognition and has a relatively broad spectrum of activity against multiple types of seizures. Three multicenter clinical studies have demonstrated its efficacy as adjunctive therapy in adults with refractory partial seizures.[2]

The only contraindication to lamotrigine is hypersensitivity to the drug. The need for monitoring drug levels has not been established. The most frequently encountered adverse reactions include dizziness, ataxia, somnolence, headache, blurred vision, nausea, vomiting and rash. Up to 10 percent of patients discontinue lamotrigine therapy because of side effects. One case of acute hepatic failure has been reported. Because lamotrigine depresses the central nervous system, patients who are taking it should be cautioned about driving or operating complex machinery.

A macular, papular or erythematous rash may develop in approximately 10 percent of patients during the first four to six weeks of

Table 19.3. Effects of Standard Anticonvulsants on Drug Levels of Newer Anticonvulsants

Newer Anticonvulsants
    Effects of Standard Anticonvulsants

Gabapentin (Neurontin)
    Phenytoin (Dilantin): No effect
    Valproic acid (Depakene): No effect
    Carbamazepine (Tegretol): No effect
    Phenobarbital: No effect

Lamotrigine (Lamictal)
    Phenytoin (Dilantin): Decreased 50%
    Valproic acid (Depakene): Increased 100%
    Carbamazepine (Tegretol): Decreased 40%
    Phenobarbital: Decreased 40%

Felbamate (Felbatol)
    Phenytoin (Dilantin): Decreased 40%
    Valproic acid (Depakene): No effect
    Carbamazepine (Tegretol): Decreased 40%
    Phenobarbital: No data

Topiramate (Topamax)
    Phenytoin (Dilantin): Decreased 48%
    Valproic acid (Depakene): Decreased 14%
    Carbamazepine (Tegretol): Decreased 40%
    Phenobarbital: No data

Fosphenytoin (Cerebyx)
    Phenytoin (Dilantin): Slight increase
    Valproic acid (Depakene): No data
    Carbamazepine (Tegretol): No effect
    Phenobarbital: Slight increase

treatment with lamotrigine. Although the rash often resolves with continued use, it may sometimes be indicative of serious systemic involvement. The occurrence of a rash or systemic symptoms such as fever or lymphadenopathy necessitates prompt discontinuation of the drug and medical evaluation. One in every 1,000 adults treated with lamotrigine develops severe, life-threatening rashes such as Stevens-Johnson syndrome, toxic epidermal necrolysis and angioedema with fever, facial swelling and lymphadenopathy. This risk is increased more than threefold with co-administration of valproic acid.

In children, the risk of developing a life-threatening rash is one in 50. Hence, use of lamotrigine is not indicated in children under 16 years of age.[7] The risk of rash may increase if lamotrigine is given at higher than recommended dosages or if initial dosing is accelerated over recommendations provided by the manufacturer.[2]

Because of the potential for severe life-threatening skin reactions, the FDA has required that the manufacturer of lamotrigine publish a special warning on the label of this product.

There is a risk of withdrawal seizures if therapy is discontinued abruptly; thus, gradual tapering of the medication over a two-week period is recommended. Caution is advised in patients with conditions that could affect elimination such as renal or hepatic impairment or the co-administration of valproic acid. Dosage reduction is mandated in patients with significant renal impairment.

Lamotrigine binds to melanin-containing tissues such as the iris of the eye, but the long-term effects of this binding and accumulation are unknown. Use in pregnant patients is recommended only if the benefit outweighs the potential risks. Lamotrigine is classified as a category C medication during pregnancy. A registry of pregnant patients using lamotrigine is maintained by the manufacturer. The drug is found in breast milk; thus nursing is not recommended during treatment. Lamotrigine is contraindicated, for use in patients under the age of 16 because of the increased risk of developing a life-threatening rash.

Overdoses of up to 10 times the usual daily dosage have been reported. Recovery occurred with supportive care. There is no specific antidote.

The starting dosage in patients who are not taking valproic acid should be 50 mg daily for two weeks, increasing to 50 mg twice daily for an additional two weeks, and then increasing by 100 mg per day weekly to a maintenance level of 150 to 250 mg twice daily.[2]

In patients who are taking valproic acid plus other anticonvulsant drugs that induce hepatic enzymes, the initial starting dosage should be reduced to 25 mg every other day for two weeks, then increased to 25 mg daily for two weeks. The dosage may be increased by 25 to 50 mg daily every one to two weeks up to a maximum of 75 mg twice daily. It is generally recommended that lamotrigine not be combined with valproic acid in a two-drug regimen. Lamotrigine is available in 25-mg, 100-mg, 150-mg and 200-mg tablets (Table 19.1). The cost of one month of therapy at the lowest recommended dosage is approximately $111.[6]

Felbamate

Felbamate (Felbatol) is approved for adjunctive or monotherapy in adults with partial seizures with or without secondary generalization. It is also approved for use in children with Lennox-Gastaut syndrome, a childhood disorder with multiple seizure types, slow spike-wave electroencephalograms, mental retardation and resistance to standard therapy with antiepileptic drugs. The mechanism of action is not known, but it has been shown to have weak inhibitory effects on GABA receptor binding sites. Because of serious potential toxicity, felbamate should be reserved for rare, compassionate use by physicians experienced in treating patients with epilepsy that is difficult to control.

Felbamate is absorbed well orally with bioavailability greater than 90 percent. Absorption is not affected by food.[8] Metabolism occurs by the hepatic cytochrome P_{450} system, but 40 to 50 percent of the drug is excreted unchanged in the urine. Felbamate affects the steady-state concentrations of other antiepileptic drugs that depend on hepatic metabolism. The addition of felbamate increases the levels of phenytoin and valproic acid and decreases the levels of carbamazepine while concurrently increasing its epoxide concentration (Table 19.2). The addition of phenytoin or carbamazepine reduces felbamate levels by 40 percent (Table 19.3). Because felbamate is only 25 percent protein bound, minimal binding effects occur with protein-bound drugs.[9]

Felbamate is also considered a category C medication during pregnancy. Because it is found in breast milk, breast feeding is not recommended for patients taking felbamate. Pediatric use is approved only for adjunctive therapy in children with Lennox-Gastaut syndrome.

The most common side effects include anorexia, vomiting, insomnia, nausea, headache, dizziness and somnolence.[10] One overdose has been reported. The patient improved with supportive care. Clinical effects of overdose included epigastric distress and tachycardia.

After initial marketing of the drug, two very serious toxic effects appeared: aplastic anemia and hepatic failure. The risk of aplastic anemia in patients taking felbamate is 100 times greater than it is in the general population. One in every 3,600 to 5,000 patients taking felbamate will have aplastic anemia. The fatality rate of this complication approaches 30 percent. Aplastic anemia may not manifest itself until several months after initiation of treatment, and patients may remain at risk for an undetermined amount of time after treatment is discontinued. The syndrome may begin without warning and may not be reliably detected by routine testing. Patients taking felbamate should remain alert for signs of infection, bleeding and easy bruising, or symptoms of anemia such as fatigue or weakness.[1,8]

Hepatotoxicity leading to hepatic failure is estimated to occur in one in every 24,000 to 34,000 patients taking felbamate. Felbamate should not be used in patients with a history of hepatic dysfunction.[1,8]

The need for monitoring drug levels has not been established. However, baseline laboratory testing should include a complete blood count, platelet count and reticulocyte count, as well as determination of liver enzyme levels. Hematologic evaluations should be performed frequently during treatment and after discontinuation of treatment. Liver enzyme levels should be determined every one to two weeks, and felbamate therapy should be discontinued if the aspartate aminotransferase, alanine aminotransferase or bilirubin levels increase above baseline.

Because of serious side effects, felbamate is not recommended as first-line therapy in the treatment of seizures. The manufacturer recommends its use only in patients who do not adequately respond to alternative therapy and whose epilepsy is so severe that the substantial risks of aplastic anemia and hepatic failure are deemed acceptable.[8] Its use requires that the physician be thoroughly familiar with the drug. The manufacturer recommends that written consent be obtained before initiation of therapy.

Monotherapy in adults should begin with 1,200 mg of felbamate daily, given in divided doses every six to eight hours. Daily dosages should increase by 600 mg every two weeks to a total daily dosage of 2,400 to 3,600 mg. As adjunctive therapy, treatment should begin at 1,200 mg daily, given in divided doses every six to eight hours. If the patient is taking phenytoin, valproic acid or carbamazepine, a 20 to 35 percent reduction in the dosage of these drugs is recommended during felbamate therapy. Levels of antiepileptic drugs should be followed as the dosage of felbamate is increased to 2,400 to 3,600 mg daily.

The beginning dosage of felbamate in children aged two to 14 years with Lennox-Gastaut syndrome is 15 mg per kg, given in three to four divided doses. Dosages of other antiepileptic drugs should be reduced by 20 percent, with further reductions based on side effects or drug levels. The daily dosage of felbamate should increase by 15 mg per kg weekly, to a maximum of 45 mg per kg.[9]

Felbamate is available in 400-mg and 600-mg tablets, and as a suspension of 600 mg per 5 mL (Table 19.1). The cost of one month of treatment at the lowest recommended maintenance dosage is approximately $52.[6]

Topiramate

Topiramate (Topamax) has been approved for adjunctive treatment in adults with partial seizures. It has a novel chemical structure derived from D-fructose that blocks voltage-sensitive sodium channels, enhances the activity of GABA, an inhibitory neurotransmitter, and blocks the action of glutamate, an excitatory neurotransmitter. It is also a weak carbonic anhydrase inhibitor.[11]

Topiramate is well absorbed orally with a bioavailability of 80 percent. It is less than 20 percent protein bound. When used alone, 20 percent of the drug is metabolized. With concurrent use of other antiepileptic drugs, 50 percent of the drug is metabolized. Excretion is primarily renal, with 50 to 80 percent of each dose excreted unchanged. The half-life is 20 to 30 hours.

A 30 percent and 48 percent median reduction in seizure frequency occurs at dosages of 200 mg and 400 mg per day, respectively. No improvement in seizure reduction occurs at dosages above 400 mg.[12] The only known contraindication is hypersensitivity to the drug. Side effects include dizziness and somnolence (which are not dose related), ataxia, impaired concentration, confusion, fatigue, paresthesias, speech difficulties, diplopia and nausea.[13] There is an increased risk of nephrolithiasis, which may be due to carbonic anhydrase inhibition.[14] Concomitant use of topiramate with other carbonic anhydrase inhibitors such as dichlorphenamide (Daranide) or acetazolamide (Diamox) should be avoided.

Topiramate increases phenytoin concentration by 25 percent and decreases valproic acid concentration by 11 percent (Table 19.2). Topiramate does not change the concentration of carbamazepine, phenobarbital or primidone when coadministered. Concentrations of topiramate decrease up to 48 percent when phenytoin is coadministered, up to 40 percent with coadministration of carbamazepine and up to 14 percent with valproic acid.

Topiramate is classified as a category C medication during pregnancy. It is not known if it is excreted in human breast milk.

Overdoses have been managed to date with prompt induction of emesis or lavage. Topiramate is effectively removed by hemodialysis.

The starting dosage is 50 mg per day given in the evening, increasing by 50 mg per week until a dosage of 200 mg given twice daily is reached. It is not necessary to monitor drug levels. Dosing beyond 400 mg per day does not increase efficacy. Topiramate can be taken with food, if desired. Patients with impaired renal function should use one half the recommended dosage.

Topiramate is available in 25-mg, 100-mg and 200-mg coated tablets. The cost of one month's therapy at 400 mg per day is approximately $181.[6]

Fosphenytoin

Fosphenytoin (Cerebyx) is a phenytoin precursor that is rapidly converted after parenteral administration. It is indicated for short-term parenteral use when the oral form is unavailable or less advantageous.[15] In addition to its use as a short-term substitute for oral phenytoin, fosphenytoin can be used to control status epilepticus and to prevent and control seizures during neurosurgery.

The use of parenteral phenytoin is complicated by poor solubility, high alkalinity, hypotension, cardiac arrhythmias and the potential for soft tissue injury with extravasation. However, fosphenytoin can be administered intravenously or intramuscularly with a low risk of tissue irritation. No significant electrocardiographic changes have been noted with either intravenous or intramuscular administration. Mild decrements in mean systolic blood pressure have been reported with intravenous administration.

Therapeutic serum levels of phenytoin are attained within 10 minutes of infusion of intravenous fosphenytoin.[16] Peak serum phenytoin levels are attained 90 minutes after intramuscular administration. Fosphenytoin administered intravenously or intramuscularly is 100 percent bioavailable and is 90 to 95 percent protein bound. A 15-mg dose of fosphenytoin is equivalent to 1 mg of phenytoin.

Fosphenytoin is contraindicated in patients with hypersensitivity to phenytoin or other hydantoins, and in patients with sinoatrial block, second- and third-degree atrioventricular block and Stokes'-Adams syndrome.[13]

Common adverse effects include pruritus, nystagmus, dizziness, somnolence, ataxia, nausea, tinnitus and hypotension. Up to 64 percent of patients experience groin discomfort on intravenous administration, which usually dissipates within 60 minutes.

Concomitant use with carbamazepine or diazepam (Valium) has shown no effect on fosphenytoin binding. Fosphenytoin binding did decrease in patients with excessive concentrations of phenobarbital or valproic acid.

For patients with status epilepticus, 22.5 to 30 mg per kg of fosphenytoin should be administered intravenously at a rate of 100 to 150 mg per minute. For nonemergent therapy or to prevent seizures, 15 to 30 mg per kg can be administered intravenously or intramuscularly in a loading dose, followed by a daily maintenance dosage of 6 to 12 mg per kg. Patients who are already at therapeutic levels of oral phenytoin can be given fosphenytoin at 1.5 times the daily oral phenytoin dose. The approximate cost of a 10-mL vial of 750 mg of fosphenytoin is $54.[6]

References

1. Dichter MA, Brodie MJ. New antiepileptic drugs. *N Engl J Med* 1996;334:1583-90.

2. Ramsay RE. Advances in the pharmacotherapy of epilepsy. *Epilepsia* 1993;34(Suppl 5):S9-16.

3. Gabapentin. Package insert. Morris Plains, N.J.: Parke-Davis, December 1994.

4. Laxer KD. Guidelines for treating epilepsy in the age of felbamate, vigabatrin, lamotrigine, and gabapentin. *West J Med* 1994; 161:309-14.

5. Rosner H, Rubin L, Kestenbaum A. Gabapentin adjunctive therapy in neuropathic pain states. *Clin J Pain* 1996;12:56-8.

6. *Red book*. Montvale, N.J.: Medical Economics Data, 1997.

7. Lamotrigine. Package insert. Research Triangle Park, N.C.: Glaxo Wellcome Inc., March 1997.

8. Palmer KJ, McTavish D. Felbamate. A review of its pharmacodynamic and phamacokinetic properties, and therapeutic efficacy in epilepsy. *Drugs* 1993; 45(6):1041-65.

9. Jensen PK. Felbamate in the treatment of refractory partial-onset seizures. *Epilepsia* 1993;34(Suppl 7):S25-9.

10. Felbamate. Package insert. Cranbury, N.J.: Wallace Laboratories, November 1995.

11. *Medical Science Bulletin* 1997;20(236):1.

12. Faught E, Wilder BJ, Ramsay RE, Reife RA, Kramer LID, Pledger GW, *et al*. Topiramate placebo-controlled dose-ranging trial in refractory partial epilepsy using 200-, 400- and 600-mg daily dosages. *Neurology* 1996;46:1684-90.

13. Olin B, ed. *Drug facts and comparisions*. St. Louis: Facts and Comparisons, Inc., 1997:283u-y.

14. Shorvon SD. Safety of topiramate: adverse events and relationships to dosing. *Epilepsia* 1996;37 (Suppl 2):18-22.

15. Fosphenytoin. Package insert. Morris Plains, N.J.: Parke-Davis, 1996.

16. Allen FH Jr, LeGarda S, *et al*. Safety, tolerance, and pharmacokinetics of intravenous fosphenytoin (Cerebyx) in status epilepticus [Abstract]. *Epilepsia* 1995;36(Suppl 4):90.

—by William J. Curry, M.D. and David L. Kulling, M.D.

William J. Curry, M.D., is co-medical director of Pennsylvania State Family Health, Middletown, and assistant professor in the Department of Family and Community Medicine at the Milton S. Hershey Medical Center, Hershey, Pa. He received his medical degree from Pennsylvania State University College of Medicine, Hershey, and completed a residency in family practice at the U.S. Air Force Regional Hospital Eglin, Eglin Air Force Base, Florida.

David L. Kulling, M.D., is assistant professor in the Department of Family and Community Medicine and the Department of Orthopaedics and Rehabilitation at the Milton S. Hershey Medical Center. He graduated from the Muntch University of Technology and completed a residency in family practice at the Allegheny Family Physicians Residency Program of the Altoona (Pa.) Hospital. He also completed a primary care sports medicine fellowship at the University of Michigan Medical School, Ann Arbor. He holds certificates of added qualification in geriatric medicine and sports medicine.

The authors thank John Y. Oh., M.D. and Robert L. Jones, D.Ed., for review of the manuscript.

Chapter 20

Hard Choices with Felbamate

The approval of felbamate for sale in August 1993 represented the first advance in the drug treatment of epilepsy in the USA in fifteen years. Before being approved felbamate had been shown to be effective in adults with partial seizures and in children with Lennox-Gastaut syndrome. Furthermore, among the 3,000 people in whom it was evaluated, it was well tolerated and did not cause dangerous side effects. Coming after such a long dry spell, many people needed and wanted better drug treatment for their seizures. Hence, between September 1993 and August 1994 approximately 150,000 people tried felbamate; 50,000 began to take it long term. However, since August of 1994 when dangerous side effects were discovered, the number of people on felbamate has dropped off sharply.

The dangerous side effects of felbamate include bone marrow failure (aplastic anemia) and hepatic failure—either of which can be fatal. By mid-September 1994 twenty-four people had developed aplastic anemia while taking felbamate and another eight had developed liver failure. Eleven of these thirty-two people died.

Confronted by these alarming figures, a majority of patients on felbamate have switched to other medications. However, an estimated 10,000 to 12,000 people including many children continue to take it. Aware of the risks, many of these people have decided to continue

Washington University (St. Louis), Comprehensive Epilepsy Program, reprinted with permission. Washington University in St. Louis, Comprehensive Epilepsy Program, Box 811, 660 S. Euclid Avenue, St. Louis, MO 63110; (314) 362-3888.

taking it because it has helped them significantly when all other drugs had failed. Others are still trying to decide.

Based on what we know today, taking felbamate entails a risk. It is clear that people who try felbamate and are not helped by it should stop taking it. Thus far, no group of people have been identified in whom felbamate is "safe." With 32 out of 50,000 people being affected, the chance of having a serious side effect calculates out to be approximately 1 in 1,500. This makes taking felbamate 25 times more dangerous than a years worth of car rides and 600 times more dangerous than taking a single flight on a commercial air line. Yet, other treatments for epilepsy are more dangerous than felbamate. For example, in a child less than two years old with uncontrolled seizures, felbamate is 3 times less dangerous than valproic acid which is associated with a 1 in 500 chance of fatal liver failure.

Those who are still deciding about felbamate have hard choices. If it has helped when nothing else did, should they continue taking it? If they keep on taking felbamate, what warning signs should they watch for? How often should they have laboratory tests done?

Ultimately it is the person with seizures or, in the case of children, the parents who must decide if the benefits of felbamate justify taking the risks based their own situation. One way of putting some of the issues in perspective is to answer several questions before deciding what to do. First, in what ways has felbamate helped? Second, how sizeable is this improvement? Third, has this improvement materially made life better, and if so, how? Finally, does this benefit justify taking a chance?

People who are considering these questions for themselves or their children need to discuss these issues with their physician plus other family members and then decide. If they decide to stop felbamate, their physician needs to be involved because seizures often increase when felbamate is discontinued.

Felbamate-related problems highlight several themes that are all too familiar among people who are affected by seizures. They routinely have to take extra chances and have to make hard decisions that those without seizures never even consider. Quality of life for people with epilepsy is a personal issue that involves more than seizure frequency and in some cases justifies making hard, even risky choices.

—by W. Edwin Dodson, M.D.

Chapter 21

Surgery for Epilepsy

Abstract

The National Institutes of Health Consensus Development Conference on Surgery for Epilepsy brought together neurologists, neurosurgeons, psychologists, other health care providers, and the public to address issues regarding epilepsy surgery including patient selection and management, localization of seizure site onset, appropriate diagnostic techniques, and postoperative outcome assessment.

The panel concluded that brain surgery is an alternative treatment when medication fails. Seizure frequency, severity type, possible brain damage or injury from frequent seizures, and effect on quality of life all must be considered in deciding to evaluate for surgery. An appropriate medication trial must have been conducted, using the correct drugs for the patient's seizure type at adequate doses and blood levels. Nonepileptic attacks must be ruled out, and diagnostic tests to detect any underlying cause should be performed.

If surgery is considered, patients should be evaluated by a team including neurologists, neurosurgeons, neuropsychologists, social workers, and, if needed, psychiatrists. Assessment of outcome should include standardized methods of information collection. Measures

National Institutes of Health Consensus Development Conference Statement, March 19-21, 1990; Surgery for Epilepsy. NIH Consensus Statement Online 1990 Mar 19-21 [cited 1998 December 31];8(2):1-20. Despite the date on this document, it was still listed as medically current when cited. The full text can be viewed at http://text.nlm.nih.gov/nih/cdc/www.77txt.html.

assessing quality of life and overall health status can compare epilepsy to other chronic conditions. Assessment of economic and social impact on the patient's family should be included.

The full text of the panel's statement follows.

Introduction

Epilepsy is common. About 10 percent of all Americans will have at least one seizure at some time. Many people have one or a few attacks and then never have another one. For those with recurrent seizures, about 70 percent are satisfactorily controlled with antiepileptic drugs. Of the 150,000 people who develop epilepsy each year, 10 to 20 percent prove to have "medically intractable epilepsy." Many of these patients and their families have to deal with a chronic disorder that impairs the quality of life for all concerned.

Brain surgery may be an alternative treatment if antiepileptic drugs fail, and it is being used more often. Several centers have reported success, and increasing numbers of patients are being referred for surgery, including many children. Improved technology has made it possible to identify more accurately where seizures originate in the brain (epileptic regions), and advances in surgery have made operative management safer. As a result, investigators have estimated that 2,000 to 5,000 new patients in the United States might be suitable for operations each year, compared with the present annual rate of about 500.

Nevertheless, controlled trials have not been done, and there is disagreement among investigators about the choices and application of methods to evaluate patients for surgery, which procedures should be done, and how best to assess outcome. For these reasons, this consensus conference was organized.

There is no precise definition of intractable epilepsy. Among the considerations are seizure frequency, seizure type, severity of attacks, and impact on quality of life. Before seizures are deemed intractable it is necessary to be certain that the correct drugs have been used in the correct amounts. Complex partial seizures are more likely to be intractable than tonic-clonic or other common forms of epilepsy. In uncontrolled complex partial seizures, the frequency of seizures varies from fewer than one a week to five or more each day. The clinical manifestations also vary in different patients. Some are not apparent to anyone but the patient; others disrupt daily activities and are socially embarrassing. If a patient falls during seizures that occur only a few times a year, repeated injuries and trips to emergency rooms can make life miserable. Even one seizure a year may disqualify a person from having a driver's license. Disability is also influenced by the reaction of the patient's family, friends, teachers, or employers. All of these factors have an impact on what is judged severe enough to warrant consideration of surgical therapy.

There are other reasons to consider surgical therapy. For instance, repeated seizures may have adverse effects on the brain, leading to progressive cerebral degeneration and more severe clinical handicaps. Chronic use of antiepileptic drugs may cause toxic syndromes and may also have adverse effects on learning, scholastic achievement, development, and job performance.

On the other hand, surgery has risks and costs that have to be considered. Before a patient is accepted for surgery, it is necessary to be certain of the diagnosis and the adequacy of previous drug therapy. Evaluation for surgery includes several methods: video-monitoring, brain imaging, different kinds of electroencephalography, and neuropsychological tests. The best combination of these studies has yet to be defined. Investigators do not agree about the preoperative need to identify areas of the brain that control speech. Similarly, there are differences of opinion about the specific surgical procedures that produce the best outcomes for different kinds of attacks. Anterior temporal lobe operations and other cortical resections involve the removal of epileptic regions from the temporal lobe and other areas of the brain and are done for complex partial seizures. Corpus callosotomy involves the severing of connections between the right and left sides of the brain and is used for some types of generalized attacks; corpus callosotomy and hemispherectomy can be used for seizures with childhood hemiplegia.

This consensus conference was designed to address the following questions:

1. How should patients be selected?
2. What evaluation is necessary to localize epileptic regions?
3. What procedures are appropriate for specific epilepsies?
4. How should outcome be assessed?
5. Directions for future research—should a controlled trial be done? If so, for what seizure types?

To address these questions, the National Institute of Neurological Disorders and Stroke and the Office of Medical Applications of Research of the National Institutes of Health convened a Consensus Development Conference on Surgery for Epilepsy on March 19-21, 1990. After a day and a half of presentations by experts and discussion by the audience, a consensus panel drawn from specialists and generalists from the medical profession and related scientific disciplines, clinical investigators, and public representatives considered the evidence and came to the following conclusions.

How Should Patients Be Selected?

Patients with unsatisfactory seizure control often seek alternative care. The number or severity of the seizures may be unacceptable to the patient, family, or treating physician. Other reasons for referral include the results of diagnostic tests that may show a structural focal brain lesion, unsatisfactory psychosocial adaptation due to poor seizure control, unacceptable sedation, or other drug side effects. Such patients, especially those with persistent complex partial seizures and some types of generalized seizures, may be candidates for surgical treatment. First, however, these patients should be referred to an adult or pediatric neurologist for further evaluation of diagnosis and treatment.

Evaluation and medical treatment of these patients may take place under the supervision of a neurologist or in an epilepsy center that provides comprehensive diagnostic and treatment services designed for patients with intractable epilepsy. By "intractable" we mean that seizures have not been brought under acceptable control with the resources available to the primary care physician or neurologist.

To be effective and comprehensive, the staff of a center should include the following: neurologists with special training and experience in epilepsy; neurosurgeons with experience in epilepsy surgery; neuropsychologists; and personnel trained to deal with social, psychological, and psychiatric problems and rehabilitation for school and work. Personnel to perform ancillary neurodiagnostic assessment must also be available, including closed-circuit TV and electroencephalography (EEG) monitoring telemetry; modern neurophysiological and EEG equipment; neuroimaging capabilities, including magnetic resonance imaging (MRI); and neuropsychological testing. Some centers also have positron emission tomography (PET), single photon emission computed tomography (SPECT), or other methods of evaluating cerebral blood flow and metabolism.

Before a patient is considered for surgery, evaluation should be sufficient to ensure the following:

- Nonepileptic attacks have been excluded and epilepsy is, in fact, present. Cardiogenic syncope, psychogenic seizures, and other nonepileptic states can closely mimic epileptic attacks.

154

- The epileptic seizure type and syndrome have been clarified. Primary and secondary epilepsies, partial seizures, and tonic-clonic seizures respond to different antiepileptic drugs and different surgical procedures.

- Diagnostic tests have been performed to define a metabolic or structural cause of the epileptic attacks.

- The patient has had a reasonable trial of the appropriate antiepileptic drugs, with adequate monitoring of compliance and the effects of the treatment.

- The patient and family have received detailed information about the specific seizure disorder, available drug treatments and side effects, and alternative treatments such as surgery. If, after this evaluation, seizures prove to be intractable or drug treatment is unsatisfactory, appropriate patients should be referred to an epilepsy center to be evaluated for surgery. Referrals should be made as soon as it is clear that medical treatment is unlikely to result in further benefit. Early referrals may prevent the development of chronic psychosocial and physical problems that result from uncontrolled seizures.

Coexisting disorders may affect the decision to operate; they may include severe psychiatric disorders, profound developmental retardation, or progressive neurodegenerative diseases. After the initial evaluation and a full unsuccessful trial of medical therapy, surgery may be considered. Patients with partial seizures and secondarily generalized seizures (attacks that begin locally and spread to both sides of the brain) are potential candidates. Secondarily generalized seizures may take the form of atonic, tonic, or tonic-clonic attacks. Patients with seizures and childhood hemiplegia may also benefit from surgery. Patients with the following seizure types are potential candidates: complex partial seizures of temporal lobe origin or other focal seizures; generalized, atonic, akinetic, or myoclonic seizures; and partial seizures with childhood hemiplegia.

What Evaluation Is Necessary to Localize Epileptic Foci?

Precise clinical, electrophysiologic, and imaging data are necessary to carry out surgical therapy. Neurological assessment is necessary to identify and exclude other forms of neurological disease. In all cases, EEG and MRI are used. Additional tests are often necessary for precise localization. The following electrophysiological techniques are used in establishing the diagnosis and focality of an epileptic disorder:

1. EEG is essential, sometimes with sleep deprivation or other activation techniques.

2. EEG monitoring with video (video-EEG) is used widely in the evaluation of potential surgical candidates to exclude nonepileptic seizures and to define the electroclinical characteristics of the seizures. It is often used to establish and localize consistency and validity of the epileptogenic region.

3. For precise cerebral localization, other more or less invasive techniques are used in some cases to establish a high degree of confidence in the electrical localization. These methods include sphenoidal leads, subdural and epidural electrodes and grids, and depth electrodes placed stereotaxically. Decisions about the need for these procedures must be individualized.

Brain Imaging Techniques

Imaging techniques include x-ray computed tomography (CT), MRI, PET, and SPECT.

CT has a limited role in the investigation of partial epilepsy because MRI is superior to CT in demonstrating brain tumors, vascular malformations, and focal brain atrophy. The diagnostic value of MRI in visualizing mesial temporal sclerosis and atrophy is under study. MRI is useful postoperatively to assess the extent of surgical resection.

PET measures regional cerebral metabolism and blood flow. PET imaging has been quite successful in identifying the focus as an area of hypometabolism between attacks. This observation may be used in selecting patients with partial and secondarily generalized seizures for resective surgery. Because of the high costs and complexities of PET, this technology has been confined to a limited number of centers.

SPECT can also be used for functional imaging of the brain because it demonstrates regional cerebral blood flow, which is linked to cerebral metabolism and can therefore be used to identify the epileptic focus. SPECT uses conventional and readily available equipment and radiopharmaceuticals. These compounds can be used to study both ictal and interictal states. In the past decade, this relatively affordable technology has become widely available. More work is needed to determine whether SPECT is as sensitive as PET in localizing the epileptic regions.

Psychological tests are essential for the evaluation of varied cerebral functions, including memory and language. The intra-arterial amobarbital test is used to localize language function and to assess memory preoperatively.

These diagnostic methods should be available at specialized epileptic centers. However, the data are insufficient to determine which particular patients require the more invasive and detailed techniques.

Combining data from the major epilepsy centers would allow the development of a data bank or registry that should clarify many unanswered questions about the use of these diagnostic techniques.

What Procedures Are Appropriate for Specific Epilepsies?

For 60 years, there has been continuous development of the surgical management of epilepsy. There have been many advances in the scientific understanding of epilepsy, in new technologies for localizing epileptic foci, and in methods for reducing operative risk. Neither randomized controlled trials nor large community-based clinical trials have been undertaken; nevertheless, several surgical approaches have been reported to be successful and rational in managing some types of intractable epilepsy. The data are not definitive and are primarily derived from single-institution studies. Surgery for epilepsy in patients with preoperatively detected neoplasms or vascular malformations depends as much on the nature and site of the lesion as on the seizure disorder.

The following discussion relates specifically to surgical procedures performed with the primary goal of alleviating a seizure disorder rather than removing a specific brain lesion. Data collected to date suggest that patients in three general categories are suitable candidates for epilepsy surgery: partial seizures of temporal or extratemporal origin, secondarily generalized seizures, or unilateral, multifocal epilepsy associated with infantile hemiplegia.

Patients with Partial Seizures

The largest group of surgical candidates comprises patients with complex partial seizures of temporal lobe origin. Preoperative evaluation identifies those patients with tumors or vascular malformations and can determine whether the epileptic focus is deep (in the amygdala or hippocampus) or superficial (cortical).

Appropriately directed, surgical resection of epileptogenic tissue has resulted in success rates of 55 to 70 percent of patients, when success was defined as no seizures (some auras may be present) for 5 years after surgery sometimes with some patients still taking anti-convulsant medication. In some patients, surgery also results in an improved psychosocial outcome, but this has not been studied adequately. Combined morbidity and mortality rates for surgery are below 5 percent. The charges for diagnostic evaluation and surgery vary from $25,000 in uncomplicated cases to over $100,000 in those who require extensive preoperative testing, with a median charge of $40–60,000.

Partial seizures of frontal origin and from other extratemporal sites may also be treated surgically when the clinical manifestations and diagnostic studies indicate an epileptic region in a resectable area. Appropriately directed surgical resection of epileptogenic tissue may result in improvement (as defined above) in 30-50 percent of cases. The mortality rates are less than 2 percent, and the charges are slightly more than the cost of temporal lobe resection.

Patients with Secondarily Generalized Seizures

Some patients with generalized seizures may be candidates for surgical management. Specifically, patients with the Lennox-Gastaut syndrome or drop-attacks may be helped by section of the corpus callosum, a procedure designed to prevent rapid bilateral generalization of epileptic discharges. The procedure is most frequently recommended in patients who are prone to violent falls that often result in head injury. The seizure disorder usually persists postoperatively but seizures may become less frequent, less disabling, and less violent. Evaluation and selection of candidates have not been standardized. There is also variability of surgical technique, particularly how completely the corpus callosum is sectioned. Postoperative mortality is low, but significant complications may occur in as many as 20 percent. The charge for the surgery is often higher than for lobectomy because the procedure as done in some centers requires two operations, but the charge for the preoperative evaluation is often less.

Seizures Associated with Infantile Hemiplegia

In patients with intractable unilateral, multifocal epilepsy associated with infantile hemiplegia, hemispherectomy or callosotomy may be beneficial. These cases are rare, accounting for about 2 percent of all patients treated surgically for epilepsy. Success is measured not only by improvement in seizure frequency and type but also by improvement in behavior. Avoidance of complications (superficial cortical hemosiderosis and hydrocephalus) is a major consideration in the selection of surgical technique and has led to a current consensus for a "functional" hemispherectomy rather than one that is "anatomically complete." Success rates of 50 to 70 percent are balanced by combined mortality and morbidity rates that, in the past, reached 50 percent with anatomical hemispherectomy. Initial charges are similar to those for callosotomy but are increased by subsequent charges of dealing with late complications.

How Should Outcome Be Assessed?

Most studies that have assessed the outcome of either medical or surgical treatment of epilepsy have emphasized a single measure: seizure elimination or reduction in frequency. This measurement of seizure frequency needs to be clarified. For example, is a 50-percent reduction in a person who has two complex partial seizures a week equivalent to a 50-percent reduction in a person who has two seizures a year? We recommend the use of standardized methods to collect information about the frequency and kinds of seizures the patients are having.

Although we recognize the importance of seizure frequency, we recommend that future studies should use "general measures" of outcome that would take advantage of validated and quantitative methods to assess the quality of life and health status of individuals. This could be achieved by a standardized survey to assess the following: short-term surgical mortality and morbidity or complications (e.g., death, paralysis, or infection in the postoperative period); physical health (symptoms, functioning, role activities, sleep-wake cycle, and mobility); mental health (psychiatric diagnoses as well as symptoms such as anxiety or depression); neuropsychological assessment, including cognitive functioning and memory, both verbal and nonverbal; social health (personal interactions, employment, sexuality, driver's license, and community interactions); and general health (health perceptions, including fear of death and pain, life satisfactions, and energy). Evaluation of children should include assessment of developmental progress and school performance.

To evaluate each of the above, we recommend using general measures of health status and quality of life so that patients with epilepsy can be compared to patients with other chronic conditions. Epilepsy is a unique condition and we also recommend that, in addition to the general measures, supplemental information should be collected about the specific aspects of the quality of life of patients with seizures, as discussed above. This information should be gathered from family members in addition to the patients themselves. Because epilepsy affects the whole family, the family's well-being should be part of the assessment.

159

The assessment of any treatment of epilepsy must include analysis of the economic impact on patients, families, and society. Economic impact includes expenditures on medical care directly (surgical and hospitalization costs, medication costs, costs of allied health personnel) as well as indirect costs such as contributed care by family members and whether a patient's income and productivity are affected positively or negatively in the future.

Assessment must be done repeatedly for several years. Data from treatment centers should be pooled to achieve statistical power sufficient to test the efficacy of treatment, as assessed by the multiple outcome measures.

We recognize that individuals will emphasize different outcomes. Some may be more concerned with the reduction in seizure frequency; others may be more concerned with the effect of treatment on memory or social function. Evaluation of any therapy for intractable epilepsy must explicitly consider these patient preferences.

For all of these considerations, there is a need for a standardized method of data collection so that results from different treatment centers can be combined and compared.

Directions for Future Research—Should a Controlled Trial Be Done? If So, for What Seizure Types?

- The panel is impressed that surgery is beneficial for selected patients, but the optimal timing of surgery is not known. Because of current referral patterns, patients considered for temporal lobe resection tend to have had uncontrolled (intractable) epilepsy for 10 to 20 years. We therefore recommend a controlled trial of early versus late surgery to determine whether early surgery or optimal medical treatment followed by later surgery of patients with complex partial seizures will result in better health status and quality of life and may prevent additional brain damage or chronic social disability.

- Investigators differ in the selection of tests for preoperative evaluation. In particular, it is not known when more extensive diagnostic tests are needed, including ictal surface EEG recording, invasive intracranial electrode recording, PET, or SPECT. A program should be developed to assess the value of these tests, and should include the development and evaluation of algorithms. This would require standardization of definitions, data collection, and central analysis of the data.

160

- We recommend development of an outcome assessment method that combines validated measures already used to assess general health status and function in a population of patients with other chronic conditions, with special items that are sensitive to the unique characteristics of people with epilepsy and those close to them, as described in the answer to question 4.

- We recommend that psychiatric and behavioral functions be systematically assessed before surgery and during followup to determine whether there are specific contraindications to any particular surgical procedure and whether these procedures subsequently affect behavior.

- In temporal lobe surgery for partial seizures, standard and "tailored" resections are used by different groups but the results are apparently similar. The circumstances in which each technique is maximally effective should be clarified by standardized data collection including documentation of extent of surgical resection and multivariate analysis so that an appropriate trial may ultimately be planned, if needed.

- Because epilepsy surgery now may be used more often in children than in the past, we recommend additional studies to determine the effects of uncontrolled seizures and antiepileptic drug therapy on the developing brain. These studies might include, but not be limited to, evaluation of sequential neurodevelopmental assessment, anatomic and metabolic imaging procedures, cognitive-linguistic-academic achievement in school, and psychosocial adaptation of the child and family.

- Surgical treatment of epilepsy might not be needed if we knew more about ways to prevent brain injury or if we had more effective and less toxic anticonvulsant drugs. It is therefore necessary to support fundamental research in the basic sciences of epilepsy: developmental neurobiology, neural science, cellular pathology, neuropharmacology, and preventive epidemiology.

Conclusions and Recommendations

- Most epilepsy surgery is performed by teams of committed physicians at sophisticated medical centers. The number of operations is increasing rapidly.

161

- As currently used, surgery for intractable epilepsy is capable of stopping seizures or reducing their frequency. Effects on overall health status and quality of life have not been adequately studied.

- Several different diagnostic studies and surgical techniques have been used but do not clearly differ in effectiveness.

- Before surgery is performed, there are three absolute requirements. First, the diagnosis of epilepsy must be ascertained. Second, there must have been an adequate trial of drug therapy; that is, the correct drugs used in the correct dosage, carefully monitored for an appropriate time. Finally, the electroclinical syndrome must be defined.

- As demand for surgery grows and it becomes available at more hospitals, quality of care must be maintained. Surgery should be performed at hospitals equipped with modern technology and staffed by multidisciplinary teams capable of preoperative diagnosis, selection of medical and surgical treatments, comprehensive postoperative evaluation, and ambulatory rehabilitative care. Rehabilitation should include the transition of patients to a seizure-free or almost seizure-free lifestyle with respect to psychological and social adjustment, education, and vocational training.

- Physicians in any center or independent hospital that offers surgery for epilepsy should agree to use standardized data collection for all patients. The data should be maintained in a central registry, with respect for confidentiality. The data should include demographic information, diagnosis, clinical history, results of preoperative evaluation, and outcome assessment of quality of life and health status for at least 5 years. Outcome information should be provided to patients considering surgery so that expectations about the benefits and risks can be discussed and assessed.

Consensus Development Panel

A complete list of the members of the Consensus Development Panel, Speakers, and Planning Committee members can be viewed at http://text.nlm.nih.gov/nih/cdc/www.77txt.html.

Chapter 22

First Device for Severe Epilepsy

Citing the potential importance of alternative treatment for some people with epilepsy, FDA approved the first medical device to help reduce frequent, uncontrolled epileptic seizures.

The NeuroCybernetic Prosthesis System is approved for use with drugs or surgery in adults and adolescents with partial onset seizures. These seizures, which begin in one part of the brain, may remain localized or spread to the entire brain.

The July 16 [1997] approval came just 19 days after an FDA advisory panel recommended the device.

The new device has an electrical generator that is implanted under the collar bone with wires to the vagus nerve in the neck, where it delivers signals that stimulate the brain to control seizures. Doctors can change nerve stimulation settings with an external programming system, and patients can turn the device on and off by holding a magnet over it.

Approximately 1.7 million Americans have epilepsy. About 200,000 of these patients have seizures that cannot be adequately controlled by drugs or surgery. Severe, ongoing seizures can lead to death.

Clinical studies of the device included 454 patients. In the most recent study, half the patients had at least a 20 percent decrease in the number of daily seizures, one in four had a decrease of more than 50 percent, and one in five had increased seizures. Nine patients died, but clinical investigators did not believe stimulation from the device

FDA Consumer, November-December 1997.

was the cause. FDA has asked the manufacturer, Cyberonics, of Houston, to provide detailed information on any further deaths.

Chapter 23

Traumatic Brain Injury and Epilepsy

Definition

Traumatic brain injury, also known as brain injury or head injury, is an injury that results in damage to the brain. Brain injury may occur in one of two ways:

- A closed brain injury occurs when the moving head is stopped rapidly, as when hitting a windshield, or when it is hit by a blunt object, causing the brain to smash into the hard bony surface inside the skull. Closed brain injury may also occur without direct external trauma to the head if the brain undergoes a rapid forward or backward movement, such as when a person experiences whiplash, or when babies are shaken.

- A penetrating brain injury occurs when a fast moving object such as a bullet pierces the skull.

Both closed and penetrating brain injuries may result in both localized and diffuse damage to the brain.

Facts

Each year, an estimated two million people sustain a brain injury. About 500,000 brain injuries each year are severe enough to require hospitalization. Brain injury is most common among males between the ages of 15-24, but can strike at any age. Many brain injuries are mild, and symptoms usually disappear over time with proper attention. Others are more severe and may result in permanent disability.

Consequences

- **Cognitive Deficits.** Cognitive deficits include shortened attention span, short-term memory problems, problem solving or judgment deficits, and the inability to understand abstract concepts. Loss of sense of time and space, as well as decreased awareness of self and others, can occur. There may also be an inability to accept more than one- or two-step commands simultaneously.

- **Motor Deficits.** Motor deficits include paralysis, poor balance, lower endurance, reduction in the ability to plan motor movements, delays in initiation, tremors, swallowing problems, and poor coordination.

- **Perceptual Deficits.** Perceptual deficits mean possible changes in hearing, vision, taste, smell and touch, loss of sensation of body parts, left or right side of body neglect. The individual may have difficulty understanding where limbs are in relation to the body.

- **Speech Deficits.** Speech deficits most commonly include speech that is not clear as a result of poor control of the speech muscles (lips, tongue, teeth, etc.) and poor breathing patterns.

- **Language Deficits.** Language deficits can mean difficulty expressing thoughts and understanding others. This may include problems identifying objects and their function as well as problems with reading, writing, and ability to work with numbers. Problems with pragmatic language, decreased vocabulary and word substitution may occur. Speech therapy may be necessary to work with language problems.

- **Social Difficulties.** Social difficulties may be apparent, such as impaired social capacity resulting in self-centered behavior in which both empathy and self-critical attitudes are greatly diminished. Brain injury can result in difficulties in making and keeping friends, as well as understanding and responding to the nuances of social interaction.

- **Regulatory Disturbances.** Regulatory disturbances include fatigue and/or changes in sleep patterns, dizziness or headache. There may be loss of bowel and bladder control.

- **Personality Changes.** Personality changes may be subtle or pronounced. Changes include apathy and decreased motivation, emotional lability, irritability, or depression. Disinhibition also may result in temper flare-ups, aggression, cursing, lowered frustration tolerance, and inappropriate sexual behavior.

Traumatic Epilepsy

Epilepsy occurs in two to five percent of all people who sustain brain injury, but it is much more common with severe or penetrating injuries. While most seizures occur immediately after the injury or within the first year, it is also possible for epilepsy to surface years later.

Epilepsy includes both major or generalized seizures and minor or partial seizures.

- **Generalized Seizures.** Generalized seizures, also called "Grand Mal," are the most dramatic type of seizure. The person falls unconscious to the ground. His or her body stiffens, then jerks convulsively. The mouth, eyes, legs and arms move. Urinary incontinence is common. After several minutes, the jerking movements slow and the seizure ends. The person will likely be drowsy afterwards and may not remember the seizure.

- **Partial Seizures.** Partial seizures, also known as "focal," may be simple (during which the person is conscious but temporarily loses control of movements or senses, such as the uncontrollable jerking of an arm or leg), or complex (during which the person appears to be in a trance and may have isolated movements, such as lip smacking or picking at their clothes). About 75% of seizures are partial, although many of these seizures may eventually generalize.

Prognosis

The extent of an individual's enduring problems after a brain injury depend on many factors. Prompt and proper diagnosis and treatment can help minimize some consequences of brain injury. However, it is usually difficult to predict the outcome of a traumatic brain injury in the first hours, days, or weeks. In fact, the outcome may remain unknown for many months or years.

Treatment

Rehabilitation of the individual with a brain injury begins immediately. The initial life-saving treatment may be provided by an EMT, emergency physician, neurosurgeon or neurologist. As the person improves, a team of specialists may be used to evaluate and treat the problems that result. This team may include experts in rehabilitation medicine (physiatrists), psychiatry, nursing, neuropsychology, social work, nutrition, special education, occupational, physical, speech and language therapies, cognitive retraining, pastoral support, activity therapy, and vocational rehabilitation. The individual and his/her family are the most important members of the team, and should be included in the rehabilitation and treatment to the greatest extent possible.

There are a variety of treatment programs along the continuum of care, including: acute rehabilitation, long-term rehabilitation, coma treatment centers, late rehabilitation, extended intensive rehabilitation, transitional living programs, behavior management programs, life-long residential, day treatment programs, independent living programs, and traumatic brain injury programs within community colleges.

Recommended Readings

Waiting to Clear, Brain Injury: Early Stages of Recovery, Mary M. Castiglione and Cynthia Johnson, 1993, Pritchett & Hull Associates, Inc., 3440 Oakcliff Rd. N.E., Suite 110, Atlanta, GA 30340-3079, (800) 841-4925.

Making Sense Out of Nonsense: Models of Head Injury Rehabilitation, Ruth A. Whitham, 1994. Available from HDI Publishers, 10131 Alfred Lane, Houston, TX 77041, (800) 321-7037.

Sexuality and the Person with Traumatic Brain Injury: A Guide for Families, Ernest R. Griffith and Sally Lemberg, 1993, F.A. Davis Company, 1915 Arch Street, Philadelphia, PA 19103 (also available from the Brain Injury Association).

Head Injury and the Family, Arthur Dell Orto and Paul Power, 1994, G.R. Press, 6959 University Blvd., Winter Park, FL 32793, (800) 438-5911.

The *HDI Coping Series* and the *HDI Professional Series* on Traumatic Brain Injury, William Burke, Michael Wesolowski and William Blacker, 1996 (revised), HDI Publishers, 10131 Alfred Lane, Houston, TX 77041, (800) 321-7037.

Through This Window: Views on Traumatic Brain Injury, Patricia I. Felton (Ed.), 1992, Exceptional Brain Trauma Survivors (EBTS), P.O. Box 500, No. Waterboro, ME 04061.

Injured Mind, Shattered Dreams: Brian's Journey From Severe Head Injury to a New Dream, Janet Miller Rife, 1994, Brookline Books, P.O. Box 1046, Cambridge, MA, (617) 868-0360.

Living with Head Injury: A Guide for Families, Richard C. Senelick and Cathy E. Ryan, 1991, Rehabilitation Institute of San Antonio, Rehabilitation Hospital Services Corporation Press, 1010 Wisconsin Avenue, N.W., Washington, D.C. 20007 (also available from the Brain Injury Association).

Traumatic Head Injury: Cause, Consequence and Challenge, Dennis P. Swiercinsky, Terrie L. Price and Lief Erick Leaf, 1993, Head Injury Association of Kansas and Greater Kansas City, 1100 Pennsylvania Ave., Suite 305, Kansas City, MO 64105 (also available from the Brain Injury Association).

Credits

Brain Injury Association, Brain Injury Resource Center, an Interactive Multi-Media Computer-Based Resource Center, 1997.

National Institute of Neurological Disorders and Stroke, February, 1989, Inter-Agency Head Injury Task Force Report, Bethesda, MD.

Soren, S. and Kraus, J.F., 1991, Occurrence, Severity and Outcomes of Brain Injury, *Journal of Head Trauma Rehabilitation*, 6(2), 1-10.

Resources

Family Caregiver Alliance
425 Bush Street, Suite 500
San Francisco, CA 94108
(415) 434-3388

(800) 445-8106 (in CA)
Website: http://www.caregiver.org
E-mail: info@caregiver.org

Family Caregiver Alliance supports and assists caregivers of brain-impaired adults through education, research, services and advocacy. FCA's information Clearinghouse covers current medical, social, public policy and caregiving issues related to brain impairments. For residents of the greater San Francisco Bay Area, FCA provides direct family support services for caregivers of those with Alzheimer's disease, stroke, brain injury, Parkinson's and other debilitating brain disorders that strike adults.

Brain Injury Association
1776 Massachusetts Avenue, N.W., Suite 100
Washington, D.C. 20036
(202) 296-6443
(800) 444-6443 (Family Helpline)

The Brain Injury Association (BIA) is a national advocacy and awareness organization which develops and distributes educational information on resources, legal rights and services. BIA is a centralized clearinghouse for information of all kinds regarding brain injury and provide referrals for state associations across the United States.

Ontario Head Injury Association
P.O. Box 2338
St. Catharines, Ontario L2M 7M7
(905) 641-8877

The Ontario Head Injury Association maintains TBI INFO, a system of on-line information on traumatic brain injury and community re-integration.

Brown Schools
National Information and Referral Service
P.O. Box 4008
Austin, TX 78765
(512) 329-8821
(800) 531-5305

The Brown Schools offer information and referral for residential and rehabilitation facilities across the U.S.

About This Text

Reviewed by Gregory J. O'Shunick, M.D., Medical Director, Mary S. Reitter, Vice President of Education and Research, and Sue Gazman, Director of Communications, Brain Injury Association, Washington, DC. Prepared by Family Caregiver Alliance in cooperation with California's Caregiver Resource Centers, a statewide system of resource centers serving families and caregivers of brain-impaired adults. Funded by the California Department of Mental Health. Revised March 1997.

California Brain Injury Organizations

California Brain Injury Association
P.O. Box 160786
Sacramento, CA 95816
(916) 442-1710 (Administrative Office)
(800) 457-2443 (Helpline)

San Diego Head Injury Foundation, Inc.
P.O. Box 84601
San Diego, CA 92138
(619) 268-4432 (Helpline)
(619) 294-6541

The Head Trauma Support Project, Inc.
Sacramento Area
2500 Marconi Ave., Suite 203
Sacramento, CA 95821
(916) 482-5770

Chapter 24

Epilepsy: Genes May Build the Road in Treatment

Epilepsy affects almost one percent of the population of the United States. It is a brain disorder causing unpredictable, uncontrolled seizures that can occur at any time or place.

Seizures result when the normal, tightly controlled electrical activity of the brain becomes excessive and disordered, interrupting normal awareness and normal activities. In the most dramatic and severe seizures (called "grand mal"), the patient loses consciousness and has wild movements of the limbs, followed by temporary suppression of conscious brain activity. The brain slowly regains its normal activity as the patient wakes up, unaware of what happened.

Epilepsy is the most common neurological disorder among young people. And because it produces problems with school, driving, and keeping a job, it has a huge economic cost (estimated by the government at $3.5 billion). It takes a social toll impossible to measure in disrupted lives for both epileptics and their families.

That cost is all the more frustrating because it seems as if it should be greatly reduced if only we had the right drugs to control the seizures. Many useful drugs exist for epilepsy, and several new ones have become available recently. But, for about one third of patients, seizures cannot be controlled by presently available medical therapy. Some epileptics can be helped by brain surgery, but thousands remain whose epilepsy cannot be controlled by any present-day treatments.

Walsh, Christoper A. "Epilepsy: Genes May Build the Road in Treatment," *The Harvard Mahoney Neuroscience Institute Letter*, Winter 1997; reprinted with permission.

So, the hunt continues for improved antiepileptic medications—a search now leading onto genetic ground.

The Genetic Picture

Epilepsy can be caused by many factors that have nothing to do with genetics; head trauma, stroke, infections, tumors, and drug or alcohol abuse can all induce epilepsy. However, up to one half of all epilepsy has no other obvious causes, and there is increasing consensus that most of these cases have some relationship to inherited genes.

Recent rapid advances in the understanding of the human genome have begun to allow the identification of genes that predispose to epilepsy. Each one of these new genes seems to cause epilepsy by interrupting key processes in the normal function of the brain's neurons.

Some rare types of epilepsy seem to be almost completely caused by the action of epilepsy genes. In families where these genes are found, anyone who inherits the epilepsy gene (which usually means half of the children of an affected parent) will eventually develop epilepsy no matter what.

However, we are coming to understand that epilepsy may be genetically more "complex," like diabetes or cancer. In these complex genetic diseases, anyone theoretically can develop the disorder, as it can be caused by the interactions of many different genes. Depending upon which combination of genes people inherit, some people will be more susceptible to epilepsy than others, but the genes do not make epilepsy inevitable.

Inherited epilepsies usually require at least four complicated, unpronounceable medical words to capture their characteristic features.

For example, some families have a remarkable epilepsy: Seizures occur in their newborn babies just during the first week of life, and then magically go away and usually never come back. The disorder is called benign (because they go away) familial neonatal (because they occur in newborns) convulsions—BFNC for short—and two different genes (BFNC1, BFCN2) can cause it. Other families have a disorder called autosomal dominant (transmitted directly from parent to child) nocturnal frontal lobe epilepsy, ADNFLE. This epilepsy causes bizarre types of movements because the seizures involve the frontal lobe; the seizures occur mostly or only just after the onset of sleep.

Researchers usually find epilepsy genes by studying families in which it is very clear that epilepsy is a genetic trait passed on from parent to child. Often such families have very rare and distinctive types of epilepsy. This makes it easier for researchers to be sure that different family members have the same kind of epilepsy and that it is caused by the action of a gene, rather than some other cause (such as drug abuse or head trauma).

For individuals who think epilepsy may run in their family, the Epilepsy Foundation of America has set up a website (www.efa.org/index/htm) that describes genetic studies in epilepsy and allows interested individuals to contact epilepsy researchers.

Table 24.1. Human Epliepsy Genes

Disorder	Chromosome	Gene Identified?
Benign familial neonatal convulsions (BFNC1)	20	no
Benign familial neonatal convulsions (BFNC2)	8	no
Juvenile myoclonic epilepsy (JME)	6	no
Idiopathic generalized epilepsy (IGE)	8	no
Partial epilepsy with auditory features (EPT)	10	no
Nocturnal frontal lobe epilepsy (ADNFLE)	20	yes
Unverricht-Lundborg disease (EPM1)	21	yes
Myoclonic epilepsy with ragged red fibers (MERRF)	mitochondrial	yes
Northern epilepsy syndrome (EPMR)	8	no
Ceroid lipofuscinosis, juvenile type (CLN3)	16	yes
Myonclonic epilepsy of Lafora (MELF)	6	no
Periventricular heterotopia (PH)	X	no
Double cortex (DC)	X	no

Another way that epilepsy genes can be found is by finding families with epilepsy in which slight abnormalities occur in the way the brain develops, since abnormalities in brain development have long been associated with seizures. The human brain can be imaged very precisely using Magnetic Resonance Imaging (MRI), and the inheritance of certain subtle malformations of the brain can then be analyzed by taking MRI pictures of everyone in a family.

Our group has used this method to localize two epilepsy genes, each one associated with subtle abnormalities of brain development that would never have been suspected before the advent of MRI imaging. The genes for the developmental epileptic disorders appear to be involved in communication between cells in the developing brain as well as in the adult brain; therefore, they may be especially central to normal brain function and thus among the most desirable targets for drug design.

Sorting through DNA

The 50,000 to 100,000 total genes present in our DNA are like individual entries in a vast encyclopedia; they collectively tell our cells what to do and when. Our 46 chromosomes are like the volumes of that encyclopedia: large DNA molecules each binding together hundreds to thousands of genes. Once a large family with inherited epilepsy is found, the tools of the international Human Genome Project can usually allow the "mapping" or localization of that gene to a place within one of the 46 chromosomes. Therefore, mapping an epilepsy gene basically means narrowing the search for the epilepsy gene down to about 500 to 1,000 genes in a smaller area of one individual chromosome.

Often, however, taking the last step to find that one disease-causing gene in a thousand takes longer than the initial mapping: It often requires painstakingly sifting through the DNA sequence of many genes to find the one that contains an error, or mutation. Finding a mutation can be like trying to find a single typographical error among a thousand encyclopedia entries, all of them written in a language that we do not yet understand! That often requires years of work and/or a stroke of good fortune.

The Road from Genes to Drug Design

Most epilepsy drugs currently on the market were discovered to have activity against seizures first, and only later did we come to understand a little bit about how or why they were effective. However, the ideal way to design epilepsy drugs would be first to understand the critical workings of the brain and the key steps that give rise to the seizures, and then make new drugs that specifically attack the key steps. Such drugs should be more specific, effective, and have fewer side effects.

The road that will lead to such drug development is beginning to be built, thanks to the rapid advances in identifying epilepsy genes. The power of genetics in opening up new avenues of investigation is unique. For example, some recently identified genes turn out to be involved in aspects of neuronal function that were previously not thought to be abnormal in epilepsy. Drug design can now be aimed at the neuronal functions mediated by these genes, without upsetting other systems. Therefore, each new epilepsy gene provides a potential new target for developing new drug therapies that may be more effective and have fewer side effects.

It is likely to take several more years to go from genes to successful epilepsy drugs: Only in 1994 were the first drugs released onto the market that were designed "rationally"—that is, by exploiting our knowledge of neuronal function to target aspects of it critical to epilepsy. However, newly released drugs (protease inhibitors) that treat AIDS interfere with processes that were not even understood a few years ago, illustrating how far and how fast "rational" drug design has come and showing its potential for new treatments given adequate understanding of epileptic mechanisms. The further study of inherited human epilepsies should provide critical information for future drug design.

—by Christoper A. Walsh

Dr. Walsh is Senior Associate in Neurology, Beth Israel Deaconess Medical Center and Assistant Professor of Neurology at Harvard Medical School.

Chapter 25

Nonepileptic Seizures

Abstract

Commonly misdiagnosed as epilepsy, nonepileptic seizures (NES) affect several hundred thousand people in the United States. Similar in appearance to epileptic seizures, NES may include altered movement, emotion, and sensation, or disturbance in consciousness unaccompanied by any epileptiform discharges in the brain. Prevalence is highest among women between 26 and 32 years of age. Patients can present with both epilepsy and NES. Most NES are psychogenic in origin. Medication, as well as hypoglycemia, migraines, hypertension, gastroesophageal reflux, and parasomnias, can be causative, as can altered functioning of the hypothalamic-pituitary-ovarian axis. Anticonvulsants can exacerbate NES, making the distinction from epilepsy critical. Diagnosis and psychiatric referral must be handled carefully to avoid alienating the patient.

Introduction

The earliest recorded descriptions of epileptic-like events are found in the writings of Hippocrates and Aretaeus. Centuries later, there is still much to be learned about nonepileptic seizures (NES), a disorder that straddles the line between neurology and psychiatry and is alternately claimed and disclaimed by each.

Thomson, LR. Nonepileptic Seizures; Avoid Misdiagnosis and Long-Term Morbidity. *Clinician Reviews*. 1996;8(3):81-96. Reprinted with permission. Copyright © Clinicians Publishing Group and Williams & Wilkins.

Nonepileptic seizures resemble epileptic seizures and may include altered movement, emotion, and sensation, or disturbance in consciousness unaccompanied by any epileptiform discharges in the brain. Several hundred thousand people in the United States are estimated to be affected by NES, which are also known as pseudoseizures, psychogenic seizures, and hysterical fits. Nonepileptic seizures are commonly misdiagnosed as epileptic seizures (ES) and inappropriately treated.

To distinguish between ES and NES on clinical grounds, researchers have compared the features of both (see Table 25.1).[1-6] These are, however, only guidelines. Each case is unique, and there are exceptions to the rules. For instance, characteristics that were once thought to be representative of NES—such as normal electroencephalogram (EEG), no loss of consciousness, sexual automatisms, and vocal obscenities—are now known to be associated with frontal lobe seizures, too.

The number of individuals who are affected by both ES and NES is greater than would be expected to occur by chance.[3] Yet, among researchers, there is great disparity in the statistical frequency of NES coexisting with epilepsy. The estimates vary from 8% to 60%, with most reporting between 10% and 25%.[7-14] Devinsky *et al.*[15] found that 32% of patients with NES had coexisting or prior epilepsy. They reported that when patients have both ES and NES, the ES tend to be stereotypic but very different and distinct from the NES, which may also be stereotypic.

Because the manifestations of NES are as varied and unique as the people who experience them, accurate diagnosis may be delayed for years. By familiarizing themselves with current diagnostic and treatment approaches, nurse practitioners and physician assistants can intervene early in the course of the disorder and avoid long-term and sometimes iatrogenic morbidity.

Etiology

"Nonepileptic seizures" describes all epileptic-like events not caused by epileptiform discharges in the brain. In the literature, terms such as "pseudoseizures" and "psychogenic seizures" are used interchangeably with NES, regardless of etiology. Cases can be further classified as psychogenic, physiogenic, or pseudoseizures, depending upon the underlying pathology.

The majority of individuals with NES are affected by seizures that are psychogenic in origin. These individuals are unaware of any underlying motivation and do not consciously cause the seizures.[16]

Table 25.1. Differential Diagnosis: NES and ES[1-6]

Characteristic	NES	ES
Onset	Gradual	Sudden
Subjective symptoms	Often present	Usually absent
Duration	Prolonged	Short
Motor features	May be less stereotypic, ictal quivering, arrhythmic jerking, nonsynchronous rhythmic movements, pelvic thrusting; bilateral motor activity with preserved consciousness	Stereotypic, phenomenological correspondence with seizure types; bilateral motor activity with preserved consciousness seen only in supplementary motor area seizures
Vocalizations	Weeping, crying, shouting, obscene language	Crying at onset, grunting, various vocalizations
Incontinence and/or injury	Incontinence and/or injury if in keeping with underlying psychopathology	May be present
Sleep	Does not occur during actual sleep	May occur during sleep
Prolactin levels	No rise	Rise
EEG	No ictal or postictal EEG changes	Ictal and postictal EEG changes (frontal lobe epilepsy may require depth electrodes)
Postictal	Lethargy and confusion less common	Postictal lethargy and confusion
Frequency	May be increased by anticonvulsant therapy and stressors, independent of anticonvulsants; may be possible to induce and abort, and to recall events that occurred during the ictus	May increase with decreasing levels of anticonvulsants, intercurrent illness, and stressors; impossible to induce and abort
Categories (e.g., absence or tonic-clonic seizures)	Often do not apply	Always apply

181

Psychogenic seizures are often the result of a conversion reaction and may function as a safety valve, protecting the individual from stress. During the seizure, stress is unconsciously converted into a physical symptom that allows the person to escape from something unpleasant. It may also serve to evoke sympathy or help from others.

Similarly, psychogenic seizures may be the manifestation of a dissociative disorder. The dissociative mechanism is used defensively to handle a traumatic event, such as physical, sexual, or emotional abuse.

Other persons experience NES that are physiologic in origin and are caused by factors including medications; conditions such as hypoglycemia, migraines, hypertension, gastroesophageal reflux, and parasomnias; and metabolic, movement, and syncopal disorders. In a previously unrecognized subset of patients who exhibit no evidence of psychopathology, NES may be caused by neuroendocrine disorders. Abnormal behavioral responses, including NES, may manifest when anomalous brain substrates are acted upon by exogenous and endogenous biochemical influences, such as drugs, hormones, and glucose.[17]

In addition, physiogenic NES are sometimes catamenial and occur because of the exquisite sensitivity of the temporolimbic structures, especially the amygdala, to hormonal influence. Patients with this type of NES typically have histories consistent with altered functioning of the hypothalamic-pituitary-ovarian axis, as evidenced by reproductive endocrine disorders, polycystic ovaries, and abnormal results on testing for luteinizing hormone-releasing hormone.

In a follow-up study of NES patients at Dartmouth Hitchcock Medical Center, 7 of 12 women (58%) felt their NES worsened premenstrually or during menses. Two experienced worsening of their seizures when placed on exogenous estrogen. One woman described dramatic improvement of her seizures while on clomiphene and progesterone, and a worsening of her seizures during labor. Another woman's seizures improved after being placed on nafarelin, an agonistic analog of gonadotropin-releasing hormone. Seventy-five percent described some type of endocrine or menstrual problem (Thomson LR *et al*, unpublished data, 1997).

The effects of estrogen in increasing epileptiform activity in the brain have been well documented, as have the therapeutic effects of progesterone and clomiphene on temporal lobe epilepsy.[18-22] Future research may further define the role of hormones both in stimulating and treating NES. The psycho-neuro-endocrine interactions of NES may be the centerpiece for research in the next century.

In some cases, psychogenic and physiogenic factors may combine to cause NES. More than 25 years ago, Niedermeyer *et al*.[23] published case studies of patients in whom NES frequency increased during anticonvulsant therapy, with the highest seizure rates seen at the highest doses. In each case, when the medication was discontinued, the seizure manifestations abated. The researchers concluded that the cerebral toxicity of anticonvulsants may be a facilitating factor for NES, when organic and/or psychodynamic-psychosocial predisposing factors are present. Cerebral toxicity may cause control mechanisms to fail; atavistic impulses then result in the motor sequences of NES.

This factor alone makes it imperative for clinicians to consider the diagnosis of NES. Mistakenly treating NES with anticonvulsants may exacerbate the condition by facilitating seizures and turning the problem into one of monumental proportions. In the study of NES patients at Dartmouth Hitchcock Medical Center, 8 of 18 patients (44%) felt that anticonvulsants made their seizures worse; 5 of 8 patients specified phenytoin. Twenty-two percent felt stopping anticonvulsants had dramatically decreased or eliminated their NES.

Pseudoseizures are those that occur as a manifestation of malingering. For instance, a patient may intentionally fake a seizure for the purpose of secondary gain, such as in the following scenarios:

- A prisoner manifests a pseudoseizure to get out of his cell and into the infirmary.

- An employee who would like to collect disability benefits fakes seizures after a job-related accident.

- A litigious patient fakes seizures following an automobile accident.

In malingering, the pseudoseizures are voluntary and intentional, and the motivation of secondary gain is well understood by the patient. Munchausen syndrome, which is a chronic factitious disorder with physical symptomatology, may appear to be a malignant form of malingering. However, the affected individual's motivation is not secondary gain. Rather, it typically is a pathological craving for attention, the psychogenesis of which may not be completely understood by the patient.

Making the Diagnosis

The longer NES continue undiagnosed, the less likely they are to come under control once the diagnosis is made.[24] The primary difficulty with diagnosis lies in distinguishing NES from ES. The two conditions may coexist, and the development of NES usually follows the onset of ES.[15] Yet when a patient who has previously been diagnosed as an epileptic presents to the emergency department with symptoms of a seizure, NES often is not considered.

Three additional factors compound the problem of differentiating between NES and ES:

- The people who experience NES are a heterogeneous group.
- The seizures themselves are extremely variable.
- Practitioners usually have only secondhand information provided by untrained observers, since seizures do not typically occur in the presence of medical personnel.

There are, however, some common historical clues as well as ictal and clinical characteristics that are red flags to NES. These signals should raise the practitioner's suspicion to the possibility of NES.

Historical and Clinical Clues

In analyses of various NES studies, which included subjects with NES of all etiologies, Lesser[4] determined that 75% of the patients affected by NES were women, with most subjects between 26 and 32 years of age. Other factors that have been cited as characterizing NES include:

- a dependent personality
- borderline personality disorder
- underlying hysterical personality disorder
- hypochondriasis
- affective disorder
- anxiety disorder
- antisocial behavior
- sexual maladjustment
- conflict avoidance
- reluctance to discuss emotions or conflicts
- depression
- prior suicide attempt
- history of alcohol consumption

There are strong indications of comorbidity with panic attacks, posttraumatic stress disorder, and depression. In a study of 50 patients with psychogenic NES, Lempert and Schmidt[12] found that 66% exhibited various psychological abnormalities, with depression most common.

A positive neurologic history, which may be the result of a developmental malformation or a traumatic, infectious, anoxic, or toxic insult, is present in the majority of patients with NES.[15] In the Dartmouth Hitchcock Medical Center study, 72% of patients had a history of head or brain injury. Various studies have found that 10% to 67% of patients with NES will have abnormal EEG findings not correlated with their nonepileptic events.[1,2,25-27] Organic cerebral dysfunction may result in compromised adaptive abilities, facilitating the onset of NES.

A large percentage of patients with NES have a history of childhood trauma, including physical and sexual abuse.[28] One study revealed a history of physical or sexual abuse in 32.6% of patients with NES.[3] In these cases, it is likely that a dissociative or conversion reaction is the psychodynamic basis for NES that are psychogenic in origin.

In summarizing the work of seven investigators who used the Minnesota Multiphasic Personality Inventory (MMPI) test to distinguish between persons with NES and those with ES, Dodrill and colleagues[29] concluded that most of the differences were found on four of the MMPI scales: hypochondriasis, depression, hysteria, and schizophrenia. In every investigation, the NES group had the more deviant findings.

These historical, behavioral, and clinical characteristics should stimulate the practitioner to explore the possibility of NES in patients diagnosed with epilepsy whose seizures are unresponsive to therapy, or who develop a distinctly new type of seizure. A patient who receives obvious secondary gain from manifesting seizures may be suspect. In patients with a history of psychiatric illness or previous abuse; a history of alcohol abuse; or a personality profile that includes hypochondriasis, depression, anxiety, hysteria, or schizophrenia, NES should be considered.

Clinicians should be careful not to allow published historical and clinical clues to limit their analysis of persons in whom NES are suspected. Most research on NES combines all patients with NES, regardless of etiology. Because psychogenic seizures are the most common, authors often focus on this group of patients in their writings. Therefore, historical clues and personality characteristics found in the literature generally refer to patients who exhibit NES as a result of a conversion reaction or dissociative response.

If the personality profile does not fit, but the ictal characteristics of gradual onset, prolonged duration, and bilateral movement without loss of consciousness are present, NES should be considered. Worsening of the seizures with the onset of additional anticonvulsants and despite therapeutic levels should raise the level of suspicion of the healthcare provider to consider the diagnosis.

Diagnostic Tools

Coupled with a thorough history and physical examination, magnetic resonance imaging is indicated (at most epilepsy centers) to rule out organic pathology.

The gold standard for diagnosing NES is the video electroencephalogram (VEEG), in which an EEG and video recording of the patient are simultaneously obtained. The film and the EEG are then compared and concurrences are identified. If a seizure-like episode is not accompanied by epileptiform discharges in the brain, the events may be diagnosed as NES.

In many centers, part of the diagnostic workup includes neuropsychological testing and an evaluation by a psychiatrist. These may be important steps in determining the etiology of the NES. Another diagnostic approach is to measure serum prolactin levels, which generally will be elevated after an ES, but not after an NES.

In some cases, NES may be induced by suggestion and terminated on command. Therefore, some epilepsy centers use the provocative saline infusion test, in which a patient is given saline and told that it may cause them to have a seizure. If there is a subsequent seizure, the patient is given more saline, and is told that the seizure will stop. If the power of suggestion appears to initiate and/or terminate the seizure, it is assumed to be nonepileptic. The ethics of this method of diagnosis are certainly questionable.

In some epilepsy centers, a provocative semistructured interview is used to determine whether emotional factors can provoke the patient's seizures. A psychiatrist leads a discussion that focuses on the person's current psychological conflicts and painful memories while the patient is monitored in the VEEG unit.

Treatment Options and Outcomes

The first step in therapeutic management is confronting the patient with the diagnosis. The manner in which this is done is of crucial clinical importance. The patient's comprehension and acceptance of the diagnosis is the first hurdle on the road to improvement and recovery.

When VEEG is used to diagnose NES, the clinician should verify with the patient and/or his or her family members that the events captured on video are typical of the seizures that have occurred previously. Once verification is made, the patient can be told that epilepsy has been completely ruled out and there is nothing wrong with the electrical activity in the brain. Any previously prescribed anticonvulsants can be discontinued.

Great caution and care must be taken when explaining that the underlying etiology may not be immediately understood. The manner in which the clinician presents this information can mean the difference between a grateful and relieved patient, and an angry, humiliated patient who doubts the diagnosis and abruptly terminates further treatment.

Since most NES patients experience psychogenic seizures, it is imperative that the patient be referred to a psychiatrist immediately. The disclosure that the seizures may be a subconscious means of communication may be painful and could have catastrophic results, particularly in the presence of severe and unacknowledged depression.

The management of NES runs the gamut of psychotherapeutics. The cornerstone to future wellness for patients with pseudoseizures and psychogenic NES is psychotherapy, which can facilitate conscious resolution of the underlying need or conflict that is the stimulus for conversion or dissociation. The approach is multimodal, and includes family and behavior therapy, which may incorporate imagery, relaxation, stress management, and biofeedback. Hypnosis has also been successfully used. Support groups give people with NES the opportunity to draw strength from each other, share coping strategies, and take responsibility for their health and future wellness.

Pharmacotherapy with anxiolytics, selective serotonin reuptake inhibitors, or antidepressants may be helpful, particularly when comorbidity exists with depression, panic attacks, mood disorders, and psychosis.

For patients with pseudoseizures who are faking the events, removing the secondary gain may resolve the problem. These patients, however, may continue to seek out other providers who will "believe them."

Patients with physiogenic NES are best served when the specific etiology is identified. When NES is an iatrogenic response to anticonvulsants, eliminating the medications may be curative. In some patients, decreasing alcohol consumption has had a dramatic effect on decreasing the frequency of NES. Hormonal therapy may benefit patients with catamenial NES. More research is needed to fully appreciate the complexity of interactions between the neurochemical and neuroendocrine systems.

The heterogeneity of the patient population with NES makes the long-term outcome highly variable. A 5-year follow-up study of 28 patients with NES found that 45% were seizure-free and 55% living on disability.[30] In the study by Lempert and Schmidt,[12] 34% of patients were seizure-free at follow-up. In another study done at Dartmouth Hitchcock Medical Center, 29% of patients at follow-up were seizure-free, 59% continued to have seizures but were improved, and 12% were worse.[31] Those patients with a long history of seizures and those with psychopathology had worse outcomes than those patients with recent onset and normal psychological status.

In patients who have both ES and NES, determining which seizure-related events occur more frequently and are most disruptive is critical for establishing appropriate therapy. Adding anticonvulsants to the treatment regimen of an epileptic whose epileptic seizures are under control, but who is having increased NES, would be counterproductive and may facilitate more nonepileptic events. In such cases, psychiatric intervention may be the treatment of choice.

Conclusion

Failure to distinguish NES from ES delays appropriate therapy by diverting attention from the psychological issues that may be associated with the diagnosis of NES. Diagnosis is complicated by the diversity of the seizures, their etiologies, and the people who experience them. Yet making the diagnosis of NES is only a small part of the challenge. Determining the cause and devising a course of treatment is typically the more difficult task. Not attending to NES can have dire consequences for the patient, who may have to contend with years of morbidity and thus a decreased quality of life.

References

1. Leis AA, Ross MA, Summers AK. Psychogenic seizures: ictal characteristics and diagnostic pitfalls. *Neurology*. 1992;42:95-99.

2. Boon PA, Williamson PD. The diagnosis of pseudoseizures. *Clin Neurol Neurosurg*. 1993;95:1-8.

3. Alper K. Nonepileptic seizures. Neurol Clin. 1994;12:153-173.

4. Lesser RP. Psychogenic seizures. In: Pedley TA, Meldrum BS, eds. *Recent Advances in Epilepsy*. Edinburgh, Scotland: Churchill Livingstone; 1985:273-296.

5. Devinsky O, Thacker K. Nonepileptic seizures. *Neurol Clin.* 1995; 13:299-319.

6. Bergen D, Ristanovic R. Weeping as a common element of pseudoseizures. *Arch Neurol.* 1993;50:1059-1060.

7. Dodrill CB. Psychosocial consequences of epilepsy. In: Filskov SB, Boll TJ, eds. *Handbook of Clinical Neuropsychology.* 2nd vol. New York, NY: John Wiley & Sons, Inc; 1986:338-363.

8. Ramani SV, Quesney LF, Olson D, *et al.* Diagnosis of hysterical seizures in epileptic patients. *Am J Psychiatry.* 1980;137:705-709.

9. Lesser RP. Psychogenic seizures. *Psychosomatics.* 1986;27:823-829.

10. Lesser RP, Lueders H, Dinner DS. Evidence for epilepsy is rare in patients with psychogenic seizures. *Neurology.* 1983;33:502-504.

11. Volow MR. Pseudoseizures: an overview. *South Med J.* 1986; 79:600-607.

12. Lempert T, Schmidt D. Natural history and outcome of psychogenic seizures: a clinical study in 50 patients. *J Neurol.* 1990;237:35-38.

13. Ozkara C, Dreifuss FE. Differential diagnosis in pseudoepileptic seizures. *Epilepsia.* 1993;34:294-298.

14. McDade G, Brown SW. Non-epileptic seizures: management and predictive factors of outcome. *Seizure.* 1992;1:7-10.

15. Devinsky O, Sanchez-Villasenor F, Vazquez B, *et al.* Clinical profile of patients with epileptic and nonepileptic seizures. *Neurology.* 1996;46:1530-1533.

16. Chabolla DR, Krahn LE, So EL, *et al.* Psychogenic nonepileptic seizures. *Mayo Clin Proc.* 1996;71:493-500.

17. Jacobs A, Herzog AG. Psychiatric classification of nonconversion nonepileptic seizures. *Arch Neurol.* 1995;52:1044-1045.

18. Herzog AG. Reproductive endocrine considerations and hormonal therapy for women with epilepsy. *Epilepsia.* 1991;32(suppl 6):S27-S33.

19. Laidlaw J. Catamenial epilepsy. *Lancet*. 1956;271:1235-1237.

20. Backstrom T. Epileptic seizures in women related to plasma estrogen and progesterone during the menstrual cycle. *Acta Neurol Scand*. 1976;54:321-347.

21. Sawyer CH. Functions of the amygdala related to the feedback actions of gonadal steroid hormones. In: Eleftheriou BE, ed. *The Neurology of the Amygdala*. New York, NY: Plenum Press; 1973:745-762.

22. Nicoletti F, Speciale C, Sortino MA, *et al*. Comparative effects of estradiol benzoate, the antiestrogen clomiphene citrate, and the progestin medroxyprogesterone acetate on kainic acid-induced seizures in male and female rats. *Epilepsia*. 1985;26:252-257.

23. Niedermeyer E, Blumen D, Holscher E, *et al*. Classical hysterical seizures facilitated by anticonvulsant toxicity. *Psychiatr Clin*. 1970;3:71-84.

24. Wyllie E, Freidman D, Luders H, *et al*. Outcome of psychogenic seizures in children and adolescents compared with adults. *Neurology*. 1991;41:742-744.

25. Roy A. Nonconvulsive psychogenic attacks investigated for temporal lobe epilepsy. *Compr Psychiatry*. 1977;18:591-593.

26. Gulick TA, Spinks IP, King DW. Pseudoseizures: ictal phenomena. *Neurology*. 1982;32:24-30.

27. Meierkord H, Will B, Fish D, *et al*. The clinical features and prognosis of pseudoseizures diagnosed using video-EEG telemetry. *Neurology*. 1991;41:1643-1646.

28. Betts T, Boden S. Diagnosis, management and prognosis of a group of 128 patients with non-epileptic attack disorder: part II: previous childhood sexual abuse in the etiology of these disorders. *Seizure*. 1992;1:27-32.

29. Dodrill CB, Wilkus RJ, Batzell LW. The MMPI as a diagnostic tool in non-epileptic seizures. In: Rowan AJ, Gates JR, eds. *Non-Epileptic Seizures*. Boston, Mass: Butterworth-Heinemann; 1993:211-219.

30. Nash JL. Pseudoseizures: etiologic and psychotherapeutic considerations. *South Med J*. 1993;86:1248-1252.

31. Siegel AM, Thomson LR, Gilbert KL, *et al*. Nonepileptic psychogenic seizures: criteria for accurate diagnosis. Abstract presented at: Annual Meeting of the American Epilepsy Society; December 1997; Boston, Mass.

— by Linda R. Thomson, MSN, CPNP

Linda R. Thomson is in practice at Pioneer Valley Pediatrics in Enfield, Connecticut, and Longmeadow, Massachusetts, and at Greater Falls Family Medicine in Bellows Falls, Vermont. She is a doctoral student in clinical hypnotherapy, and is part of a team doing research on nonepileptic seizures at Dartmouth Hitchcock Medical Center, Lebanon, New Hampshire. The author wishes to express her appreciation to Peter D. Williamson, MD, an epileptologist at Dartmouth Hitchcock Medical Center, for his input in the development of this article.

Chapter 26

Febrile Seizures

What are febrile seizures?

Febrile seizures are convulsions brought on by a fever in infants or small children. During a febrile seizure, a child often loses consciousness and shakes, moving limbs on both sides of the body. Less commonly, the child becomes rigid or has twitches in only a portion of the body, such as an arm or a leg, or on the right or the left side only. Most febrile seizures last a minute or two, although some can be as brief as a few seconds while others last for more than 15 minutes.

The majority of children with febrile seizures have rectal temperatures greater than 102° F. Most febrile seizures occur during the first day of a child's fever.

Children prone to febrile seizures are not considered to have epilepsy, since epilepsy is characterized by recurrent seizures that are *not* triggered by fever.

How common are febrile seizures?

Approximately one in every 25 children will have at least one febrile seizure, and more than one-third of these children will have additional febrile seizures before they outgrow the tendency to have them. Febrile seizures usually occur in children between the ages of

National Institute of Neurological Disorders and Stroke (NINDS), NIH Pub. No. 95-3930, September 1995.

6 months and 5 years and are particularly common in toddlers. Children rarely develop their first febrile seizure before the age of 6 months or after 3 years of age. The older a child is when the first febrile seizure occurs, the less likely that child is to have more.

What makes a child prone to recurrent febrile seizures?

A few factors appear to boost a child's risk of having recurrent febrile seizures, including young age (less than 15 months) during the first seizure, frequent fevers, and having immediate family members with a history of febrile seizures. If the seizure occurs soon after a fever has begun or when the temperature is relatively low, the risk of recurrence is higher. A long initial febrile seizure does not substantially boost the risk of recurrent febrile seizures, either brief or long.

Are febrile seizures harmful?

Although they can be frightening to parents, the vast majority of febrile seizures are harmless. During a seizure, there is a small chance that the child may be injured by falling or may choke from food or saliva in the mouth. Using proper first aid for seizures can help avoid these hazards (see section entitled "What should be done for a child having a febrile seizure?").

There is no evidence that febrile seizures cause brain damage. Large studies have found that children with febrile seizures have normal school achievement and perform as well on intellectual tests as their siblings who don't have seizures. Even in the rare instances of very prolonged seizures (more than 1 hour), most children recover completely.

Between 95 and 98 percent of children who have experienced febrile seizures do *not* go on to develop epilepsy. However, although the absolute risk remains very small, certain children who have febrile seizures face an increased risk of developing epilepsy. These children include those who have febrile seizures that are lengthy, that affect only part of the body, or that recur within 24 hours, and children with cerebral palsy, delayed development, or other neurological abnormalities. Among children who don't have any of these risk factors, only one in 100 develops epilepsy after a febrile seizure.

What should be done for a child having a febrile seizure?

Parents should stay calm and carefully observe the child. To prevent accidental injury, the child should be placed on a protected surface such as the floor or ground. The child should not be held or restrained during a convulsion. To prevent choking, the child should be placed on his or her side or stomach. When possible, the parent should gently remove all objects in the child's mouth. The parent should never place anything in the child's mouth during a convulsion. Objects placed in the mouth can be broken and obstruct the child's airway. If the seizure lasts longer than 10 minutes, the child should be taken immediately to the nearest medical facility for further treatment. Once the seizure has ended, the child should be taken to his or her doctor to check for the source of the fever. This is especially urgent if the child shows symptoms of stiff neck, extreme lethargy, or abundant vomiting.

How are febrile seizures diagnosed and treated?

Before diagnosing febrile seizures in infants and children, doctors sometimes perform tests to be sure that seizures are not caused by something other than simply the fever itself. For example, if a doctor suspects the child has meningitis (an infection of the membranes surrounding the brain), a spinal tap may be needed to check for signs of the infection in the cerebrospinal fluid (fluid that bathes the brain and spinal cord). If there has been severe diarrhea or vomiting, dehydration could be responsible for seizures. Also, doctors often perform other tests such as examining the blood and urine to pinpoint the cause of the child's fever.

A child who has a febrile seizure usually doesn't need to be hospitalized. If the seizure is prolonged or is accompanied by a serious infection, or if the source of the infection cannot be determined, a doctor may recommend that the child be hospitalized for observation.

How are febrile seizures prevented?

If a child has a fever most parents will use fever-lowering drugs such as acetaminophen or ibuprofen to make the child more comfortable, although there are no studies that prove that this will reduce the risk of a seizure. One preventive measure would be to try to reduce the number of febrile illnesses, although this is often not a practical possibility.

Prolonged daily use of oral anticonvulsants, such as phenobarbital or valproate, to prevent febrile seizures is usually not recommended because of their potential for side effects and questionable effectiveness for preventing such seizures.

Children especially prone to febrile seizures may be treated with the drug diazepam orally or rectally, whenever they have a fever. The majority of children with febrile seizures do not need to be treated with medication, but in some cases a doctor may decide that medicine given only while the child has a fever may be the best alternative. This medication may lower the risk of having another febrile seizure. It is usually well tolerated, although it occasionally can cause drowsiness, a lack of coordination, or hyperactivity. Children vary widely in their susceptibility to such side effects.

What research is being done on febrile seizures?

The National Institute of Neurological Disorders and Stroke (NINDS), a part of the National Institutes of Health (NIH), sponsors research on febrile seizures in medical centers throughout the country. NINDS-supported scientists are exploring what environmental and genetic risk factors make children susceptible to febrile seizures. Some studies suggest that women who smoke or drink alcohol during their pregnancies are more likely to have children with febrile seizures, but more research needs to be done before this link can be clearly established. Scientists are also working to pinpoint factors that can help predict which children are likely to have recurrent or long-lasting febrile seizures.

Investigators continue to monitor the long-term impact that febrile seizures might have on intelligence, behavior, school achievement, and the development of epilepsy. For example, scientists conducting studies in animals are assessing the effects of seizures and anticonvulsant drugs on brain development.

Investigators also continue to explore which drugs can effectively treat or prevent febrile seizures and to check for side effects of these medicines.

Where can I get more information?

Additional information for patients, families, and physicians is available from:

Epilepsy Foundation of America
4351 Garden City Drive
Landover, Maryland 20785
(301) 459-3700
(800) EFA-1000 (332-1000)

For more information on research on febrile seizures, you may wish to contact:

Office of Scientific and Health Reports
NIH Neurological Institute
P.O. Box 5801
Bethesda, Maryland 20824
(301) 496-5751
(800) 352-9424

Part Four

Amyotrophic Lateral Sclerosis (ALS)/Lou Gehrig's Disease

Chapter 27

Amyotrophic Lateral Sclerosis (ALS)/Lou Gehrig's Disease

What Is ALS?

Amyotrophic lateral sclerosis (ALS) is a progressive disease of the nervous system. The cause is not known and there is no cure, although progress is being made on both fronts. ALS is also known as Lou Gehrig's disease after the famous baseball player who died from it.

ALS attacks motor neurons, which are among the largest of all nerve cells in the brain and spinal cord. These cells send messages to muscles throughout the body. In ALS, motor neurons die and the muscles do not receive these messages. As a result, muscles weaken as they lose their ability to move. Eventually, most muscle action is affected, including those which control swallowing and breathing, as well as major muscles in the arms, legs, back and neck. There is, however, no loss of sensory nerves, so people with ALS retain their sense of feeling, sight, hearing, smell, and taste. The mind is not affected by this disease and people with ALS remain fully alert and aware of events. The course of ALS is extremely variable and it is difficult to predict the rate of progression in any single patient. For the majority of people with ALS, weakness tends to progress over a three-to-five year period.

ALS can strike anyone, at any age, but generally ALS occurs between the ages of 40 and 70. According to the National Institutes of

Health, some 4,600 people in the United States are newly diagnosed with ALS each year. About 4 to 6 people per 100,000 worldwide get ALS. In a small percentage of patients, ALS is genetic.

What Are the Symptoms?

The first signs of ALS are often arm and leg weakness, muscle wasting and faint muscle rippling. These symptoms occur because muscles are no longer receiving the nutrient signals they need for

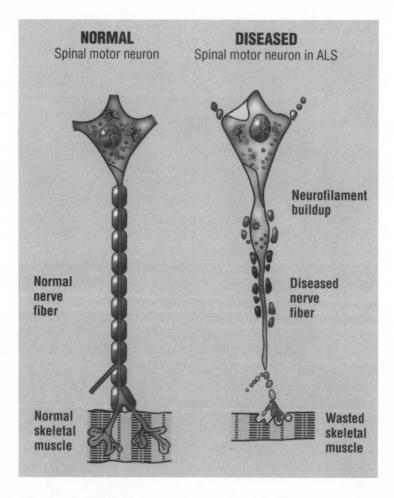

Figure 27.1. *ALS attacks motor neurons (Source for illustration: U.S. Food and Drug Administration).*

growth and maintenance—a result of motor neurons dying. ALS nerve degeneration may also cause muscle cramps and vague pains, or problems with speech and swallowing. Some people with the disease may lose some control over their emotional responses. They may laugh or cry much more easily than in the past. Eventually, all voluntary muscle action is affected.

How Is ALS Diagnosed?

There is no specific test for diagnosing ALS. However, several tests—including nerve conduction studies and electromyogram (EMG)—are used to measure how well and quickly the nerves are working. Ruling out other causes of muscular weakness is important because ALS often mimics other treatable diseases. Diagnosis requires special skills and neurologic tests. People with ALS symptoms usually are referred to neurologists, who specialize in the nervous system. Diagnosis may take several months since an important part of the diagnostic process is to confirm disease progression.

What Causes ALS?

The cause of ALS is unknown. It attacks its victims at random. However, it was recently discovered that five to ten percent of those with ALS show a definite genetic pattern. In this rare form, about one-half of the offspring may develop ALS. These people show a gene defect that affects an enzyme called superoxide dismutase. This enzyme eliminates toxic substances called free radicals. Free radicals can cause nerve cells to die and are associated with a number of diseases and even implicated in aging itself. For most people with ALS, the vast majority of their children are not at any greater risk of developing this disease than the general population. This type of ALS is often called "sporadic ALS" due to its unpredictable nature.

ALS researchers have found no difference between the symptoms and disease progression in the sporadic and genetic forms of ALS. Therefore, since the genetic and acquired forms of ALS appear to be similar, an understanding of the cause of the genetic form could lead to treatment for all forms of the disease.

Treatment

While there is no cure for ALS, research to solve the ALS puzzle is ongoing. Scientific advances have led to approval of the first treatment for the disease—a medication that may increase survival time. Other treatments under investigation include several nerve growth factors which may help maintain quality of life by maintaining nerve function. While each of these therapies represent a step forward for people with ALS, a cure remains to be discovered.

For the majority of people with ALS, the primary treatment remains the management of ALS symptoms. Patients need to take an active role in the design of their treatment regimen. Ideally, ALS management involves physical, occupational, speech, respiratory, and nutrition therapy. For instance, certain drugs and the application of heat or whirlpool therapy may help to relieve muscle cramping. Exercise can help maintain muscle strength and function. Exercise, however, is recommended in moderation. Drugs also may be used to help combat fatigue, but in some patients may worsen muscle cramps.

As the disease progresses, various assistive devices will help persons with ALS maintain their independence and ensure personal safety. For example, an ankle/foot brace can improve function and conserve energy, as well as help avoid injury. When neck, trunk, and shoulder weakness makes walking or sitting difficult, cervical collars, perhaps with an additional chest and head strap, provide helpful support. A reclining chair is preferable to a headrest to relieve fatigue of neck muscles. There are also numerous devices to assist in feeding, dressing, and maintaining personal hygiene. Eventually, more substantial equipment, such as wheelchairs, scooters, lifts, and hospital beds may be required.

It is important to know that speech therapists can help with speech and swallowing difficulties as they develop. Also, drug treatments can help patients who develop excessive saliva and drooling. Family members of people with ALS should be instructed in the Heimlich maneuver to provide assistance in a life-threatening choking episode. Feeding tubes may be necessary to maintain nutrition, as may breathing devices when the disease affects the muscles of the chest. However, with these supportive devices, there are physical, emotional, and financial implications, and their use should be discussed with a physician well in advance of when the need arises. Managing the symptoms is a process that is challenging for people with ALS, their caregivers, and their medical team.

Of all the disabilities that affect a person with ALS, one of the most devastating and most common is the progressive loss of the ability to communicate. However, advances in computer technology mean that persons with ALS today have vital new electronic communications options that can be adapted to their individual capabilities.

Progress Through Research

Significant progress is being made in the study of ALS. Although there is still no cure, recent clinical trials have shown that some drugs affect nerve cell activity and may increase the survival time for people with ALS. Newly developed animal models of the genetic form of the disease, so-called transgenic ALS mice, offer neurologic researchers the ability to test therapies in mice. There is great hope that this and other neuroscientific advances will lead to a cure in humans. Talk with your doctor about being involved in future clinical trials or about the drugs currently available for the treatment of this disease.

For More Information

American Academy of Neurology
2221 University Ave. SE, Suite 335
Minneapolis, MN 55414
(612) 623-8115
E-mail: aan@aan.com

The Amyotrophic Lateral Sclerosis Association (ALSA)
21021 Ventura Boulevard, #321
Woodland Hills, CA 91364
(818) 340-7500
(800) 782-4747 Patient Hotline

Muscular Dystrophy Association
3300 East Sunrise Drive
Tucson, AZ 85718
(602) 529-2000

Chapter 28

Living with ALS

Minimizing ALS Fatigue

Although the course of ALS is unpredictable, fatigue is one outcome that is predictable, resulting from muscle weakness and spasticity. Fatigue can range from mild lassitude to extreme exhaustion.
People often complain of tiredness, dwindling strength, and lack of
energy. Despite the adverse effects of fatigue, symptoms can be mini-
mized through effective management. By recognizing the signs of fatigue, knowing which factors worsen symptoms, and learning how to
conserve energy, persons with ALS can greatly improve their quality
of living.

Noticeable signs of fatigue include: Slower body movement, slower
speech responses, short answers, lower voice volume, dull tone of
voice, shortness of breath, increased sighing, anorexia, irritability,
anxiety, crying episodes, decreased smiling, lack of enjoyment of previously enjoyed experiences, decreased caring about things that were
previously important, deterioration in appearance and grooming, increased forgetfulness, increased preference for being alone, and dis-
interest in decision making daily plans.

Factors which may aggravate fatigue include: Immobility, overexertion, sleep disruption, pain, excessive weight loss, protein malnutrition, breathing weakness, stress, anxiety, hopelessness, grief, too hot or cold weather, certain medications (such as tranquilizers, sedatives, pain relievers, antihistamines, muscle relaxants), alcohol, smoking, the unavailability of people when help is needed, the lack of financial resources to provide for needs to make life easier, and an inaccessible home environment which has steps and long distances between rooms.

Anti-Fatigue Strategies

1. Learn methods of making every task easier. Use assistive devices when needed. See an occupational therapist for determining what is best for your needs. If you have trouble walking, don't resist getting a wheelchair. A motorized wheelchair will spare you the exertion of manually wheeling around in a standard model.

2. Pace yourself. Move slowly and easily. Stop and rest often and take a few breaths before you start again. If you become breathless during a task, it is time to stop. Schedule heavier tasks during predicted times of higher energy. Plan your activities and gather everything you need before you start. Don't stand when you can sit. Utilize possible shortcuts. Obtain assistance in completing tasks if you need help. Always allow enough energy to enjoy at least one valued experience each day.

3. Alternate activities with periods of rest. Schedule regular rest periods each day, perhaps a half hour after morning care and an hour in the early afternoon. Rest before going away.

4. Get a handicapped parking sticker. Your local department of motor vehicles has the form that your physician will need to fill out.

5. Try to establish a regular sleeping pattern. If you have problems waking up at night, determine why and what to do about it.

6. Avoid prolonged bathing in warm water, as it may worsen muscle fatigue. Be cautious of extreme outdoor temperatures.

7. Maintain your nutritional requirements each day, and prevent unnecessary weight loss. You may need to consult with a dietitian.

8. Avoid stressful situations as much as possible. Understanding fatigue will help family members cope better with emotional upsets, realizing they are not personal attacks, but normal responses to fatigue.

9. If you feel noticeably weaker or have difficulty breathing after taking a medication, let your doctor know. Perhaps your medication needs to be substituted for another one or the dosage altered. Trouble breathing, however, may be related to breathing fatigue and may warrant an evaluation by your doctor for a breathing remedy.

10. Making your living environment accessible for daily activities, and remove barriers to energy conservation. Moving a bed to another location or relocating personal items are some examples.

Failure to manage fatigue can result in unnecessary suffering, social isolation, and rapid physical deterioration. However, effective management will maximize your wellness and abilities, giving you the desire to keep living and the strength to carry on. Although in ALS you can't take away fatigue, you can learn to overcome fatigue and not let it overcome you.

—Excerpted from an article by Pamela A. Cazzolli, R.N.

Dressing with Ease, Style, and Comfort

Dressing and undressing are often challenging tasks among people with limited mobility. While buttons and zipping zippers are frustrating for some folks, others may find reaching arms through armholes or putting legs through legholes as tedious chores. Besides the obstacles people face for dressing independently, it is not always easy for their assistants. Wearing accessible clothes and selecting attire to meet individual needs will make dressing easier, sparing unnecessary aggravation and fatigue. Getting dressed everyday, even if not leaving the house, is really important for boosting self-esteem.

In general, clothing should not restrict joint motion. Light-weight or stretch-knit fabrics allow greater freedom of movement. Roomy armholes and garments which open in the front, eliminating the need to raise arms over the head, are easier to put on and take off. Large buttons, which require little finger/hand coordination can replace standard fasteners, and be hidden in shirts, blouses, dresses and pants. Zippered fronts on tops and dresses also offer convenience. Buttons sewn on with elastic thread are easier to manage.

Sewing fabric loops inside pants and underwear makes pulling them on and off much simpler. Trousers with elastic waistbands or drawstrings and French-cut underpants with wide leg openings, like boxer shorts, make dressing and toileting easier. Leg brace wearers should choose knit pants loose enough to pull on easily over braces. Wraparound skirts go on better than skirts which fasten in the back, and accommodate weight changes. Wearing a wraparound skirt with the opening in the back, as well as drop-seat pants, are ideal for using the toilet when traveling. By wearing culottes, ladies can enjoy the look of a skirt and the convenience of pants. Pulling a slip over the head can be avoided by wearing a half slip. Front-fastening bras or all-stretch bras permit more independence in dressing.

Some people find dressing safer and easier while lying down, especially when pulling up pants. Others prefer to sit on the edge of the bed or chair. Those who have one side weaker than the other should dress the weaker side first. Dressing aids are also available to help persons put on and take off garments. Some devices include: a dressing stick with a hook on the end to assist in pulling up pants without bending over; a buttoner to pull buttons through button holes; a zipper pull to open and close zippers; a stocking aid to pull on stockings; long wooden scissors for reaching clothing; and a long-handled shoehorn to help get shoes on.

What to wear on the feet depends on one's ability to walk. Persons with weak ankles and feet may warrant an evaluation by an occupational or physical therapist. Lightweight, supportive shoes may be recommended for walking and possibly brace support too. Some persons prefer moccasins, as rubber-soled shoes may cause tripping, although they help keep the feet from slipping off wheelchair footplates. To put laced shoes on and off with ease and without having to retie them, replace standard shoelaces with elastic laces. Other kinds of easy access shoes are shoes with Velcro fasteners across the top, or loafers. For added convenience, women can wear thigh-high hosiery or knee socks with skirts instead of pantyhose. Wearing knee-high fashion boots or calf high leg warmers are ideal for hiding leg braces on skirt wearers.

Persons who sit a lot should choose clothes that not only feel comfortable but look attractive while sitting. Wearing a flexible fabric, such as a soft cotton/polyester blend, that moves with the body provides the most comfort. Wearing loose tops that are worn on the outside of pants and skirts looks and feels the best. Wheelchair users find short jackets, ponchos, or capes more convenient than long coats. Men who wear suits may need to alter their suits, adding extra room in the shoulders and the seat. The use of clip-on ties or ready-tied ties with a Velcro fastener may spare the hassle of tie tying. Dresses and skirts that are cut fuller in the hips prevent riding up when sitting. Although outfits with fullness are comfortable, excess fullness in sleeves, pant legs, and skirts can get caught in wheelchair spokes and can also cause tripping. Sitters should avoid wearing pants with heavy seams that may cause pressure areas when sitting.

Whether a fabric is comfortable depends on how it feels, how much heat it retains, and how well it absorbs moisture. Because immobility and loss of subcutaneous fat can cause some persons to feel cold, wearing several layers of light clothing traps in heat and is more effective in keeping warm than using heavy clothes. The wearer can remove layers when feeling overly warm. Light clothing made of terrycloth or cotton flannelette fabric may be more comfortable.

In addition to accessibility and comfort, color and texture should be key factors in clothing choices. Colorful tops add brilliance to basic slacks and skirts. Fleecewear is both functional and fashionable, and is easy to wear anytime, anywhere. The young-at-hearts who like denims, will find stonewashed cotton the softest. Slippery fabrics, such as those used in nylon lingerie, allow the body to slide easily from one surface to another, like from bed to chair. Wearing nylon pajamas or gowns will help the wearer turn over in bed. Persons with breathing problems may breathe better with wide open necklines, and should avoid hairy fabrics, like mohair, as floating filaments may be inhaled.

Dressing for success means wearing clothes that are easy to wear, good-looking, and comfortable day and night. Finding solutions to dressing problems will take the stressing out of dressing. And feeling your best begins by looking your best.

—Excerpted from an article written by Pamela A. Cazzolli, R.N.,
Nurse Consultant, Eastern Ohio Chapter

Orthotic Devices

It is not unusual to notice the first symptoms of ALS in the arms or legs. There may be only a slight weakness or clumsiness in the affected limb at first and the person with ALS (PALS) may be able to go about as the weakness progresses to a more noticeable level; however, adaptability, comfort, and independence can be greatly enhanced with the proper orthopedic devices and/or products.

The first step to getting help at this point is to provide your doctor with a simple, clear description of the problem: "I can't button my shirt"; "I can't hold a pencil or a knife and fork"; "My foot drags when I walk"; "My wrist will no longer hold my hand in an extended position." Your doctor may then write a prescription for a visit to an orthotist, a physical therapist, an occupational therapist, any two of them, or even all three, as there may be a device or new way of doing things to compensate for the problems the PALS are experiencing.

An orthotist designs and makes appliances or devices for support, such as a foot-angle brace or splint or hand splints. A physical therapist can recommend exercises, such as range of motion, to help the weakening limb stay functional longer. The occupational therapist can evaluate the way you perform activities of daily living and suggest ways to modify your home and ways of doing things for more convenience and safety, such as using special eating utensils, dressing aids, bathing aids, etc.

Many of the items that these specialists may recommend are available locally in medical supply stores and these professionals can guide you in making a wise purchase or rental. The vast array of products (new ones are constantly coming on to the market) and where to find them can be confusing and costly if poor or unsuitable choices are made.

Insurance companies, including Medicare, will pay for some items if a physician has prescribed it. Remember, too, that some of these items may be available through your local ALS chapter or MDA clinic. Seek advice and assistance before you purchase or rent a major item.

For example, there are many kinds of wheelchairs for different needs: motorized, reclining, etc. There is even a special wheelchair for using on the beach. Some people use several kinds. It is also important to know that a good wheelchair must fit. People buying wheelchairs should be measured to fit the particular chair. Never buy or rent a wheelchair without first trying it on.

Some of the best devices are those created by the ingenuity of persons with ALS or their families (and passed on to others at support group meetings).

The most common devices that many people use during the beginning stages of ALS are: button holder; reacher; key holder; cane; electric toothbrush; shower attachment with flexible hose; hand grips for shower and bathtub; pullover shirts/blouses; elastic waist pants/skirts; slip-on shoes; and Velcro for fastening practically anything.

For the middle stages, many persons with ALS use: a raised toilet seat; shower chair; urinal; walker with wheels and hand brakes; lightweight folding wheelchair to put in the car; neck collar; ankle-foot splints; hand splints; reclining chair with footrest; a chair with an electric rising seat or lift; and a transfer board.

For the advanced stages persons with ALS and their caregivers usually use: electric bed; highback wheelchair with headrest that reclines and has removable arms, leg rests, and lap tray; bedside commode; hydraulic lift; foot support boot; arm supports; suction machine; and communication devices.

Admittedly, many people manage without some of these devices, but life may not be as comfortable for either caregivers or patients. Care and comfort depend on taking the time to research and find the items that will be most helpful.

—Excerpted from Reaching Out, *Orange County, California Chapter, 1991 written by Betty Scharf, R.N.*

Breathing Difficulties

Breathing difficulties do not happen to everyone with ALS, but when they occur it is generally a gradual process. This means that breathing failure does not usually come on all at once. Many people with ALS have gone through this disease without any respiratory emergencies.

Shortness of Breath (Dyspnea)

Shortness of breath (or dyspnea), also referred to as air hunger, may be an early warning sign of breathing difficulties. It is usually noted first on exertion, later on, it may occur even at rest. You may think, "I'm getting out of shape" or "I'm getting old." You may note you get winded with less and less activity.

We all have favorite positions for falling asleep. You may notice that this position is no longer comfortable and you get restless. Elevating the head and chest with a blanket folded under the head of the mattress or using an elevated position in a hospital bed can make breathing easier.

The solution to shortness of breath is to do activity within your range. Stop soon enough and rest until your breath comes back. Exercises to strengthen breathing muscles wastes precious breath. There is no exercise that can bring back muscles that have lost a good nerve supply. But you can protect your muscles from fatigue.

Changes in Breathing Pattern

Normally, breathing is an efficient process. The diaphragm, largest muscle in the body, does 70–80% of the work. The belly, shoulders, neck and rib muscles do a minor but necessary job. Think of oxygen as you do gasoline for your car. Normal breathing uses about 2% of the body's oxygen to perform this quiet constant movement throughout your life. Labored breathing can take up to 50% of your oxygen.

If you are using the smaller muscles more and more, you will tire more readily. Take a look at a person with normal breathing. Then take a look at yourself in the mirror. If you note any differences, ask your doctor or nurse to explain. It may be your body build, or it may be a sign of oncoming problems.

Respiratory Infections

People with ALS are more susceptible to infections than others because they have a harder time clearing infection. ALS does no damage to lungs or heart tissue.

Your cough may not be strong enough, there may be a tendency to get food down the wrong way or mucous accumulates. Infections may occur simply because you don't breathe deeply enough to keep all the delicate areas of the lungs open and moving air. This is called stasis. Resulting infection is termed hypostasis pneumonia.

What can be done to prevent chest infections? It is important to avoid crowds and family members with colds. Flu shots in the Fall are valuable. Activity and frequent position change help keep the lungs open—even turning in bed helps.

Mechanical aerosol devices can be used under medical prescription. Water is better than a device if you can drink enough to keep your chest secretions thin. This makes it easier to clear your throat. Sometimes, choking on saliva or mucous cannot be avoided. If you are able to keep your secretions thin by good fluid intake, choking may never occur. If it does, staying relaxed and peaceful is very difficult, but is the best way to restore easy breathing. An open airway is a relaxed airway. If you do get a chest infection, seek medical treatment early before it gets a hold on you. This is very important!

—Excerpted from an article by Barbara Beal, R.N., M.N.

To Cough or Not to Cough

It is beneficial for persons with ALS to take some time each day for deep breathing and coughing exercises to keep the lungs free of troublesome secretions (see Managing Breathing Problems above).

Especially after eating, persons with ALS may cough for a long time, due to food particles or saliva that are stuck in the throat. This is uncomfortable for persons with ALS and for those around them but the far greater and more serious problem is the depletion of available energy and strength that leaves person fatigued and vulnerable.

The cause for this kind of coughing is an inadequate swallowing mechanism and weakened chest and abdominal muscles that fail to produce a strong enough cough to clear the offending food particles or saliva. A simple maneuver called "assisted coughing" may be all that is necessary. Caregivers can learn to do this procedure, or persons with ALS by themselves if they have adequate strength in their arms and hands.

The best position for assisted coughing is sitting upright and leaning slightly forward. Place a small pillow or a folded towel against the upper abdomen (about five inches above the navel). After the patient take as deep a breath as possible, the caregiver, with an open palm over the pillow, gives a gentle push (in and up) exactly at the moment of the cough. This push greatly enhances the cough and usually is enough to clear the airway.

The towel may also be used folded the long way and wrapped around the mid-body, with the caregiver standing behind person with ALS and holding the towel ends. At the moment of the cough, the towel is pulled tight. The towel should be released immediately at the end of the cough. This effectively splints the weakened chest muscles and gives added strength to the cough. Occasionally a stronger method is required. This method uses the palm of the hand or even the fist. A push is required up and under the right lower rib just to the right of the sternum. (The stomach lies to the left and is to be avoided.) Again, push exactly at the moment of the cough and then release.

Caution: Caution is in order against pressing directly over the stomach, especially if the person with ALS has eaten recently. The stomach lies in the upper part of the abdominal cavity with most of its pouch-like structure to the left of the sternum. If the force of the push is too strong it could cause regurgitation of food into the throat and serious risks of choking or aspiration.

Practice to get just the right amount of force into the push. a person with ALS can guide the caregiver or the caregiver can try it on himself or herself to get just the right feel.

Another necessary skill for the caregiver is to learn the Heimlich Maneuver (call your local hospital or Red Cross Chapter for lessons). The Heimlich differs from the assisted cough in that it is for dislodging a large piece of food that is completely cutting off all air. If not cleared immediately, this kind of obstruction will end in death.

The Heimlich push uses the fist very strongly and directly under the sternum, usually with the person administering it standing behind. Slapping hard at the mid-back with an open palm exactly at the moment of cough remains a standard procedure for any kind of choking. However, it is essential to be timed with the cough or it is more harmful than beneficial.

The cough is usually our friend and is helpful. But if it is not doing its job and just wearing a patient out, try a little assisted coughing.

—Excerpted from an article by Betty Scharf, R.N.

Chapter 29

Basic Home Care for ALS Patients

Brief Overview of ALS

Amyotrophic lateral sclerosis (ALS) is a neurological disorder, characterized by progressive degeneration of motor cells in the spinal cord and brain.

When the motor neuron cell can no longer send the impulses to the muscles there is increased muscle weakness, especially in the arms and legs, speech, swallowing, and breathing. When muscles no longer receive the messages they require to function, they begin to atrophy (waste away). ALS is very often referred to as "Lou Gehrig's disease." Neither its cause nor cure is known.

Three known classifications of ALS have been described:

- Sporadic—the most common form of ALS in the United States.

- Familial—suggests genetic dominant inheritance and accounts for a very small number of cases in the United States. Familial ALS requires further investigation before the significance of the hereditary factor can be firmly established.

- Guamanian—an extremely high incidence of ALS has been observed in Guam and the Trust Territories of the Pacific.

©1987, revised 1989, 1990, 1992, 1997 The Amyotrophic Lateral Sclerosis Association (ALSA), 21021 Ventura Blvd., Suite 321, Woodland Hills, CA 91364, (818) 340-7500; reprinted with permission. Visit ALSA on the internet at http://www.alsa.org, or call ALSA's patient hotline: (800) 782-4747.

At the onset of ALS the symptoms may be so slight that they are frequently overlooked. With regard to the progression of the illness, and the appearance of symptoms, the course of the disease may include the following:

- twitching and cramping of muscles, especially those in the hands and feet

- impairment of the use of the arms and legs

- "thick speech" and difficulty in projecting the voice

- in more advanced stages, shortness of breath, difficulty in breathing and swallowing

ALS is individual in each person—in the area of the body affected as well as in the rate of progression.

It is important to stress that ALS does not affect the intellectual functioning. Nor does it interfere with the ability to taste, see, smell, hear, or recognize touch.

Diet and Nutrition

Nutrition is an important consideration in the health care of any person and the patient with ALS is no exception. Care should be taken to provide a well balanced diet at all times. As the disease progresses, difficulties in maintaining good nutrition will be encountered. The following suggestions should be kept in mind:

- Eat to prevent weight loss.

- Continue vitamins as prescribed. Liquid vitamins may be prescribed for patients experiencing swallowing difficulty. Care must be taken to avoid choking on pills.

- Consider supplementing meals with high calorie shakes, or a packaged product such as Ensure.

- Dietary limitations for other diseases such as diabetes, etc. should be maintained.

- If at all possible, patients should feed themselves. However, it is important to stress here that the patient should not be urged to try if he/she is too weak or tired. This is unkind and proves nothing.

- Alcoholic beverages should not be taken by the patient without the approval of one's physician, since alcohol can affect the central nervous system and exaggerate the ALS symptoms. Similarly, drugs such as sleeping pills, pain killers, barbiturates, and opiates should not be taken without the advice of the physician, as they tend to depress the respiratory centers.

- Most patients benefit from eating with the family rather than alone.

- A sufficient amount of time should be provided for eating; rushing increases anxiety, making choking a greater risk, and usually results in eating less than one would otherwise.

- The patient should not be the focus of the family's attention during meals, but rather, the family should engage in normal mealtime conversation; conversely, the patient should be included (especially by eye contact) in the mealtime conversation. This rule should apply whenever the patient is part of a group. Even if one cannot respond, the person hears and understands everything.

- If a patient finds eating tiring, he/she may find it easier to eat five or six small meals rather than three large ones.

- When the amount of calories expended in energy used in eating exceeds the number of calories taken in, (i.e., if it takes more than one hour to eat) it may be time to consider an alternate method of assuring proper nutrition.

- Swallowing can be tested with water if there is any doubt in the patient's mind about his swallowing ability. Slightly thickened liquids are easier and less of a choking problem than are thin liquids.

Swallowing

Almost all ALS patients experience some degree of swallowing difficulty during the course of the disease. If the patient experiences a coughing or choking sensation after food, in particular after water, some changes in consistency or posture is needed. A slight decrease in swallowing ability usually requires little alteration from the regular family diet other than chopping or mincing of hard to chew foods such as meats. With more severe limitations in swallowing ability, the patient may only be able to tolerate food of a semisolid consistency similar to that of commercially prepared baby food. This is known as blenderized or texture modified diet. There are several creative cookbooks containing recipes and techniques to expand the variety of foods for easy swallowing.

Food Preparation

An alternative to the purchase of commercially prepared pureed food is the use of a blender in the home to puree food regularly served to the family. Not only is this significantly less expensive, but it also provides the psychological advantage of allowing the patient to eat the same food as the rest of the family. There is no need to purchase a multiple speed blender; a one-speed is adequate. For families "on the go," blenderized diets resembling convenience dinners are available.

Self-Feeding Aids

There are various modifications in eating utensils which may make it easier to feed oneself. Some examples of these modifications include:

- Plastic glassware and dishes; these may allay the fear of feeding oneself because of the risk of breakage. Plastic glassware is also lighter in weight and easier for the patient to handle.

- Built-up handles for flatware and utensils that attach to the hand are especially useful to those with impaired grasping ability.

Check with a rehabilitation therapist about special devices to assist with self feeding.

Feeding Tube

If an ALS patient is unable to swallow blenderized foods, an alternative method of obtaining nutrition is available. This is called a feeding tube.

Elimination

Since smooth or involuntary muscles are not usually involved in ALS, the patient will probably always have control of some urinary and bowel muscles.

If the patient uses the family toilet, several adaptations may make usage easier for him or her. An elevated seat makes rising from a sitting position less of a strain on weakened leg muscles. A handrail on the side of the toilet may provide similar assistance by allowing the patient to steady himself when sitting and to pull up to a standing position when rising. Patients with limited mobility may benefit from having a bedside commode near the bed.

A bedpan is necessary for patients confined to bed. It should be heated with warm water and dried prior to use. The patient should not be permitted to sit or lie on the bedpan for prolonged periods of time because the pressure from the bedpan decreases circulation to the affected skin and predisposes the patient to the development of bedsores. In some cases, patients find it more comfortable and family members find it easier to use smaller bedpans known as orthopedic or "fracture" bedpans. Protective pads for use under the bedpan can be purchased at a surgical supply house or pharmacy that carries sickroom equipment.

Bowel Function

Constipation is the most common disorder of bowel functioning encountered by ALS patients although diarrhea is not rare. Several factors increase the risk of development of constipation: 1) decreased activity; 2) decreased roughage in the diet; 3) decreased fluid intake; and 4) inability to swallow the saliva.

Careful attention to activity and diet may prevent constipation in some cases. Patient activity should be encouraged within the limits of strength. If swallowing ability permits, and there are no dietary restrictions, the addition of vegetables, raw fruits, bran cereals, and prunes may help promote normal bowel functioning.

As it is important to recognize constipation as soon as possible, a record should be kept of the dates of bowel movements. This will make detection of constipation easier. Treatment of constipation should, of course, be discussed with your physician; but in general, overuse of laxatives or enemas should be avoided as dependency is easily acquired. Mineral oil is not usually suggested.

Bladder Function

Unless otherwise indicated by previously existing medical problems, a fluid intake of two or three quarts per day is one of the best methods of preventing bladder problems. The high fluid intake helps keep the urinary tract well "flushed" and decreases the risk of infection. Both the patient and family should be aware of the signs and symptoms of urinary tract infection which include: frequent urination (especially in small amounts), pain during urination, low back pain, fever, and cloudy, foul smelling urine.

Hygiene

Bathing

Patients only mildly affected by ALS can usually continue their pre-illness hygiene patterns with only slight modifications. A handrail can be attached to the side of the bathtub. Non-skid tape or decals should be put on the bottom of the tub to prevent slipping. A small stool with sides can be placed in the bathtub for the patient to sit on while bathing. As weakness increases, the patient will need assistance getting into and out of the tub and supervision during bathing.

Here is where an elevated tub chair can help. It allows the patient to sit down outside the tub and slide across while lifting the legs over the side and into the tub. With the use of a portable shower head, the chair can make it possible for a patient to continue taking tub baths.

A power operated bath lift is even more convenient, though more expensive as well. It can be used throughout a longer period as disability increases and even be operated by the patient. It allows the patient to be immersed nearly waist high in water.

A portable whirlpool can be mounted on the tub to help the relaxation of muscles.

Shower benches are also available with some designed so the shower curtain slides through a space in the seat helping to keep water inside the directed area. Portable wall and hand-held shower heads can bring the shower to the patient and can be used in either a tub or shower stall.

More severely affected patients may not be able to use the bathtub and must depend on bedbaths. In this case, the patient should be responsible for as much of this bath as possible, although assistance with washing the back and feet is frequently needed. A basin for water, soap, a washcloth, and towel are all the equipment necessary for a bedbath. If you wish, protective pads can be placed around the patient to keep the bed dry. Washing equipment should be placed near the patient. The warm water in the basin should be changed whenever it becomes cool or soapy. Some patients and families have found it helpful to use two basins—one for fresh water and the other for rinsing the soapy washcloth. In some cases, small buckets may be preferred over shallow basins to minimize spillage. The patient's room should be warm and draft-free during the bath and privacy should be protected. Alcohol rubs on the back, stomach, and limbs are comforting to the patient. (Be careful to avoid the genital area with alcohol). Small body areas (such as an arm or the chest) should be washed, rinsed and dried completely before proceeding to another area. This helps prevent chilling. Generally, normal scrubbing need not be avoided as the friction produced increases circulation to the area. The perineal area (the area around the genitalia and the rectum) should be washed last and from front to back. This is especially important for female patients to avoid introducing bacteria from the rectal area into the vagina and/or urinary tract.

A daily complete bath is not necessary in most cases; on the day or days between complete baths, a partial bath will usually be sufficient. A partial bath includes washing the face, underarm, and genital area. If the patient is confined to bed or a wheelchair for long periods, either he/she or a family member should inspect the skin daily. Bath time is usually the most convenient time to do this. Areas of redness, particularly over bony prominence such as the elbows, shoulders, heels, knees, hips, and coccyx (the lower end of the backbone) indicate that there has been pressure on that body part for too long, resulting in decreased circulation. Reddened areas should be massaged gently with lotion and future pressure on that area limited to one or two hours at the most. Bath oil added to the bath water may prevent drying and itching of the skin. Foam cushions and other devices are available to help reduce pressure.

Oral hygiene is very important for the ALS patient. Some patients with limited grasping ability may find electric toothbrushes easier to use than manual ones. Chapsticks or petroleum jelly can be applied to the lips to prevent drying and cracking. Some patients who have decreased swallowing ability experience problems with drooling the accumulated saliva. Tissues should be readily accessible for these patients. If use of tissues to prevent drooling does not solve the problem, a protective absorbent terry cloth bib (which may be purchased or easily made from a towel) may be used to prevent wetting of the clothes. This type of bib can be easily washed.

Fingernails and toenails should be kept short and clean. Toenails should be cut straight across to prevent the development of ingrown nails. Patients who are unable to manage a nail file can still retain responsibility for nail care if the file is taped to an easily accessible flat surface.

Many sources of assistance are available to family members responsible for washing and cutting the patient's hair. Patients with significant weakness usually find short hair easier to manage than long hair. In many cases, the patient can sit in a chair and lean back over a sink to facilitate hair washing. A spray attachment for the sink spigot may also be helpful. Shallow shampoo trays are available which make washing hair at the sink or in bed easier. These trays funnel the water used into the sink or into a bucket on the floor. Dry shampoos are also available. In some communities, beauticians will make home visits to wash or cut the hair of the homebound. It should be remembered that clean hair adds to the feeling of comfort and well being of the patient.

Clothing

Whenever possible, patients should be encouraged to dress in street clothes during the day as this usually has a positive effect on morale. They may find it easier to dress themselves if certain modifications in clothing are made. The modifications may include the use of:

- Light clothes—weather permitting.

- Loose fitting pullover shirts and blouses without buttons. Sweatshirts and jogging attire can be comfortable and fashionable as well.

- Slip-on elastic tie rather than string tie shoes. All footwear worn by the patient should provide support and slip resistance.

- Slacks or trousers with elastic tops.

- Shoe horns with long thick handles.

- Wearing apparel of all kinds—slacks, shirts, ties, blouses, dresses, shoes, etc. are available with Velcro fasteners and should be utilized.

It should be mentioned here that if a patient is unsteady on his/ her feet it is well to put a loose leather belt around the waist so that the patient may be grabbed by the attendant should he/she start to fall. Those caring for female patients who are confined to bed may find back-tie gowns easier to manage than conventional gowns or pajamas.

Physical Therapy

Physical therapy can play an important role in the overall well-being of the ALS patient. Certain exercises can prove very beneficial to the patient in easing the discomfort of contracture and fluid retention and improving circulation. Physical therapy is also important in maintaining mobility. It is important to contact a physician or rehabilitation therapist who can demonstrate and train members of the family to do these exercises with the patient.

Equipment

ALS patients in the latter stages of the disease may require special equipment and aids to assist them. A variety of aids and equipment that can make the patient more comfortable and help him to maneuver are available through medical supply houses. Following is but a partial list of such equipment: wheelchairs (electric and manual); form-fitted seats for wheelchairs; walkers; wheelchair lifts and stair lifts; patient lifts (lifts the patient from one place to another); sliding boards; electric beds or mattresses; page turners; bathroom aids such as raised toilet seats; commode seats for wheelchairs; waterbeds (to avoid bedsores); sheepskin (goes under the patient to avoid bedsores); folding wheelchair ramps; external catheter for bed patients; leg support weights; and IPPB Machines (to ease respiratory difficulty). The above equipment should be used on the advice of a medical professional. The importance of a hospital bed (electrical or manual) should be stressed here. Changing position is imperative to the ALS patient. In some instances, when the patient cannot move himself, poor circulation, fluid retention, stiffness and bedsores can occur. A hospital bed can alleviate these stresses and prevent discomfort. Hospital beds are available for rental from medical supply houses.

The patient who has lost the use of his/her legs can experience a "flopping" outward of the legs when in bed, causing sudden pain in the joints and groin area. Legs should he propped on the sides with pillows or leg support weights to prevent this from occurring. If weights are metal and cold, be sure they are covered with a soft warm fabric for comfort.

Activity

Activity is a very important consideration for those with ALS. Patients should be encouraged to be as active as their strength permits but not to the point of fatigue. Safety should always be stressed, but it is important patients understand they are the best ones to assess their capabilities. The physical therapist will instruct the patient and family members in any exercises that are considered necessary.

Some patients have leg weakness that makes use of a walker advisable. If a walker is prescribed, the patient should be given careful instruction in its use. Special care should be taken to be certain that the patient is strong enough to use a walker. A wheelchair should be properly prescribed and fitted with appropriate back and seat cushions, belts, and leg rests. It is important to have professional guidance before borrowing or buying a wheelchair. Wheelchairs can be purchased with many attachments that can make the patient more comfortable. Personalized, molded seats are available. There are many foot and leg supports available for wheelchairs. Some of these supports are adjustable and can be moved into different positions. The need of a wheelchair for mobility should not mean that the patient is housebound. If weather permits, family members should try to spend short periods of time outdoors with the patient, as well as having her/him accompany them on outings. The change of scene and routine can be very beneficial. Dinner out can be just as much fun for the patient as it is for you, even when feeding is required. A rehabilitation therapist or a physical therapist can provide instruction in transferring techniques to assist the patient in moving to and from a wheelchair. A sliding board can be very helpful here. Many patients have found it easier to make a wheelchair-automobile transfer if the wheelchair is on the same level as the car rather than being on the curb.

Patients who are unable to use a walker or wheelchair may still be able to sit in a comfortable chair for variable periods of time. Also, there are many foot and leg supports available for wheelchairs. Some of these supports are adjustable and can be moved into different positions.

Patients who are confined to bed should not be permitted to remain in one position for longer than two hours during the day; longer periods are often permissible during the night. If the patient is unable to turn himself, he must be assisted. The following is a partial listing of points to be considered.

- A physical therapist or rehabilitation therapist should demonstrate the positions to be used for the individual patient.

- Family members who will be assisting in turning the patient should receive thorough instruction in turning techniques and proper body mechanics from a physical therapist or other qualified medical professional. Use of proper body mechanics can prevent muscle strain in the person doing the turning.

- The patient should always be positioned in good body alignment with no strain on any joint. Always ask the patient if he or she is comfortable when positioning is completed.

- Pillows can be very useful for propping the patient in a particular position.

- The patient should always be lifted and never dragged through a position change. A turning sheet placed over the bottom sheet can be very helpful in lifting the patient in bed.

- The skin areas on which the patient has been lying should be examined after turning for any redness which would indicate that pressure has been applied to that area for too long; a massage to these areas is soothing and also increases circulation to the areas. Positioning is particularly important with bony points of pressure over the entire body—hips, shoulders, elbows, ankles, heels, knees and base of spine. Patients must be turned on a regular basis (every two hours) and pillows or a sheepskin used to avoid pressure over these areas. To not do so will bring about pressure sores and ultimately skin ulcers.

- Check with a physical or rehabilitation therapist about the use of foot-boards and elastic stockings.

Respiration

Although it is largely involuntary, breathing is a muscular activity with the diaphragm and intercostal muscles being the major muscles involved. The diaphragm is the more important, and causes the most serious problems when it is weakened by ALS. This means that any stress that requires increased respiratory effort will have a greater effect on the ALS patient than on the unaffected person. The person with ALS must avoid respiratory infection. "Flu" and pneumonia vaccines are available to the patient. People with colds or the "flu" should not come in contact with the patient.

It is often easier for the patient to breath when sitting up than when lying down, as in the vertical or semi-vertical position the abdominal contents do not press against the diaphragm.

It is not unusual for the ALS patient to have difficulty sleeping. Television in the patient's room at night can be very comforting. Many patients sleep better if they use several pillows.

If breathing becomes a problem, a pulmonary specialist should be contacted immediately. Breathing aids are available to lessen the patient's labor and discomfort. And today patients can adapt readily to mechanical respiratory assistance at home. It is important here that the patient understands he or she has a choice—whether or not they want to avail themselves of life sustaining devices, such as the home respirator, or not. If not, a "living will" or Durable Power of Attorney for medical care may be called for. And these decisions should be made before the necessity for them arises.

Communication

Many patients with ALS experience difficulty with speaking during the course of their illness. This difficulty may be caused by the inability to project the voice or by the inability to form the words—both of which result from muscle weakness. The patient should be encouraged to continue speaking even though he or she may feel discouraged. Speaking more slowly and using two or three syllable words is helpful. Family members should resist the temptation to speak to others for the patient even if they know what the patient is attempting to say. Most patients do better in a relaxed atmosphere and when they are not being rushed.

There are a number of alternate communication devices and systems available. Some possibilities include a homemade speaking board, magic slates, voice amplifiers, portable tape typewriters, and computers. Please contact The ALS Association for specific information.

Psychological Support

Psychological manifestations such as denial, anger, withdrawal, and depression are common, normal reactions of both the patient with a chronic, progressive illness and the family members. An atmosphere in which everyone feels comfortable in discussing their feelings will keep the lines of communication open. Family members should not give false assurances that "everything will be all right," but instead, should listen and, in fact encourage the patient to voice his/her fears and concerns and respond honestly. In most cases, with this kind of support the patient (and incidentally, the family members themselves) can be helped to reach an acceptance of the illness and prognosis. At the same time, it is important to recognize that the acceptance does not mean defeat. Hope is an integral part of survival and should go hand in hand with acceptance. Each patient is individual; the symptoms are individual; the case is individual and it is always best not to generalize.

Neurological research is moving at a faster pace now and no one can predict what tomorrow's findings will bring.

It should be stressed again that ALS patients have no impairment of intelligence, judgement, or other mental facilities. They are still a member of the family and should be treated with the same respect as always, especially with regard to being included in family discussions and decisions. Their opinion should be sought, as before. This attitude will acknowledge that, while their bodily functions are severely impaired, their minds are not. They must be given this recognition that they are alive and a (mentally) healthy and functioning member of the family system. In the past few years, many books have been written about helping the patient with a chronic, debilitating illness and the patient with terminal illness. One of the best of these is *On Death and Dying* by Dr. Elisabeth Kubler-Ross which discusses dying and how it is faced by patients, families, and the medical professionals responsible for their care. Information presented in this book is also applicable to understanding and dealing with the emotional reactions to chronic illness and could possibly answer many of your questions. This book is widely available in paperback and may be useful to patients and their families.

Recreation

Recreation activities become very important to those with limited activity. Mildly affected ALS patients can usually continue to pursue their pre-illness recreational activities. More severely affected patients will need to modify their activities within the limitations imposed by the disease. Some examples of recreational activities suitable for people with limited mobility and significant weakness include:

- Cards: Patients with limited grasping ability may find it easier to use trays that hold the cards for easy viewing.

- Radio/TV

- Reading: Automatic page turners can be purchased or obtained on loan if the patient is unable to do this. If reading is tiring for the patient, talking book services are available in many communities.

If these services are not available in your public library, you should request them. Family members may also take turns reading to the patient.

- The Braille Institute Library offers a free talking book service including listening equipment for individuals certified as qualified by a physician. For information call: 1-800-808-2555.

- Playing chess by mail or other board games at home.

Of course, when selecting alternative recreational activities, the patient's interests should be kept in mind.

Patient Services of the ALS Association

The ALS Association National Office provides information about the following services for the patient and family:

Referral Services

- **Medical and Home Health Services.** Referrals are made covering all areas of medical needs from hospitals to nursing homes and in-home care.

- **Information Assistance.** Questions on managing ALS are answered or if necessary, persons are given information on whom to contact for additional data.

- **Psychological Support.** Through a volunteer organization network, referrals are given to provide proper counseling.

- **Resource Equipment List.** Recommendations and referrals are made on all types of equipment for handicapped persons. Contacts are maintained with manufacturers and suppliers to make sure the most up-to-date materials are presented.

- **Certified ALSA Centers.** Outpatient clinical care facilities providing a multidisciplinary team approach to provide a continuum of care as well as appropriate diagnostic capabilities for ALS patients.

"Living with ALS" Manuals

Six comprehensive manuals explaining day-to-day living with ALS. (See descriptions under "Suggested Readings.")

Local Chapters and Support Groups

Throughout the United States, The ALS Association has local chapters and support groups which provide referrals and other patient programs on a local level.

Information and Education

Besides working to increase public awareness of ALS, The Association provides an ongoing information and education program to the health care community to assist them in better meeting the needs of the ALS patient and family. For information on any of the above services, contact The ALS Association National Office at (818) 340-7500 or (800) 782-4747.

Suggested Readings

The following books are available through The ALS Association:

- *Living with ALS* manuals by The ALS Association

  What's It All About? This manual provides an overview of ALS, what it is and how it affects your body. It also provides information on what kinds of resources are available to help you deal with ALS more effectively.

  Coping with Change. This manual addresses the psychological, emotional, and social issues that you must deal with when your life is affected by ALS. It provides information on how to cope with the many lifestyle changes and adjustments that occur when you live with ALS.

  Managing Your Symptoms and Treatment. This manual discusses the symptoms that can occur when you have ALS and how to treat them. It also covers the most recent breakthroughs in medications and how these treatments can improve the quality and duration of your life.

  Functioning When Your Mobility Is Affected. This manual covers the spectrum of mobility issues that occur with ALS. It specifically discusses exercises to maximize your mobility as well as how to adapt your home and activities of daily living to help you function more effectively.

Adjusting to Swallowing and Speaking Difficulties. This manual discusses how your speech can be affected by ALS. It covers specific techniques and devices available for improving communication. In addition, swallowing difficulties and how to maintain a balanced diet are also covered.

Adapting to Breathing Changes. This manual explains how normal breathing is affected by ALS. Specifically, it explains how to determine if you have breathing problems and what options are available to assist you as your breathing capacity changes.

- *Maintaining Good Nutrition with ALS* from The ALS Association.

The ALS Association National Office maintains a reading list of recommended books available through the publisher or book stores. Please contact the Patient Services Department at (818) 340-7500, or (800) 782-4747.

Conclusion

As mentioned previously, it is not possible for this chapter to provide all answers to all questions asked by all patients with ALS and by their family members. For this reason, close communication with members of the medical profession is essential. There should be no hesitation about referring any questions or problems to them; this includes physicians, nurses, physical and rehabilitation therapists, psychologist, psychiatrists, social workers, etc.

The ALS Association is a major source of information and support for the ALS patient and his/her family. We care and we want to help you. Patients and caregivers may use our toll-free telephone number: 1-800-782-4747. Please feel free to call on us! Thank you.

Chapter 30

Mealtime Challenges for ALS Patients

Swallowing Tips

General Body Positioning and Environment

Head Positioning—DO

- Keep head level or tilted slightly forward.

- If you have difficulty holding up your head, speak with your doctor, physical therapist or occupational therapist regarding strategies or assistive devices.

- Pillows can be positioned so the head cannot fall backwards.

Head Positioning—DON'T

- Avoid letting your head lean backwards, even momentarily when you swallow. This action exposes your airway to food.

Trunk Positioning—DO

- Keep your trunk at approximately 90% whenever possible, especially when drinking liquids.

Trunk Positioning — DON'T

- Avoid eating or drinking when reclining.

Environment — DO

- Take one bite at a time. This method is slower but safer. If you have trouble with 1 bite and you take a second bite, what will you do with it if you start to choke?

    1. Gasp in for air and breathe in the second bite? or

    2. Cough them both out?

    Please take one bite at a time.

- Eating and speaking should be separated. The same mechanism cannot perform both functions at once.

- When swallowing is difficult, it becomes even more important to make mealtime as pleasant and relaxed as possible.

Environment — DON'T

- Avoid answering questions with a mouthful of food. Our mothers were right! Never speak with your mouthful. One breathes in before one speaks. You don't want to 'breathe' your last bite of food into your lungs.

- Avoid distractions if eating is very difficult. Think about each bite.

Mouth Stage
(Oral Transit)

Lip Seal — DO

- Be aware of your lip position. Lip balm, especially flavored, can increase your self-monitoring. Keep your lips tightly closed after inserting food or liquids.

Lip Seal — DON'T

- Avoid keeping your lips open continually, otherwise your mouth will become extremely dry and seepage will be a problem.

Jaw Position — DO

- Keep jaw closed whenever possible. As soon as food has been inserted, close your lips and teeth tightly before you begin to chew and swallow.

Jaw Position — DON'T

- If your jaw is weak, don't fall into the habit of ignoring your jaw and letting it fall open. Try to determine how much your jaw will close. If it is a problem contact your physician or occupational therapist about a chin strap or other assistive devices.

- If your jaw is difficult to open completely and chewing is a problem, avoid tough, chewy foods. Talk to your dietitian about a change in the consistency of your diet.

Drooling — DO

- Swallow often. If swallowing saliva is a problem, there are several options your physician can discuss with you (including a suction machine or medication) to determine which is best for you. Close monitoring of your diet can be of assistance. Milk or milk products in some people can thicken saliva. Sweet items can increase saliva flow while citrus products can thin the saliva somewhat.

- Keep your teeth and lips closed. Keep a handkerchief or facial tissue near. While eating, watch out for seepage of liquids. Follow the above suggestions. Refer to lip seal suggestions, especially.

Drooling — DON'T

- Avoid poor positioning. When you are not eating or drinking, keep your head level.

- When you are not eating or drinking, avoid the head down position.

Tongue — DO

- If one side is 'better' than another, place food midway on tongue on the 'good' side and chew on that side.

- If food sticks to your upper plate of your dentures, speak to your dentist to determine if something can be applied to decrease the likelihood of this.

- If it is difficult to move food in your mouth, perhaps a change in consistency can help. Speak to your dietitian about a 'mechanical soft' or 'pureed' (blenderized) diet.

- If room temperature liquids are a problem, change the temperature to cool or warm.

- Carbonated beverages (soft drinks, beer, etc.) can often be taken when plain liquids cannot.

Tongue — DON'T

- Avoid placing food on the tip of your tongue, if tongue movement is difficult, place the food in the mid-to-back area of the tongue.

- You may need to avoid very hot or very cold foods or drinks. Use your discretion. Cool or warm temperatures are better.

Throat State
(Pharyngeal Transit)

DO

- If it is very easy to gag, place the food toward the back of your tongue in a gentle, slow, firm movement. Use your own discretion, you may need to place the food closer to the middle portion of the tongue to avoid a premature gag.

- If taking pills with water is a problem, experiment with placing a pill with a small bite of mashed potatoes or pudding.

- If thin liquids seem to make you choke more readily, change to thicker liquids. (Freeze and put into a blender to make a slushy drink or add gelatin or potato flakes to thicken.) Speak to your dietitian for information.

- If dry foods are hard to swallow, change the texture and consistency. Cut up into small bites, add gravy, etc. Speak to your dietitian about strategies with diet modification.

- Coughing is a protective mechanism and can help avoid aspiration. Ask your speech-language pathologist about the Supraglottic Swallow.

DON'T
- Don't drop the food in the back area of your tongue without first running the spoon from the front to the back of the tongue with a firm slow movement if gagging is a problem.

- Don't ignore difficulties with periodic intermittent problems with choking or strangling on liquids. Contact your physician and your speech-language pathologist immediately.

- Don't be embarrassed to cough if you are in public. Coughing can save your life.

- Don't breathe in when you are in mid-swallow. Complete your chew, then swallow, then take a breath.

Information about Feeding Tubes

The digestive systems prepares the food we eat for absorption by the body. This process changes all food into proteins, carbohydrates, fats, vitamins, mineral salts, and water. The intestinal mucous then is able to absorb these products for transportation by the blood to their final destination.

The organs of the digestive system form a tube (gastrointestinal tract) that begins with the mouth and ends with the large intestine. These organs are the mouth, pharynx, esophagus, stomach, and intestines. The intestines are divided into three sections: the duodenum, the jejunum, and the ileum.

The issues that arise for persons with ALS are:

1. Should I have a feeding tube? Will it prolong my life?

2. If I chose to have one, when should it be done?

3. Can I still eat by mouth?

4. What's the difference between a nasogastric tube, esophagostomy tube, gastrostomy tube, jejunostomy tube, PEG tube, and a Button or key tube?

5. What is involved in managing a feeding tube? Are there problems?

6. What do I put down the tube, when, and how?

Should I have a feeding tube? Will it prolong my life?

Many people with ALS (PALS) choose to have a feeding tube. A few do refuse to have one and they have a right to refuse. If a decision is made not to have a feeding tube, weight loss and poorer health can be difficult for caregivers to manage. Physicians can make an opening in the abdomen and food can be transported through a feeding tube. The feeding tube ends in our stomach, or in the jejunum (part of the small intestine).

Some advantages to having a feeding tube:

• Feeding times are simpler and take 10-15 minutes.

• There are no choking, chewing, and swallowing problems.

• Adequate nutrition helps to maintain weight, prevent deficiencies, improves PALS general health and resistance to infection.

• Fluids can be given without choking.

• Life will probably be prolonged.

• Energy expended in the chore of eating may be saved for other activities.

The disadvantages may include:

• You may not want your life prolonged.

• The idea of a feeding tube may be intolerable.

• The insertion of a feeding tube is a surgical procedure requiring a hospital stay from one half to several days.

• Potential infections or discomfort with the opening for the tube.

• Cost of special food such as Ensure. Insurance may or may not pay for these products.

When should I get one?

If you wait until your respiratory system is compromised and you can no longer cough well, the risk of choking and pneumonia increases. Physicians recommend getting a tube early.

Do it now if you are spending more than an hour for your meals; if you have lost ten percent of your weight or more—you may be seriously undernourished; if eating by mouth means frequent choking; if you are dehydrated from lack of sufficient fluids; if your time and attentions are consumed with getting adequate food and water.

Can I still eat by mouth?

Usually by the time you get a tube eating by mouth has become a lengthy, unpleasant chore and you are happy to give it up. However, if you get one early, you may still enjoy eating by mouth for the taste, etc. The tube can be used to take in extra fluids and calories.

What are the Pro's and Con's of the various types of feeding tubes?

Nasogastric Tube. The NG tube is used for temporary or short term use. The tube is inserted through the nose, down the esophagus, and into the stomach secured to the nose with tape. The nose and back of the throat can become irritated and even ulcerated from the pressure of the tube left in place for more than a few weeks. It is uncomfortable to remove and reinsert. There is also danger of the tube moving and going into the airway instead of the esophagus.

Esophageal Tube. The opening for this tube is in the side of the neck. A long catheter is inserted down through the esophagus into the stomach. After the opening is well-healed, the tube may be removed between feedings. This method is not used very often. One obvious disadvantage is that it is noticeably visible unless a scarf is worn to cover it. For persons with ALS that chose to use a ventilator, a second opening in the neck area may create problems. The advantage is no gastric juices can leak through the opening and cause irritations or problems.

PEG Tube. The percutaneous endoscopic gastrostomy (PEG) tube is currently used most often. The tube is approximately 10 inches long. A large endoscope (instrument) is passed through the mouth and down into the stomach. This feeding tube is threaded down and out through an opening in the abdominal wall. Some physicians use a simple method that doesn't involve an endoscopy. One of the strongest advantages of this method is that usually no general anesthesia is needed, only heavy sedation. With a skilled physician, this procedure can be done quickly with few problems. You may be able to come home the same day. Problems with initial feedings can be dealt with by experienced personnel while in the hospital. It is important that patients and caregivers feel knowledgeable and confident before going home. Arrangements can be made for visits by home care nurses until you feel confident.

Some of the problems with PEG tubes include aspiration pneumonia (fluid gets into the airway and lungs, causing infection). Gastric reflux and aspiration can be minimize by close adherence to elevating the head at least 45 degrees during and after feeding, for a period of 30 to 60 minutes. Liquid medications rather than crushed pills are preferred through a PEG. Bulk-forming agents such as Metamucil, should not be given through a PEG tube. Blenderized foods may be used if they are able to pass through the eyelets at the end of the tube. Have your doctor show you a tube before he inserts it. Careful routine flushing with water is a necessity to keep it from clogging.

Gastrostomy Tube. The term gastrostomy can simply mean a feeding tube; however, it usually refers to the placement of the tube via a more complicated surgical procedure to create an opening in the abdominal wall into the stomach. This procedure usually means a longer hospital stay and may require the use of general anesthesia.

Jejunostomy Tube. The jejunostomy is a long thin tube placed via fluoroscopy through the stomach ending in the jejunum (in the small intestine). Proponents of this type of feeding tube believe that there is less problem from aspiration pneumonia due to reflux (the return flow of formula into the back of the throat). Critics say a J-tube should be used after all other methods of controlling reflux and aspiration into the lungs have failed. The J-tube has a greater incidence of diarrhea, clogging, and abdominal distention.

Another important disadvantage is that formula must be infused at a much slower rate than a Gastrostomy tube, requiring the use and added expense of a pump. It also may interfere with the quality of life for may persons with ALS who want to remain active, and find so much time attached to a piece of machinery a hindrance. J-tubes also require a more expensive product for problem free digestion. Lastly, placement of the J-tube is more expensive due to the need for fluoroscopy for proper placement. If aspiration pneumonia becomes an uncontrollable problem, a J-tube may be required.

Button Tube. The Button tube is a new short tube that lies even with the skin. An extension tube is attached for feedings. The advantage to this type of tube is that there is no tubing left hanging on the abdomen.

What is involved in managing a feeding tube? Are there problems?

Patency of Tube. The preferred tube requires pouring a liquid product "down" the tube about five times a day. This is followed by water. Home care nurses have a variety of things they like to do to "clean" the inside of the tube. The tube is always flushed with water usually at least one cup after a feeding. This may be followed with about ¼ cup of "cleanser." The products used as cleansers I am most familiar with are Coca-Cola, cranberry juice, meat tenderizer (one part tenderizer to 4 parts water) and vinegar water (one part vinegar to four parts water); Viokase, a commercially prepared product is available by prescription. Viokase is mixed with a small amount of water and used to unclog tubes or as a routine cleanser. After the insertion of these "cleansers," the tube is plugged quickly and the solutions are allowed to set in the tubing and do their work for 15 minutes to an hour or more. Then these solutions are flushed with a cup of water.

Dumping. In the beginning, the liquid feedings should flow in over 15 to 20 minutes or more to prevent stomach cramps, regurgitation, diarrhea, etc. Sometimes skin flushing, perspiration, clamminess, or other unpleasant symptoms may follow too fast feedings. This is referred to as "dumping syndrome." Diarrhea is a common problem that requires care and attention. Abdominal distention may be severe enough to compromise respirations. Dumping syndrome may be lessened with diluted feedings, a different product, or slower infusion.

Insertion Site. The insertion site on the abdomen (around the feeding tube) should be cleaned with hydrogen peroxide. A cotton-tipped swab can be used. Usually this is all that is required. Provodine-Iodine ointment or solution may be placed at the exit site until it is heated. The ointment/solution helps prevent an infection while the fistula or "tunnel" heals. A small dressing may be placed around the opening to absorb the small amounts of secretions that tend to ooze out on the skin. These may be acidic stomach secretions which can irritate the skin. A thin layer of a liquid antacid can be spread around the tube insertion site and allowed to dry. This counteracts the acid.

Infection in the Tube "Tunnel." On rare occasions, stomach juices will leak into the abdominal tissues and infection may result. You should press around the opening with your finger to check for any

secretions that might look like pus. Any white/yellow pus-looking secretions require a physician for treatment.

Outer Tube. The feeding tube should not be too long. If it is too
long, that length and weight will pull on the opening and be uncomfortable. Sometimes it is helpful to tape it to the abdomen with
hypoallergenic tape. You may take a shower without concern. Immers-
ing the opening in bathtub water could cause a problem from unclean
water.

Replacement. The tube may need to be replaced if it stops working or the parts wear out. Some tubes can be replaced by a nurse or
caregiver, but others must be reinserted in a hospital setting. Replacement routine depends on the physician. Most tubes are replaced every 6–12 months.

What do I put down the tube?

If your tube is the type that ends in the stomach, anything you can
get down the tube is all right. That includes all drinks, blenderized
thinned soups and foods, crushed medicines (check with your phar-
macists first; some medications cannot be crushed, some will harden
when mixed with water and clog the tube). A tuberculin syringe filled
with water may provide enough pressure to unclog the tube. If the
feeding tube ends in the jejunum (intestine) a predigested product may
be preferable to lessen such dumping symptoms as abdominal distention, diarrhea, stomach cramps, etc. Normally a formula such as
Jevity is tolerated.

Customarily, a registered dietitian will give you exact directions
as to the kind of and amount of feedings, beginning slowly and building up the amount according to tolerance. You may take several days
or even a week or so to tolerate the feedings without diarrhea, flushing, perspiration, etc. Occasional blood tests to evaluate your nutritional status is optimal care.

Ensure, Jevity, Pulmocare, or other such products are normally
used. They come in easy to use cans or some can be purchased in pow-
der form as the most economical way. These products may be purchased in pharmacies, medical supply companies, and even in some
grocery stores. Carnation Breakfast with a small amount of oil added
makes a fair substitute if you need one for a few feedings (Note: Carnation Breakfast should not be used as sole means of nutrition). These
products should be used at room temperature to prevent gastric complications.

The stomach should be checked to see if the previous feeding has emptied into the intestine. This is done by aspirating with a syringe. If more than 100 cc's of fluid are obtained, the new feeding should be delayed or skipped. This is most important in the beginning weeks. If it is not a problem, you may skip it!

There are several methods of nutrition through the feeding tube. I have tried to review the most often used:

Kangaroo Bag/Gravity Method. The Kangaroo Bag method uses a plastic bag connected to a long piece of extension tubing. This tubing is then attached to the feeding tube. The liquid then flows via gravity into the stomach. The bag can be hung on a hook, an IV pole, literally anything that is stable and approximately 18 inches higher than the stomach. After the supplement has been administered, one to two cups of water should follow for rinsing purposes. Although the manufacturer recommends daily replacement of the bag, I have found that it can be reused several times if strict attention is paid to abundant flushing and storage of the bag in the refrigerator. The bag should be changed more frequently when the weather is hot.

Kangaroo Bag/Pump Method. This method is essentially the same procedure as above, except that instead of letting the liquid infuse by gravity, it is infused by a pump at a rate you set. This method is always used with jejunostomy tubes. J-tubes require a slower rate of infusion and are more problematic.

There is nothing wrong with using a simple funnel for introducing liquid down the tube—whatever works! Essentially what is happening is that the food is by-passing the mouth and esophagus.

The person receiving the feeding should remain in a semi-upright position for 30 to 60 minutes after each feeding. Those who are able to walk would benefit from a short, slow walk. This helps to prevent regurgitation and aspiration problems. Aspirating any of the feeding puts you at risk for pneumonia, a problem that can be avoided with a little care.

Bolus Method. While the fastest and simplest method, it can be the most dangerous method! The "bolus" method uses a large syringe which is attached to the feeding tube. (Syringes can be purchased from the pharmacy). The outer part of the syringe is the only part used. The plunger is not used! Liquid is poured into the syringe and allowed to flow in as fast as gravity will allow. USE EXTREME CAUTION IF CHOOSING TO USE THE PLUNGER TO FORCE THE LIQUID INTO THE STOMACH! Serious problems of respiratory depression, cramping, regurgitation aspiration, and over expansion of the stomach do occur more frequently with the bolus method. In the first few weeks, caution should be taken not to give too much formula too fast. Small frequent feedings is the best method. The bolus method is not the best method of administration to use in the first few weeks. Time for adjusting to a liquid diet should be allowed.

Conclusion

A person with ALS has the right to make their own decision about feeding tubes. Experience has shown us that choosing a feeding tube does not lengthen the quantity of life as much as it improves the quality of life. If problems with swallowing come early in the disease, it seems to be a kindness to both the patient and the caregiver to have a tube placed. It is emotionally difficult for the caregivers to watch the process of losing ground in weight and health due to inadequate nutrition.

—Excerpted from an article by Betty Scharf, R.N.

Chapter 31

ALS Drug Development Update

Drug Development Update: Latest Developments as of March 20, 1998

Amgen and Guilford Pharmaceuticals Inc.

Small Molecule Neurotrophic Agents

These two companies announced in mid-August that they have entered into an agreement granting Amgen worldwide rights for Guilford's FKBO-neuroimmunophilin ligands, a novel class of small molecule neurotrophic agents that may represent a new approach in the treatment of neurodegenerative disorders. These orally active neurotrophic agents are being developed by Guilford to promote nerve regeneration and repair for a number of neurodegenerative diseases. Guilford is a biopharmaceutical company engaged in the development of polymer-based therapeutics for cancer and novel products for the diagnosis and treatment of neurological diseases such as Parkinson's diseases and ALS.

Under the agreement, Amgen receives worldwide rights to the compounds for all human therapeutic and diagnostic applications. Amgen will conduct and pay for all clinical development and manufacturing of products, and will market products worldwide.

The small molecule neurotrophic compounds (neuroimmunophilin ligands) consist of small organic molecules which have activity comparable to NGF, BDNF, and other protein neurotrophic factors, but are active following *oral* administration. This means that, even in small doses given orally, they cross the blood/brain barrier and perform their function. Also, they appear to specifically target damaged nerve cells while leaving healthy cells alone which may translate into fewer side effects. To date, Guilford has conducted tests of their compounds in culture and in animal models.

Amgen-Regeneron Partners

BDNF

Since late 1996 when the results of a large Phase III clinical trial of BDNF demonstrated no significant difference in survival between the groups on BDNF versus the placebo group, Amgen has pursued development of BDNF for ALS using intrathecal delivery. A small, one-year trial using BDNF has been completed and evaluated. Using intrathecal delivery, BDNF was delivered directly to the cerebrospinal fluid, also called the intrathecal space. In order to deliver the BDNF into the intrathecal space, a drug pump was implanted beneath the skin with an attached catheter extending into the cerebrospinal fluid. During the first three months, one out of every five patients received placebo drug during a double-blinded trial. After the three months, all patients received intrathecal BDNF.

The objectives of the small trial were to evaluate the safety and tolerability of BDNF using this infusion system, and to assess any biological effects seen. This trial involved a *total* of 25 patients conducted in two sites—one in the U.S. (Chicago) and one in Germany.

A Phase II intrathecal trial will begin at eight sites in mid-Spring 1998.

For further information, please call Amgen at (805) 447-1000 or ALSA's Patient Hotline at (800) 782-4747.

Cephalon, Inc.

Myotrophin®

1998. The U.S. Food and Drug Administration (FDA) has scheduled its Peripheral and Central Nervous Systems Drugs Advisory Committee to further consider the efficacy of the New Drug Application (NDA) for Myotrophin. The Committee meeting will be held on April 9, 1998 at the Holiday Inn in Bethesda, Maryland from 8:30 a.m. to 5:00 p.m. with a one-hour open public hearing from 8:30–9:30 a.m.

As in the past, the Committee can vote to recommend approval to the FDA of Myotrophin® or it can vote not to recommend FDA approval. The FDA is not bound by either recommendation in reaching their decision on Myotrophin® by the target goal of May 11, 1998.

Although the FDA apparently has one or more issues for consideration, the nature of the issue or question has not been disclosed and an agenda has not been developed as of this date.

1997. On November 11, 1997 Cephalon, Inc. and Chiron Corporation announced that they have withdrawn and resubmitted to the FDA the companies' new drug application (NDA) to market Myotrophin® Injection in the U.S. By withdrawing and resubmitting the NDA, the companies enable the FDA to continue its review.

The move was made at the request of the FDA in order to give the FDA the additional time it requires for more in-depth analysis. While the regulations concerning such a resubmission now give the FDA six months for more analysis, neither Cephalon, Chiron, or ALSA know at this time if the FDA will need to take that full amount of time.

In the meantime, the treatment IND (expanded access program) remains the same. People who are taking the drug will be able to continue. To make inquiries about the program, call 1-800-829-3054.

1996-97. The FDA's Peripheral & Central Nervous System Drugs Advisory Committee, after reviewing Cephalon's New Drug Application for Myotrophin® Injection in a formal public meeting on May 8, 1997 voted not to recommend FDA approval of Myotrophin. The final vote was six to three against recommending approval. Those voting against approval felt the evidence was not substantial enough to demonstrate Myotrophin's effectiveness.

Even though the FDA *generally* follows the advice of its advisory panels, that does not mean *always*. The FDA designated Myotrophin® Injection an orphan drug for the treatment of ALS in 1991. It was made available to a limited number of patients with ALS in the U.S. under a Treatment Investigational New Drug protocol (expanded access program) approved by the FDA in June 1996.

In February of this year, Cephalon, Inc. and Chiron Corporation submitted a new drug application (NDA) to the U.S. Food and Drug Administration (FDA) seeking clearance to market Myotrophin® Injection in the United States for the treatment of ALS.

Eli Lilly and Company

Glutamate Antagonist

Eli Lilly and Company recently received FDA approval to begin a 50-patient, two-center study at Johns Hopkins and Indiana University. The study will be double-blind, 9 months in duration, and will test a glutamate antagonist (LY300164) versus placebo.

For further information, please call Bob Pascuzzi, M.D., at Indiana University at (317) 630-6146 or Jeff Rothstein, M.D., at Johns Hopkins at (410) 955-6435 or ALSA's Patient Hotline at (800) 782-4747.

SANOFI Pharmaceuticals, Inc.

SR57746A

Sanofi is a French-based, multi-national health care corporation which acquired Sterling Winthrop in 1994. SR57746A is an original Sanofi compound which exhibits neurotrophic and neuroprotective effects. It is being developed primarily as a potential treatment for ALS.

This year, Sanofi has initiated two 18-month, randomized, double-blind, placebo-controlled, multicenter trials of its compound SR57746A. These Phase III clinical trials will evaluate the effectiveness, safety, and tolerability of two doses of SR57746A in patients with ALS at 60 large investigational centers in North America and Europe. One study will include 1200 patients who take the approved, marketed drug Riluzole® and the other study will include 800 patients not taking the drug.

SR57746A is a nonpeptide which possesses neurotrophin-like activity. The compound reduces the histological (tissue), neurochemical, and functional deficiencies produced in widely divergent models of experimental neurodegeneration. The ability of SR 57746A to increase innervation of human muscle and to prolong the survival of mice suffering from progressive motor neuropathy (as demonstrated in a prior clinical trial) suggests the compound might be an effective therapy for the treatment of ALS. Even though the mechanism by which SR57746A produces its neurotrophic and neuroprotective effects is not fully understood, it is probably related to the compound's ability to mimic the activity or stimulate the biosynthesis of a number of neurotrophins (such as NGF and BDNF) originating within the body.

An exploratory Phase II trial, evaluating the effect of SR57746A in patients with ALS provided encouraging results. It was not possible to draw a definitive conclusion about the activity of SR57746A due to the small number of patients enrolled in this Phase II trial, therefore, further studies were required.

Current Sanofi Phase III trial sites include the following:

U.S. Centers

ARIZONA
Mayo Clinic, Scottsdale
E. Peter Bosch, M.D.
Contact: Camille Brouzes (602) 301-7583

CALIFORNIA
Center for Neurologic Study, San Diego
Richard Smith, M.D.
Contact: Stephanie Darby (619) 455-5463

California Pacific Medical Center, San Francisco
Robert G. Miller, M.D.
Contact: (415) 923-3904

University of California, Los Angeles
Michael C. Graves, M.D.
Contact: Linda de Sepulveda (310) 825-9816

COLORADO
University of Colorado, Denver
Hans Neville, M.D.
Contact: Donna Burns (303) 315-7046

CONNECTICUT
University of Connecticut Health Center, Farmington
Kevin Felice, M.D.
Contact: Candace Kiely (860) 679-4837

FLORIDA
University of Miami
Walter G. Bradley, M.D.
Contact: Julie Steele (305) 243-7526

GEORGIA
Emory University, Atlanta
Jeffrey Rosenfeld, M.D.
Contact: Meraida Polah (404) 778-3754

ILLINOIS
Northwestern University, Chicago
Robert L. Sufit, M.D.
Contact: Pat Casey (312) 908-0774

MARYLAND
Johns Hopkins University, Baltimore
Jeffrey D. Rothstein, M.D.
Contact: Lora Clawson (410) 955-6435

MISSOURI
Washington University Medical School, St. Louis
Alan Pestronk, M.D.
Contact: Julaine Florence (314) 362-6981

NEW MEXICO
University of New Mexico
Raul N. Mandler, M.D.
Contact: Martha Meister (505) 272-3342

NEW YORK
Columbia Presbyterian Neurological Institute, New York
Dale Lange, M.D.
Contact: Maura Del Bene (212) 305-5706

State University of New York, Syracuse
Jeremy Shefner, M.D.
Contact: Karyn Kushner (315) 464-5358

NORTH CAROLINA
Bowman Gray School of Medicine, Winston-Salem
Peter D. Donofrio, M.D.
Contact: Carolyn Ashburn, RN (910) 716-9056

OHIO
The Cleveland Clinic Foundation
Hiroshi Mitsumoto, M.D.
Contact: Doreen Andrews (216) 444-5538, (800) 223-2273, ext. 45538

Ohio State University, Columbus
Jerry R. Mendell, M.D.
Contact: Karen Downing (614) 292-1234

PENNSYLVANIA
Allegheny University, Hahneman Campus, Philadelphia

Terry Heiman-Patterson, M.D.
Contact: Donna Sandler (215) 893-6217 or (215) 893-2103

TEXAS
Baylor College of Medicine, Houston
Yadollah Harati, M.D.
Contact: (713) 798-5993 or (713) 798-5975

Veterans Affairs Medical Center, Houston
Yadollah Harati, M.D.
Contact: Carol Echols (713) 794-7393

VERMONT
University of Vermont, Burlington
Rup Tandan, M.D.
Contact: Patty Krusinski (802) 656-4177

WISCONSIN
University of Wisconsin, Madison
Benjamin R. Brooks, M.D.
Contact: Jennifer Parnell (608) 263-0170

Canadian Centers

ALBERTA
Foothills Hospital, Calgary
Thomas E. Feasby, M.D.
Doug Zochodne, M.D.
Contact: (403) 670-4418

University of Alberta, Edmonton
Michael H. Brooks, M.D.
Contact: Corrina Boyd (403) 492-4019

BRITISH COLUMBIA
Vancouver General Hospital
Andrew Eisen, M.D.
Contact: Jean Pearmain (604) 875-4405

ONTARIO
London Health Sciences Center, London
Michael Strong, M.D.
Contact: Ann Rowe (519) 663-3934

McMaster Medical Center, Hamilton
John D. Turnbull, M.D.
Contact: Joan Martin (905) 521-2100, ext. 6365

The Rehabilitation Centre, Ottawa
Anthony Newall, M.D.
Contact: Nancy Ridgeway (613) 737-7350

Sunny Brook Health Science Center, North York
Marek Gawel, M.D.
Contact: Kristen Boyer (416) 480-4959

QUEBEC
Montreal Neurologic Institute, Montreal
Neil R. Cashman, M.D.
Contact: Sharon Runions (514) 398-8532, (514) 398-5262

Pavillon Deschamps, Montreal
Pierre Duquette, M.D.
Contact: (514) 281-6000, ext. 5068

For further information, please call ALSA's Patient Hotline at (800) 782-4747.

On-Going Progress of Other Drugs in Development for Treatment of ALS

Amgen

GDNF

Glial cell-derived neurotrophic factor (GDNF) is a naturally occurring neurotrophic factor that in preclinical animal studies was shown to produce significant protective and survival-promoting effects on motor neurons. In prior studies GDNF applied locally to the nerve, injected subcutaneously or administered directly into the cerebrospinal fluid has been shown to protect motor neurons from undergoing degenerative changes following severing of the nerves.

Amgen filed an Investigational New Drug application with the FDA and will be proceeding with clinical trials at six sites utilizing GDNF in persons with ALS. Patient enrollment is restricted to a small number of patients. In this study, GDNF will be administered into the ventricles of the brain after surgical placement of an intracerebroventricular access port and catheter. This route of administration provides the best distribution of GDNF to all motor neurons. As a Phase I study, the initial objectives must first establish the safety of the agent in humans.

For further information, please call Amgen at (805) 447-1000 or ALSA's Patient Hotline at (800) 782-4747.

CytoTherapeutics

NT 4/5 and CT- I

Trials evaluating peripherally (e.g. orally) administered single growth factors to treat ALS have provided questionable evidence of the desired effect in humans to date. Two factors may account for these results: single factors may be insufficient for clinically relevant effects, and systemic delivery may produce an unfavorable therapeutic ratio by concentrating protein outside of the nervous system rather than within it. Experimental evidence indicates that two growth factors from complementary molecular families are more powerful than single factors, and preclinical and clinical data suggest that *central administration* of factors is less toxic and more effective than peripheral administration.

CytoTherapeutics, Inc., in collaboration with Genentech, Inc., has established a program to evaluate the use of its proprietary cellular encapsulation technology to deliver two growth factors, neurotrophin 4/5 and cardiotrophin 1, directly into the cerebrospinal fluid to treat patients with ALS.

For further information, please call CytoTherapeutics, Inc. at (401) 272-3310 or ALSA's Patient Hotline at (800) 782-4747.

Parke-Davis

Gabapentin (Neurontin®)

A Phase II double-blind, placebo-controlled study of gabapentin (Neurontin®) in patients with ALS was initiated by investigators of the Western ALS study group and received support from the Parke-Davis Company, the manufacturer of gabapentin. Gabapentin is an anti-glutamate used in the treatment of epilepsy.

ALS patients treated with gabapentin declined more slowly than those on placebo. The rate of weakening of arm muscles in patients on gabapentin was slower than patients taking placebo. These findings were not conclusive, but were considered to show a trend towards a beneficial effect. Confirmation of an effect will require additional testing. Gabapentin was generally well tolerated. The most common side effects were dizziness or lightheadedness, drowsiness, fatigue, and foot swelling. For most patients who experienced these side effects, they were temporary and mild.

Based on the findings of this screening study, a second multi-center placebo-controlled trial began February 1997. For further information, please call ALSA's Patient Hotline at (800) 782-4747.

Rhône-Poulenc Rorer

Rilutek® and Gene Therapy

Rilutek®, the first ALS drug ever approved by the FDA, is on the market. There are no ALS clinical trials being conducted by RPR at this time. However, that does not preclude future trials.

The April 1997 issue of *Nature Medicine* featured a study on the use of gene therapy for the treatment of ALS in an animal model. These results are the first ever demonstration of an impact of *in vivo* gene transfer on life span in a genetic animal model of any disease. Researchers from RPR Gencell, a division of Rhône-Poulenc Rorer, INSERM, CNRS, and the Institute of Medical Physiology in Denmark found that after intramuscular injection of the neurotrophin-3 adenoviral vector in pmn-mice, a 50% increase in lifespan was observed as well as a reduced loss of motor axons and improved neuromuscular function. It is important to remember that although these results are encouraging, several important scientific questions need to be answered before a Phase I trial can begin. This process is expected to take up to 18 months.

For further information, please call Rhône-Poulenc Rorer at (610) 454-8000 or ALSA's Patient Hotline at (800) 782-4747.

Transcend Therapeutics, Inc.

Procysteine®

Transcend Therapeutics, Inc. is a developmental stage, privately funded pharmaceutical company located in Cambridge, Massachusetts and currently focusing its efforts on drugs which treat diseases in which depletion of the body's primary antioxidant, glutathione, is depleted. A Phase I study in patients with ALS who received oral and intravenous dosage to the company's lead compound, Procysteine®, has been completed at Massachusetts General Hospital, under the direction of Dr. Robert Brown and Dr. Merit Cudkowicz.

The initial study of Procystein® determined preliminary safety and that the drug entered the CSF (crossed the blood/brain barrier). The company is awaiting results of some ongoing additional mouse model studies being conducted by Drs. Brown and Cudkowicz before making a decision about a Phase II study to look at effectiveness.

For further information, please call ALSA's Patient Hotline at (800) 782-4747.

Chapter 32

New Hope for People with ALS

Sunday, May 2, 1939, will be forever remembered in the annals of baseball as the day New York Yankees' first baseman Lou Gehrig voluntarily benched himself, ending a streak of 2,130 consecutive games.

For months the once great player's game had been in decline. His reflexes were off. He stumbled, fumbled, and struggled to hit or catch the ball. No one understood why, least of all Gehrig himself.

A few weeks after Gehrig benched himself, doctors diagnosed his illness as amyotrophic lateral sclerosis (ALS), a progressive disease of the central nervous system that remains incurable to this day.

Two years later, on June 2, 1941, Gehrig died at the age of 37. The disease that took his life became known to Americans as Lou Gehrig's disease. His consecutive games record stood for 56 years until it was broken by the Baltimore Orioles' Cal Ripken Jr. on Sept. 6, 1995.

In the years since Gehrig's death, many drugs have been tried for the treatment of ALS. For 54 years, none was found to be effective. But one recent drug approval and the granting of early access to another drug give reason for hope.

The Food and Drug Administration approved Rilutek (riluzole) in December 1995. It was the first drug found to have an effect, albeit a modest one, on the course of ALS. In clinical trials conducted in the United States and Europe, the drug appeared to prolong patients' survival by about three months.

Before the agency approved Rilutek, the drug had been made available to more than 3,000 ALS patients in the United States under the

FDA Consumer, September 1996.

Treatment IND (investigational new drug) program. This program gives patients access, under certain circumstances, to promising investigational new drugs for serious and life-threatening diseases for which there is no adequate treatment.

A second drug, Myotrophin (somatomedin C), was granted a Treatment IND by FDA last June 24 [1996]. Myotrophin is a recombinant insulin-like growth factor that appears to prevent neuron loss and promote neuron regeneration in animal studies. The drug has been studied in humans since 1992 in two completed international trials and a third ongoing in Japan. FDA granted treatment IND status to Myotrophin based on the results from the drug's first trial in humans, which indicated the drug has a modest effect in reducing the rate of disease progression.

Disabling and Often Deadly

More than 30,000 Americans have ALS, according to the ALS Association, a nonprofit organization that supports ALS research and public and patient education about the disease. Around 3,000 to 5,000 new cases of the disease are diagnosed every year.

Although ALS can strike at any age, it usually appears between the ages of 40 and 70. Men and women of all ethnic and racial groups are about equally affected.

The disease attacks the motor neurons, nerve cells in the brain and spinal cord that control the body's voluntary muscles. As the motor neurons begin to die, the muscles weaken and shrink. Early symptoms of ALS may include unusual fatigue and clumsiness, muscle weakness, slurred speech, and difficulty swallowing.

As the disease progresses, patients gradually lose the use of their hands, arms, legs, and neck muscles, ultimately becoming paralyzed. They can speak and swallow only with great difficulty. However, thinking ability, bladder and bowel function, sexual function, and the senses—sight, hearing, smell, taste, and touch—are unaffected.

About half of people with ALS die within three to five years of diagnosis. In rare cases, a person may survive with the disease for many years. The usual cause of death is failure of the diaphragm muscles that control breathing. Some individuals with ALS choose to prolong their lives by using a ventilator, but prolonged use of a ventilator may increase the risk of death from an infection such as pneumonia.

No single test can diagnose ALS. Because of the slow onset of the disease, it can be difficult to diagnose in the early stages, said Jeffrey Rothstein, M.D., Ph.D., associate professor of neurology at Johns

Hopkins University School of Medicine in Baltimore. Johns Hopkins is one of the nation's leading centers for ALS research.

"We do a number of tests to rule out other diseases that might mimic ALS. Because it's a fatal disease, you want to be absolutely certain of your diagnosis. The patient is generally about 20 to 50 percent into the disease by the time it is diagnosed," he said.

Exceptional Survivor

The brilliant British theoretical physicist Stephen W. Hawking, who is probably best known to the general public as the author of *A Brief History of Time*, is one of a very few people who have survived for many years with amyotrophic lateral sclerosis (ALS).

Hawking, now 54, was diagnosed with ALS in 1963 when he was a 21-year-old graduate student at Cambridge University in England. Hawking's life demonstrates that ALS impairs neither intellect nor sexual function. His work on the origin and nature of the universe has been, in the words of biographers Michael White and John Gribbin, "ground-breaking and revolutionary." Hawking also married and fathered three children after his diagnosis.

In 1985, after suffering a windpipe blockage, Hawking had a breathing device surgically implanted in his throat. The surgery resulted in the loss of his voice. He now "speaks" by using a voice synthesizer connected to a computer that he operates by squeezing a switch in his hand.

In *Stephen Hawking: A Life in Science*, White and Gribbin write that Hawking has a very strong personality and has "never [given] in to the symptoms of ALS more than he is physically compelled to."

Cause a Mystery

Doctors have known about ALS since 1874 (it was first identified by a French physician, J.M. Charcot), but its cause remains a mystery. Inability to pinpoint the cause of ALS has hindered efforts to find an effective treatment, said Marc Walton, M.D., Ph.D., a medical officer in the clinical trials division of FDA's Center for Biologics Evaluation and Research.

Doctors once thought that ALS might be caused by the same virus that causes polio and that exposure to polio would increase the risk of ALS, said Ralph Kuncl, M.D., Ph.D., associate professor of neurology at Johns Hopkins. However, he said, no evidence has been found to support this theory.

Another conjecture was that an environmental toxin might cause ALS. This theory arose in part because some places—the South Pacific island of Guam and parts of Japan—have some what higher than normal rates of ALS.

The cicad nut, a traditional food in Guam, contains toxic substances capable of killing motor neurons, said Kuncl. "But the toxicity level is not enough to cause the degeneration seen in ALS."

The "surprisingly uniform" incidence of ALS in the rest of the world "would not be expected if the disease were caused by an environmental toxin," Kuncl added. However, the reason for the increased rate of ALS in Guam and Japan remains unknown.

Some doctors believe that ALS is an autoimmune disease—that is, a disease in which the body attacks itself with antibodies normally produced to protect against infection. In ALS, according to this theory, antibodies attack and kill the motor neurons. However, "very potent autoimmune therapies have been tried in ALS and have all failed to alter the course of the disease," said Rothstein.

Another theory is that ALS is caused by toxic levels of glutamate in the brain. Glutamate is a constituent of protein that cells in the body use to help break down food and build up body tissues. In the central nervous system, nerve cells (neurons) use glutamate to communicate with one another.

Because too much glutamate can be toxic, the brain usually regulates the substance, keeping levels to those needed for body functioning. Abnormally high levels of glutamate have been found in the cerebrospinal fluid (the clear watery fluid that surrounds the brain and the spinal cord) of some patients with ALS.

In experiments, scientists have found that a protein responsible for removing excess glutamate from the brain appears not to work properly in people with ALS. They theorize that toxicity resulting from excessive glutamate might be killing motor neurons. The death of these cells leads to progressive muscle wasting in patients with ALS. One of the characteristics of Rilutek is that it inhibits the release of glutamate in the brain.

Rilutek is taken by mouth. Everyone who takes the drug must be monitored regularly for signs of Rilutek's most important side effect, a rise in the level of liver enzymes, which indicates abnormal liver function.

The drug's labeling states that treatment should be discontinued if liver enzymes increase to 10 times their normal level.

About five out of every 100 people who get ALS have an inherited, or familial, form of the disease; that is, one or more of their immediate family members—parents, brothers, sisters, or grandparents—also have the disease. Children of people with familial ALS have a fifty-fifty chance of developing the disease themselves.

In 1993, scientists identified a gene that, when defective, is associated with some cases of familial ALS. This gene carries the operating instructions for a protein whose function is to neutralize cell-damaging substances called free radicals. Some scientists think that when the gene is defective, an excessive build-up of free radicals may kill motor neurons.

However, this genetic mutation is found in only about one-fifth of people with familial ALS, according to Rothstein, and it has not been detected in anyone with the sporadic (noninherited) form of the disease, which is far more common.

Searching for Treatments

Even if the cause of the disease is eventually found, the development of effective treatments presents enormous challenges, said Rothstein. "The drugs have to be potent and they have to get into the nervous system, which has a very tight barrier—the blood-brain barrier—that prevents entry by many drugs."

Some doctors think that neurotrophic growth factors, substances produced by the body that stimulate nerve cells to grow and multiply, may be useful for treating ALS. These substances can now be produced in the laboratory using the techniques of biotechnology. Myotrophin is one such factor.

"No one thinks that neurotrophic factors, or the lack of them, cause ALS," said Rothstein. "But in animal experiments they seem to work quite well in preventing injury to motor neurons."

FDA's Walton said the agency is working with investigators and the drugs' manufacturers to try to design trials "that will tell us as quickly and efficiently as possible whether or not these products can be effective in the treatment of ALS."

Until more effective drugs are developed and approved to treat ALS, measures to improve patients' mobility and quality of life remain the mainstay, said Rothstein. "Nutrition is very important. A recent study in Italy showed increased survival in ALS patients who received good nutrition using a feeding tube.

"There's also a mask that patients can use to assist their breathing, and physical therapy can help to make them more comfortable. A speech pathologist can help them to learn different swallowing techniques as their swallowing muscles become weaker. Support groups for patients and their families are also very important."

On Sept. 6, 1995—the day Cal Ripken Jr. broke Lou Gehrig's record for consecutive games played—the Baltimore Orioles and the Johns Hopkins Medical Institutions announced the launch of the Cal Ripken/ Lou Gehrig Fund for Neuromuscular Research.

Ticket sales to the record-breaking game and an Orioles contribution raised $2 million for the fund. Kuncl said the money will support research at Johns Hopkins on neuromuscular diseases, with an emphasis on ALS.

Johns Hopkins' Rothstein said that though the drugs available do not thus far seem to give dramatic improvement, he is not discouraged.

"This is against the background of decades when no drug ever did anything for the disease. Initial therapies for many diseases, like leukemia and other cancers, had the same kind of effect ... a modest increase in survival. But they were followed by better therapies that, over time, increased patients' survival.

"It's a daunting task, but I envision that some day it will be possible to develop drugs that will not only stop motor neurons from dying but replace them and reverse the course of ALS."

Part Five

Parkinson's Disease

Chapter 33

Parkinson's Disease

Introduction

Parkinson's disease may be one of the most baffling and complex of the neurological disorders. Its cause remains a mystery but research in this area is active, with new and intriguing findings constantly being reported.

Parkinson's disease was first described in 1817 by James Parkinson, a British physician who published a paper on what he called "the shaking palsy." In this paper, he set forth the major symptoms of the disease that would later bear his name. For the next century and a half, scientists pursued the causes and treatment of the disease. They defined its range of symptoms, distribution among the population, and prospects for cure.

In the early 1960s, researchers identified a fundamental brain defect that is a hallmark of the disease: the loss of brain cells that produce a chemical—*dopamine*—that helps direct muscle activity. This discovery pointed to the first successful treatment for Parkinson's disease and suggested ways of devising new and even more effective therapies.

Society pays an enormous price for Parkinson's disease. According to the National Parkinson Foundation, each patient spends an average of $2,500 a year for medications. After factoring in office visits, Social Security payments, nursing home expenditures, and lost

National Institute of Neurological Disorders and Stroke (NINDS), NIH Pub. No. 94-139, September 1994.

income, the total cost to the Nation is estimated to exceed $5.6 billion annually.

What Is Parkinson's Disease?

Parkinson's disease belongs to a group of conditions called motor system disorders. The four primary symptoms are *tremor* or trembling in hands, arms, legs, jaw, and face; *rigidity* or stiffness of the limbs and trunk; *bradykinesia* or slowness of movement; and *postural instability* or impaired balance and coordination. As these symptoms become more pronounced, patients may have difficulty walking, talking, or completing other simple tasks.

The disease is both chronic, meaning it persists over a long period of time, and progressive, meaning its symptoms grow worse over time. It is not contagious nor is it usually inherited—that is, it does not pass directly from one family member or generation to the next.

Parkinson's disease is the most common form of *parkinsonism*, the name for a group of disorders with similar features (see section below entitled "What are the Other Forms of Parkinsonism?"). These disorders share the four primary symptoms described above, and all are the result of the loss of dopamine-producing brain cells. Parkinson's disease is also called primary parkinsonism or idiopathic Parkinson's disease; idiopathic is a term describing a disorder for which no cause has yet been found. In the other forms of parkinsonism either the cause is known or suspected or the disorder occurs as a secondary effect of another, primary neurological disorder.

What Causes the Disease?

Parkinson's disease occurs when certain nerve cells, or neurons, in an area of the brain known as the *substantia nigra* die or become impaired. Normally, these neurons produce an important brain chemical known as dopamine. Dopamine is a chemical messenger responsible for transmitting signals between the substantia nigra and the next "relay station" of the brain, the *corpus striatum*, to produce smooth, purposeful muscle activity. Loss of dopamine causes the nerve cells of the striatum to fire out of control, leaving patients unable to direct or control their movements in a normal manner. Studies have shown that Parkinson's patients have a loss of 80 percent or more of dopamine-producing cells in the substantia nigra. The cause of this cell death or impairment is not known but significant findings by research scientists continue to yield fascinating new clues to the disease.

266

One theory holds that free radicals—unstable and potentially damaging molecules generated by normal chemical reactions in the body—may contribute to nerve cell death thereby leading to Parkinson's disease. Free radicals are unstable because they lack one electron; in an attempt to replace this missing electron, free radicals react with neighboring molecules (especially metals such as iron), in a process called oxidation. Oxidation is thought to cause damage to tissues, including neurons. Normally, free radical damage is kept under control by antioxidants, chemicals that protect cells from this damage. Evidence that oxidative mechanisms may cause or contribute to Parkinson's disease includes the finding that patients with the disease have increased brain levels of iron, especially in the substantia nigra, and decreased levels of ferritin, which serves as a protective mechanism by chelating or forming a ring around the iron, and isolating it.

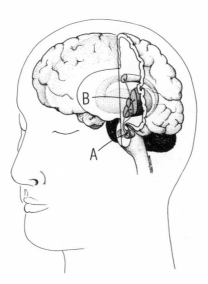

Figure 33.1. *This drawing shows a cut-away view of one side of the brain. In the healthy brain, nerve cells in a region known as the substantia nigra (A) produce the chemical messenger dopamine. Dopamine sends signals to another brain region called the corpus striatum (B) that allow the body to move smoothly and purposefully. In Parkinson's disease, the substantia nigra fails to produce sufficient supplies of dopamine.*

Some scientists have suggested that Parkinson's disease may occur when either an external or an internal toxin selectively destroys dopaminergic neurons. An environmental risk factor such as exposure to pesticides or a toxin in the food supply is an example of the kind of external trigger that could hypothetically cause Parkinson's disease. The theory is based on the fact that there are a number of toxins, such as 1-methyl-4-phenyl-1,2,3,6,-tetrahydropyridine (MPTP) and neuroleptic drugs, known to induce parkinsonian symptoms in humans. So far, however, no research has provided conclusive proof that a toxin is the cause of the disease.

A relatively new theory explores the role of genetic factors in the development of Parkinson's disease. Fifteen to twenty percent of Parkinson's patients have a close relative who has experienced parkinsonian symptoms (such as a tremor). After studies in animals showed that MPTP interferes with the function of mitochondria within nerve cells, investigators became interested in the possibility that impairment in mitochondrial DNA may be the cause of Parkinson's disease. Mitochondria are essential organelles found in all animal cells that convert the energy in food into fuel for the cells.

Yet another theory proposes that Parkinson's disease occurs when, for unknown reasons, the normal, age-related wearing away of dopamine-producing neurons accelerates in certain individuals. This theory is supported by the knowledge that loss of antioxidative protective mechanisms is associated with both Parkinson's disease and increasing age.

Many researchers believe that a combination of these four mechanisms—oxidative damage, environmental toxins, genetic predisposition, and accelerated aging—may ultimately be shown to cause the disease.

Who Gets Parkinson's Disease?

About 50,000 Americans are diagnosed with Parkinson's disease each year, with more than half a million Americans affected at any one time. Getting an accurate count of the number of cases may be impossible however, because many people in the early stages of the disease assume their symptoms are the result of normal aging and do not seek help from a physician. Also, diagnosis is sometimes difficult and uncertain because other conditions may produce some of the symptoms of Parkinson's disease. People with Parkinson's disease may be told by their doctors that they have other disorders or, conversely, people with similar diseases may be initially diagnosed as having Parkinson's disease.

Parkinson's disease strikes men and women in almost equal numbers and it knows no social, economic, or geographic boundaries. Some studies show that African-Americans and Asians are less likely than whites to develop Parkinson's disease. Scientists have not been able to explain this apparent lower incidence in certain populations. It is reasonable to assume, however, that all people have a similar probability of developing the disease.

Age, however, clearly correlates with the onset of symptoms. Parkinson's disease is a disease of late middle age, usually affecting people over the age of 50. The average age of onset is 60 years. However, some physicians have reportedly noticed more cases of "early-onset" Parkinson's disease in the past several years, and some have estimated that 5 to 10 percent of patients are under the age of 40.

What Are the Early Symptoms?

Early symptoms of Parkinson's disease are subtle and occur gradually. Patients may be tired or notice a general malaise. Some may feel a little shaky or have difficulty getting out of a chair. They may notice that they speak too softly or that their handwriting looks cramped and spidery. They may lose track of a word or thought, or they may feel irritable or depressed for no apparent reason. This very early period may last a long time before the more classic and obvious symptoms appear.

Friends or family members may be the first to notice changes. They may see that the person's face lacks expression and animation (known as "masked face") or that the person remains in a certain position for a long time or does not move an arm or leg normally. Perhaps they see that the person seems stiff, unsteady, and unusually slow.

As the disease progresses, the shaking, or tremor, that affects the majority of Parkinson's patients may begin to interfere with daily activities. Patients may not be able to hold utensils steady or may find that the shaking makes reading a newspaper difficult. Parkinson's tremor may become worse when the patient is relaxed. A few seconds after the hands are rested on a table, for instance, the shaking is most pronounced. For most patients, tremor is usually the symptom that causes them to seek medical help.

What Are the Major Symptoms of the Disease?

Parkinson's disease does not affect everyone the same way. In some people the disease progresses quickly, in others it does not. Although some people become severely disabled, others experience only minor motor disruptions. Tremor is the major symptom for some patients, while for others tremor is only a minor complaint and different symptoms are more troublesome.

Tremor. The tremor associated with Parkinson's disease has a characteristic appearance. Typically, the tremor takes the form of a rhythmic back-and-forth motion of the thumb and forefinger at three beats per second. This is sometimes called "pill rolling." Tremor usually begins in a hand, although sometimes a foot or the jaw is affected first. It is most obvious when the hand is at rest or when a person is under stress. In three out of four patients, the tremor may affect only one part or side of the body, especially during the early stages of the disease. Later it may become more general. Tremor is rarely disabling and it usually disappears during sleep or improves with intentional movement.

Rigidity. Rigidity, or a resistance to movement, affects most parkinsonian patients. A major principle of body movement is that all muscles have an opposing muscle. Movement is possible not just because one muscle becomes more active, but because the opposing muscle relaxes. In Parkinson's disease, rigidity comes about when, in response to signals from the brain, the delicate balance of opposing muscles is disturbed.

The muscles remain constantly tensed and contracted so that the person aches or feels stiff or weak. The rigidity becomes obvious when another person tries to move the patient's arm, which will move only in ratchet-like or short, jerky movements known as "cogwheel" rigidity.

Bradykinesia. Bradykinesia, or the slowing down and loss of spontaneous and automatic movement, is particularly frustrating because it is unpredictable. One moment the patient can move easily. The next moment he or she may need help. This may well be the most disabling and distressing symptom of the disease because the patient cannot rapidly perform routine movements. Activities once performed quickly and easily—such as washing or dressing—may take several hours.

Postural instability. Postural instability, or impaired balance and coordination, causes patients to develop a forward or backward lean and to fall easily. When bumped from the front or when starting to walk, patients with a backward lean have a tendency to step backwards, which is known as *retropulsion*. Postural instability can cause patients to have a stooped posture in which the head is bowed and the shoulders are drooped.

As the disease progresses, walking may be affected. Patients may halt in mid-stride and "freeze" in place, possibly even toppling over. Or patients may walk with a series of quick, small steps as if hurrying forward to keep balance. This is known as *festination*.

Are There Other Symptoms?

Various other symptoms accompany Parkinson's disease; some are minor, others are more bothersome. Many can be treated with appropriate medication or physical therapy. No one can predict which symptoms will affect an individual patient, and the intensity of the symptoms also varies from person to person. None of these symptoms is fatal, although swallowing problems can cause choking.

Depression. This is a common problem and may appear early in the course of the disease, even before other symptoms are noticed. Depression may not be severe, but it may be intensified by the drugs used to treat other symptoms of Parkinson's disease. Fortunately, depression can be successfully treated with antidepressant medications.

Emotional changes. Some people with Parkinson's disease become fearful and insecure. Perhaps they fear they cannot cope with new situations. They may not want to travel, go to parties, or socialize with friends. Some lose their motivation and become dependent on family members. Others may become irritable or uncharacteristically pessimistic.

Memory loss and slow thinking may occur, although the ability to reason remains intact. Whether people actually suffer intellectual loss (also known as *dementia*) from Parkinson's disease is a controversial area still being studied.

Difficulty in swallowing and chewing. Muscles used in swallowing may work less efficiently in later stages of the disease. In these cases, food and saliva may collect in the mouth and back of the throat, which can result in choking or drooling. Medications can often alleviate these problems.

Speech changes. About half of all parkinsonian patients have problems with speech. They may speak too softly or in a monotone, hesitate before speaking, slur or repeat their words, or speak too fast. A speech therapist may be able to help patients reduce some of these problems.

Urinary problems or constipation. In some patients bladder and bowel problems can occur due to the improper functioning of the autonomic nervous system, which is responsible for regulating smooth muscle activity. Some people may become incontinent while others have trouble urinating. In others, constipation may occur because the intestinal tract operates more slowly. Constipation can also be caused by inactivity, eating a poor diet, or drinking too little fluid. It can be a persistent problem and, in rare cases, can be serious enough to require hospitalization. Patients should not let constipation last for more than several days before taking steps to alleviate it.

Skin problems. In Parkinson's disease, it is common for the skin on the face to become very oily, particularly on the forehead and at the sides of the nose. The scalp may become oily too, resulting in dandruff. In other cases, the skin can become very dry. These problems are also the result of an improperly functioning autonomic nervous system. Standard treatments for skin problems help. Excessive sweating, another common symptom, is usually controllable with medications used for Parkinson's disease.

Sleep problems. These include difficulty staying asleep at night, restless sleep, nightmares and emotional dreams, and drowsiness during the day. It is unclear if these symptoms are related to the disease or to the medications used to treat Parkinson's disease. Patients should never take over-the-counter sleep aids without consulting their physicians.

What Are the Other Forms of Parkinsonism?

Other forms of parkinsonism include the following:

Postencephalitic parkinsonism. Just after the first World War, a viral disease, encephalitis lethargica, attacked almost 5 million people throughout the world, and then suddenly disappeared in the 1920s. Known as sleeping sickness in the United States, this disease killed one third of its victims and in many others led to post-encephalitic parkinsonism, a particularly severe form of movement disorder in which some patients developed, often years after the acute phase of the illness, disabling neurological disorders, including various forms of catatonia. (In 1973, neurologist Oliver Sacks published *Awakenings*, an account of his work in the late 1960s with surviving postencephalitic patients in a New York hospital. Using the then-experimental drug levodopa, Dr. Sacks was able to temporarily "awaken" these patients from their statue-like state. A film by the same name was released in 1990.) In rare cases, other viral infections, including western equine encephalomyelitis, eastern equine encephalomyelitis, and Japanese B encephalitis, can leave patients with parkinsonian symptoms.

Drug-induced parkinsonism. A reversible form of parkinsonism sometimes results from use of certain drugs—chlorpromazine and haloperidol, for example—prescribed for patients with psychiatric disorders. Some drugs used for stomach disorders (metoclopramide) and high blood pressure (reserpine) may also produce parkinsonian symptoms. Stopping the medication or lowering the dosage causes the symptoms to abate.

Striatonigral degeneration. In this form of parkinsonism, the substantia nigra is only mildly affected, while other brain areas show more severe damage than occurs in patients with primary Parkinson's disease. People with this type of parkinsonism tend to show more rigidity and the disease progresses more rapidly.

Arteriosclerotic parkinsonism. Sometimes known as pseudoparkinsonism, arteriosclerotic parkinsonism involves damage to brain vessels due to multiple small strokes. Tremor is rare in this type of parkinsonism, while *dementia*—the loss of mental skills and abilities—is common. Antiparkinsonian drugs are of little help to patients with this form of parkinsonism.

Toxin-induced parkinsonism. Some toxins—such as manganese dust, carbon disulfide, and carbon monoxide—can also cause parkinsonism. A chemical known as MPTP (1-methyl-4-phenyl-1,2,5,6-tetrahydropyridine) causes a permanent form of parkinsonism that closely resembles Parkinson's disease. Investigators discovered this reaction in the 1980s when heroin addicts in California who had taken an illicit street drug contaminated with MPTP began to develop severe parkinsonism. This discovery, which demonstrated that a toxic substance could damage the brain and produce parkinsonian symptoms, caused a dramatic breakthrough in Parkinson's research: for the first time scientists were able to simulate Parkinson's disease in animals and conduct studies to increase understanding of the disease.

Parkinsonism-dementia complex of Guam. This form occurs among the Chamorro populations of Guam and the Mariana Islands and may be accompanied by a disease resembling amyotrophic lateral sclerosis (Lou Gehrig's disease). The course of the disease is rapid, with death typically occurring within 5 years. Some investigators suspect an environmental cause, perhaps the use of flour from the highly toxic seed of the cycad plant. This flour was a dietary staple for many years when rice and other food supplies were unavailable ·in this region, particularly during World War II. Other studies, however, refute this link.

Parkinsonism accompanying other conditions. Parkinsonian symptoms may also appear in patients with other, clearly distinct neurological disorders such as Shy-Drager syndrome (sometimes called multiple system atrophy), progressive supranuclear palsy, Wilson's disease, Huntington's disease, Hallervorden-Spatz syndrome, Alzheimer's disease, Creutzfeldt-Jakob disease, olivopontocerebellar atrophy, and post-traumatic encephalopathy.

How Do Doctors Diagnose Parkinson's Disease?

Even for an experienced neurologist, making an accurate diagnosis in the early stages of Parkinson's disease can be difficult. There are, as yet, no sophisticated blood or laboratory tests available to diagnose the disease. The physician may need to observe the patient for some time until it is apparent that the tremor is consistently present and is joined by one or more of the other classic symptoms. Since other forms of parkinsonism have similar features but require different treatments, making a precise diagnosis as soon as possible is essential for starting a patient on proper medication.

How is the Disease Treated?

At present, there is no cure for Parkinson's disease. But a variety of medications provide dramatic relief from the symptoms.

When recommending a course of treatment, the physician determines how much the symptoms disrupt the patient's life and then tailors therapy to the person's particular condition. Since no two patients will react the same way to a given drug, it may take time and patience to get the dose just right. Even then, symptoms may not be completely alleviated. In the early stages of Parkinson's disease, physicians often begin treatment with one or a combination of the less powerful drugs—such as the anticholinergics or amantadine (see section below entitled "Are There Other Medications Available for Managing Disease Symptoms?"), saving the most powerful treatment, specifically levodopa, for the time when patients need it most.

Levodopa

Without doubt, the gold standard of present therapy is the drug levodopa (also called L-dopa). L-Dopa (from the full name L-3,4-dihydroxyphenylaianine) is a simple chemical found naturally in plants and animals. Levodopa is the generic name used for this chemical when it is formulated for drug use in patients. Nerve cells can use levodopa to make dopamine and replenish the brain's dwindling supply. Dopamine itself cannot be given because it doesn't cross the blood-brain barrier, the elaborate meshwork of fine blood vessels and cells that filters blood reaching the brain. Usually, patients are given levodopa combined with carbidopa. When added to levodopa, carbidopa delays the conversion of levodopa into dopamine until it reaches the brain, preventing or diminishing some of the side effects that often accompany levodopa therapy. Carbidopa also reduces the amount of levodopa needed.

Levodopa's success in treating the major symptoms of Parkinson's disease is a triumph of modern medicine. First introduced in the 1960s, it delays the onset of debilitating symptoms and allows the majority of parkinsonian patients—who would otherwise be very disabled—to extend the period of time in which they can lead relatively normal, productive lives.

Although levodopa helps at least three-quarters of parkinsonian cases, not all symptoms respond equally to the drug. Bradykinesia and rigidity respond best, while tremor may be only marginally reduced. Problems with balance and other symptoms may not be alleviated at all.

People who have taken other medications before starting levodopa therapy may have to cut back or eliminate these drugs in order to feel the full benefit of levodopa. Once levodopa therapy starts people often respond dramatically, but they may need to increase the dose gradually for maximum benefit.

Because a high-protein diet can interfere with the absorption of levodopa, some physicians recommend that patients taking the drug restrict protein consumption to the evening meal.

Levodopa is so effective that some people may forget they have Parkinson's disease. But levodopa is not a cure. Although it can diminish the symptoms, it does not replace lost nerve cells and it does not stop the progression of the disease.

Side Effects of Levodopa

Although beneficial for thousands of patients, levodopa is not without its limitations and side effects. The most common side effects are nausea, vomiting, low blood pressure, involuntary movements, and restlessness. In rare cases patients may become confused. The nausea and vomiting caused by levodopa are greatly reduced by the combination of levodopa and carbidopa which enhances the effectiveness of a lower dose. A slow-release formulation of this product, which gives patients a longer lasting effect, is also available.

Dyskinesias, or involuntary movements such as twitching, nodding, and jerking, most commonly develop in people who are taking large doses of levodopa over an extended period. These movements may be either mild or severe and either very rapid or very slow. The only effective way to control these drug-induced movements is to lower the dose of levodopa or to use drugs that block dopamine, but these remedies usually cause the disease symptoms to reappear. Doctors and patients must work together closely to find a tolerable balance between the drug's benefits and side effects.

Other more troubling and distressing problems may occur with long-term levodopa use. Patients may begin to notice more pronounced symptoms before their first dose of medication in the morning, and they can feel when each dose begins to wear off (muscle spasms are a common effect). Symptoms gradually begin to return. The period of effectiveness from each dose may begin to shorten, called the *wearing-off effect*. Another potential problem is referred to as the *on-off effect* — sudden, unpredictable changes in movement, from normal to parkinsonian movement and back again, possibly occurring several times during the day. These effects probably indicate that the patient's response to the drug is changing or that the disease is progressing.

One approach to alleviating these side effects is to take levodopa more often and in smaller amounts. Sometimes, physicians instruct patients to stop levodopa for several days in an effort to improve the response to the drug and to manage the complications of long-term levodopa therapy. This controversial technique is known as a "drug holiday." Because of the possibility of serious complications, drug holidays should be attempted only under a physician's direct supervision, preferably in a hospital. Parkinson's disease patients should never stop taking levodopa without their physician's knowledge or consent because of the potentially serious side effects of rapidly withdrawing the drug.

Are There Other Medications Available for Managing Disease Symptoms?

Levodopa is not a perfect drug. Fortunately, physicians have other treatment choices for particular symptoms or stages of the disease. Other therapies include the following:

Bromocriptine and pergolide. These two drugs mimic the role of dopamine in the brain, causing the neurons to react as they would to dopamine. They can be given alone or with levodopa and may be used in the early stages of the disease or started later to lengthen the duration of response to levodopa in patients experiencing wearing-off or on-off effects. They are generally less effective than levodopa in controlling rigidity and bradykinesia. Side effects may include paranoia, hallucinations, confusion, dyskinesias, nightmares, nausea, and vomiting.

Selegiline. Also known as deprenyl, selegiline has become a commonly used drug for Parkinson's disease. Recent studies supported by the NINDS have shown that the drug delays the need for levodopa therapy by up to a year or more. When selegiline is given with levodopa, it appears to enhance and prolong the response to levodopa and thus may reduce wearing-off fluctuations. In studies with animals, selegiline has been shown to protect the dopamine-producing neurons from the toxic effects of MPTP. Selegiline inhibits the activity of the enzyme monoamine oxidase B (MAO-B), the enzyme that metabolizes dopamine in the brain, delaying the breakdown of naturally occurring dopamine and of dopamine formed from levodopa. Dopamine then accumulates in the surviving nerve cells. Some physicians, but not all, favor starting all parkinsonian patients on selegiline because of its possible protective effect. Selegiline is an easy drug to take, although side effects may include nausea, orthostatic hypotension, or insomnia (when taken late in the day). Also, toxic reactions have occurred in some patients who took selegiline with fluoxetine (an antidepressant) and meperidine (used as a sedative and an analgesic).

Research scientists are still trying to answer questions about selegiline use: How long does the drug remain effective? Does long-term use have any adverse effects? Evaluation of the long-term effects will help determine its value for all stages of the disease.

Anticholinergics. These drugs were the main treatment for Parkinson's disease until the introduction of levodopa. Their benefit is limited, but they may help control tremor and rigidity. They are particularly helpful in reducing drug-induced parkinsonism. Anticholinergics appear to act by blocking the action of another brain chemical, acetylcholine, whose effects become more pronounced when dopamine levels drop. Only about half the patients who receive anticholinergics respond, usually for a brief period and with only a 30 percent improvement. Although not as effective as levodopa or bromocriptine, anticholinergics may have a therapeutic effect at any stage of the disease when taken with either of these drugs. Common side effects include dry mouth, constipation, urinary retention, hallucinations, memory loss, blurred vision, changes in mental activity, and confusion.

Amantadine. An antiviral drug, amantadine, helps reduce symptoms of Parkinson's disease. It is often used alone in the early stages of the disease or with an anticholinergic drug or levodopa. After several months amantadine's effectiveness wears off in a third to a half of the patients taking it, although effectiveness may return after a brief withdrawal from the drug. Amantadine has several side effects, including mottled skin, edema, confusion, blurred vision, and depression.

Is Surgery Ever Used to Treat Parkinson's Disease?

Treating Parkinson's disease with surgery was once a common practice. But after the discovery of levodopa, surgery was restricted to only a few cases. One of the procedures used, called *cryothalamotomy*, requires the surgical insertion of a supercooled metal tip of a probe into the thalamus (a "relay station" deep in the brain) to destroy the brain area that produces tremors. This and related procedures are coming back into favor for patients who have severe tremor or have the disease only on one side of the body. Investigators have also revived interest in a surgical procedure called *pallidotomy* in which a portion of the brain called the globus pallidus is lesioned. Some studies indicate that pallidotomy may improve symptoms of tremor, rigidity, and bradykinesia, possibly by interrupting the neural pathway between the globus pallidus and the striatum or thalamus. Further research on the value of surgically destroying these brain areas is currently being conducted.

Can Diet or Exercise Programs Help Relieve Symptoms?

Diet. Eating a well-balanced, nutritious diet can be beneficial for anybody. But for preventing or curing Parkinson's disease, there does not seem to be any specific vitamin, mineral, or other nutrient that has any therapeutic value. A high protein diet, however, may limit levodopa's effectiveness.

Despite some early optimism, recent studies have shown that tocopherol (a form of vitamin E) does not delay Parkinson's disease. This conclusion came from a carefully conducted study supported by the NINDS called DATATOP (Deprenyl and Tocopherol Antioxidative Therapy for Parkinson's Disease) that examined, over 5 years, the effects of both deprenyl (selegiline) and vitamin E on early Parkinson's disease. While deprenyl was found to slow the early symptomatic progression of the disease and delay the need for levodopa, there was no evidence of therapeutic benefit from vitamin E.

Exercise. Because movements are affected in Parkinson's disease, exercising may help people improve their mobility. Some doctors prescribe physical therapy or muscle-strengthening exercises to tone muscles and to put underused and rigid muscles through a full range of motion. Exercises will not stop disease progression, but they may improve body strength so that the person is less disabled. Exercises also improve balance, helping people overcome gait problems, and can strengthen certain muscles so that people can speak and swallow better. Exercises can also improve the emotional well-being of parkinsonian patients by giving them a feeling of accomplishment. Although structured exercise programs help many patients more general physical activity, such as walking, gardening, swimming, calisthenics, and using exercise machines, is also beneficial.

What Are the Benefits of Support Groups?

One of the most demoralizing aspects of the disease is how completely the patient's world changes. The most basic daily routines may be affected—from socializing with friends and enjoying normal and congenial relationships with family members to earning a living and taking care of a home. Faced with a very different life, people need encouragement to remain as active and involved as possible. That's when support groups can be of particular value to parkinsonian patients, their families, and their caregivers.

A list of national volunteer organizations that can help patients locate support groups in their communities appears at the end of this chapter.

Can Scientists Predict or Prevent Parkinson's Disease?

As yet, there is no way to predict or prevent the disease. However, researchers are now looking for a biomarker—a biochemical abnormality that all patients with Parkinson's disease might share—that could be picked up by screening techniques or by a simple chemical test given to people who do not have any parkinsonian symptoms.

Positron emission tomography (PET) scanning may lead to important advances in our knowledge about Parkinson's disease. PET scans of the brain produce pictures of chemical changes as they occur in the living brain. Using PET, research scientists can study the brain's dopamine receptors (the sites on nerve cells that bind with dopamine) to determine if the loss of dopamine activity follows or precedes degeneration of the neurons that make this chemical. This information could help scientists better understand the disease process and may potentially lead to improved treatments.

What Research is Being Done?

In the last decade research has laid the groundwork for many of today's promising new clinical trials, technologies, and drug treatments. Scientists, physicians, and patients hope that today's progress means tomorrow's cure and prevention.

Parkinson's disease research focuses on many areas. Some investigators are studying the functions and anatomy of the motor system and how it regulates movement and relates to major command centers in the brain. Scientists looking for the cause of Parkinson's disease will continue to search for possible environmental factors, such as toxins that may trigger the disorder, and to study genetic factors to determine if one or many defective genes play a role. Although Parkinson's disease is not directly inherited, it is possible that some people are genetically more or less susceptible to developing it. Other scientists are working to develop new protective drugs that can delay, prevent, or reverse the disease.

Since the accidental discovery that MPTP causes parkinsonian symptoms in humans, scientists have found that by injecting MPTP into laboratory animals, they can reproduce the brain lesions that cause these symptoms. This allows them to study the mechanisms of the disease and helps in the development of new treatments. For instance, it was from animal studies that researchers discovered that the drug selegiline can prevent the toxic effects of MPTP. This discovery helped spark interest in studying selegiline as a preventive treatment in humans.

Scientists are also investigating the role of mitochondria, structures in cells that provide the energy for cellular activity, in Parkinson's disease. Because MPTP interferes with the function of mitochondria within nerve cells, some scientists suspect that similar abnormalities may be involved in Parkinson's disease.

Today, an array of promising research involves studying brain areas other than the substantia nigra that may be involved in the disease. One group of NINDS-supported scientists is studying the consequences of dopamine cell degeneration in the basal ganglia—brain structures located deep in the forebrain that help control voluntary movement. In laboratory animals, MPTP-induced reduction of dopamine results in overactivity of nerve cells in a region of the brain called the subthalamic nucleus, producing tremors and rigidity and suggesting that these symptoms may be related to excessive activity in this region. Destroying the subthalamic nucleus results in a reversal of parkinsonian symptoms in the animal models.

Scientists supported by the NINDS are also looking for clues to the cause of Parkinson's disease by studying malfunctions in the structures called "dopamine transporters" that carry dopamine in and out of the synapse, or narrow gap between nerve cells. For example, one research group recently found an age-related decrease in the concentration of dopamine transporters in healthy human nerve cells taken from areas of the brain damaged by Parkinson's. This decline in transporter concentration means that any further threat to the remaining dopamine transporters could result in Parkinson's disease.

The search for more effective medications for Parkinson's disease is likely to be aided by the recent isolation of at least five individual brain receptors for dopamine. New information about the unique effects of each individual dopamine receptor on different brain areas has led to new treatment theories and clinical trials.

Scientists are also studying new methods for delivering dopamine to critical areas in the brain. NINDS-supported investigators, using an animal model of the disease, implanted tiny dopamine-containing particles into brain regions affected by the disease. They found that such implants can partially ameliorate the movement problems exhibited by these animals. The results suggest that similar techniques may one day work for people with Parkinson's disease.

A recent study revealed that when the experimental drug Ro 40-7592 is added to the standard drug treatment for Parkinson's disease, levodopa-carbidopa, symptom relief is prolonged by more than 60 percent. Although levodopa-carbidopa restores normal movement early in the disease's course, the treatment loses effectiveness as the disease progresses (wearing-off effect). NINDS scientists found, however, that patients treated with both levodopa-carbidopa and Ro 40-7592 experienced longer periods of improved movement. This promising new drug that blocks the breakdown of dopamine and levodopa would allow patients to take fewer doses and smaller

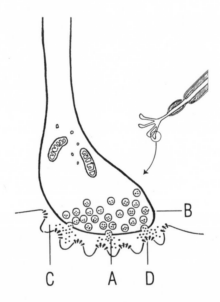

Figure 33.2. *This drawing shows the release of neurochemicals (A), such as dopamine, from the end of the neuron (B) into the synapse (C)—the place where a signal passes from the neuron to another cell. Neurochemicals cross the synapse and attach to neuroreceptors (D) on neighboring cells. Scientists are searching for clues to the cause of Parkinson's disease by studying malfunctions in structures called dopamine transporters that carry dopamine in and out of the synapse.*

amounts of levodopa-carbidopa and to decrease the problems of the wearing-off effect. At the present time, Ro 40-7592 is still in the experimental stage. Scientists are continuing to study the drug to learn whether it can be given in multiple daily doses to provide even further improvement.

Also under investigation are additional controlled-release formulas of Parkinson's disease drugs and implantable pumps that give a continuous supply of levodopa to help patients who have problems with fluctuating levels of response. Another promising treatment method involves implanting capsules containing dopamine-producing cells into the brain. The capsules are surrounded by a biologically inert membrane that lets the drug pass through at a timed rate.

Neural grafting, or transplantation of nerve cells, is an experimental technique proposed for treating the disease. NINDS-supported investigators have shown in animal models that implanting fetal brain tissue from the substantia nigra into a parkinsonian brain causes damaged nerve cells to regenerate. In January 1994, the NINDS awarded a research grant to a group of scientists from three institutions to conduct a controlled clinical trial of fetal tissue implants in humans. The treatment attempts to replace the lost or damaged dopamine-producing neurons with healthy, fetal neurons, and thereby improve movement and response to medications. A new and promising approach may be the use of genetically engineered cells—that is, cells such as modified skin cells that do not come from the nervous system but are grown in tissue culture—that could have the same beneficial effects. Skin cells would be much easier to harvest and patients could serve as their own donors.

What is the Role of the NINDS?

As a world leader in research on neurological disorders, including Parkinson's disease, the NINDS supports a wide range of basic laboratory studies and clinical trials at its Bethesda, Maryland, location and at grantee institutions around the world. Current research programs funded by the NINDS include using animal models to study how the disease progresses, developing new drug therapies, and implanting tissue in animals and humans. Through these and other research projects, scientists are moving ever closer to unraveling the mysteries of Parkinson's disease. For patients and families of patients, this research should offer encouragement and hope for the future.

The Institute also sponsors an active information program that provides patients and the general public with educational materials and research highlights. Among the NINDS publications that may be of interest to those concerned about Parkinson's disease is "Know Your Brain," an 8-page fact sheet that explains how the healthy brain works tute's address and phone number, as well as information on other organizations that offer various services to those affected by Parkinson's disease, are provided in the "Information Resources" section below.

What Can I Do to Help?

The NINDS and the National Institute of Mental Health jointly support two national brain specimen banks. These banks supply research scientists around the world with nervous system tissue from patients with neurological and psychiatric disorders. They need tissue from patients with Parkinson's disease so that scientists can study and understand the disorder. Those who may be interested in donating should write to:

Dr. Wallace W. Tourtellotte, Director
National Neurological Research Specimen Bank
VAMC-West Los Angeles
11301 Wilshire Boulevard
Los Angeles, CA 90073
(310) 824-4307

Dr. Edward D. Bird, Director
Brain Tissue Resource Center
McLean Hospital
115 Mill Street
Belmont, MA 02178
(617) 855-2400
1-800-BRAIN-BANK (1-800-272-4622)

Two organizations, not funded by the NINDS, also provide research scientists with nervous system tissue from patients with neurological disorders. Interested donors should write or call:

National Disease Research Interchange (NDRI)
1880 JFK Boulevard
6th Floor
Philadelphia, PA 19103
(215) 557-7361
1-800-222-NDRI (1-800-222-6374)

University of Miami Brain Endowment Bank
Department of Neurology (D4-5)
1501 NW 9th Avenue
Miami, FL 33136
(305) 547-6219
1-800-UM-BRAIN (1-800-86-27246)

Information Resources

NIH Neurological Institute
P.O. Box 5801
Bethesda, MD 20824
(301) 496-5751
1-800-352-9424

The National Institute of Neurological Disorders and Stroke, a component of the National Institutes of Health, is the leading Federal supporter of research on disorders of the brain and nervous system. The Institute also sponsors an active public information program and can answer questions about diagnosis, treatment, and research related to Parkinson's disease.

Private voluntary organizations that provide the public with information on treatment, diagnosis, and services include the following:

American Parkinson Disease Association
1250 Hylan Blvd.
Staten Island, NY 10305
(718) 981-8001
800-223-APDA (800-223-2732)

This association funds research; sponsors support groups, symposia, and information and referral centers; and publishes a newsletter and other educational manuals.

National Parkinson Foundation, Inc.
1501 N.W. 9th Avenue (Bob Hope Road)
Miami, FL 33136-1494
(305) 547-6666
1-800-327-4545 (in Florida 1-800-433-7022)

This foundation supports research, clinical services, and physical, occupational, speech, and psychological therapies. It also offers public education, disseminates information by means of its brochures, and raises public awareness of Parkinson's disease.

Parkinson's Disease Foundation
650 West 168th Street
New York, NY 10032-9982
(212) 923-4700
1-800-457-6676

This foundation supports research; promotes the formation of support groups; and offers professional training fellowships and symposia, patient and professional information, counseling, advocacy, and referral.

The Parkinson's Institute
1170 Morse Avenue
Sunnyvale, CA 94089-1605
(408) 734-2800

This foundation operates a clinic and research facility, publishes a newsletter, and offers many services for patients and their families.

Parkinson's Support Groups of America
11376 Cherry Hill Road, # 204
Beltsville, MD 20705
(301) 937-1545

This organization promotes research; maintains a library; and sponsors a speakers' bureau, support groups, and an annual convention. The organization also offers a variety of services and programs for the public.

United Parkinson Foundation
833 West Washington Boulevard
Chicago, IL 60607
(312) 733-1893

This foundation funds research; offers information for patients, families, and professionals; and publishes a newsletter, brochures, and fact sheets.

Chapter 34

Parkinson's Disease: Diagnosis and Drug Therapies

Introduction

Parkinson's disease is a progressive neurodegenerative condition of unknown cause and with no known cure. The diagnosis is based on clinical findings of rest tremor, muscle rigidity, bradykinesia, and gait instability. Over 40% of patients develop a dementia syndrome that is largely distinct from Alzheimer's disease. Depression is common, also occurring in more than 40% of patients with PD. Careful evaluation is necessary to help distinguish Parkinson's disease from secondary causes of parkinsonism. Carbidopa/levodopa, dopamine agonists, and monoamine oxidase type B inhibitors are the mainstays of treatment. Anticholinergics and other agents may also be useful. Pharmacologic treatment must be carefully titrated to control symptoms and to avoid side effects. In advanced disease, dose-related dyskinesias, end-of-dose wearing-off effect, and unpredictable sudden motor fluctuations become very disabling and difficult to manage.

Example

Mrs. Cavanaugh is only 55, but as she shuffles into the examination room you can see there's something wrong. Her face seems frozen without expression, and you have to lean closer to hear her faint answer to your greeting. You glance at her name and address on the patient history form and note that her handwriting is small and cramped. Your first impression: Parkinson's disease (PD). Parkinsonism is a clinical syndrome comprised of a tremor at rest, rigidity, bradykinesia, and gait instability. When this syndrome results from a specific degenerative disorder, it is called PD; when it results from other definable diseases, it is called secondary or symptomatic parkinsonism. In this chapter, we discuss the clinical workup of the patient with suspected PD—what to look for and how to exclude other diagnoses. Once the diagnosis is confirmed, we discuss the challenge of tailoring drug therapy to control symptoms and avoid side effects in both the newly-diagnosed and later-stage patient.

Parkinson's Disease: Clinical Background

Parkinson's disease affects about 1 million Americans, most over the age of 50, according to the American Parkinson Disease Association, Inc. The age-specific incidence peaks around age 70 and then declines,[1] whereas the age-specific prevalence increases almost exponentially for ages beyond 65, affecting 1 to 2% of the population over age 80. Men and women are equally likely to develop PD.

For secondary parkinsonism, incidence and prevalence rates vary widely according to the underlying disorders (*see* Table 34.1). Drug-induced parkinsonism and arteriosclerotic parkinsonism are the most common, whereas many of the neurodegenerative diseases are rare.

Clinical Course

PD is a progressive degenerative condition resulting in a gradual worsening of symptoms. The progressive immobility of PD patients makes them susceptible to infection and inanition. Untreated PD patients progress to death within 8 to 10 years, whereas treatment extends their survival to about 15 years following diagnosis.

Etiology

The etiology of PD is unknown. Viral infections, premature aging, environmental toxins, and genetic factors have all been suggested as potential causes. Von Economo's encephalitis, an epidemic caused by a viral agent that occurred in the early 20th century, often resulted in a syndrome that was very similar to PD.

Early onset of PD has been associated with living in rural areas of industrialized nations, suggesting exposure to an environmental

Table 34.1. Causes of Secondary Parkinsonism

Cause	Examples
Atherosclerosis	
Degeneration	Basal ganglia calcification (Fahr's disease)
	Cortical Lewy body disease
	Olivopontocerebellar atrophy
	Parkinson-dementia complex (of Guam)
	Progressive supranuclear palsy (PSP)
	Shy-Drager syndrome
	Striatonigral degeneration
	Wilson's disease
Drug-induced	Antipsychotics
	Lithium
	Metoclopramide
	Methyldopa
	Reserpine
Endocrine	Hypoparathyroidism
	Hypothyroidism
Hydrocephalus, normal pressure	
Infection	AIDS
	Jakob-Creutzfeldt disease
	Pbsi-encephalitic (Von Economo's)
Intoxication	Carbon monoxide
	Manganese
	Methylphanyltetrahydropyridine (MPTP)
Traumatic encephelopathy	
Tumors, basal ganglia	Arteriovenous malformations
	Neoplasms

Source: Prepared for Geriatrics by Douglas W. Scharre, MD, and Michael E. Mahler, MD.

toxin.[2] An example of a toxin causing parkinsonism is methylphenyl-tetrahydropyridine (MPTP), a byproduct of a synthetic narcotic.[3] MPTP is transformed by monoamine oxidase type B to the free radical species MPP+, which selectively enters and destroys cells in the substantia nigra and locus ceruleus. It is possible that similar environmental toxins may produce PD in individuals who have an inherited vulnerability to these toxins.[4]

Finally, despite the fact that PD appears to be a sporadic disease with occasional familial incidence, genetic factors may play a role, possibly through the mitochondrial DNA.[5]

Pathology

In PD, there is a loss of pigmented neurons and the appearance of intraneuronal Lewy bodies in the pars compacta of the substantia nigra and in the ventral tegmental area (VTA). These changes result in the denervation of both the nigrostriatal and VTA-mesocortical dopaminergic pathways. Denervation in noradrenergic pathways to the cortex also occur secondary to neuronal loss in the locus ceruleus. However, dopamine deficiency in the striatum is the major factor in the pathogenesis of PD and secondary parkinsonism. Clinical symptoms begin when there is approximately 80% depletion of the striatal dopamine.

Diagnosis of PD: The Cardinal Signs

The diagnosis of PD is based on clinical findings. The cardinal signs of PD are the resting tremor, rigidity, bradykinesia, and gait instability. Although more than one-half of all PD patients present with a tremor, the other features of the disease are usually present at the time of diagnosis. PD is often mildly asymmetric at the outset, but it generally evolves to affect both sides of the body relatively equally. The tremor frequency is typically between 4 and 7 Hz and consists of coarse, alternating agonist-antagonist muscle movements. It is a rest tremor that is present when the patient is alert but not moving volitionally. With purposeful movements, the tremor decreases. In addition, it is not uncommon for some PD patients to have a high frequency, low amplitude action tremor.

To test for tremor, have the patient rest his arms on his legs while sitting. Observe for resting tremor on one or both sides. Note the frequency and amplitude, and watch for changes when the arms are then lifted straight away from the body.

Muscle rigidity, an increase in resistance to passive stretching, occurs throughout the range of motion. The cogwheel phenomenon results from the resting tremor superimposed on the muscle rigidity. Rigidity is also evident in the typical posture of PD patients: flexion of the neck and trunk, flexion of the arms, hips, and knees. Despite the rigidity, there is no loss of muscle strength.

In the patient examination, check the muscle tone in all four extremities and the neck to assess the degree of rigidity and to feel for "cogwheeling." The rigidity becomes more pronounced with activating procedures. Ask the patient to draw a large square in the air with a finger or toe while you are assessing muscle tone in the opposite extremity.

Bradykinesia literally means slow-moving and is probably the earliest and most disabling feature of PD.[6] PD patients have difficulty initiating movements and are slowed in all volitional and many involuntary acts. Bradykinesia and paucity of movements cause:

- the mask-like, expressionless face (decreased eye-blink and emotional grimace)
- drooling (the result of decreased swallowing)
- hypophonia (soft, mumbled speech)
- micrographia (small, illegible handwriting).

Abnormal gait and postural instability occur frequently. The typical gait for a patient with PD consists of:

- a forward stooped posture
- shortened, shuffling steps (marche a petits pas)
- decreased arm-swing
- tendency to propel forwards with increasing speed (Destination).

To test for postural instability, stand behind the patient and quickly pull backward on his shoulders. The appropriately prepared patient will typically start to fall or adjust the feet in order to maintain an upright posture.

When turning, the patient does not pivot but takes several small steps and turns en bloc. The balance is unsteady when turning and numerous falls may result. This imbalance can be severe enough to impair standing and even unsupported sitting.

Patients may also experience autonomic nervous system dysfunction resulting in hyperhidrosis, orthostatic hypotension, impotence, constipation, and incontinence. Many PD patients also complain of insomnia.

Neurobehavioral Symptoms: Dementia, Depression

Although James Parkinson originally wrote that "the senses and intellects [are] uninjured" in PD, most contemporary investigations demonstrate that many patients exhibit cognitive decline. PD pathology without evidence of any concurrent Alzheimer features is sufficient to cause the intellectual decline. More than 40% of PD patients have an obvious dementia syndrome, whereas more than 90% have subtle but measurable neuropsychological deficits.[7]

Dementia is most common in patients with postural instability and gait disturbance and least common in patients with marked tremor.[8] Although the pattern of cognitive deficits can be varied, this dementia is largely distinct from Alzheimer's dementia.[9]

Many of those with intellectual loss display a subcortical dementia syndrome characterized by poor retrieval memory, slowing of information processing, difficulty with frontal lobe-executive tasks, and sparing of language function. The intellectual decline is insidious and gradual. Some PD patients probably have Alzheimer's disease as well.[10]

Depression is common, affecting 40 to 60% of PD patients. It is often highlighted with anxiety but does not correlate well with disease severity or disability. In some cases, the depression could represent a psychological response to disability. However, many studies suggest that depression in PD is related to the loss of frontal dopaminergic projections.

Depression in PD patients typically responds to treatment with conventional tricyclic antidepressants or electroconvulsive therapy. Nortriptyline HCI (Aventyl, Pamelor), desipramine HCI (Norpramin, Pertofrane), and imipramine HCI (Janimine, Tofranil) have all proven to be efficacious. The usual dose is about one-half that used in depressed patients without PD. Medications should be continued for 9 to 12 months for maximal effectiveness.

The anticholinergic properties of the tricyclics may improve tremor and rigidity symptoms in some patients but may cause worsening of cognition in those who are also demented. Trazodone HCI (Desyrel) may be useful for patients with both depression and dementia.

Differential Diagnosis: Secondary Causes

Secondary causes of parkinsonism may be difficult to differentiate from PD. Resting tremor is less prominent or absent in many of these conditions. Although the diagnosis of PD is based on clinical findings, laboratory evaluations including serum chemistries, thyroid function tests, heavy metal screens, and brain imaging may be indicated in newly-diagnosed patients to differentiate those with secondary parkinsonism.

Marked asymmetry of symptoms, limb weakness, and abnormal reflexes are likely to be present in arteriosclerotic parkinsonism. In progressive supranuclear palsy (PSP), patients have supranuclear ophthalmoplegia, pseudobulbar palsy, and axial rigidity in addition to parkinsonism.

Some of the other degenerative conditions are multisystem disorders that display combinations of extrapyramidal, corticospinal, spinocerebellar, and autonomic dysfunction. The multisystem atrophies generally have a more rapid progression, a tendency for familial inheritance, and a poor response to levodopa.[11] In drug-induced parkinsonism, the symptoms may linger as long as 6 months after removal of the offending agent.

Drug Therapy: Symptom Control and Side Effects

Antiparkinson pharmacologic treatment is necessary when the tremor and bradykinesia begin to interfere with the patient's occupational and social functioning, independence, and self-care activities. Drug therapy must be carefully titrated to control symptoms and to avoid side effects.

Anticholinergics

For patients younger than age 65 with mild symptoms, anticholinergic medications help to restore the balance between the decreased dopamine levels and the normal levels of acetylcholine within the striatum. Anticholinergics help with drooling and are more effective for the resting tremor than for rigidity or bradykinesia.

Amantadine (Symadine, Symmetrel) increases the release of dopamine in the brain. In the treatment of early PD, both amantadine and anticholinergic medications have been used alone or in combination with carbidopa/levodopa (Sinemet) for additive effects. However, because of the high incidence of serious side effects from anticholinergics and amantadine, these agents should be used with caution—if at all—in patients age 65 and older.

Selegiline

The secondary parkinsonism seen with MPTP sparked the development of neuroprotective therapy for PD. Selegiline HCl (Eldepryl) selectively inhibits monoamine oxidase type B and protects pretreated animals then exposed to MPTP from developing parkinsonism by blocking its conversion to the toxic free radical MPP+.

Several randomized placebo-controlled studies in humans have concluded that selegiline delays the need for levodopa for up to 9 months in early PD.[12,13] It is not clear yet whether this benefit will be apparent throughout the course of the illness.[14]

All newly diagnosed PD patients should be started on selegiline for its potential neuroprotective effect, and levodopa should be added later only if symptoms are disabling. The effective dose of selegiline is 5 mg bid, with the second dose in the early afternoon to avoid insomnia. No dietary restrictions are necessary.

Carbidopa/Levodopa

Dopamine replacement has been the mainstay of treatment for PD. The combination of levodopa and carbidopa (Sinemet) is the most efficient way to get dopamine into the brain. Dopamine does not pass the blood-brain barrier, but levodopa does, and it is converted in the brain to dopamine through decarboxylation. Carbidopa inhibits only the peripheral decarboxylation of levodopa, thereby reducing the peripheral side effects and enhancing the availability of dopamine in the brain. Levodopa is dramatically effective; bradykinesia and rigidity improve markedly, whereas tremor responds variably.

The usual initial dose of carbidopa/levodopa for middle-age adults is a 25/100 tablet three times a day. However, elderly patients—who are most sensitive to side effects—should start with one-half tablet twice a day and increase the dose every week by increments of one-half to one tablet.

The serum half-life of levodopa is 3 hours, so a more frequent schedule is necessary as the daily dose increases while titrating to an optimal effect. Substitute the 10/100 or 25/250 carbidopa/levodopa tablets when the dose exceeds six of the 25/100 tablets a day, because only 75 to 100 mg/day of carbidopa is needed to maximally inhibit peripheral decarboxylation.

The immediate side effects of levodopa include nausea, dizziness, confusion, and psychosis. These are limited by careful titration of the dose. After several years of therapy, the response to levodopa changes and dose-related dyskinesias (chorea, dystonia, myoclonus), end-of-dose wearing-off effect, and unpredictable sudden fluctuations between mobility and immobility (the "on-off" phenomenon) can emerge.[15] These complications may be caused by progression of the illness, altered pharmacokinetics, or receptor changes. The use of the lowest dose that controls symptoms early in the disease may forestall the development of these disabling and difficult-to-manage response fluctuations.

The controlled-release preparation of carbidopa/levodopa (Sinemet-CR, 50/200), helps to reduce the wearing-off phenomenon but may increase dyskinesias.[16] Because the controlled-release preparation takes longer to reach maximum plasma levels, a standard tablet may also be required to control symptoms, especially with the first dose of the day.

Dopamine Agonists

When a levodopa dosage of 1,000 mg/d is not sufficient to control the symptoms, add a dopamine agonist such as bromocriptine mesylate (Parlodel) or pergolide mesylate (Permax). Used alone, dopamine agonists have less antiparkinson effect than levodopa, but they have a longer duration of action. In combination with levodopa, these agents appear no more effective than levodopa alone in new onset PD. However, they may improve efficacy and smooth out the motor fluctuations that appear after the patient has had PD for several years.[18] Dopamine agonists and levodopa have similar side effects, so dosing them apart in time or reducing their dosage will help decrease these effects.

Nondrug Therapies: Maximizing Function

Dietary factors can affect the clinical response to levodopa. Neutral amino acids in proteins compete with levodopa for absorption across the intestinal mucosa and for active transport across the blood-brain barrier.[19]

Patients may avoid fluctuating responses to levodopa by taking the dose at least 30 minutes before meals. Reducing protein intake to the minimum daily allowance or eating most of the day's protein at the evening meal—when motor fluctuations are most tolerable—can also be beneficial.

Calcium supplementation may be necessary for protein-restricted diets. An alternative to protein restriction or redistribution is a diet with a carbohydrate-to-protein ratio of up to 7 to 1, as carbohydrate loads tend to reduce circulating amino acid levels.

Other important ways to maximize patient function include:

- regular exercise to counteract physical disability

- hearing and vision care to avoid social and sensory deprivation

- education concerning disease progression, complications of drug treatments, and neurobehavioral symptoms to help prepare the patient or caregiver for declining or fluctuating abilities

- individual psychotherapy or support groups to help patients and family deal with feelings of loss, grief, and guilt.

Conclusion

Because there is no known cure for PD, its management focuses on the control of symptoms and the avoidance of drug side effects. By individualizing therapy and making changes in drugs and dosages as needed, the primary care physician aims to increase the span of independent function. Neurologic consultation should be obtained to assist with proper diagnosis in atypical presentations and to help with management of fluctuating motor responses to treatment and neurobehavioral symptoms. Research for a more definitive treatment of PD continues. Surgical transplantations of adrenal medulla tissue were not very successful and were plagued by comphcations.[20] However, transplantation of catecholaminergic cells from fetal brain tissue into the striatum may decrease the severity of PD and increase the effectiveness of levodopa.[21]

References

1. Schoenberg BS. Epidemiology of movement disorders. In: Marsden CD, Fahn S, eds. *Movement disorders (2nd ed)*. London: Butterworth, 1987:7-32.

2. Stern M, Dulaney E, Gruber S, *et al*. The epidemiology of Parkinson's disease: A case-control study of young onset and old onset patients. *Arch Neural* 1991; 48:903-7.

3. Langston JW, Ballard P, Tetrud JW, Irwin I. Chronic parkinsonism in humans due to a product of meperidine-analog synthesis. *Science* 1983; 219:979-80.

4. Jenner P, Schapira AHV, Marsden CD. New insights into the cause of Parkinson's disease. *Neurology* 1992; 42:2241-50.

5. Jankovic I. Theories on the etiology and pathogenesis of Parkinson's disease. *Neurology* 1993; 43(suppl 1):21-3.

6. Watts RL, Mandir AS, Ahn KJ, Juncos JL, Zakers GO, Freeman A. Electrophysiologic analysis of early Parkinson's disease. *Neurology* 1991; 41(suppl 2):44-8.

7. Cummings JL. Intellectual impairment in Parkinson's disease: Clinical, pathologic, and biochemical correlates. *Geriatr Psychiatry Neural* 1988; 1:24-36.

8. Jankovic I, McDermott M, Carter J, *et al*. Parkinson Study Group. Variable expression of Parkinson's disease: A baseline analysis of the DATATOP cohort. *Neurology* 1990; 40:1529-34.

9. Mahler ME, Cummings JL. Alzheimer disease and the dementia of Parkinson disease: Comparative investigations. *Alzheimer Dis Assoc Disord* 1990; 4:133-49.

10. Hakim AM, Mathieson G. Dementia in Parkinson's disease: A neuropathologic study. *Neurology* 1979; 29:1209-14.

11. Langston JW, Koller WC, Giron LT. Etiology of Parkinson's disease. In: Olanow CW, Lieberman AN, eds. *The scientific basis for the treatment of Parkinson's disease*. Park Ridge, NJ. Parthenon Publishing Group, 1992:33-58.

12. Myllyla VV, Sotaniemi KA, Vuorinen JA, Heinonen EH. Selegiline as initial treatment in de novo parkinsonian patients. *Neurology* 1992; 42:339-43.

13. The Parkinson Study Group. Effects of tocopherol and deprenyl on the progression of disability in early Parkinson's disease. *N Engl J Med* 1993; 328:176-83.

14. Olanow CW, Caine D. Does selegiline monotherapy in Parkinson's disease act by symptomatic or protective mechanisms? *Neurology* 1991; 42(suppl 4):13-26.

15. Jankovic J. Natural course and limitations of levodopa therapy. *Neurology* 1993, 43(suppl 1):14-7.

16. Sage JI, Mark M. Comparison of controlled-release Sinemet (CR4) and standard Sinemet (25 mg/100 mg) in advanced Parkinson's disease: A double-blind, crossover study. *Clin Neuropharmacol* 1988; 11:174-9.

17. Weiner WJ, Factor SA, Sanchez-Ramos JR, *et al*. Early combination therapy (bromocriptine and levodopa) does not prevent

motor fluctuations in Parkinson's disease. *Neurology* 1993; 43:21-7.

18. Goetz CG. Dopaminergic agonists in the treatment of Parkinson's disease. *Neurology* 1990; (Suppl 3):50-4.

19. Kempster PA, Wahlquist ML. Dietary factors in the management a Parkinson's disease. *Nutr Rev* 1994; 52:51-8.

20. Olanow CW, Koller WC, Goetz CG, *et al*. Autologous transplantation of adrenal medulla in Parkinson's disease: 18-month results. *Arch Neural* 1990; 47:1286-9.

21. Fahn S. Fetal-tissue transplants in Parkinson's disease. *N Engl J Med* 1992; 327:1589-90.

— by Douglas W. Scharre and Michael E. Mahler

Dr. Scharre was a neurobehavior fellow and clinical instructor, UCLA School of Medicine, when this article was written. He is now assistant professor of neurology, department of neurology, Ohio State University, Columbus. Dr. Mahler is director, Neurobehavior Unit, West Los Angeles VA Medical Center and associate clinical professor of neurology, UCLA School of Medicine, Reed Neurological Research Center, Los Angeles. This article was supported by a National Institute on Aging training grant and the Department of Veterans Affairs.

Chapter 35

Parkinson's Disease: Adapting to a Nursing Home

Even in the best of circumstances, residing in a nursing home can bring overwhelming challenges, and when you add a chronic progressive neurological disease such as Parkinson's disease (PD), the challenges add up and may seem insurmountable. The word "challenge" can be defined as: to take a stand against or to confront boldly and courageously. The challenges that come with being a resident with PD in a nursing home are surmountable when appropriately confronted. To accomplish this, one must be educated about the issues, willing to educate others, take a stand when needed, and be patient, creative and adaptable. One must also be willing to look at the changing family roles and at the issues that come to the forefront when adapting to these changes.

The number of people living to an older age continues to increase: 43% of Americans age 65 or older will spend some time in a long term facility, and 50% of the stays in a long term facility will average 2.6 years. Even if you don't end up needing nursing home care, it is likely you will be involved with someone who does. Nursing homes are staffed with a minimal number of professional people and many of the staff members may not have experience with chronic diseases. The nursing assistants are often transient individuals within the nursing home industry, and even with training being done by the nursing home administration, it is an uphill battle to provide skilled care.

Those in administration have dealt with the problem by making nursing homes more institutional: a classic example is medications given only at set times.

Individualized Care

How important is individualized care to the person with PD? Parkinson's disease manifests itself differently among those affected. The goal in its treatment is: decrease symptoms, increase mobility, and improve quality of living. The uniqueness of the symptoms of the disease in each person leads to the need for care tailored to that person. Fine tuning can take a while and be challenging and/or frustrating to all involved. A former American Parkinson Disease Association (APDA) I & R [Information and Referral] Center Coordinator, Glenda Whitsett, gave the following scenario:

Bob has PD and is a nursing home resident. He has an order for Sinemet 25/100 T.I.D (T.I.D. means three times a day, dividing the patient's waking hours). Bob gets his medications at 7 a.m. (with breakfast), 2 p.m., and 9 p.m. Bob wakes up stiff and rigid and is unable to feed himself. The aide cheerfully places a bib on Bob and feeds him. He feels humiliated but is unable to express himself clearly because his speech is also affected by PD. Bob pushes the food away after only a few bites and motions the aide out of the room. Confused and offended by his seemingly rude behavior, the aide leaves the room. A few minutes later, the nurse comes and gives Bob his medication. Since his breakfast is over, it is time to bathe and change linens. The medication is taking a while to "kick in," especially on top of a fat and protein laden meal of bacon and eggs. Bob is still stiff and cannot get out of bed to shower, so he is given a sponge bath. He is cross and barely cooperative. After his bath, it takes two aides on either side of him to safely move Bob into a chair next to his bed. By now, Bob is beginning to loosen up and can dress himself with assistance. Within another 30 minutes, he can walk down the hall. Physically, he is now able to interact with others and participate in activities, but emotionally Bob is angry, frustrated, and depressed, so he chooses to isolate himself. By noon his medication is wearing off. In an effort to maintain some dignity, he insists on feeding himself lunch, but because of the tremor and rigidity, he manages little more than a few bites. By 2 p.m. he is once again very stiff and rigid. His speech is also impaired again so he avoids talking to others. He sits alone in his room and waits for his Sinemet. The evening meal is easier since he has had Sinemet on board for about three hours. By 7 p.m. though, it is wearing off, movements are quite difficult, speech is barely audible. Once again he goes to his room alone. At 8 p.m., it is time to get ready for bed, but Bob's tremor and stiffness make it impossible to unbutton his shirt, wash his face, or even brush his teeth without assistance. It is 9 p.m. and his last dose of Sinemet comes and he goes to bed. However, his sleep is fitful (a common side effect of Sinemet). Restraints are used to prevent him from falling from his bed due to his thrashing. Bob is tired and depressed.

What would happen with a few changes? At 6 a.m. the nurse brings Bob his morning dose of Sinemet. By 7 a.m. when breakfast arrives, he is able to move well enough to feed himself without assistance. At 8 a.m., he gets out of bed, and walks down the hall to shower. He is slow and asks for help with the buttons, but otherwise functions on his own. It is much easier to change the linens and tidy up with Bob out of the bed. By 9 a.m., he is feeling well enough to join others in the recreation room for stretching exercises. Afterwards, he plays cards for a while. At 11 a.m., his symptoms are creeping back. The nurse brings him his Sinemet. By noon, when lunch is served, his tremor and rigidity are fairly well controlled so he eats lunch in the dining room. It takes a good 30 to 45 minutes, but he finishes his meal without assistance. In the afternoon, Bob takes a slow stroll in the courtyard, enjoying the fresh air and sunshine. He might play cards or join others in an organized activity. By 5 p.m. his Sinemet is wearing off again, and the nurse brings his medication. When dinner is served at 8 p.m., he can eat without assistance. In the evening, he enjoys the company of visitors or others in the nursing home. At 9 p.m., he is fatigued and moving slower. Since the main reason for taking Sinemet is to help him move, he doesn't really need to take it before going to bed. He sleeps better without it anyway, no more nightmares and thrashing about. Occasionally, he may need to urinate in the middle of the night, in which case he has to use a nearby urinal or ask for assistance. Overall, his quality of life has greatly improved and he needs much less assistance from the nursing staff.

The employees of the nursing home are required to take care of patients with a variety of acute, chronic, and often complicated illnesses. Unless they know someone with PD, they may not know anything about the disease or the patient's needs. The employees are concerned with accomplishing their assigned tasks and are usually kept on the run. Often, the Parkinson's patient is thought to be malingering or just trying to get his own way. The family can take an active role and help the employees become knowledgeable about Parkinson's.

The Ability to Partner with the Nursing Home Staff

The ability of the nurses in charge to think critically is of benefit to the PD patient. Critical thinking is the ability to look at a situation and be able to come up with options, evaluate them, and understand why something is occurring. A nurse with this ability strives to find a solution that is a win/win for all involved and results into a better quality of life for the patient. The ability of problem solving should be a desired quality of the charge nurse. This quality gives the patient and family an increased chance of partnering with nursing home employees to provide the care that encourages a loved one to function at the highest level possible of his or her capabilities.

The Nursing Home Decision

The decision to enter a nursing home facility is usually made after all parties have agreed that care in the home is no longer manageable or safe. Making the decision is often heart wrenching, a difficult process in the best of circumstances and even more difficult when made during a crisis. Our society puts emphasis on taking care of people in their own home. However, caregiving can be exhausting and difficult. Many times when a family member is placed in a nursing home a sense of failure is felt or projected upon the caregiver. Recognizing when one is physically and emotionally spent, and then taking steps to remedy the situation is healthy for all involved.

Where do you start? Begin by assessing your support system. For example, what is your relationship with others in the family? If there has not been a close relationship for years, you can probably assume that there won't be much help or support. On the other hand, if there has been positive relationships that have remained close, include them in the decision making process. Do you have close friends? Are you involved with a church? Seek their input. Ask your physician for advice regarding the situation. Make a list of the people in your support system and a list of suggested nursing homes. What location is most convenient for them to make frequent visits? Next, you'll need to make a decision about the level of care your loved one will need, and your physician can definitely help you with it:

- **Custodial care**—is suitable for a person who does not need the care of a practical nurse but needs help with meals, personal hygiene, and getting dressed.

- **Intermediate care**—is suitable for a person who does not require 24-hour nursing and is not able to live alone.

- **Skilled care**—is for a person who needs intensive 24-hour supervision by a registered nurse.

Now you are ready to make an assessment of the financial situation. Does the individual have any financial assets to pay for his/her care? Is there any long-term care insurance? Can the family contribute any financial help? Is there any provision with the medical insurance for care in a nursing home and if so, what does the insurance require for the patient to qualify for this assistance?

How do you choose? Visit each of the homes being considered. Make sure you have a list of questions you want to ask. I suggest you plan on a scheduled and an unscheduled visit. There shouldn't be any difference. If the unscheduled visit is first, do they offer to give you a tour? Before the final decision is made, drive by the home in the evening and on a weekend. If possible, make a visit during one of these times. Check out the lighting outside. Is there a security system? Is there any difference seen in the care provided during these times and that of during the day? You will also want to eat a meal at the facility to evaluate food quality. Also think about the loved one's personality and lifestyle. Where will they be happiest and have their needs met? What quality of life does the person have and what environment would encourage the highest quality possible for this person? Take a friend or pastor along on these visits if possible. Having an objective perspective can help make the decision clearer.

Changing Roles

Prior to nursing home admission the patient and family probably have already dealt with some changing roles, such as the patient being dependent on the caregiver for assistance. A spouse or child may be providing financially where previously the Parkinson's patient has been the provider. The degree of adaptation to these changing roles affects the transition to nursing home placement. Good communication and cooperation of all parties involved will go a long way to encourage the highest quality of life possible for the situation. How the individual or family weathers the storm of nursing home placement depends on how healthy the relationships are prior to the move. Also, one must realize that dealing with a chronic illness such as PD stresses family relationships. This can overshadow the initial transition.

Another important fact to remember is that the first couple of weeks in a nursing home can be overwhelming for all involved. At home the resident lives with a spouse or other family members. In the nursing home they are suddenly in the midst of a large number of unfamiliar people. The employees assigned to the resident will also be responsible for a number of other patients, whereas at home, the caregiver was available much quicker. One must remember that each person involved is unique and each person will exhibit their own individual coping style. How a person previously adapted and accepted change plays a large role in how he/she reacts to nursing home placement. Feelings such as denial, anger, resentment, guilt, and depression are normal in such transitions. Acceptance and adaptation to nursing home placement is important for optimum functioning and quality of life providing there is proper support for the nursing home resident.

Adequate Care

How do you know if a loved one is receiving adequate care? Even when you made careful assessments of needs and evaluated the options available you may find yourself uncomfortable with the results. First, remember that a lot of emotional energy will be spent during this transition. Initially, be careful making a judgment that maybe emotionally based. Ask the following questions:

1. How is the individual functioning compared with prior to nursing home admission?

2. Is the resident clean and dry?

3. Is the individual being encouraged to be as active as possible?

4. Is your loved one receiving individualized care that is fostering mobility, functioning, and dignity?

The caregiver or family is encouraged to maintain an active role in the resident's life. Make frequent visits at varying times to the nursing home. Upon admission you should receive a copy of the "Resident's Rights." Know these!

When a question or problem arises, confront the issues at the beginning. Small problems allowed to fester become volcanoes just waiting to erupt. When confronting an issue follow the chain of command in the facility and the grievance policy they have in place. After trying all these avenues, if you still are not satisfied contact your "Area on Aging Agency" and ask for a consultation with an ombudsman. Sometimes, having an objective outside person involved can have a profound effect on solving a problem. Remember when confronting a problem, no one likes or wants to be attacked. Approach the subject with the facts and the determination to work together to solve the problem.

Conclusion

Moving someone into a nursing home is never easy. Do your homework, educate yourself, and plan ahead. These steps will provide a smooth transition when the time arrives. Living in a nursing home can be a challenge. When families, caregivers, patients, and nursing home employees confront and understand the issues involved with PD and work as a team to coordinate the care of individual PD patients, the move is successful. Parkinson's patients are courageous and able to face the challenge of long term care.

— by Karla Tolson, R.N., B.S.N.
Coordinator, APDA Information and Referral Center
Tulsa, Oklahoma

Part Six

Other Brain Disorders

Chapter 36

Brain Tumors

Each year more than 17,000 people in the United States find out they have a brain tumor. The National Cancer Institute (NCI) has written this text to help patients and their families and friends better understand brain tumors. We also hope others will read it to learn more about these tumors.

This text describes the symptoms, diagnosis, and treatment of brain tumors. Other NCI booklets about cancer, its treatment, and living with the disease are listed at the end of this chapter. We know that booklets cannot answer every question about brain tumors. They cannot take the place of talks with doctors, nurses, and other members of the health care team, but we hope our information will help with these talks.

Our knowledge about brain tumors keeps increasing. For up-to-date information, call the NCI-supported Cancer Information Service (CIS) toll free at 1-800-4-CANCER (1-800-422-6237).

The Brain

Together, the brain and spinal cord form the central nervous system. This complex system is part of everything we do. It controls the things we choose to do—like walk and talk—and the things our body does automatically—like breathe and digest food. The central nervous

"What You Need to Know about Brain Tumors," National Cancer Institute (NCI), NIH Pub. No. 95-1558, March 1995.

309

system is also involved with our senses—seeing, hearing, touching, tasting, and smelling—as well as our emotions, thoughts, and memory.

The brain is a soft, spongy mass of nerve cells and supportive tissue. It has three major parts: the cerebrum, the cerebellum, and the brain stem. The parts work together, but each has special functions.

The cerebrum, the largest part of the brain, fills most of the upper skull. It has two halves called the left and right cerebral hemispheres. The cerebrum uses information from our senses to tell us what's going on around us and tells our body how to respond. The right hemisphere controls the muscles on the left side of the body, and the left hemisphere controls the muscles on the right side of the body. This part of the brain also controls speech and emotions as well as reading, thinking, and learning.

The cerebellum, under the cerebrum at the back of the brain, controls balance and complex actions like walking and talking.

The brain stem connects the brain with the spinal cord. It controls hunger and thirst and some of the most basic body functions, such as body temperature, blood pressure, and breathing.

The brain is protected by the bones of the skull and by a covering of three thin membranes called meninges. The brain is also cushioned

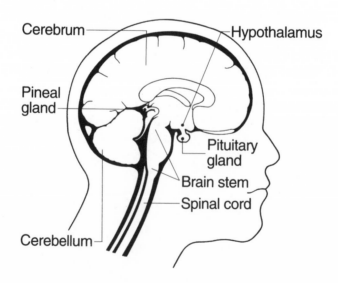

Figure 36.1. The brain and spinal cord.

and protected by cerebrospinal fluid. This watery fluid is produced by special cells in the four hollow spaces in the brain, called ventricles. It flows through the ventricles and in spaces between the meninges. Cerebrospinal fluid also brings nutrients from the blood to the brain and removes waste products from the brain.

The spinal cord is made up of bundles of nerve fibers. It runs down from the brain through a canal in the center of the bones of the spine. These bones protect the spinal cord. Like the brain, the spinal cord is covered by the meninges and cushioned by cerebrospinal fluid.

Spinal nerves connect the brain with the nerves in most parts of the body. Other nerves go directly from the brain to the eyes, ears, and other parts of the head. This network of nerves carries messages back and forth between the brain and the rest of the body.

About Brain Tumors

The body is made up of many types of cells. Each type of cell has special functions. Most cells in the body grow and then divide in an orderly way to form new cells as they are needed to keep the body healthy and working properly. When cells lose the ability to control their

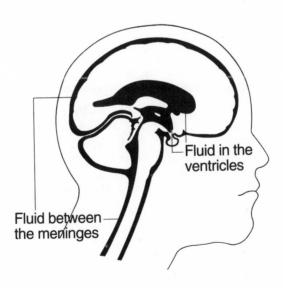

Figure 36.2. Spaces that contain cerebrospinal fluid.

growth, they divide too often and without any order. The extra cells form a mass of tissue called a tumor. Tumors are benign or malignant.

- Benign brain tumors do not contain cancer cells. Usually these tumors can be removed, and they are not likely to recur. Benign brain tumors have clear borders. Although they do not invade nearby tissue, they can press on sensitive areas of the brain and cause symptoms.

- Malignant brain tumors contain cancer cells. They interfere with vital functions and are life threatening. Malignant brain tumors are likely to grow rapidly and crowd or invade the tissue around them. Like a plant, these tumors may put out "roots" that grow into healthy brain tissue. If a malignant tumor remains compact and does not have roots, it is said to be encapsulated. When an otherwise benign tumor is located in a vital area of the brain and interferes with vital functions, it may be considered malignant (even though it contains no cancer cells).

Doctors refer to some brain tumors by grade—from low grade (grade I) to high grade (grade IV). The grade of a tumor refers to the way the cells look under a microscope. Cells from higher grade tumors are more abnormal looking and generally grow faster than cells from lower grade tumors; higher grade tumors are more malignant than lower grade tumors.

Possible Causes

The causes of brain tumors are not known. Researchers are trying to solve this problem. The more they can find out about the causes of brain tumors, the better the chances of finding ways to prevent them. Doctors cannot explain why one person gets a brain tumor and another doesn't, but they do know that no one can "catch" a brain tumor from another person. Brain tumors are not contagious.

Although brain tumors can occur at any age, studies show that they are most common in two age groups. The first group is children 3 to 12 years old; the second is adults 40 to 70 years old.

By studying large numbers of patients, researchers have found certain risk factors that increase a person's chance of developing a brain tumor. People with these risk factors have a higher-than-average risk of getting a brain tumor. For example, studies show that some types of brain tumors are more frequent among workers in certain industries, such as oil refining, rubber manufacturing, and drug manufacturing.

Other studies have shown that chemists and embalmers have a higher incidence of brain tumors. Researchers also are looking at exposure to viruses as a possible cause. Because brain tumors sometimes occur in several members of the same family, researchers are studying families with a history of brain tumors to see whether heredity is a cause. At this time, scientists do not believe that head injuries cause brain tumors to develop.

In most cases, patients with a brain tumor have no clear risk factors. The disease is probably the result of several factors acting together.

Primary Brain Tumors

Tumors that begin in brain tissue are known as primary brain tumors. (Secondary tumors that develop when cancer spreads to the brain are discussed in the next section.) Primary brain tumors are classified by the type of tissue in which they begin. The most common brain tumors are gliomas, which begin in the glial (supportive) tissue. There are several types of gliomas:

- **Astrocytomas** arise from small, star-shaped cells called astrocytes. They may grow anywhere in the brain or spinal cord. In adults, astrocytomas most often arise in the cerebrum. In children, they occur in the brain stem, the cerebrum, and the cerebellum. A grade III astrocytoma is sometimes called anaplastic astrocytoma. A grade IV astrocytoma is usually called glioblastoma multiforme.

- **Brain stem gliomas** occur in the lowest, stemlike part of the brain. The brain stem controls many vital functions. Tumors in this area generally cannot be removed. Most brain stem gliomas are high-grade astrocytomas.

- **Ependymomas** usually develop in the lining of the ventricles. They may also occur in the spinal cord. Although these tumors can develop at any age, they are most common in childhood and adolescence.

- **Oligodendrogliomas** arise in the cells that produce myelin, the fatty covering that protects nerves. These tumors usually arise in the cerebrum. They grow slowly and usually do not spread into surrounding brain tissue. Oligodendrogliomas are rare. They occur most often in middle-aged adults but have been found in people of all ages.

There are other types of brain tumors that do not begin in glial tissue. Some of the most common are described below:

- **Medulloblastomas** were once thought to develop from glial cells. However, recent research suggests that these tumors develop from primitive (developing) nerve cells that normally do not remain in the body after birth. For this reason, medulloblastomas are sometimes called primitive neuroectodermal tumors (PNET). Most medulloblastomas arise in the cerebellum; however, they may occur in other areas as well. These tumors occur most often in children and are more common in boys than in girls.

- **Meningiomas** grow from the meninges. They are usually benign. Because these tumors grow very slowly, the brain may be able to adjust to their presence; meningiomas often grow quite large before they cause symptoms. They occur most often in women between 30 and 50 years of age.

- **Schwannomas** are benign tumors that begin in Schwann cells, which produce the myelin that protects the acoustic nerve—the nerve of hearing. Acoustic neuromas are a type of schwannoma. They occur mainly in adults. These tumors affect women twice as often as men.

- **Craniopharyngiomas** develop in the region of the pituitary gland near the hypothalamus. They are usually benign; however, they are sometimes considered malignant because they can press on or damage the hypothalamus and affect vital functions. These tumors occur most often in children and adolescents.

- **Germ cell tumors** arise from primitive (developing) sex cells, or germ cells. The most frequent type of germ cell tumor in the brain is the germinoma.

- **Pineal region tumors** occur in or around the pineal gland, a tiny organ near the center of the brain. The tumor can be slow growing (pineocytoma) or fast growing (pineoblastoma). The pineal region is very difficult to reach, and these tumors often cannot be removed.

Secondary Brain Tumors

Metastasis is the spread of cancer. Cancer that begins in other parts of the body may spread to the brain and cause secondary tumors.

These tumors are not the same as primary brain tumors. Cancer that spreads to the brain is the same disease and has the same name as the original (primary) cancer. For example, if lung cancer spreads to the brain, the disease is called metastatic lung cancer because the cells in the secondary tumor resemble abnormal lung cells, not abnormal brain cells.

Treatment for secondary brain tumors depends on where the cancer started and the extent of the spread, as well as other factors, including the patient's age, general health, and response to previous treatment.

Symptoms of Brain Tumors

The symptoms of brain tumors depend mainly on their size and their location in the brain. Symptoms are caused by damage to vital tissue and by pressure on the brain as the tumor grows within the limited space in the skull. They also may be caused by swelling and a buildup of fluid around the tumor, a condition called edema. Symptoms may also be due to hydrocephalus, which occurs when the tumor blocks the flow of cerebrospinal fluid and causes it to build up in the ventricles. If a brain tumor grows very slowly, its symptoms may appear so gradually that they are overlooked for a long time.

The most frequent symptoms of brain tumors include:

- Headaches that tend to be worse in the morning and ease during the day,
- Seizures (convulsions),
- Nausea or vomiting,
- Weakness or loss of feeling in the arms or legs,
- Stumbling or lack of coordination in walking (ataxic gait),
- Abnormal eye movements or changes in vision,
- Drowsiness,
- Changes in personality or memory, and
- Changes in speech.

These symptoms may be caused by brain tumors or by other problems. Only a doctor can make a diagnosis.

Diagnosis

To find the cause of a person's symptoms, the doctor asks about the patient's personal and family medical history and performs a complete physical examination. In addition to checking general signs of health, the doctor does a neurologic exam. This includes checks for alertness, muscle strength, coordination, reflexes, and response to pain. The doctor also examines the eyes to look for swelling caused by a tumor pressing on the nerve that connects the eye and the brain.

Depending on the results of the physical and neurologic examinations, the doctor may request one or both of the following:

- **A CT (or CAT) scan** is a series of detailed pictures of the brain. The pictures are created by a computer linked to an x-ray machine. In some cases, a special dye is injected into a vein before the scan. The dye helps to show differences in the tissues of the brain.

- **MRI (magnetic resonance imaging)** gives pictures of the brain, using a powerful magnet linked to a computer. MRI is especially useful in diagnosing brain tumors because it can "see" through the bones of the skull to the tissue underneath. A special dye may be used to enhance the likelihood of detecting a brain tumor.

The doctor may also request other tests such as:

- **A skull x-ray** can show changes in the bones of the skull caused by a tumor. It can also show calcium deposits, which are present in some types of brain tumors.

- **A brain scan** reveals areas of abnormal growth in the brain and records them on special film. A small amount of a radioactive material is injected into a vein. This dye is absorbed by the tumor, and the growth shows up on the film. (The radiation leaves the body within 6 hours and is not dangerous.)

- **An angiogram, or arteriogram**, is a series of x-rays taken after a special dye is injected into an artery (usually in the area where the abdomen joins the top of the leg). The dye, which flows through the blood vessels of the brain, can be seen on the x-rays. These x-rays can show the tumor and the blood vessels that lead to it.

- **A myelogram** is an x-ray of the spine. A special dye is injected into the cerebrospinal fluid in the spine, and the patient is tilted to allow the dye to mix with the fluid. This test may be done when the doctor suspects a tumor in the spinal cord.

Treatment

Treatment for a brain tumor depends on a number of factors. Among these are the type, location, and size of the tumor, as well as the patient's age and general health. Treatment methods and schedules often vary for children and adults. The doctor develops a treatment plan to fit each patient's needs.

The patient's doctor may want to discuss the case with other doctors who treat brain tumors. Also, the patient may want to talk with the doctor about taking part in a research study of new treatment methods. Such studies, called clinical trials, are discussed below.

Many patients want to learn all they can about their disease and their treatment choices so they can take an active part in decisions about their medical care. A person with a brain tumor will have many questions, and the doctor is the best person to answer them. Most patients want to know what kind of tumor they have, how it can be treated, how effective the treatment is likely to be, and how much it's likely to cost. Here are some important questions to ask the doctor:

- What type of treatment will I receive?
- What are the expected benefits of treatment?
- What are the risks and possible side effects of treatment?
- What can be done about side effects?
- Would a clinical trial be appropriate for me?
- Will I need to change my normal activities? If so, for how long?
- How often will I need to have checkups?

Many people find it helpful to make a list of their questions before they see the doctor. Taking notes can make it easier to remember what the doctor says. Some patients find that it also helps to have a family member or friend with them when they talk with the doctor—either to take part in the discussion or just to listen.

Patients and their families have a lot to learn about brain tumors and their treatment. They should not feel that they need to understand everything the first time they hear it. They will have other chances to ask the doctor to explain things that are not clear.

Planning Treatment

Decisions about treatment for brain tumors are complex. Before starting treatment, the patient might want a second doctor to review the diagnosis and treatment plan. There are several ways to find a doctor to consult:

- The patient's doctor may be able to suggest a doctor who specializes in treating brain tumors.

- The Cancer Information Service, at 1-800-4-CANCER, can tell callers about cancer centers and other NCI-supported programs in their area.

- Patients can get the names of specialists from their local medical society, a nearby hospital or cancer center, or a medical school.

Treatment Methods

Brain tumors are treated with surgery, radiation therapy, and chemotherapy. Depending on the patient's needs, several methods may be used. The patient may be referred to doctors who specialize in different kinds of treatment and work together as a team. This medical team often includes a neurosurgeon, a medical oncologist, a radiation oncologist, a nurse, a dietitian, and a social worker. The patient may also work with a physical therapist, an occupational therapist, and a speech therapist.

Before treatment begins, most patients are given steroids, which are drugs that relieve swelling (edema). They may also be given anticonvulsant medicine to prevent or control seizures. If hydrocephalus is present, the patient may need a shunt to drain the cerebrospinal fluid. A shunt is a long, thin tube placed in a ventricle of the brain and then threaded under the skin to another part of the body, usually the abdomen. It works like a drainpipe: Excess fluid is carried away from the brain and is absorbed in the abdomen. (In some cases, the fluid is drained into the heart.)

Surgery. Surgery is the usual treatment for most brain tumors. To remove a brain tumor, a neurosurgeon makes an opening in the skull. This operation is called a craniotomy.

Whenever possible, the surgeon attempts to remove the entire tumor. However, if the tumor cannot be completely removed without damaging vital brain tissue, the doctor removes as much of the tumor as possible. Partial removal helps to relieve symptoms by reducing pressure on the brain and reduces the amount of tumor to be treated by radiation therapy or chemotherapy.

Some tumors cannot be removed. In such cases, the doctor may do only a biopsy. A small piece of the tumor is removed so that a pathologist can examine it under a microscope to determine the type of cells it contains. This helps the doctor decide which treatment to use.

318

Sometimes, a biopsy is done with a needle. Doctors use a special headframe (like a halo) and CT scans or MRI to pinpoint the exact location of the tumor. The surgeon makes a small hole in the skull and then guides a needle to the tumor. (Using this technique to do a biopsy or for treatment is called stereotaxis.)

Radiation therapy. Radiation therapy (also called radiotherapy) is the use of high-powered rays to damage cancer cells and stop them from growing. It is often used to destroy tumor tissue that cannot be removed with surgery or to kill cancer cells that may remain after surgery. Radiation therapy is also used when surgery is not possible.

Radiation therapy may be given in two ways. External radiation comes from a large machine. Generally, external radiation treatments are given 5 days a week for several weeks. The treatment schedule depends on the type and size of the tumor and the age of the patient. Giving the total dose of radiation over an extended period helps to protect healthy tissue in the area of the tumor.

Radiation can also come from radioactive materials placed directly in the tumor (implant radiation therapy). Depending on the material used, the implant may be left in the brain for a short time or permanently. Implants lose a little radioactivity each day. The patient stays in the hospital for several days while the radiation is most active.

External radiation may be directed just to the tumor and the tissue close to it or, less often, to the entire brain. (Sometimes the radiation is also directed to the spinal cord.) When the whole brain is treated, the patient often receives an extra dose of radiation to the area of the tumor. This boost can come from external radiation or from an implant.

Stereotactic radiosurgery is another way to treat brain tumors. Doctors use the techniques described above to pinpoint the exact location of the tumor. Treatment is given in just one session; high-energy rays are aimed at the tumor from many angles. In this way, a high dose of radiation reaches the tumor without damaging other brain tissue. (This use of radiation therapy is sometimes called the gamma knife.)

Chemotherapy. Chemotherapy is the use of drugs to kill cancer cells. The doctor may use just one drug or a combination, usually giving the drugs by mouth or by injection into a blood vessel or muscle. Intrathecal chemotherapy involves injecting the drugs into the cerebrospinal fluid.

319

Chemotherapy is usually given in cycles: a treatment period followed by a recovery period, then another treatment period, and so on. Patients often do not need to stay in the hospital for treatment. Most drugs can be given in the doctor's office or the outpatient clinic of a hospital. However, depending on the drugs used, the way they are given, and the patient's general health, a short hospital stay may be necessary.

Clinical Trials

Researchers are looking for treatment methods that are more effective against brain tumors and have fewer side effects. When laboratory research shows that a new method has promise, doctors use it to treat cancer patients in clinical trials. These trials are designed to answer scientific questions and to find out whether the new approach is both safe and effective. Patients who take part in clinical trials make an important contribution to medical science and may have the first chance to benefit from improved treatment methods.

Many clinical trials of new treatments for brain tumors are under way. Doctors are studying new types and schedules of radiation therapy, new anticancer drugs, new drug combinations, and combinations of chemotherapy and radiation.

Scientists are trying to increase the effectiveness of radiation therapy by giving treatments twice a day instead of once. Also, they are studying drugs called radiosensitizers. These drugs make the cancer cells more sensitive to radiation. Another method under study is hyperthermia, in which the tumor is heated to increase the effect of radiation therapy.

Many drugs cannot reach brain cells because of the blood-brain barrier, a network of blood vessels and cells that filters blood going to the brain. Researchers continue to look for new drugs that will pass through the blood-brain barrier. Studies are under way using different techniques to temporarily disrupt the barrier so that drugs can reach the tumor.

In other studies, scientists are exploring new ways to give the drugs. Drugs may be injected into an artery leading to the brain or may be put directly into the ventricles. Doctors are also studying the effectiveness of placing tiny wafers containing anticancer drugs directly into the tumor. (The wafers dissolve over time.)

Researchers are also testing the use of very high doses of anticancer drugs. Because these higher doses may damage healthy bone marrow, doctors combine this treatment with bone marrow transplantation to replace the marrow that has been destroyed.

Biological therapy is a new way of treating brain tumors that is currently under study. This type of treatment is an attempt to improve the way the body's immune system fights disease.

Patients interested in taking part in a clinical trial should discuss this option with their doctor. They may want to read *What Are Clinical Trials All About?*, an NCI booklet that explains some of the possible benefits and risks of treatment studies.

One way to learn about clinical trials is through PDQ, a computerized resource developed by the National Cancer Institute. This resource contains information about cancer treatment and about clinical trials in progress all over the country. The Cancer Information Service can provide PDQ information to patients and the public (see "Resources").

Side Effects of Treatment

Cancer treatment often causes side effects. These side effects occur because treatment to destroy cancer cells damages some healthy cells as well.

The side effects of cancer treatment vary. They depend on the type of treatment used and on the area being treated. Also, each person reacts differently. Doctors try to plan the patient's therapy to keep side effects to a minimum. They also watch patients very carefully so they can help with any problems that occur.

A craniotomy is a major operation. The surgery may damage normal brain tissue, and edema may occur. Weakness, coordination problems, personality changes, and difficulty in speaking and thinking may result. Patients may also have seizures. In fact, for a short time after surgery, symptoms may be worse than before. Most of the side effects of surgery lessen or disappear with time.

Most of the side effects of radiation therapy go away soon after treatment is over. However, some side effects may occur or persist long after treatment is complete.

Some patients have nausea for several hours after treatment. Patients receiving radiation therapy may become very tired as treatment continues. Resting is important, but doctors usually advise their patients to try to stay reasonably active. Radiation therapy to the scalp causes most patients to lose their hair. When it grows back, the new hair is sometimes softer and may be a slightly different color. In some cases, hair loss is permanent.

Skin reactions in the treated area are common. The scalp and ears may be red, itchy, or dark; these areas may look and feel sunburned. The treated area should be exposed to the air as much as possible but

321

should be protected from the sun. Patients should not wear anything on the head that might cause irritation. Good skin care is important at this time. The doctor may suggest certain kinds of soap or ointment, and patients should not use any other lotions or creams on the scalp without the doctor's advice.

Sometimes brain cells killed by radiation form a mass in the brain. The mass may look like a tumor and may cause similar symptoms, such as headaches, memory loss, or seizures. Doctors may suggest surgery or steroids to relieve these problems. About 4 to 8 weeks after radiation therapy, patients may become quite sleepy or lose their appetite. These symptoms may last several weeks, but they usually go away on their own. Still, patients should notify the doctor if they occur.

Children who have had radiation therapy for a brain tumor may have learning problems or partial loss of eyesight. If the pituitary gland is damaged, children may not grow or develop normally.

The side effects of chemotherapy depend on the drugs that are given. In general, anticancer drugs affect rapidly growing cells, such as blood cells that fight infection, cells that line the digestive tract, and cells in hair follicles. As a result, patients may have a lower resistance to infection, loss of appetite, nausea, vomiting, or mouth sores. Patients may also have less energy and may lose their hair. These side effects usually go away gradually after treatment stops.

Some anticancer drugs can cause infertility. Women taking certain anticancer drugs may have symptoms of menopause (hot flashes and vaginal dryness; periods may be irregular or stop). Some drugs used to treat children and teenagers may affect their ability to have children later in life.

Certain drugs used in the treatment of brain tumors may cause kidney damage. Patients are given large amounts of fluid while taking these drugs. Patients may also have tingling in the fingers, ringing in the ears, or difficulty hearing. These problems may not clear up after treatment stops.

Treatment with steroids to reduce swelling in the brain may cause increased appetite and weight gain. Swelling of the face and feet is common. Steroids can also cause restlessness, mood swings, burning indigestion, and acne. However, patients should not stop using steroids or change their dose without consulting the doctor. The use of steroids must be stopped gradually to allow the body to adjust to the change.

Loss of appetite can be a problem for patients during therapy. People may not feel hungry when they are uncomfortable or tired. Some of the common side effects of cancer treatment, such as nausea and vomiting, can also make it hard to eat. Yet good nutrition is important because patients who eat well generally feel better and have more energy. Eating well means getting enough calories and protein to help prevent weight loss, regain strength, and rebuild normal tissues. Many patients find that eating several small meals and snacks during the day works better than trying to have three large meals.

Patients being treated for a brain tumor may develop a blood clot and inflammation in a vein, most often in the leg. This is called thrombophlebitis. A patient who notices swelling in the leg, leg pain, and/or redness in the leg should notify the doctor right away.

Doctors, nurses, and dietitians can explain the side effects of cancer treatment and can suggest ways to deal with them. In addition, the NCI booklets *Radiation Therapy and You*, *Chemotherapy and You*, and *Eating Hints* contain helpful information about cancer treatment and coping with side effects. *Young People With Cancer: A Handbook for Parents* provides information to help children handle the side effects of treatment.

Rehabilitation

Rehabilitation is a very important part of the treatment plan. The goals of rehabilitation depend on the patient's needs and how the tumor has affected his or her daily activities. The medical team makes every effort to help patients return to their normal activities as soon as possible.

Patients and their families may need to work with an occupational therapist to overcome any difficulty in activities of daily living, such as eating, dressing, bathing, and using the toilet. If an arm or leg is weak or paralyzed, or if a patient has problems with balance, physical therapy may be necessary. Speech therapy may be helpful for individuals having trouble speaking or expressing their thoughts. Speech therapists also work with patients who are having difficulty swallowing.

If special arrangements are necessary for school-age children, they should be made as soon as possible. Sometimes, children have tutors in the hospital or after they go home from the hospital. Children who have problems learning or remembering what they learn may need tutors or special classes when they return to school.

Follow-up Care

Regular follow-up is very important after treatment for a brain tumor. The doctor will check closely to make sure that the tumor has not returned. Checkups usually include general physical and neurologic exams. From time to time, the patient will have CT scans or MRI.

Patients who receive radiation therapy to large areas of the brain or certain anticancer drugs may have an increased risk of developing leukemia or a second tumor at a later time. Also, radiation that affects the eyes may lead to the development of cataracts. Patients should carefully follow their doctor's advice on health care and checkups. If any unusual health problem occurs, they should report it to the doctor as soon as it appears.

Living with a Brain Tumor

The diagnosis of a brain tumor can change the lives of patients and the people who care about them. These changes can be hard to handle. Patients and their families and friends may have many different and sometimes confusing emotions.

At times, patients and those close to them may feel frightened, angry, or depressed. These are normal reactions when people face a serious health problem. Most patients, including children and teenagers, find it helps to share their thoughts and feelings with loved ones. Sharing can help everyone feel more at ease and can open the way for others to show their concern and offer their support.

Worries about tests, treatments, hospital stays, rehabilitation, and medical bills are common. Parents may worry about whether their children will be able to take part in normal school or social activities. Doctors, nurses, social workers, and other members of the health care team may be able to calm fears and ease confusion. They can also provide information and suggest helpful resources.

Patients and their families are naturally concerned about what the future holds. Sometimes they use statistics to try to figure out whether the patient will be cured or how long he or she will live. It is important to remember, however, that statistics are averages based on large numbers of patients. They can't be used to predict what will happen to a certain patient because no two cancer patients are alike. The doctor who takes care of the patient and knows that person's medical history is in the best position to discuss the patient's outlook (prognosis).

People should feel free to ask the doctor about their prognosis, but it is important to keep in mind that not even the doctor can tell exactly what will happen. When doctors talk about recovering from a brain tumor, they may use the term remission rather than cure. Even though many people recover completely, doctors use this term because a brain tumor can recur.

Support for Cancer Patients

Living with a serious disease is not easy. Everyone involved faces many problems and challenges. Finding the strength to cope with these difficulties is easier when people have helpful information and support services.

The doctor can explain the disease and give advice about treatment, going back to work or school, or other activities. If patients want to discuss concerns about the future, family relationships, and finances, it may also help to talk with a nurse, social worker, counselor, or clergy member.

Friends and relatives who have had personal experience with cancer can be very supportive. Also, it helps many patients to meet and talk with other people who are facing problems like theirs. Cancer patients often get together in self-help and support groups, where they can share what they have learned about cancer and its treatment and about coping with the disease. In addition to groups for adults with cancer, special support groups for children or teens with cancer or for parents whose children have cancer are available in many cities. It's important to keep in mind, however, that each patient is different. Treatments and ways of dealing with cancer that work for one person may not be right for another—even if they both have the same kind of cancer. It's always a good idea to discuss the advice of friends and family members with the doctor.

Often, a social worker at the hospital or clinic can suggest local and national groups that will help with rehabilitation, emotional support, financial aid, transportation, or home care. The American Cancer Society is one such group. This nonprofit organization has many services for patients and their families. The American Brain Tumor Association is another organization that can help patients find support groups in local areas. Candlelighters Childhood Cancer Foundation sponsors support groups for parents of children with cancer. In some cities, the Foundation has special groups for children or teens with cancer, as well. Information about other programs and services for cancer patients and their families is available through the Cancer Information Service. The toll-free number is 1-800-4-CANCER. Information about these and other resources can be found at the end of this chapter or in the "Additional Help and Information" section at the end of this book.

The public library is also a good place to find books and articles on living with cancer. Cancer patients and their families can also find helpful suggestions in the NCI booklets listed at the end of this chapter.

Medical Terms

Acoustic (ah-KOOS-tik): Related to sound or hearing.

Anaplastic (an-ah-PLAS-tik): A term used to describe cancer cells that divide rapidly and bear little or no resemblance to normal cells.

Angiogram (AN-jee-o-gram): An x-ray of blood vessels. A dye is injected into an artery to outline the blood vessels on the x-ray picture. Also called an arteriogram (ar-TEER-ee-o-gram).

Anticonvulsant (an-ti-kon-VUL-sant): Medicine to stop, prevent, or control seizures (convulsions).

Astrocytoma (as-tro-sy-TO-ma): A type of brain tumor.

Ataxic gait (ah-TAK-sik): Awkward, uncoordinated walking.

Benign (bee-NINE): Not cancerous; a benign brain tumor may be life threatening, depending on its size and location.

Biological therapy: Treatment with substances called biological response modifiers that can stimulate the immune system to fight disease more effectively. Also called immunotherapy.

Biopsy (BY-op-see): The removal of a sample of tissue for examination under a microscope to check for cancer cells.

Bone marrow: The soft, spongy tissue in the center of many bones. Red bone marrow produces blood cells (white blood cells, red blood cells, and platelets).

Bone marrow transplantation (tranz-plan-TAYshun): A procedure in which doctors use marrow taken from a patient before treatment or from another person to replace marrow destroyed by high doses of radiation or anticancer drugs.

Brain stem: The stemlike part of the brain that is connected to the spinal cord.

Brain stem glioma (glee-O-ma): A type of brain tumor.

Cancer: A term for more than 100 diseases in which abnormal cells grow out of control.

Central nervous system: The brain and the spinal cord. Also called CNS.

Cerebellum (sair-uh-BELL-um): The portion of the brain in the back of the head between the cerebrum and the brain stem.

Cerebral hemispheres (seh-REE-bral HEM-iss-feerz): The two halves of the cerebrum.

Cerebrospinal fluid (seh-REE-bro-SPY-nal): The watery fluid flowing around the brain and spinal cord. Also called CSF.

Cerebrum (seh-REE-brum): The largest part of the brain. It is divided into two hemispheres, or halves.

Chemotherapy (kee-mo-THER-ah-pee): Treatment with anticancer drugs.

Clinical trials: Studies in which new cancer treatments are tested in cancer patients. Each study is designed to answer scientific questions and to find better ways to treat patients.

Craniopharyngioma (KRAY-nee-o-fah-rin-jee-O-ma): A type of brain tumor.

Craniotomy (kray-nee-OT-o-mee): An operation in which an opening is made in the skull so the doctor can reach the brain.

CT (or CAT) scan: An x-ray procedure using a computer to produce detailed pictures of areas inside the body.

Cyst: A closed sac or capsule, usually filled with fluid or semisolid material.

Edema (eh-DEE-ma): Swelling; an abnormal buildup of fluid.

Encapsulated (en-KAP-soo-lay-ted): Confined to a specific area; the tumor remains in a compact form.

Ependymoma (eh-PEN-di-MO-ma): A type of brain tumor.

Gamma knife: Radiation therapy in which high-energy rays are aimed at a tumor from many angles in a single treatment session.

Germ cell tumors: A type of brain tumor.

Germinoma (jer-mih-NO-ma): A type of germ cell tumor.

Glioblastoma multiforme (glee-o-blas-TO-ma mul-tih-FOR-may): A type of brain tumor.

Glioma (glee-O-ma): A name for brain tumors that begin in the glial cells, or supportive cells, in the brain. "Glia" is the Greek word for glue.

Hair follicle (FOL-i-kul): A sac from which a hair grows.

Hydrocephalus (hy-dro-SEF-uh-lus): The abnormal buildup of cerebrospinal fluid in the ventricles of the brain.

Hyperthermia (hy-per-THER-mee-a): Treatment that involves heating a tumor.

Hypothalamus (hy-po-THAL-uh-mus): The area of the brain that controls body temperature, hunger, and thirst.

Immune system (im-MYOON): The complex group of organs and cells that defends the body against infection or disease.

Infertility: Inability to have children.

Intrathecal chemotherapy (in-tra-THEE-kal): Injection of anticancer drugs into cerebral fluid.

Malignant (mah-LIG-nant): Cancerous (see Cancer); life threatening. A malignant brain tumor seriously threatens vital functions.

Medulloblastoma (MED-yoo-lo-blas-TO-ma): A type of brain tumor.

Membrane: A very thin layer of tissue that covers a surface.

Meninges (meh-NIN-jeez): The three membranes that cover the brain and spinal cord.

Meningioma (meh-nin-jee-O-ma): A type of brain tumor.

Menopause: The time of a woman's life when menstrual periods permanently stop. Also called "change of life."

Metastasis (meh-TAS-ta-sis): The spread of cancer from one part of the body to another. Cells in the metastatic (secondary) tumor are like those in the original (primary) tumor.

MRI: A test using a magnet linked to a computer to create pictures of areas inside the body. Also called magnetic resonance imaging.

Myelin (MY-eh-lin): The fatty substance that covers and protects nerves.

Myelogram (MY-eh-lo-gram): An x-ray of the spinal cord and the bones of the spine.

Neurologist (new-ROL-o-jist): A doctor who specializes in the diagnosis and treatment of disorders of the nervous system.

Neuroma (new-RO-ma): A tumor that arises in nerve cells.

Neurosurgeon (NEW-ro-SER-jun): A doctor who specializes in surgery on the brain and other parts of the nervous system.

Nitrosoureas (ny-TRO-so-yur-EE-ahz): A group of anticancer drugs that can cross the blood-brain barrier. Carmustine (BCNU) and lomustine (CCNU) are nitrosoureas.

Oligodendroglioma (OL-i-go-den-dro-glee-O-ma): A type of brain tumor.

Oncologist (on-KOL-o-jist): A doctor who specializes in treating cancer. Some oncologists specialize in a particular type of cancer treatment. For example, a radiation oncologist treats cancer with radiation therapy.

Ophthalmoscope (off-THAL-mo-skope): A lighted instrument used to examine the inside of the eye, including the retina and the optic nerve.

Optic nerve: The nerve that carries messages from the retina to the brain.

Papilledema (pap-il-eh-DEE-ma): Swelling around the optic nerve, usually due to pressure on the nerve by a tumor.

Paralysis (pa-RAL-i-sis): Loss of ability to move all or part of the body.

Pathologist (path-OL-o-jist): A doctor who identifies diseases by studying cells and tissues under a microscope.

Pineal gland (PIN-ee-al): A small gland located in the cerebrum.

Pineal region tumors: Types of brain tumors.

Pineoblastoma (PIN-ec-o-blas-TO-ma): A type of brain tumor.

Pineocytoma (PIN-ee-o-sy-TO-ma): A type of brain tumor.

Pituitary gland (pi-TOO-i-tare-ee): The main endocrine gland; it produces hormones that control other glands and many body functions, especially growth.

Primitive neuroectodermal tumors (NEW-ro-ek-toDER-mul): A type of brain tumor.

Prognosis (prog-NO-sis): The probable outcome or course of a disease.

Radiation therapy (ray-dee-AY-shun): Treatment with high-energy rays (such as x-rays) to kill cancer cells. The radiation may come from outside the body (external radiation) or from radioactive materials placed directly in the tumor (implant radiation).

Radiosensitizers: Drugs that make cells more sensitive to radiation.

Recur: To occur again. Recurrence is the reappearance of cancer cells at the same site or in another location.

Remission: Disappearance of the signs and symptoms of cancer. When this happens, the disease is said to be in remission. A remission can be temporary or permanent.

Risk factor: Something that increases a person's chances of getting a disease.

Schwannoma (shwah-NO-ma): A type of brain tumor.

Seizures (SEE-zhurz): Convulsions; sudden, involuntary movements of the muscles.

Shunt: A catheter (tube) that carries cerebrospinal fluid from a ventricle in the brain to another area of the body.

Stereotaxis (stair-ee-o-TAK-sis): Use of a computer and scanning devices to create three-dimensional pictures. This method can be used to direct a biopsy, external radiation, or the insertion of radiation implants.

Steroids (STEH-roidz): Drugs used to relieve swelling and inflammation.

Surgery: An operation.

Thrombophlebitis (throm-boe-fleh-BY-tis): Inflammation of a vein that occurs when a blood clot forms.

Tissue: A group or layer of similar cells that perform a special function.

Tumor: An abnormal mass of tissue.

Ventricles (VEN-trih-kulz): Four connected cavities (hollow spaces) in the brain.

Vital: Necessary to maintain life. Breathing is a vital function.

X-ray: High-energy radiation. It is used in low doses to diagnose diseases and in high doses to treat cancer.

Resources

Information about brain tumors is available from many sources. Several are listed below. You may also wish to check for additional information at your local library or bookstore or from support groups in the community or consult "Additional Help and Information" at the back of this book.

Cancer Information Service (CIS)
1-800-4-CANCER

The Cancer Information Service, a program of the National Cancer Institute, provides a nationwide telephone service for cancer patients and their families and friends, the public, and health care professionals. The staff can answer questions and can send booklets about cancer. They also have information about local resources and services. One toll-free number, 1-800-4-CANCER (1-800-422-6237), connects callers with the office that serves their area. Spanish-speaking staff members are available.

American Cancer Society (ACS)
1-800-ACS-2345

The American Cancer Society is a national voluntary organization with local units all over the country. It supports research, conducts educational programs, and publishes booklets about cancer. It also offers many services to patients and their families. To obtain booklets or to learn about services and activities in local areas, call the Society's toll-free number, 1-800-ACS-2345 (1-800-227-2345), or the number listed under "American Cancer Society" in the white pages of the telephone book.

American Brain Tumor Association (ABTA)
2720 River Road, Suite 146
Des Plaines, IL 60018
1-800-886-ABTA

The American Brain Tumor Association supports research on brain tumors and provides information to the public through booklets and newsletters. This organization also provides resource listings of doctors, treatment facilities, and support groups throughout the country. The Association's toll-free number is 1-800-886-ABTA (1-800-886-2282).

Candlelighters Childhood Cancer Foundation (CCCF)
7910 Woodmont Avenue, Suite 460
Bethesda, MD 20814
1-800-366-CCCF

Candlelighters is a national organization of parents whose children have or have had cancer. It operates a patient information service and publishes newsletters for parents and young people. Local chapters sponsor family support groups. The toll-free number is 1-800-366-CCCF (1-800-366-2223).

National Institute of Neurological Disorders and Stroke (NINDS)
NINDS Information Center
Post Office Box 5801
Bethesda, MD 20824
1-800-352-9424

The National Institute of Neurological Disorders and Stroke, an agency of the Federal Government, supports research on brain tumors and other disorders that affect the brain and nervous system. The Information Center can send free printed materials on brain tumors. Its toll-free number is 1-800-352-9424.

Booklets

Cancer patients, their families and friends, and others may find the following booklets useful. They are available free of charge from the National Cancer Institute. You may request them by calling 1-800-4-CANCER.

Booklets about Cancer Treatment

- *Radiation Therapy and You: A Guide to Self-Help During Treatment*
- *Chemotherapy and You: A Guide to Self-Help During Treatment*
- *Eating Hints for Cancer Patients*
- *What Are Clinical Trials All About?*

Booklets about Living with Cancer

- *Taking Time: Support for People With Cancer and the People Who Care About Them*
- *Facing Forward: A Guide For Cancer Survivors*
- *Young People With Cancer: A Handbook for Parents*
- *When Cancer Recurs: Meeting the Challenge Again*
- *Advanced Cancer: Living Each Day*

Chapter 37

Survival Rates for Brain Tumor Patients Increasing

Five-year survival rates for brain tumor patients have improved over the last 25 years, according to a study published in the January [1998] issue of the *Journal of Neurosurgery*. The population-based study followed more than 25,000 brain tumor patients in 8 geographic regions in the United States from 1973–1991.

"This study describes survival rates for brain tumor patients by type of tumor and by age over an extended period of time," said Faith Davis, PhD, Director of the Division of Epidemiology and Biostatistics, School of Public Health, University of Illinois at Chicago, and primary author of the paper. "What the study determined was that we have made significant progress in treating certain types of tumors, particularly medulloblastomas, oligodendrogliomas and astrocytomas, and there has been increased survival rates for some age groups, particularly children and young adults. Unfortunately, it also shows there's been very little improvement in the outcome of one of the most common brain tumors, glioblastoma multiforme."

Brain tumors affect approximately 11 in every 100,000 people, according to the Central Brain Tumor Registry of the United States. There currently are not any known risk factors and brain tumors affect people of all ages and races. There are more than a dozen different types of brain tumors, and tumors are classified by level of malignancy, size and the degree to which the cancer has spread to different parts of the brain or body.

Steven Brem, MD, a neurosurgeon at H. Lee Moffitt Cancer Center in Tampa, Florida and co-author of the study, credits the increased survival rates to better diagnostic equipment and improved surgical techniques. The computerized tomography (CT) and magnetic resonance imaging (MRI) scans were both developed in the 1980s and create computer images of the brain that allow doctors to see tumors without opening up the skull. This not only helps doctors detect tumors but also allows them to see the exact size and location of the tumor before and after treatment. Surgical procedures have also changed in the last 25 years with neurosurgeons relying more on surgical microscopes, lasers, radiosurgery and better anesthesia.

"There's a delicate balance in brain tumor surgery between removing as much of the tumor as possible and not disrupting healthy brain tissue," Dr. Brem said. "The more detailed and precise the instruments allow us to be, the better."

Survival rates for pediatric brain tumor patients have also increased in recent years, showing an increase of over 30 percent for certain types of tumors. About 4 in every 100,000 children under age 15 suffer from a brain tumor, according to the Central Brain Tumor Registry. In general, the study showed the younger a patient was diagnosed with a brain tumor, the longer the survival rate was. This is attributed to children and young adults developing different types of brain tumors than adults, and these types of tumors often respond better to radiation therapy.

Glioblastoma multiforme brain tumors remain the most intractable of tumors for all ages groups with survival rates increasing less than 5 percent in the past 25 years. "These remain the most challenging tumors to treat because the biology and genetic make-up of the tumor is so unstable," Dr. Brem said. "This tumor is also incredibly fast-growing and can double in size in about 10 days. A neurosurgeon can do the most pristine removal of this tumor, but inevitably, there are at least a few stray tumor cells left that immediately start multiplying all over again."

Like glioblastomas multiforme, many types of malignant tumors in the body cannot be completely removed surgically. These tumors often require strong chemotherapy drugs and radiation to successfully complete treatment. However, the brain is protected by a blood-brain barrier that makes this difficult.

"The brain-blood barrier is a wonderful natural barrier that stops poison, bacteria, and anything harmful from reaching the nervous system," Dr. Brem said. "Unfortunately, this barrier also prevents us from getting significant doses of needed drugs into the brain to fight the cancerous cells."

Another difference between brain tumors and tumors occurring in other parts of the body is that brain tumors, especially glioblastomas multiforme, tend to mutate themselves several times creating a variety of abnormal cells. "If we find a way to kill off one type of cell, there's often another one waiting to take over," Dr. Brem said.

Researchers are currently working on an "all fronts attack" to address the special challenges of brain tumors. Therapies under research include gene therapy, biological therapies, stereotactic radiosurgery, drug therapy, focal radiation, and microsurgery. There are more than 100 different types of clinical trials being conducted nationwide on various brain tumor treatment options.

"The amount of research information coming out of the neurosurgical community on tumors right now is quite incredible," Dr. Brem said. "Different researchers are taking completely different approaches to addressing the same issues and that's encouraging. It just takes time to investigate and prove each approach. This study helps us determine exactly which areas we've made progress in and which areas need more work."

"Patients need to remember that this study, or any neurosurgeon, cannot predict any one patient's outcome," Dr. Brem said. "This study only gives us a baseline to compare a patient to. Each tumor, each patient is different. By being population-based, this study gives us a lot of statistical information to work with and gives us some hope that we've made progress, but it also shows we have a ways to go when it comes to treating brain tumors."

The Journal of Neurosurgery is a peer-reviewed, scientific publication of The American Association of Neurological Surgeons (AANS). The Journal is the most widely read neurosurgical publication in the world and has been published monthly since 1944. Both the Journal and the AANS are dedicated to advancing the specialty of neurological surgery in order to provide the highest quality of neurosurgical care to the public. All active members of the AANS must be certified by the American Board of Neurosurgery. Neurological surgery is the medical specialty concerned with the diagnosis and treatment of disorders affecting the nervous system, the brain, spinal cord and spinal column.

Chapter 38

Cerebral Palsy

Introduction

In the 1860s, an English surgeon named William Little wrote the first medical descriptions of a puzzling disorder that struck children in the first years of life, causing stiff, spastic muscles in their legs and, to a lesser degree, their arms. These children had difficulty grasping objects, crawling, and walking. They did not get better as they grew up nor did they become worse. Their condition, which was called Little's disease for many years, is now known as *spastic diplegia*. It is just one of several disorders that affect control of movement and are grouped together under the term cerebral palsy.

Because it seemed that many of these children were born following complicated deliveries, Little suggested their condition resulted from a lack of oxygen during birth. This oxygen shortage damaged sensitive brain tissues controlling movement, he proposed. But in 1897, the famous physician Sigmund Freud disagreed. Noting that children with cerebral palsy often had other problems such as mental retardation, visual disturbances, and seizures, Freud suggested that the disorder might sometimes have roots earlier in life, during the brain's development in the womb. "Difficult birth, in certain cases," he wrote, "is merely a symptom of deeper effects that influence the development of the fetus."

National Institute of Neurological Disorders and Stroke (NINDS), NIH Pub. No. 93-159, September 1993.

337

Despite Freud's observation, the belief that birth complications cause most cases of cerebral palsy was widespread among physicians, families, and even medical researchers until very recently. In the 1980s, however, scientists analyzed extensive data from a government study of more than 35,000 births and were surprised to discover that such complications account for only a fraction of cases—probably less than 10 percent. In most cases of cerebral palsy, no cause could be found. These findings from the National Institute of Neurological Disorders and Stroke (NINDS) perinatal study have profoundly altered medical theories about cerebral palsy and have spurred today's researchers to explore alternative causes.

At the same time, biomedical research has also led to significant changes in understanding, diagnosing, and treating persons with cerebral palsy. Identification of infants with cerebral palsy very early in life gives youngsters the best opportunity for developing to their full capacity. Biomedical research has led to improved diagnostic techniques—such as advanced brain imaging and modern gait analysis— that are making this easier. Certain conditions known to cause cerebral palsy, such as *rubella* (German measles) and *jaundice*, can now be prevented or treated. Physical, psychological, and behavioral therapy that assist with such skills as movement and speech and foster social and emotional development can help children who have cerebral palsy to achieve and succeed. Medications, surgery, and braces can often improve nerve and muscle coordination, help treat associated medical problems, and either prevent or correct deformities.

Much of the research to improve medical understanding of cerebral palsy has been supported by the NINDS, one of the Federal Government's National Institutes of Health. The NINDS is America's leading supporter of biomedical research into cerebral palsy and other neurological disorders. Through this information, the NINDS hopes to help the more than 4,500 American babies and infants diagnosed each year, their families, and others concerned about cerebral palsy benefit from these research results.

What is Cerebral Palsy?

Cerebral palsy is an umbrella-like term used to describe a group of chronic disorders impairing control of movement that appear in the first few years of life and generally do not worsen over time. The term *cerebral* refers to the brain's two halves, or hemispheres, and *palsy* describes any disorder that impairs control of body movement. Thus, these disorders are not caused by problems in the muscles or nerves.

Instead, faulty development or damage to motor areas in the brain disrupts the brain's ability to adequately control movement and posture.

Symptoms of cerebral palsy lie along a spectrum of varying severity. An individual with cerebral palsy may have difficulty with fine motor tasks, such as writing or cutting with scissors; experience trouble with maintaining balance and walking; or be affected by involuntary movements, such as uncontrollable writhing motion of the hands or drooling. The symptoms differ from one person to the next, and may even change over time in the individual. Some people with cerebral palsy are also affected by other medical disorders, including seizures or mental impairment. Contrary to common belief, however, cerebral palsy does not always cause profound handicap. While a child with severe cerebral palsy might be unable to walk and need extensive, lifelong care, a child with mild cerebral palsy might only be slightly awkward and require no special assistance. Cerebral palsy is not contagious nor is it usually inherited from one generation to the next. At this time, it cannot be cured, although scientific research continues to seek improved treatments and methods of prevention.

How Many People Have This Disorder?

The United Cerebral Palsy Associations estimate that more than 500,000 Americans have cerebral palsy. Despite advances in preventing and treating certain causes of cerebral palsy, the number of children and adults it affects has remained essentially unchanged or perhaps risen slightly over the past 30 years. This is partly because more critically premature and frail infants are surviving through improved intensive care. Unfortunately, many of these infants have developmental problems of the nervous system or suffer neurological damage. Research is under way to improve care for these infants, as in ongoing studies of technology to alleviate troubled breathing and trials of drugs to prevent bleeding in the brain before or soon after birth.

What Are the Different Forms?

Spastic diplegia, the disorder first described by Dr. Little in the 1860s, is only one of several disorders called cerebral palsy. Today doctors classify cerebral palsy into four broad categories—spastic, athetoid, ataxic, and mixed forms—according to the type of movement disturbance.

Spastic cerebral palsy. In this form of cerebral palsy, which affects 70 to 80 percent of patients, the muscles are stiffly and permanently contracted. Doctors will often describe which type of spastic cerebral palsy a patient has based on which limbs are affected. The names given to these types combine a Latin description of affected limbs with the term *plegia* or *paresis*, meaning paralyzed or weak. The four commonly diagnosed types of spastic cerebral palsy are shown in Figure 38.1.

When both legs are affected by spasticity, they may turn in and cross at the knees. This abnormal leg posture, called scissoring, can interfere with walking.

Individuals with spastic hemiparesis may also experience *hemiparetic tremors*, in which uncontrollable shaking affects the limbs on one side of the body. If these tremors are severe, they can seriously impair movement.

Athetoid, or dyskinetic, cerebral palsy. This form of cerebral palsy is characterized by uncontrolled, slow, writhing movements.

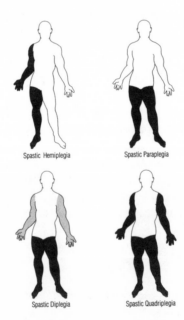

Spastic Hemiplegia   Spastic Paraplegia

Spastic Diplegia   Spastic Quadriplegia

Figure 38.1. The four key forms of spastic cerebral palsy. Doctors name them by combining the terms plegia (meaning paralyzed) or paresis (weak) with a Latin description of the affected limbs.

These abnormal movements usually affect the hands, feet, arms, or legs and, in some cases, the muscles of the face and tongue, causing grimacing or drooling. The movements often increase during periods of emotional stress and disappear during sleep. Patients may also have problems coordinating the muscle movements needed for speech, a condition known as *dysarthria*. Athetoid cerebral palsy affects about 10 to 20 percent of patients.

Ataxic cerebral palsy. This rare form affects balance and coordination. Affected persons may walk unsteadily with a wide-based gait, placing their feet unusually far apart, and experience difficulty when attempting quick or precise movements, such as writing or buttoning a shirt. They may also have intention tremor. In this form of tremor, beginning a voluntary movement, such as reaching for a book, causes a trembling that affects the body part being used. The tremor worsens as the individual gets nearer to the desired object. The ataxic form affects an estimated 5 to 10 percent of cerebral palsy patients.

Mixed forms. It is common for patients to have symptoms of more than one form of cerebral palsy mentioned above. The most common combination includes spasticity and athetoid movements but other combinations are possible.

What Other Medical Disorders Are Associated with Cerebral Palsy?

Many individuals who have cerebral palsy have no associated medical disorders. However, disorders that involve the brain and impair its motor function can also cause seizures and impair an individual's intellectual development, attentiveness to the outside world, activity and behavior, and vision and hearing. Medical disorders associated with cerebral palsy include:

Mental impairment. About one-third of children who have cerebral palsy are mildly intellectually impaired, one-third are moderately or severely impaired, and the remaining third are intellectually normal. Mental impairment is more commonly seen in children with spastic quadriplegia.

Seizures or epilepsy. As many as half of all children with cerebral palsy have seizures. During a seizure, the normal, orderly pattern of

341

electrical activity in the brain is disrupted by uncontrolled bursts of electricity. When seizures recur without a direct trigger, such as fever, the condition is called epilepsy. In the person who has cerebral palsy and epilepsy, this disruption may be spread throughout the brain and cause varied symptoms all over the body—as in tonic-clonic seizures—or may be confined to just one part of the brain and cause more specific symptoms—as in partial seizures.

Tonic-clonic seizures generally cause patients to cry out and are followed by loss of consciousness, twitching of both legs and arms, convulsive body movements, and loss of bladder control.

Partial seizures are classified as simple or complex. In simple partial seizures, the individual has localized symptoms, such as muscle twitches, numbness, or tingling. In complex partial seizures, the individual may hallucinate, stagger, perform automatic and purposeless movements, or experience impaired consciousness or confusion.

Growth problems. A syndrome called *failure to thrive* is common in children with moderate-to-severe cerebral palsy, especially those with spastic quadriparesis. Failure to thrive is a general term physicians use to describe children who seem to lag behind in growth and development despite having enough food. In babies, this lag usually takes the form of too little weight gain; in young children, it can appear as abnormal shortness; in teenagers, it may appear as a combination of shortness and lack of sexual development. Failure to thrive probably has several causes, including, in particular, poor nutrition and damage to the brain centers controlling growth and development.

In addition, the muscles and limbs affected by cerebral palsy tend to be smaller than normal. This is especially noticeable in some patients with spastic hemiplegia, because limbs on the affected side of the body may not grow as quickly or as large as those on the more normal side. This condition usually affects the hand and foot most severely. Since the involved foot in hemiplegia is often smaller than the unaffected foot even among patients who walk, this size difference is probably not due to lack of use. Scientists believe the problem is more likely to result from disruption of the complex process responsible for normal body growth.

Impaired vision or hearing. A large number of children with cerebral palsy have *strabismus*, a condition in which the eyes are not aligned because of differences in the left and right eye muscles. In an adult, this condition causes double vision. In children, however, the brain often adapts to the condition by ignoring signals from one of the misaligned eyes. Untreated, this can lead to very poor vision in one eye and can interfere with certain visual skills, such as judging distance. In some cases, physicians may recommend surgery to correct strabismus.

Children with hemiparesis may have *hemianopia*, which is defective vision or blindness that impairs the normal field of vision. For example, when hemianopia affects the right field of vision, a child looking straight ahead might have perfect vision except on the far right. In homonymous hemianopia, the impairment affects the same part of the visual field of both eyes.

Impaired hearing is also more frequent among those with cerebral palsy than in the general population.

Abnormal sensation and perception. Some children with cerebral palsy have impaired ability to feel simple sensations like touch and pain. They may also have *stereognosia*, or difficulty perceiving and identifying objects using the sense of touch. A child with stereognosia, for example, would have trouble identifying a hard ball, sponge, or other object placed in his hand without looking at the object.

What Causes Cerebral Palsy?

Cerebral palsy is not one disease with a single cause, like chicken pox or measles. It is a group of disorders that are related but have different causes. When physicians try to uncover the cause of cerebral palsy in an individual child, they look at the form of cerebral palsy, the mother's and child's medical history, and onset of the disorder.

About 10 to 20 percent of children who have cerebral palsy acquire the disorder after birth. Acquired cerebral palsy results from brain damage in the first few months or years of life and often follows brain infections, such as bacterial meningitis or viral encephalitis, or results from head injury—most often from a motor vehicle accident, a fall, or child abuse.

Congenital cerebral palsy, on the other hand, is present at birth, although it may not be detected for several months. In most cases, the cause of congenital cerebral palsy is unknown. Thanks to research, however, scientists have pinpointed some specific events during pregnancy or around the time of birth that can damage motor centers in the developing brain. Some of these causes of congenital cerebral palsy include:

Infections during pregnancy. German measles, or rubella, is caused by a virus that can infect pregnant women and, therefore, the fetus in the uterus, to cause damage to the developing nervous system. Other infections that can cause brain injury in the developing fetus include cytomegalovirus and toxoplasmosis.

Jaundice in the infant. Bile pigments, compounds that are normally found in small amounts in the bloodstream, are produced when blood cells are destroyed. When many blood cells are destroyed in a short time, as in the condition called Rh incompatibility (see below), the yellow-colored pigments can build up and cause jaundice. Severe, untreated jaundice can damage brain cells.

Perinatal asphyxia. During labor and delivery, a shortage of oxygen in the blood, reduced brain blood flow, or both can impair the supply of oxygen to the newborn's brain, causing the condition known as perinatal asphyxia. When asphyxia is severe enough to put the newborn at risk for long-term brain damage, it immediately causes problems with brain function (as in moderate-to-severe hypoxic-ischemic encephalopathy). Asphyxia this severe is very uncommon, is always linked to dysfunction of other body organs, and is often accompanied by seizures.

Rh incompatibility. In this blood condition, the mother's body produces immune cells called antibodies that destroy the fetus's blood cells, leading to a form of jaundice in the newborn.

In the past, physicians and scientists attributed most cases of cerebral palsy to asphyxia or other complications during birth if they could not identify another cause. However, extensive research by NINDS scientists and others has shown that very few babies who experience asphyxia during birth develop encephalopathy after birth. Research also shows that most babies who experience asphyxia do not grow up to have cerebral palsy or other neurological disorders. In fact, current evidence suggests that cerebral palsy is associated with asphyxia and other birth complications in no more than 10 percent of cases.

Stroke/intracranial hemorrhage. Bleeding in the brain (intracranial hemorrhage) has several causes—including broken blood vessels in the brain, clogged blood vessels, or abnormal blood cells—and is one form of stroke. Newborn respiratory distress, a breathing disorder that is particularly common in premature infants, is one cause. Although strokes are better known for their effects on older adults, they can also occur in the fetus during pregnancy or the newborn around the time of birth, damaging brain tissue and causing neurological problems. Ongoing research is testing potential treatments that may one day help prevent stroke in fetuses and newborns.

What Are the Risk Factors?

Research scientists have examined thousands of expectant mothers, followed them through childbirth, and monitored their children's early neurological development. As a result, they have uncovered certain characteristics, called risk factors, that increase the possibility that a child will later be diagnosed with cerebral palsy:

Breech presentation. Babies with cerebral palsy are more likely to present feet first, instead of head first, at the beginning of labor.

Complicated labor and delivery. Vascular or respiratory problems of the baby during labor and delivery may sometimes be the first sign that a baby has suffered brain damage or that a baby's brain has not developed normally during the pregnancy. Such complications can cause permanent brain damage.

Inborn malformations outside the nervous system. Babies with physical birth defects—including faulty formation of the spinal bones, hernia (a protrusion of organs through an abnormal opening inside the body) in the groin area, or an abnormally small jaw bone—are at an increased risk for cerebral palsy.

Low Apgar score. The *Apgar score* (named for anesthesiologist Virginia Apgar) is a numbered rating that reflects a newborn's condition. To determine an Apgar score, doctors periodically check the baby's heart rate, breathing, muscle tone, reflexes, and skin color in the first minutes after birth. They then assign points; the higher the score, the more normal the baby's condition. A low score at 10–20 minutes after delivery is often considered an important sign of potential problems.

Low birthweight and premature birth. The risk of cerebral palsy is higher among babies who weigh less than 2500 grams (5 lbs.,

7½ oz.) at birth and among babies who are born less than 37 weeks into pregnancy. This risk increases as birthweight falls.

Multiple births. Twins, triplets, and other multiple births are linked to an increased risk of cerebral palsy.

Nervous system malformations. Some babies born with cerebral palsy have visible signs of nervous system malformation, such as an abnormally small head (microcephaly). This suggests that problems occurred in the development of the nervous system while the baby was in the womb.

Maternal bleeding or severe proteinuria late in pregnancy. Vaginal bleeding during the sixth to ninth months of pregnancy and severe proteinuria (the presence of excess proteins in the urine) are linked to a higher risk of having a baby with cerebral palsy.

Maternal hyperthyroidism, mental retardation, or seizures. Mothers with any of these conditions are slightly more likely to have a child with cerebral palsy.

Seizures in the newborn. An infant who has seizures faces a higher risk of being diagnosed, later in childhood, with cerebral palsy.

Knowing these warning signs helps doctors keep a close eye on children who face a higher risk for long-term problems in the nervous system. However, parents should not become too alarmed if their child has one or more of these factors. Most such children do not have and do not develop cerebral palsy.

Can Cerebral Palsy Be Prevented?

Several of the causes of cerebral palsy that have been identified through research are preventable or treatable:

- **Head injury** can be prevented by regular use of child safety seats when driving in a car and helmets during bicycle rides, and elimination of child abuse. In addition, common sense measures around the household—like close supervision during bathing and keeping poisons out of reach—can reduce the risk of accidental injury.

- **Jaundice** of newborn infants can be treated with phototherapy. In phototherapy, babies are exposed to special blue lights that break down bile pigments, preventing them from building up and threatening the brain. In the few cases in which this treatment is not enough, physicians can correct the condition with a special form of blood transfusion.

- **Rh incompatibility** is easily identified by a simple blood test routinely performed on expectant mothers and, if indicated, expectant fathers. This incompatibility in blood types does not usually cause problems during a woman's first pregnancy, since the mother's body generally does not produce the unwanted antibodies until after delivery. In most cases, a special serum given after each childbirth can prevent the unwanted production of antibodies. In unusual cases, such as when a pregnant woman develops the antibodies during her first pregnancy or antibody production is not prevented, doctors can help minimize problems by closely watching the developing baby and, when needed, performing a transfusion to the baby while in the womb or an exchange transfusion (in which a large volume of the baby's blood is removed and replaced) after birth.

- **Rubella**, or German measles, can be prevented if women are vaccinated against this disease *before* becoming pregnant.

In addition, it is always good to work toward a healthy pregnancy through regular prenatal care and good nutrition and by eliminating smoking, alcohol consumption, and drug abuse. Despite the best efforts of parents and physicians, however, children will still be born with cerebral palsy. Since in most cases the cause of cerebral palsy is unknown, little can currently be done to prevent it. As investigators learn more about the causes of cerebral palsy through basic and clinical research, doctors and parents will be better equipped to help prevent this disorder.

What Are the Early Signs?

Early signs of cerebral palsy usually appear before 3 years of age, and parents are often the first to suspect that their infant is not developing motor skills normally. Infants with cerebral palsy are frequently slow to reach developmental milestones, such as learning to roll over, sit, crawl, smile, or walk. This is sometimes called developmental delay.

Some affected children have abnormal muscle tone. Decreased muscle tone is called *hypotonia*; the baby may seem flaccid and relaxed, even floppy. Increased muscle tone is called *hypertonia*, and the baby may seem stiff or rigid. In some cases, the baby has an early period of hypotonia that progresses to hypertonia after the first 2 to 3 months of life. Affected children may also have unusual posture or favor one side of their body.

Parents who are concerned about their baby's development for any reason should contact their physician, who can help distinguish normal variation in development from a developmental disorder.

How is Cerebral Palsy Diagnosed?

Doctors diagnose cerebral palsy by testing an infant's motor skills and looking carefully at the infant's medical history. In addition to checking for those symptoms described above—slow development, abnormal muscle tone, and unusual posture—a physician also tests the infant's reflexes and looks for early development of hand preference.

Reflexes are movements that the body makes automatically in response to a specific cue. For example, if a newborn baby is held on its back and tilted so the legs are above its head, the baby will automatically extend its arms in a gesture, called the Moro reflex, that looks like an embrace. Babies normally lose this reflex after they reach 6 months, but those with cerebral palsy may retain it for abnormally long periods. This is just one of several reflexes that a physician can check.

Doctors can also look for hand preference—a tendency to use either the right or left hand more often. When the doctor holds an object in front and to the side of the infant, an infant with hand preference will use the favored hand to reach for the object, even when it is held closer to the opposite hand. During the first 12 months of life, babies do not usually show hand preference. But infants with spastic hemiplegia, in particular, may develop a preference much earlier, since the hand on the unaffected side of their body is stronger and more useful.

The next step in diagnosing cerebral palsy is to rule out other disorders that can cause movement problems. Most important, doctors must determine that the child's condition is not getting worse. Although its symptoms may change over time, cerebral palsy by definition is not progressive. If a child is continuously losing motor skills, the problem is probably due to other causes—including genetic diseases, muscle diseases, disorders of metabolism, or tumors in the nervous system. The child's medical history, special diagnostic tests, and, in some cases, repeated check-ups can help confirm that other disorders are not the cause.

The doctor may also order specialized tests to learn more about the possible cause of cerebral palsy. One such test is *computed tomography*, or CT, a sophisticated imaging technique that uses X rays and a computer to create an anatomical picture of the brain's tissues and structures. A CT scan may reveal brain areas that are underdeveloped, abnormal cysts (sacs that are often filled with liquid) in the brain, or other physical problems. With the information from CT scans, doctors may be better equipped to judge the long-term outlook for an affected child.

Magnetic resonance imaging, or MRI, is a relatively new brain imaging technique that is rapidly gaining widespread use for identifying brain disorders. This technique uses a magnetic field and radio waves, rather than X rays. MRI gives better pictures of structures or abnormal areas located near bone than CT.

A third test that can expose problems in brain tissues is *ultrasonography*. This technique bounces sound waves off the brain and uses the pattern of echoes to form a picture, or sonogram, of its structures. Ultrasonography can be used in infants before the bones of the skull harden and close. Although it is less precise than CT and MRI scanning, this technique can detect cysts and structures in the brain, is less expensive, and does not require long periods of immobility.

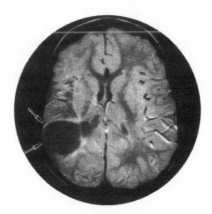

Figure 38.2. Like a scar that records an old injury to the skin, the large cyst (arrows) seen in this MRI scan reflects earlier damage or faulty development in the brain.

Finally, physicians may want to look for other conditions that are linked to cerebral palsy, including seizure disorders, mental impairment, and vision or hearing problems.

When the doctor suspects a seizure disorder, an *electroencephalogram*, or EEG, may be ordered. An EEG uses special patches called electrodes placed on the scalp to record the natural electrical currents inside the brain. This recording can help the doctor see telltale patterns in the brain's electrical activity that suggest a seizure disorder.

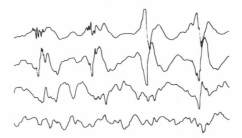

Figure 38.3. Sharp peaks and valleys on this EEG tracing reveal bursts of abnormal electrical activity in the brain during seizures in a 2-year-old child.

Intelligence tests are often used to determine if a child with cerebral palsy is mentally impaired. Sometimes, however, a child's intelligence may be underestimated because problems with movement, sensation, or speech due to cerebral palsy make it difficult for him or her to perform well on these tests.

If problems with vision are suspected, the doctor may refer the patient to an ophthalmologist for examination; if hearing impairment seems likely, an otologist may be called in.

Identifying these accompanying conditions is important and is becoming more accurate as ongoing research yields advances that make diagnosis easier. Many of these conditions can then be addressed through specific treatments, improving the long-term outlook for those with cerebral palsy.

How is Cerebral Palsy Managed?

Cerebral palsy can not be cured, but treatment can often improve a child's capabilities. In fact, progress due to medical research now means that many patients can enjoy near-normal lives if their neurological problems are properly managed. There is no standard therapy that works for all patients. Instead, the physician must work with a team of health care professionals first to identify a child's unique needs and impairments and then to create an individual treatment plan that addresses them.

Some approaches that can be included in this plan are drugs to control seizures and muscle spasms, special braces to compensate for muscle imbalance, surgery, mechanical aids to help overcome impairments, counseling for emotional and psychological needs, and physical, occupational, speech, and behavioral therapy. In general, the earlier treatment begins, the better chance a child has of overcoming developmental disabilities or learning new ways to accomplish difficult tasks.

The members of the treatment team for a child with cerebral palsy should be knowledgeable professionals with a wide range of specialties. A typical treatment team might include:

- **a physician**, such as a pediatrician, a pediatric neurologist, or a pediatric physiatrist, trained to help developmentally disabled children. This physician, often the leader of the treatment team, works to synthesize the professional advice of all team members into a comprehensive treatment plan, implements treatments, and follows the patient's progress over a number of years.

- **an orthopedist**, a surgeon who specializes in treating the bones, muscles, tendons, and other parts of the body's skeletal system. An orthopedist might be called on to predict, diagnose, or treat muscle problems associated with cerebral palsy.

- **a physical therapist**, who designs and implements special exercise programs to improve movement and strength.

- **an occupational therapist**, who can help patients learn skills for day-to-day living, school, and work.

- **a speech and language pathologist**, who specializes in diagnosing and treating communication problems.

- **a social worker**, who can help patients and their families locate community assistance and education programs.

- **a psychologist**, who helps patients and their families cope with the special stresses and demands of cerebral palsy. In some cases, psychologists may also oversee therapy to modify unhelpful or destructive behaviors or habits.

- **an educator**, who may play an especially important role when mental impairment or learning disabilities present a challenge to education.

Individuals who have cerebral palsy and their family or caregivers are also key members of the treatment team, and they should be intimately involved in all steps of planning, making decisions, and applying treatments. Studies have shown that family support and personal determination are two of the most important predictors of which individuals who have cerebral palsy will achieve long-term goals.

Too often, however, physicians and parents may focus primarily on an individual symptom—especially the inability to walk. While mastering specific skills is an important focus of treatment on a day-to-day basis, the ultimate goal is to help individuals grow to adulthood and have maximum independence in society. In the words of one physician, "After all, the real point of walking is to get from point A to point B. Even if a child needs a wheelchair, what's important is that they're able to achieve this goal."

What Specific Treatments Are Available?

Physical, Behavioral, and Other Therapies

Therapy—whether for movement, speech, or practical tasks—is a cornerstone of cerebral palsy treatment. The skills a 2-year-old needs to explore the world are very different from those that a child needs in the classroom or a young adult needs to become independent. Cerebral palsy therapy should be tailored to reflect these changing demands.

Physical therapy. Physical therapy usually begins in the first few years of life, soon after the diagnosis is made. Physical therapy programs use specific sets of exercises to work toward two important goals: preventing the weakening or deterioration of muscles that can follow lack of use (called disuse atrophy) and avoiding *contracture*, in which muscles become fixed in a rigid, abnormal position.

Contracture is one of the most common and serious complications of cerebral palsy. A contracture is a chronic shortening of a muscle due to abnormal tone and weakness associated with cerebral palsy. A muscle contracture limits movement of a bony joint, such as the elbow, and can disrupt balance and cause loss of previous motor abilities.

Physical therapy alone, or in combination with special braces (sometimes called *orthotic devices*), works to prevent this complication by stretching spastic muscles. For example, if a child has spastic hamstrings (tendons located behind the knee), the therapist and parents should encourage the child to sit with the legs extended to stretch them.

A third goal of some physical therapy programs is to improve the child's motor development. A widespread program of physical therapy that works toward this goal is the Bobath technique, named for a husband and wife team who pioneered this approach in England. This program is based on the idea that the primitive reflexes retained by many children with cerebral palsy present major roadblocks to learning voluntary control. A therapist using the Bobath technique tries to counteract these reflexes by positioning the child in an opposing movement. So, for example, if a child with cerebral palsy normally keeps his arm flexed, the therapist would repeatedly extend it.

A second such approach to physical therapy is "patterning," which is based on the principle that motor skills should be taught in more or less the same sequence that they develop normally. In this controversial approach, the therapist guides the child with movement problems along the path of normal motor development. For example, the child is first taught elementary movements like pulling himself to a standing position and crawling before he is taught to walk—regardless of his age. Some experts and organizations, including the American Academy of Pediatrics, have expressed strong reservations about the patterning approach, because studies have not documented its value.

Physical therapy is usually just one element of an infant development program that also includes efforts to provide a varied and stimulating environment. Like all children, the child with cerebral palsy needs new experiences and interactions with the world around him in order to learn. Stimulation programs can bring this valuable experience to the child who is physically unable to explore.

As the child with cerebral palsy approaches school age, the emphasis of therapy shifts away from early motor development. Efforts now focus on preparing the child for the classroom, helping the child master activities of daily living, and maximizing the child's ability to communicate.

Physical therapy can now help the child with cerebral palsy prepare for the classroom by improving his or her ability to sit, move independently or in a wheelchair, or perform precise tasks, such as writing. In **occupational therapy**, the therapist works with the child to develop such skills as feeding, dressing, or using the bathroom. This can help reduce demands on caregivers and boost self-reliance and self-esteem. For the many children who have difficulty communicating, **speech therapy** works to identify specific difficulties and overcome them through a program of exercises. For example, if a child has difficulty saying words that begin with "b," the therapist may suggest daily practice with a list of "b" words, increasing their difficulty as each list is mastered. Speech therapy can also work to help the child learn to use special communication devices, such as a computer with voice synthesizers.

Behavioral therapy. Behavioral therapy provides yet another avenue to increase a child's abilities. This therapy, which uses psychological theory and techniques, can complement physical, speech, or occupational therapy. For example, behavioral therapy might include hiding a toy inside a box to reward a child for learning to reach into the box with his weaker hand. Likewise, a child learning to say his "b" words might be given a balloon for mastering the word. In other cases, therapists may try to discourage unhelpful or destructive behaviors, such as hair-pulling or biting, by selectively presenting a child with rewards and praise during other, more positive activities.

As a child with cerebral palsy grows older, the need for and types of therapy and other support services will continue to change. Continuing physical therapy addresses movement problems and is supplemented by vocational training, recreation and leisure programs, and special education when necessary. Counseling for emotional and psychological challenges may be needed at any age, but is often most critical during adolescence. Depending on their physical and intellectual abilities, adults may need attendant care, living accommodations, transportation, or employment opportunities.

Regardless of the patient's age and which forms of therapy are used, treatment does not end when the patient leaves the office or treatment center. In fact, most of the work is often done at home. The therapist functions as a coach, providing parents and patients with the strategy and drills that can help improve performance at home, at school, and in the world. As research continues, doctors and parents can expect new forms of therapy and better information about which forms of therapy are most effective for individuals with cerebral palsy.

Drug Therapy

Physicians usually prescribe drugs for those who have seizures associated with cerebral palsy, and these medications are very effective in preventing seizures in many patients. In general, the drugs given to individual patients are chosen based on the type of seizures, since no one drug controls all types. However, different people with the same type of seizure may do better on different drugs, and some individuals may need a combination of two or more drugs to achieve good seizure control.

Drugs are also sometimes used to control spasticity, particularly following surgery. The three medications that are used most often are diazepam, which acts as a general relaxant of the brain and body; baclofen, which blocks signals sent from the spinal cord to contract the muscles; and dantrolene, which interferes with the process of muscle contraction. Given by mouth, these drugs can reduce spasticity for short periods, but their value for long-term control of spasticity has not been clearly demonstrated. They may also trigger significant side effects, such as drowsiness, and their long-term effects on the developing nervous system are largely unknown. One possible solution to avoid such side effects may lie in current research to explore new routes for delivering these drugs.

Patients with athetoid cerebral palsy may sometimes be given drugs that help reduce abnormal movements. Most often, the prescribed drug belongs to a group of chemicals called anticholinergics that work by reducing the activity of acetylcholine. Acetylcholine is a chemical messenger that helps some brain cells communicate and that triggers muscle contraction. Anticholinergic drugs include trihexyphenidyl, benztropine, and procyclidine hydrochloride.

Occasionally, physicians may use alcohol "washes"—or injections of alcohol into a muscle—to reduce spasticity for a short period. This technique is most often used when physicians want to correct a developing contracture. Injecting alcohol into a muscle that is too short weakens the muscle for several weeks and gives physicians time to work on lengthening the muscle through bracing, therapy, or casts. In some cases, if the contracture is detected early enough, this technique may avert the need for surgery. In addition, a number of experimental drug therapies are under investigation.

Surgery

Surgery is often recommended when contractures are severe enough to cause movement problems. In the operating room, surgeons can lengthen muscles and tendons that are proportionately too short. First, however, they must determine the exact muscles at fault, since lengthening the wrong muscle could make the problem worse.

Finding problem muscles that need correction can be a difficult task. To walk two strides with a normal gait, it takes more than 30 major muscles working at exactly the right time and exactly the right force. A problem in any one muscle can cause abnormal gait. Furthermore, the natural adjustments the body makes to compensate for muscle problems can be misleading. A new tool that enables doctors to spot gait abnormalities, pinpoint problem muscles, and separate real problems from compensation is called *gait analysis*. Gait analysis combines cameras that record the patient while walking, computers

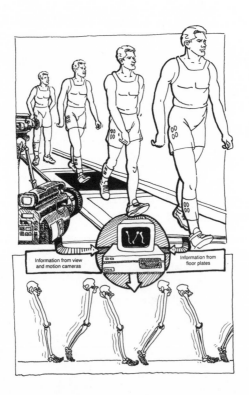

Figure 38.4. *In gait analysis, video cameras, sensitive force plates on the floor, and a computer help tease apart the hundreds of individual movements needed to take a single stride. This process can help physicians spot and treat problems with specific muscles and tendons in cerebral palsy.*

that analyze each portion of the patient's gait, force plates that detect when feet touch the ground, and a special recording technique that detects muscle activity (known as *electromyography*). Using these data, doctors are better equipped to intervene and correct significant problems. They can also use gait analysis to check surgical results.

Because lengthening a muscle makes it weaker, surgery for contractures is usually followed by months of recovery. For this reason, doctors try to fix all of the affected muscles at once when it is possible or, if more than one surgical procedure is unavoidable, they may try to schedule operations close together.

A second surgical technique, known as *selective dorsal root rhizotomy*, aims to reduce spasticity in the legs by reducing the amount of stimulation that reaches leg muscles via nerves. In the procedure, doctors try to locate and selectively sever some of the overactivated nerve fibers that control leg muscle tone. Although there is scientific controversy over how selective this technique actually is, recent research results suggest it can reduce spasticity in some patients, particularly those who have spastic diplegia. Ongoing research is evaluating this surgery's effectiveness.

Experimental surgical techniques include chronic cerebellar stimulation and stereotaxic thalamotomy. In chronic cerebellar stimulation, electrodes are implanted on the surface of the cerebellum—the part of the brain responsible for coordinating movement—and are used to stimulate certain cerebellar nerves. While it was hoped that this technique would decrease spasticity and improve motor function, results of this invasive procedure have been mixed. Some studies have reported improvements in spasticity and function, others have not.

Stereotaxic thalamotomy involves precise cutting of parts of the thalamus, which serves as the brain's relay station for messages from the muscles and sensory organs. This has been shown effective only for reducing, hemiparetic tremors.

Mechanical Aids

Whether they are as humble as velcro shoes or as advanced as computerized communication devices, special machines and gadgets in the home, school, and workplace can help the child or adult with cerebral palsy overcome limitations.

The computer is probably the most dramatic example of a new device that can make a difference in the lives of those with cerebral palsy. For example, a child who is unable to speak or write but can make head movements may be able to learn to control a computer using a special light pointer that attaches to a headband. Equipped with a computer and voice synthesizer, this child could communicate with others. In other cases, technology has led to new versions of old devices, such as the traditional wheelchair and its modern offspring that runs on electricity.

What Other Major Problems Are Associated with Cerebral Palsy?

A common complication is incontinence, caused by faulty control over the muscles that keep the bladder closed. Incontinence can take the form of bed-wetting (also known as enuresis), uncontrolled urination during physical activities (or stress incontinence), or slow leaking of urine from the bladder. Possible medical treatments for incontinence include special exercises, biofeedback, prescription drugs, surgery, or surgically implanted devices to replace or aid muscles. Specially designed undergarments are also available.

Poor control of the muscles of the throat, mouth, and tongue sometimes leads to drooling. Drooling can cause severe skin irritation and, because it is socially unacceptable, can lead to further isolation of affected children from their peers. Although numerous treatments for drooling have been tested over the years, there is no one treatment that always helps. Drugs called anticholinergics can reduce the flow of saliva but may cause significant side effects, such as mouth dryness and poor digestion. Surgery, while sometimes effective, carries the risk of complications, including worsening of swallowing problems. Some patients benefit from a technique called biofeedback that can tell them when they are drooling or having difficulty controlling muscles that close the mouth. This kind of therapy is most likely to work if the patient has a mental age of more than 2 or 3 years, is motivated to control drooling, and understands that drooling is not socially acceptable.

Difficulty with eating and swallowing—also triggered by motor problems in the mouth—can cause poor nutrition. Poor nutrition, in turn, may make the individual more vulnerable to infections and cause or aggravate "failure to thrive"—a lag in growth and development that is common among those with cerebral palsy. When eating is difficult, a therapist trained to address swallowing problems can help by instituting special diets and teaching new feeding techniques. In severe cases of swallowing problems and malnutrition, physicians may recommend tube feeding, in which a tube delivers food and nutrients down the throat and into the stomach, or *gastrostomy*, in which a surgical opening allows a tube to be placed directly into the stomach.

What Research is Being Done?

Investigators from many arenas of medicine and health are using their expertise to help improve treatment and prevention of cerebral palsy. Much of their work is supported through the National Institute of Neurological Disorders and Stroke (NINDS), the National Institute of Child Health and Human Development, other agencies within the Federal Government, nonprofit groups such as the United Cerebral Palsy Research and Educational Foundation, and private institutions.

The ultimate hope for overcoming cerebral palsy lies with prevention. In order to prevent cerebral palsy, however, scientists must first understand the complex process of normal brain development and what can make this process go awry.

Between early pregnancy and the first months of life, one cell divides to form first a handful of cells, and then hundreds, millions, and, eventually, billions of cells. Some of these cells specialize to become brain cells. These brain cells specialize into different types and migrate to their appropriate site in the brain. They send out branches to form crucial connections with other brain cells. Ultimately, the most complex entity known to us is created: a human brain with its billions of interconnected neurons.

Mounting evidence is pointing investigators toward this intricate process in the womb for clues about cerebral palsy. For example, a group of researchers has recently observed that more than one-third of children who have cerebral palsy also have missing enamel on certain teeth. This tooth defect can be traced to problems in the early months of fetal development, suggesting that a disruption at this period in development might be linked both to this tooth defect and to cerebral palsy.

As a result of this and other research, many scientists now believe that a significant number of children develop cerebral palsy because of mishaps early in brain development. They are examining how brain cells specialize, how they know where to migrate, how they form the right connections—and they are looking for preventable factors that can disrupt this process before or after birth.

Scientists are also scrutinizing other events—such as bleeding in the brain, seizures, and breathing and circulation problems—that threaten the brain of the newborn baby. Through this research, they hope to learn how these hazards can damage the newborn's brain and to develop new methods for prevention.

Some newborn infants, for example, have life-threatening problems with breathing and blood circulation. A recently introduced treatment to help these infants is extracorporeal membrane oxygenation (ECMO), in which blood is routed from the patient to a special machine that takes over the lungs' task of removing carbon dioxide and adding oxygen. Although this technique can dramatically help many such infants, some scientists have observed that a substantial fraction of treated children later experience long-term neurological problems, including developmental delay and cerebral palsy. Investigators are studying infants through pregnancy, delivery, birth, and infancy, and are tracking those who undergo this treatment. By observing them at all stages of development, scientists can learn whether their problems developed before birth, result from the same breathing problems that made them candidates for the treatment, or spring from errors in the treatment itself. Once this is determined, they may be able to correct any existing problems or develop new treatment methods to prevent brain damage.

Other scientists are exploring how brain insults like hypoxic-ischemic encephalopathy (brain damage from a shortage of oxygen or blood flow), bleeding in the brain, and seizures can cause the abnormal release of brain chemicals and trigger brain damage. For example, research has shown that bleeding in the brain unleashes dangerously high amounts of a brain chemical called glutamate. While glutamate is normally used in the brain for communication, too much glutamate overstimulates the brain's cells and causes a cycle of destruction. Scientists are now looking closely at glutamate to detect how its release harms brain tissue and spreads the damage from stroke. By learning how such brain chemicals that normally help us function can hurt the brain, scientists may be equipped to develop new drugs that block their harmful effects.

In related research, some investigators are already conducting studies to learn if certain drugs can help prevent neonatal stroke. Several of these drugs seem promising because they appear to reduce the excess production of potentially dangerous chemicals in the brain and may help control brain blood flow and volume. Earlier research has linked sudden changes in blood flow and volume to stroke in the newborn.

Low birthweight itself is also the subject of extensive research. In spite of improvements in health care for some pregnant women, the incidence of low birth-weight babies born each year in the United States remains at about 7 ½ percent. Some scientists currently investigating this serious health problem are working to understand how infections, hormonal problems, and genetic factors may increase a woman's chances of giving birth prematurely. They are also conducting more applied research that could yield: 1) new drugs that can safely delay labor, 2) new devices to further improve medical care for premature infants, and 3) new insight into how smoking and alcohol consumption can disrupt fetal development.

While this research offers hope for preventing cerebral palsy in the future, ongoing research to improve treatment brightens the outlook for those who must face the challenges of cerebral palsy today. An important thrust of such research is the evaluation of treatments already in use so that physicians and parents have the information they need to choose the best therapy. A good example of this effort is an ongoing NINDS-supported study that promises to yield new information about which patients are most likely to benefit from selective dorsal root rhizotomy, a recently introduced surgery that is becoming increasingly in demand for reduction of spasticity.

Similarly, although physical therapy programs are a popular and widespread approach to managing cerebral palsy, little scientific evidence exists to help physicians, other health professionals, and parents determine how well physical therapy works or to choose the best approach among many. Current research on cerebral palsy aims to provide this information through careful studies that compare the abilities of children who have had physical and other therapy with those who have not.

As part of this effort, scientists are working to create new measures to judge the effectiveness of treatment, as in ongoing research to precisely identify the specific brain areas responsible for movement. Using such techniques as magnetic pulses, researchers can locate brain areas that control specific actions, such as raising an arm or lifting a leg, and construct detailed maps. By comparing charts made before and after therapy among children who have cerebral palsy, researchers may gain new insights into how therapy affects the brain's organization and new data about its effectiveness.

Investigators are also working to develop new drugs—and new ways of using existing drugs—to help relieve cerebral palsy's symptoms. In one such set of studies, early research results suggest that doctors may improve the effectiveness of the anti-spasticity drug called baclofen by giving the drug through spinal injections, rather than by mouth. In addition, scientists are also exploring the use of tiny implanted pumps that deliver a constant supply of anti-spasticity drugs into the fluid around the spinal cord, in the hope of improving these drugs' effectiveness and reducing side effects, such as drowsiness.

Other experimental drug development efforts are exploring the use of minute amounts of the familiar toxin called botulinum. Ingested in large amounts, this toxin is responsible for botulism poisoning, in which the body's muscles become paralyzed. Injected in tiny amounts into specific muscles, however, this toxin has shown early promise in reducing local spasticity.

A large research effort is also directed at producing more effective, nontoxic drugs to control seizures. Through its Antiepileptic Drug Development Program, the NINDS screens new compounds developed by industrial and university laboratories around the world for toxicity and anticonvulsant activity and coordinates clinical studies of efficacy and safety. To date, this program has screened more than 13,000 compounds and, as a result, five new antiepileptic drugs— carbamazepine, clonazepam, valproate, clorazepate, and felbamate— have been approved for marketing. A new project within the program is exploring how the structure of a given antiseizure medication relates to its effectiveness. If successful, this project may enable scientists to design better antiseizure medications more quickly and cheaply.

As researchers continue to explore new treatments for cerebral palsy and to expand our knowledge of brain development, we can expect significant medical advances to prevent cerebral palsy and many other disorders that strike in early life.

Where Can I Find More Information?

The NINDS is the Federal Government's leading supporter of biomedical research on brain and nervous system disorders, including cerebral palsy. The NINDS conducts research in its own laboratories at the National Institutes of Health in Bethesda, MD, and supports research at institutions worldwide. The Institute also sponsors an active public information program. Other NINDS publications that may be of interest to those concerned about cerebral palsy include "Epilepsy: Hope Through Research" and "The Dystonias." The Institute's address and phone number, as well as information on other organizations that offer various services to those affected by cerebral palsy, are provided below.

Information Resources

NIH Neurological Institute
P.O. Box 5801
Bethesda, MD 20824
(301) 496-5751
(800) 352-9424

The National Institute of Neurological Disorders and Stroke, a component of the National Institutes of Health, is the leading federal supporter of research on brain and nervous system disorders. The Institute also sponsors an active public information program and can answer questions about diagnosis, treatment, and research related to cerebral palsy.

In addition, a number of private organizations offer a variety of services and information that can help those affected by cerebral palsy. They include:

March of Dimes Birth Defects Foundation
1275 Mamaroneck Avenue
White Plains, NY 10605
(914) 428-7100

This foundation funds research, medical services, public education, and genetic counseling. Resources include fact sheets, brochures, educational kits, and audiovisual materials.

National Easter Seal Society
230 W. Monroe, 18th floor
Chicago, IL 60606
(312) 726-6200
(312) 726-4258 (TDD)

This organization includes state and local affiliates and operates facilities and programs across the country. They offer a range of rehabilitation services, research and public education programs, and assistive technology services. Their programs also include therapy, counseling, training, social clubs, camping, transportation, and referrals. In addition, the society sponsors a grants program for research on disabling conditions and rehabilitation, provides low-cost booklets and pamphlets to the public, and publishes a bimonthly journal.

United Cerebral Palsy Associations and
The United Cerebral Palsy Research and Educational Foundation
1522 K Street, NW
Suite 1112
Washington, DC 20005
(202) 842-1266
(800) USA-5UCP (outside Washington, DC)

This coalition of associations provides family support, legislative advocacy, public information and education, and training, specifically for issues of importance to those who have cerebral palsy. It also publishes newsletters and various brochures and pamphlets. The UCP Research and Educational Foundation supports research to prevent cerebral palsy and develop therapies to improve the quality of life for those affected by this disorder.

More information about seizures and epilepsy is available from:

Epilepsy Foundation of America
4351 Garden City Drive
Landover, MD 20785
(301) 459-3700
(800) EFA-1000

This foundation sponsors programs for patient and public education, legal and government affairs, and employment training and placement. The foundation also supports research, maintains the National Epilepsy Library (800-EFA-4050), publishes a variety of patient/family and professional education materials, and sponsors affiliates.

Chapter 39

Headache

Introduction

An estimated 45 million Americans experience chronic headaches. For at least half of these people, the problem is severe and sometimes disabling. It can also be costly: headache sufferers make over 8 million visits a year to doctors' offices. Migraine victims alone lose over 157 million workdays because of headache pain.

Understanding why headaches occur and improving headache treatment are among the research goals of the National Institute of Neurological Disorders and Stroke (NINDS). As the leading supporter of brain research in the Federal Government, the NINDS also supports and conducts studies to improve the diagnosis of headaches and to find ways to prevent them.

Why Does it Hurt?

What hurts when you have a headache? Several areas of the head can hurt, including a network of nerves which extends over the scalp and certain nerves in the face, mouth, and throat. Also sensitive to pain, because they contain delicate nerve fibers, are the muscles of the head and blood vessels found along the surface and at the base of the brain.

The bones of the skull and tissues of the brain itself, however, never hurt, because they lack pain-sensitive nerve fibers.

National Institute of Neurological Disorders and Stroke (NINDS), NIH Pub. No. 96-158, October 1996.

The ends of these pain-sensitive nerves, called *nociceptors*, can he stimulated by stress, muscular tension, dilated blood vessels, and other triggers of headache. Once stimulated, a nociceptor sends a message up the length of the nerve fiber to the nerve cells in the brain, signaling that a part of the body hurts. The message is determined by the location of the nociceptor. A person who suddenly realizes "My toe hurts," is responding to nociceptors in the foot that have been stimulated by the stubbing of a toe.

A number of chemicals help transmit pain-related information to the brain. Some of these chemicals are natural painkilling proteins called *endorphins*, Greek for "the morphine within." One theory suggests that people who suffer from severe headache and other types of chronic pain have lower levels of endorphins than people who are generally pain free.

When Should You See a Physician?

Not all headaches require medical attention. Some result from missed meals or occasional muscle tension and are easily remedied. But some types of headache are signals of more serious disorders, and call for prompt medical care. These include:

- Sudden, severe headache
- Headache associated with convulsions
- Headache accompanied by confusion or loss of consciousness
- Headache following a blow on the head
- Headache associated with pain in the eye or ear
- Persistent headache in a person who was previously headache free
- Recurring headache in children
- Headache associated with fever
- Headache which interferes with normal life

A headache sufferer usually seeks help from a family practitioner. If the problem is not relieved by standard treatments, the patient may then be referred to a specialist—perhaps an internist or neurologist. Additional referrals may be made to psychologists.

What Tests are Used to Diagnose Headache?

Diagnosing a headache is like playing Twenty Questions. Experts agree that a detailed question-and-answer session with a patient can often produce enough information for a diagnosis. Many types of headaches have clear-cut symptoms which fall into an easily recognizable pattern.

Patients may be asked: How often do you have headaches? Where is the pain? How long do the headaches last? When did you first develop headaches? The patient's sleep habits and family and work situations may also be probed.

Most physicians will also obtain a full medical history from the patient, inquiring about past head trauma or surgery and about the use of medications. A blood test may be ordered to screen for thyroid disease, anemia, or infections which might cause a headache. X-rays may be taken to rule out the possibility of a brain tumor or blood clot.

A test called an *electroencephalogram* (EEG) may be given to measure brain activity. EEG's can indicate a malfunction in the brain, but they cannot usually pinpoint a problem that might be causing a headache. A physician may suggest that a patient with unusual headaches undergo a *computed tomographic (CT) scan* and/or *magnetic resonance imaging (MRI)*. The CT scan produces images of the brain that show structures or variations in the density of different types of tissue. The scan enables the physician to distinguish, for example, between a bleeding blood vessel in the brain and a brain tumor, and is an important diagnostic tool in cases of headache associated with brain lesions or other serious disease. MRI uses magnetic fields and radio waves to produce an image that provides information about the structure and biochemistry of the brain.

An eye exam is usually performed to check for weakness in the eye muscle or unequal pupil size. Both of these symptoms are evidence of an aneurysm—an abnormal ballooning of a blood vessel. A physician who suspects that a headache patient has an aneurysm may also order an *angiogram*. In this test, a special fluid which can be seen on an X-ray is injected into the patient and carried in the bloodstream to the brain to reveal any abnormalities in the blood vessels there.

Thermography, an experimental technique for diagnosing headache, promises to become a useful clinical tool. In thermography, an infrared camera converts skin temperature into a color picture or thermogram with different degrees of heat appearing as different colors. Skin temperature is affected primarily by blood flow. Research scientists have found that thermograms of headache patients show strikingly different heat patterns from those of people who never or rarely get headaches.

A physician analyzes the results of all these diagnostic tests along with a patient's medical history in order to arrive at a diagnosis.

Headaches are diagnosed as

- Vascular
- Muscle contraction (tension)
- Traction
- Inflammatory

Vascular headaches—a group that includes the well-known *migraine* are so named because they are thought to involve abnormal function of the brain's blood vessels or vascular system. Muscle contraction headaches appear to involve the tightening or tensing of facial and neck muscles. Traction and inflammatory headaches are symptoms of other disorders, ranging from stroke to sinus infection. Some people have more than one type of headache.

What are Migraine Headaches?

The most common type of vascular headache is migraine. Migraine headaches are usually characterized by severe pain on one or both sides of the head, an upset stomach, and at times disturbed vision.

Former basketball star Kareem Abdul-Jabbar remembers experiencing his first migraine at age 14. The pain was unlike the discomfort of his previous mild headaches.

"When I got this one I thought, *'This* is a headache'," he says. "The pain was intense and I felt nausea and a great sensitivity to light. All I could think about was when it would stop. I sat in a dark room for an hour and it passed."

Symptoms of Migraine

Abdul-Jabbar's sensitivity to light is a standard symptom of the two most prevalent types of migraine-caused headache: classic and common.

The major difference between the two types is the appearance of neurological symptoms 10 to 30 minutes before a classic migraine attack. These symptoms are called an *aura*. The person may see flashing lights or zigzag lines, or may temporarily lose vision. Other classic symptoms include speech difficulty, weakness of an arm or leg, tingling of the face or hands, and confusion.

The pain of a classic migraine headache is described as intense, throbbing, or pounding and is felt in the forehead, temple, ear, jaw, or around the eye. Classic migraine starts on one side of the head but

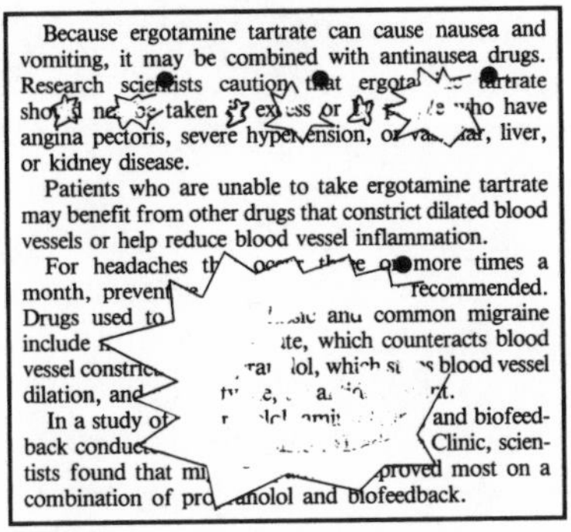

Because ergotamine tartrate can cause nausea and vomiting, it may be combined with antinausea drugs. Research scientists caution that ergotamine tartrate should never be taken in excess or by those who have angina pectoris, severe hypertension, or vascular, liver, or kidney disease.

Patients who are unable to take ergotamine tartrate may benefit from other drugs that constrict dilated blood vessels or help reduce blood vessel inflammation.

For headaches that occur three or more times a month, prevention is recommended. Drugs used to treat classic and common migraine include methysergite, which counteracts blood vessel constriction, propranolol, which slows blood vessel dilation, and amitriptyline.

In a study of biofeedback conducted at the Menninger Clinic, scientists found that migraine patients improved most on a combination of propranolol and biofeedback.

Figure 39.1. If you were about to experience a classic migraine headache, you might find it difficult to read this pamphlet. You could lose part of your vision temporarily and see zigzag lines and black dots. Such visual problems—and other neurological symptoms—often precede classic migraine.

may eventually spread to the other side. An attack lasts 1 to 2 pain-wracked days.

The common migraine—a term that reflects the disorder's greater occurrence in the general population—is not preceded by an aura. But some people experience a variety of vague symptoms beforehand, including mental fuzziness, mood changes, fatigue, and unusual retention of fluids. During the headache phase of a common migraine, a person may have diarrhea and increased urination, as well as nausea and vomiting. Common migraine pain can last 3 or 4 days.

Both classic and common migraine can strike as often as several times a week, or as rarely as once every few years. Both types can occur at any time. Some people, however, experience migraines at predictable times—near the days of menstruation or every Saturday morning after a stressful week of work.

The Migraine Process

Research scientists are unclear about the precise cause of migraine headaches. There seems to be general agreement, however, that a key element is blood flow changes in the brain. People who get migraine headaches appear to have blood vessels that overreact to various triggers.

Scientists have devised one theory of migraine which explains these blood flow changes and also certain biochemical changes that may be involved in the headache process. According to this theory, the nervous system responds to a trigger such as stress by creating a spasm in the nerve-rich arteries at the base of the brain. The spasm closes down or constricts several arteries supplying blood to the brain, including the scalp artery and the carotid or neck arteries.

As these arteries constrict, the flow of blood to the brain is reduced. At the same time, blood-clotting particles called platelets clump together—a process which is believed to release a chemical called *serotonin*. Serotonin acts as a powerful constrictor of arteries, further reducing the blood supply to the brain.

Reduced blood flow decreases the brain's supply of oxygen. Symptoms signaling a headache, such as distorted vision or speech, may then result, similar to symptoms of stroke.

Reacting to the reduced oxygen supply, certain arteries within the brain open wider to meet the brain's energy needs. This widening or dilation spreads, finally affecting the neck and scalp arteries. The dilation of these arteries triggers the release of pain-producing substances called *prostaglandins* from various tissues and blood cells. Chemicals which cause inflammation and swelling and substances which increase sensitivity to pain are also released. The circulation of these chemicals and the dilation of the scalp arteries stimulate the pain-sensitive nociceptors. The result, according to this theory: a throbbing pain in the head.

Women and Migraine

Although both males and females seem to be affected by migraine, the condition is more common in adult women. Both sexes may develop migraine in infancy, but most often the disorder begins between the ages of 5 and 35.

The relationship between female hormones and migraine is still unclear. Women may have "menstrual migraine"—headaches around the time of their menstrual period—which may disappear during pregnancy. Other women develop migraine for the first time when they are pregnant. Some are first affected after menopause.

The effect of oral contraceptives on headaches is perplexing. Scientists report that some women with migraine who take birth control pills experience more frequent and severe attacks. However, a small percentage of women have fewer and less severe migraine headaches when they take birth control pills. And normal women who do not suffer from headaches may develop migraines as a side effect when they use oral contraceptives. Investigators around the world are studying hormonal changes in women with migraine in the hope of identifying the specific ways these naturally occurring chemicals cause headaches.

Triggers of Headache

Although many sufferers have a family history of migraine, the exact hereditary nature of this condition is still unknown. People who get migraines are thought to have an inherited abnormality in the regulation of blood vessels.

"It's like a cocked gun with a hair trigger," explains one specialist. "A person is born with a potential for migraine and the headache is triggered by things that are really not so terrible."

These triggers include stress and other normal emotions, as well as biological and environmental conditions. Fatigue, glaring or flickering fights, the weather, and certain foods can set off migraine. It may seem hard to believe that eating such seemingly harmless foods as yogurt, nuts, and lima beans can result in a painful migraine headache. However, some scientists believe that these foods and several others contain chemical substances, such as tyramine, which constrict arteries—the first step of the migraine process. Other scientists believe that foods cause headaches by setting off an allergic reaction in susceptible people.

While a food-triggered migraine usually occurs soon after eating, other triggers may not cause immediate pain. Scientists report that people can develop migraine not only during a period of stress but also afterwards when their vascular systems are still reacting. For example, migraines that wake people up in the middle of the night are believed to result from a delayed reaction to stress.

Other Forms of Migraine

In addition to classic and common, migraine headache can take several other forms:

Patients with *hemiplegic migraine* have temporary paralysis on one side of the body, a condition known as hemiplegia. Some people may experience vision problems and vertigo—a feeling that the world is spinning. These symptoms begin 10 to 90 minutes before the onset of headache pain.

In *ophthalmoplegic migraine*, the pain is around the eye and is associated with a droopy eyelid, double vision, and other sight problems.

Basilar artery migraine involves a disturbance of a major brain artery. Preheadache symptoms include vertigo, double vision, and poor muscular coordination. This type of migraine occurs primarily in adolescent and young adult women and is often associated with the menstrual cycle.

Benign exertional headache is brought on by running, lifting, coughing, sneezing, or bending. The headache begins at the onset of activity, and pain rarely lasts more than several minutes.

Status migrainosus is a rare and severe type of migraine that can last 72 hours or longer. The pain and nausea are so intense that people who have this type of headache must be hospitalized. The use of certain drugs can trigger status migrainosus. Neurologists report that many of their status migrainosus patients were depressed and anxious before they experienced headache attacks.

Headache-free migraine is characterized by such migraine symptoms as visual problems, nausea, vomiting, constipation, or diarrhea. Patients, however, do not experience head pain. Headache specialists have suggested that unexplained pain in a particular part of the body, fever, and dizziness could also be possible types of headache-free migraine.

How Is Migraine Headache Treated?

During the Stone Age, pieces of a headache sufferer's skull were cut away with flint instruments to relieve pain. Another unpleasant remedy used in the British Isles around the ninth century involved drinking "the juice of elderseed, cow's brain, and goat's dung dissolved in vinegar." Fortunately, today's headache patients are spared such drastic measures.

Drug therapy, biofeedback training, stress reduction, and elimination of certain foods from the diet are the most common methods of preventing and controlling migraine and other vascular headaches.

Regular exercise, such as swimming or vigorous walking, can also reduce the frequency and severity of migraine headaches.

During a migraine headache, temporary relief can sometimes he obtained by using cold packs or by pressing on the bulging artery found in front of the ear on the painful side of the head.

Drug Therapy

There are two ways to approach the treatment of migraine headache with drugs: prevent the attacks, or relieve symptoms after the headache occurs.

For infrequent migraine, drugs can be taken at the first sign of a headache in order to stop it or to at least ease the pain. People who get occasional mild migraine may benefit by taking aspirin or acetaminophen at the start of an attack. Aspirin raises a person's tolerance to pain and also discourages clumping of blood platelets. Small amounts of caffeine may be useful if taken in the early stages of migraine. But for most migraine sufferers who get moderate to severe headaches, and for all cluster patients, stronger drugs may be necessary to control the pain.

One of the most commonly used drugs for the relief of classic and common migraine symptoms is *ergotamine tartrate*, a vasoconstrictor which helps counteract the painful dilation stage of the headache. For optimal benefit, the drug is taken during the early stages of an attack. If a migraine has been in progress for about an hour and has passed into the final throbbing stage, ergotamine tartrate will probably not help.

Because ergotamine tartrate can cause nausea and vomiting, it may be combined with antinausea drugs. Research scientists caution that ergotamine tartrate should not be taken in excess or by people who have angina pectoris, severe hypertension, or vascular, liver, or kidney disease.

Patients who are unable to take ergotamine tartrate may benefit from other drugs that constrict dilated blood vessels or help reduce blood vessel inflammation.

For headaches that occur three or more times a month, preventive treatment is usually recommended. Drugs used to prevent classic and common migraine include methysergide maleate, which counteracts blood vessel constriction; propranolol hydrochloride, which stops blood vessel dilation; and amitriptyline, an antidepressant.

Antidepressants called MAO inhibitors also prevent migraine. These drugs block an enzyme called monoamine oxidase which normally helps nerve cells absorb the artery-constricting brain chemical, serotonin.

MAO inhibitors can have potentially serious side effects—particularly if taken while ingesting foods or beverages that contain tyramine, a substance that constricts arteries.

Several drugs for the prevention of migraine have been developed in recent years, including serotonin agonists which mimic the action of this key brain chemical. Prompt administration of these drugs is important.

Many antimigraine drugs can have adverse side effects. But like most medicines they are relatively safe when used carefully and under a physician's supervision. To avoid long-term side effects of preventive medications, headache specialists advise patients to reduce the dosage of these drugs and then to stop taking them as soon as possible.

Biofeedback and Relaxation Training

Drug therapy for migraine is often combined with biofeedback and relaxation training. Biofeedback refers to a technique that can give people better control over such body function indicators as blood pressure, heart rate, temperature, muscle tension, and brain waves. *Thermal biofeedback* allows a patient to consciously raise hand temperature. Some patients who are able to increase hand temperature can reduce the number and intensity of migraines. The mechanisms underlying these self-regulation treatments are being studied by research scientists.

"To succeed in biofeedback," says a headache specialist, "you must be able to concentrate and you must be motivated to get well."

A patient learning thermal biofeedback wears a device which transmits the temperature of an index finger or hand to a monitor. While the patient tries to warm his hands, the monitor provides feedback either on a gauge that shows the temperature reading or by emitting a sound or beep that increases in intensity as the temperature increases. The patient is not told how to raise hand temperature, but is given suggestions such as "Imagine that your hands feel very warm and heavy."

"I have a good imagination," says one headache sufferer who traded in her medication for thermal biofeedback. The technique decreased the number and severity of headaches she experienced.

In another type of biofeedback called *electromyographic or EMG training*, the patient learns to control muscle tension in the face, neck, and shoulders.

Either kind of biofeedback may be combined with relaxation training, during which patients learn to relax the mind and body.

Biofeedback can be practiced at home with a portable monitor. But the ultimate goal of treatment is to wean the patient from the machine. The patient can then use biofeedback anywhere at the first sign of a headache.

The Antimigraine Diet

Scientists estimate that a small percentage of migraine sufferers will benefit from a treatment program focused solely on eliminating headache-provoking foods and beverages.

Other migraine patients may be helped by a diet to prevent low blood sugar. Low blood sugar, or hypoglycemia, can cause dilation of the blood vessels in the head. This condition can occur after a period without food: overnight, for example, or when a meal is skipped. People who wake up in the morning with a headache may be reacting to the low blood sugar caused by the lack of food overnight.

Treatment for headaches caused by low blood sugar consists of scheduling smaller, more frequent meals for the patient. A special diet designed to stabilize the body's sugar-regulating system is sometimes recommended.

For the same reason, many specialists also recommend that migraine patients avoid oversleeping on weekends. Sleeping late can change the body's normal blood sugar level and lead to a headache.

Besides Migraine, What are Other Types of Vascular Headaches?

After migraine, the most common type of vascular headache is the toxic headache produced by fever. Pneumonia, measles, mumps, and tonsillitis are among the diseases that can cause severe toxic vascular headaches. Toxic headaches can also result from the presence of foreign chemicals in the body. Other kinds of vascular headaches include "*clusters*," which cause repeated episodes of intense pain, and headaches resulting from a rise in blood pressure.

Chemical Culprits

Repeated exposure to nitrite compounds can result in a dull, pounding headache that may be accompanied by a flushed face. Nitrite, which dilates blood vessels, is found in such products as heart medicine and dynamite, but is also used as a chemical to preserve meat. Hot dogs and other processed meats containing sodium nitrite can cause headaches.

Eating foods prepared with monosodium glutamate (MSG) can result in headache. Soy sauce, meat tenderizer, and a variety of packaged foods contain this chemical which is touted as a flavor enhancer.

Headache can also result from exposure to poisons, even common household varieties like insecticides, carbon tetrachloride, and lead. Children who ingest flakes of lead paint may develop headaches. So may anyone who has contact with lead batteries or lead-glazed pottery.

Artists and industrial workers may experience headaches after exposure to materials that contain chemical solvents. Solvents, like benzene, are found in turpentine, spray adhesives, rubber cement, and inks.

Drugs such as amphetamines can cause headaches as a side effect. Another type of drug-related headache occurs during withdrawal from long-term therapy with the antimigraine drug ergotamine tartrate.

Jokes are often made about alcohol hangovers but the headache associated with "the morning after" is no laughing matter. Fortunately, there are several suggested remedies for the pain, including ergotamine tartrate. The hangover headache may also be reduced by taking honey, which speeds alcohol metabolism, or caffeine, a constrictor of dilated arteries. Caffeine, however, can cause headaches as well as cure them. Heavy coffee drinkers often get headaches when they try to break the caffeine habit.

Cluster Headaches

Cluster headaches, named for their repeated occurrence in groups or clusters, begin as a minor pain around one eye, eventually spreading to that side of the face. The pain quickly intensifies, compelling the victim to pace the floor or rock in a chair. "You can't lie down, you're fidgety," explains a cluster patient. "The pain is unbearable." Other symptoms include a stuffed and runny nose and a droopy eyelid over a red and tearing eye.

Cluster headaches last between 30 and 45 minutes. But the relief people feel at the end of an attack is usually mixed with dread as they await a recurrence. Clusters can strike several times a day or night for several weeks or months. Then, mysteriously, they may disappear for months or years. Many people have cluster bouts during the spring and fall. At their worst, chronic cluster headaches can last continuously for years.

Cluster attacks can strike at any age but usually start between the ages of 20 and 40. Unlike migraine, cluster headaches are more common in men and do not run in families. Research scientists have observed certain physical similarities among people who experience cluster headache. The typical cluster patient is a tall, muscular man with a ragged facial appearance and a square, jutting or dimpled chin. The texture of his coarse skin resembles an orange peel. Women who get clusters may also have this type of skin.

Studies of cluster patients show that they are likely to have hazel eyes and that they tend to be heavy smokers and drinkers. Paradoxically, both nicotine, which constricts arteries, and alcohol, which dilates them, trigger cluster headaches. The exact connection between these substances and cluster attacks is not known.

Despite a cluster headache's distinguishing characteristics, its relative infrequency and similarity to such disorders as *sinusitis* can lead to misdiagnosis. Some cluster patients have had tooth extractions, sinus surgery, or psychiatric treatment in futile efforts to cure their pain.

Research studies have turned up several clues as to the cause of cluster headache, but no answers. One clue is found in the thermograms of untreated cluster patients, which show a "cold spot" of reduced blood flow above the eye.

Figure 39.2. *A thermogram of a normal person shows a symmetrical heat pattern on the individual's forehead.*

Figure 39.3. *A cluster headache patient's thermogram shows a cold area (appears white) of reduced blood flow on the left side of the forehead.*

The sudden start and brief duration of cluster headaches can make them difficult to treat; however, research scientists have identified several effective drugs for these headaches. The antimigraine drug ergotamine tartrate can subdue a cluster, if taken at the first sign of an attack. Injections of *dihydroergotamine*, a form of ergotamine tartrate, are sometimes used to treat clusters.

Some cluster patients can prevent attacks by taking propranolol or methysergide. Investigators have also discovered that mild solutions of cocaine hydrochloride applied inside the nose can quickly stop cluster headaches in most patients. This treatment may work because it both blocks pain impulses and constricts blood vessels.

Another option that works for some cluster patients is rapid inhalation of pure oxygen through a mask for 5 to 15 minutes. The oxygen seems to ease the pain of cluster headache by reducing blood flow to the brain.

In chronic cases of cluster headache, certain facial nerves may be surgically cut or destroyed to provide relief. These procedures have had limited success. Some cluster patients have had facial nerves cut only to have them regenerate years later.

Painful Pressure

Chronic high blood pressure can cause headache, as can rapid rises in blood pressure like those experienced during anger, vigorous exercise, or sexual excitement.

The severe "orgasmic headache" occurs right before orgasm and is believed to be a vascular headache. Since sudden rupture of a cerebral blood vessel can occur, this type of headache should be evaluated by a doctor.

What are Muscle-Contraction Headaches?

It's 5:00 p.m. and your boss has just asked you to prepare a 20-page briefing paper. Due date: tomorrow. You're angry and tired and the more you think about the assignment, the tenser you become. Your teeth clench, your brow wrinkles, and soon you have a splitting tension headache.

Tension headache is named not only for the role of stress in triggering the pain, but also for the contraction of neck, face, and scalp muscles brought on by stressful events. Tension headache is a severe but temporary form of muscle-contraction headache. The pain is mild to moderate and feels like pressure is being applied to the head or neck. The headache usually disappears after the period of stress is over. Ninety percent of all headaches are classified as tension/muscle-contraction headaches.

By contrast, chronic muscle-contraction headaches can last for weeks, months, and sometimes years. The pain of these headaches is often described as a tight band around the head or a feeling that the head and neck are in a cast. "It feels like somebody is tightening a giant vise around my head," says one patient. The pain is steady, and is usually felt on both sides of the head. Chronic muscle-contraction headaches can cause sore scalps—even combing one's hair can be painful.

Many scientists believe that the primary cause of the pain of muscle-contraction headache is sustained muscle tension. Other studies suggest that restricted blood flow may cause or contribute to the pain.

Occasionally, muscle-contraction headaches will be accompanied by nausea, vomiting, and blurred vision, but there is no preheadache syndrome as with migraine. Muscle-contraction headaches have not been linked to hormones or foods, as has migraine, nor is there a strong hereditary connection.

Research has shown that for many people, chronic muscle-contraction headaches are caused by depression and anxiety. These people tend to get their headaches in the early morning or evening when conflicts in the office or home are anticipated.

Emotional factors are not the only triggers of muscle-contraction headaches. Certain physical postures that tense head and neck muscles—such as holding one's chin down while reading—can lead to head and neck pain. So can prolonged writing under poor light, or holding a phone between the shoulder and ear, or even gum-chewing.

More serious problems that can cause muscle-contraction headaches include degenerative arthritis of the neck and *temporomandibular joint dysfunction*, or TMD. TMD is a disorder of the joint between the temporal bone (above the ear) and the mandible or lower jaw bone. The disorder results from poor bite and jaw clenching.

Treatment for muscle-contraction headache varies. The first consideration is to treat any specific disorder or disease that may be causing the headache. For example, arthritis of the neck is treated with anti-inflammatory medication and TMD may be helped by corrective devices for the mouth and jaw.

Acute tension headaches not associated with a disease are treated with muscle relaxants and analgesics like aspirin and acetaminophen.

Stronger analgesics, such as propoxyphene and codeine, are sometimes prescribed. As prolonged use of these drugs can lead to dependence, patients taking them should have periodic medical checkups and follow their physicians' instructions carefully.

Nondrug therapy for chronic muscle-contraction headaches includes biofeedback, relaxation training, and counseling. A technique called cognitive restructuring teaches people to change their attitudes and responses to stress. Patients might be encouraged, for example, to imagine that they are coping successfully with a stressful situation. In progressive relaxation therapy, patients are taught to first tense and then relax individual muscle groups. Finally, the patient tries to relax his or her whole body. Many people imagine a peaceful scene such as lying on the beach or by a beautiful lake. Passive relaxation does not involve tensing of muscles. Instead, patients are encouraged to focus on different muscles, suggesting that they relax. Some people might think to themselves, *Relax* or *My muscles feel warm*.

People with chronic muscle-contraction headaches may also be helped by taking antidepressants or MAO inhibitors. Mixed muscle-contraction and migraine headaches are sometimes treated with barbiturate compounds, which slow down nerve function in the brain and spinal cord.

People who suffer infrequent muscle-contraction headaches may benefit from a hot shower or moist heat applied to the back of the neck. Cervical collars are sometimes recommended as an aid to good posture. Physical therapy, massage, and gentle exercise of the neck may also be helpful.

When Is Headache a Warning of a More Serious Condition?

Like other types of pain, headaches can serve as warning signals of more serious disorders. This is particularly true for headaches caused by traction or inflammation.

Traction headaches can occur if the pain-sensitive parts of the head are pulled, stretched, or displaced, as, for example, when eye muscles are tensed to compensate for eyestrain. Headaches caused by *inflammation* include those related to meningitis as well as those resulting from diseases of the sinuses, spine, neck, ears, and teeth. Ear and tooth infections and glaucoma can cause headaches. In oral and dental disorders, headache is experienced as pain in the entire head, including the face.

Traction and inflammatory headaches are treated by curing the underlying problem. This may involve surgery, antibiotics or other drugs.

Characteristics of the various types of traction and inflammatory headaches vary by disorder:

Brain tumor. Brain tumors are diagnosed in about 11,000 people every year. As they grow, these tumors sometimes cause headache by pushing on the outer layer of nerve tissue that covers the brain or by pressing against pain-sensitive blood vessel walls. Headache resulting from a brain tumor may be periodic or continuous. Typically, it feels like a strong pressure is being applied to the head. The pain is relieved when the tumor is destroyed by surgery, radiation, or chemotherapy.

Stroke. Headache may accompany several conditions that can lead to stroke, including hypertension or high blood pressure, arteriosclerosis, and heart disease. Headaches are also associated with completed stroke, when brain cells die from lack of sufficient oxygen.

Many stroke-related headaches can be prevented by careful management of the patient's condition through diet, exercise, and medication.

Mild to moderate headaches are associated with transient ischemic attacks (TIAs), sometimes called "mini-strokes," which result from a temporary lack of blood supply to the brain. The head pain occurs near the clot or lesion that blocks blood flow. The similarity between migraine and symptoms of TIA can cause problems in diagnosis. The rare person under age 40 who suffers a TIA may be misdiagnosed as having migraine; similarly, TIA-prone older patients who suffer migraine may be misdiagnosed as having stroke-related headaches.

Spinal tap. About one-fourth of the people who undergo a lumbar puncture or spinal tap develop a headache. Many scientists believe these headaches result from leakage of the cerebrospinal fluid that flows through pain-sensitive membranes around the brain and down to the spinal cord. The fluid, they suggest, drains through the tiny hole created by the spinal tap needle, causing the membranes to rub painfully against the bony skull. Since headache pain occurs only when the patient stands up, the "cure" is to remain lying down until the headache runs its course—anywhere from a few hours to several days.

Head trauma. Headaches may develop after a blow to the head, either immediately or months later. There is little relationship between the severity of the trauma and the intensity of headache pain. One cause of trauma headache is scar formation in the scalp. Another is ruptured blood vessels which result in an accumulation of blood called a hematoma. This mass of blood can displace brain tissue and cause headaches as well as weakness, confusion, memory loss, and seizures. Hematomas can be drained to produce rapid relief of symptoms.

Arteritis and meningitis. Arteritis, an inflammation of certain arteries in the head, primarily affects people over age 50. Symptoms include throbbing headache, fever, and loss of appetite. Some patients experience blurring or loss of vision. Prompt treatment with corticosteroid drugs helps to relieve symptoms.

Headaches are also caused by infections of meninges, the brain's outer covering, and phlebitis, a vein inflammation.

Trigeminal neuralgia. Trigeminal neuralgia, or tic douloureux, results from a disorder of the trigeminal nerve. This nerve supplies the face, teeth, mouth, and nasal cavity with feeling and also enables the mouth muscles to chew. Symptoms are headache and intense facial pain that comes in short, excruciating jabs set off by the slightest touch to or movement of trigger points in the face or mouth. People with trigeminal neuralgia often fear brushing their teeth or chewing on the side of the mouth that is affected. Many trigeminal neuralgia patients are controlled with drugs, including carbamazepine. Patients who do not respond to drugs may be helped by surgery on the trigeminal nerve.

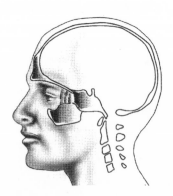

Figure 39.4. Acute sinusitis headaches can occur when one or all four of the sinus cavities fill with bacterial or viral fluid. The particular cavity affected determines the location of the sinus headache.

Sinus infection. In a condition called acute sinusitis, a viral or bacterial infection of the upper respiratory tract spreads to the membrane which lines the sinus cavities. When one or all four of these cavities are filled with bacterial or viral fluid, they become inflamed, causing pain and sometimes headache. Treatment of acute sinusitis includes antibiotics, analgesics, and decongestants. Chronic sinusitis may be caused by an allergy to such irritants as dust, ragweed, animal hair, and smoke. Research scientists disagree about whether chronic sinusitis triggers headache.

What Causes Headache in Children?

Like adults, children experience the infections, trauma, and stresses that can lead to headaches. In fact, research shows that as young people enter adolescence and encounter the stresses of puberty and secondary school, the frequency of headache increases.

Migraine headaches often begin in childhood or adolescence. According to recent surveys, as many as half of all schoolchildren experience some type of headache.

Children with migraine often have nausea and excessive vomiting. Some children have periodic vomiting, but no headache—the so-called "abdominal migraine." Research scientists have found that these children usually develop headaches when they are older.

Physicians have many drugs to treat migraine in children. Different classes that may be tried include analgesics, antiemetics, anticonvulsants, beta-blockers, and sedatives. A diet may also be prescribed to protect the child from foods that trigger headache. Sometimes psychological counseling or even psychiatric treatment for the child and the parents is recommended.

Childhood headache can be a sign of depression. Parents should alert the family pediatrician if a child develops headaches along with other symptoms such as a change in mood or sleep habits. Antidepressant medication and psychotherapy are effective treatments for childhood depression and related headache.

Conclusion

If you suffer from headaches and none of the standard treatments help, do not despair. Some people find that their headaches disappear once they deal with a troubled marriage, pass their law board exams, or resolve some other stressful problem. Others find that if they control their psychological reaction to stress, the headaches disappear.

"I had migraines for several years," says one woman, "and then they went away. I think it was because I lowered my personal goals in life. Today, even though I have 100 things to do at night, I don't worry about it. I learned to say no."

For those who cannot say no, or who get headaches anyway, today's headache research offers hope. The work of NINDS-supported scientists around the world promises to improve our understanding of this complex disorder and provide better tools to treat it.

Information Resources

NIH Neurological Institute
P.O. Box 5801
Bethesda, MD 20824
(301) 496-5751
(800) 352-9424

The National Institute of Neurological Disorders and Stroke, a component of the National Institutes of Health, is the leading Federal supporter of research on disorders of the brain and nervous system. The Institute also sponsors an active public information program and can answer questions about diagnosis, treatment, and research related to headache.

Private voluntary organizations that offer information and services to those affected by headache include the following:

American Council for Headache Education (ACHE)
875 Kings Highway
Suite 200
Woodbury, NJ 08096
(609) 384-8760
(800) 255-ACHE (2243)
http://www.achenet.org

This organization is a nonprofit patient/health professional partnership dedicated to advancing treatment and management of headache and to raising the public awareness of headache as a valid, biologically based illness. ACHE offers headache brochures, a quarterly newsletter, the book *Migraine: The Complete Guide*, assistance through in-person support groups, and support via the Internet and commercial on-line service providers.

National Headache Foundation
428 W. St. James Place
2nd Floor
Chicago, IL 60614-2750
(312) 388-6399
(800) 843-2256

The foundation promotes research and public education, publishes a quarterly newsletter, and offers many publications including a state-by-state list of physician members, a headache chart, a handbook, brochures, and fact sheets.

Chapter 40

Narcolepsy

What Is Narcolepsy?

Narcolepsy is a chronic sleep disorder with no known cause. The main characteristic of narcolepsy is excessive and overwhelming daytime sleepiness, even after adequate nighttime sleep. A person with narcolepsy is likely to become drowsy or to fall asleep, often at inappropriate times and places. Daytime sleep attacks may occur with or without warning and may be irresistible. These attacks can occur repeatedly in a single day. Drowsiness may persist for prolonged periods of time. In addition, nighttime sleep may be fragmented with frequent wakenings.

Three other classic symptoms of narcolepsy, which may not occur in all patients, are:

- **Cataplexy:** sudden episodes of loss of muscle function, ranging from slight weakness (such as limpness at the neck or knees, sagging facial muscles, or inability to speak clearly) to complete body collapse. Attacks may be triggered by sudden emotional reactions such as laughter, anger, or fear and may last from a few seconds to several minutes. The person remains conscious throughout the episode.

- **Sleep paralysis:** temporary inability to talk or move when failing asleep or waking up. It may last a few seconds to minutes.

National Heart, Lung, and Blood Institute (NHLBI), NIH Pub. No. 96-3649, October 1996.

- **Hypnagogic hallucinations:** vivid, often frightening, dream-like experiences that occur while dozing or falling asleep.

Daytime sleepiness, sleep paralysis, and hypnagogic hallucinations can also occur in people who do not have narcolepsy.

In most cases, the first symptom of narcolepsy to appear is excessive and overwhelming daytime sleepiness. The other symptoms may begin alone or in combination months or years after the onset of the daytime sleep attacks. There are wide variations in the development, severity, and order of appearance of cataplexy, sleep paralysis, and hypnagogic hallucinations in individuals. Only about 20 to 25 percent of people with narcolepsy experience all four symptoms. The excessive daytime sleepiness generally persists throughout life, but sleep paralysis and hypnagogic hallucinations may not.

The symptoms of narcolepsy, especially the excessive daytime sleepiness and cataplexy, often become severe enough to cause serious disruptions in a person's social, personal, and professional lives and severely limit activities.

When Should You Suspect Narcolepsy?

You should be checked for narcolepsy if:

- you often feel excessively and overwhelmingly sleepy during the day, even after having had a full night's sleep;

- you fall asleep when you do not intend to, such as while having dinner, talking, driving, or working;

- you collapse suddenly or your neck muscles feel too weak to hold up your head when you laugh or become angry, surprised, or shocked;

- you find yourself briefly unable to talk or move while falling asleep or waking up.

How Common Is Narcolepsy?

Although it is estimated that narcolepsy afflicts as many as 200,000 Americans, fewer than 50,000 are diagnosed. It is as widespread as Parkinson's disease or multiple sclerosis and more prevalent than cystic fibrosis, but it is less well known. Narcolepsy is often mistaken for depression, epilepsy, or the side effects of medications.

Who Gets Narcolepsy?

Narcolepsy can occur in both men and women at any age, although its symptoms are usually first noticed in teenagers or young adults. There is strong evidence that narcolepsy may run in families; 8 to 12 percent of people with narcolepsy have a close relative with the disease.

What Happens in Narcolepsy?

Normally, when an individual is awake, brain waves show a regular rhythm. When a person first falls asleep, the brain waves become slower and less regular. This sleep state is called non-rapid eye movement (NREM) sleep. After about an hour and a half of NREM sleep, the brain waves begin to show a more active pattern again, even though the person is in deep sleep. This sleep state, called rapid eye movement (REM) sleep, is when dreaming occurs.

In narcolepsy, the order and length of NREM and REM sleep periods are disturbed, with REM sleep occurring at sleep onset instead of after a period of NREM sleep. Thus, narcolepsy is a disorder in which REM sleep appears at an abnormal time. Also, some of the aspects of REM sleep that normally occur only during sleep—lack of muscle tone, sleep paralysis, and vivid dreams—occur at other times in people with narcolepsy. For example, the lack of muscle tone can occur during wakefulness in a cataplexy episode. Sleep paralysis and vivid dreams can occur while falling asleep or waking up.

How Is Narcolepsy Diagnosed?

Diagnosis is relatively easy when all the symptoms of narcolepsy are present. But if the sleep attacks are isolated and cataplexy is mild or absent, diagnosis is more difficult.

Two tests that are commonly used in diagnosing narcolepsy are the polysomnogram and the multiple sleep latency test. These tests are usually performed by a sleep specialist. The polysomnogram involves continuous recording of sleep brain waves and a number of nerve and muscle functions during nighttime sleep. When tested, people with narcolepsy fall asleep rapidly, enter REM sleep early, and may awaken often during the night. The polysomnogram also helps to detect other possible sleep disorders that could cause daytime sleepiness.

For the multiple sleep latency test, a person is given a chance to sleep every 2 hours during normal wake times. Observations are made of the time taken to reach various stages of sleep. This test measures the degree of daytime sleepiness and also detects how soon REM sleep begins. Again, people with narcolepsy fall asleep rapidly and enter REM sleep early.

How Is Narcolepsy Treated?

Although there is no cure for narcolepsy, treatment options are available to help reduce the various symptoms. Treatment is individualized depending on the severity of the symptoms, and it may take weeks or months for an optimal regimen to be worked out. Complete control of sleepiness and cataplexy is rarely possible. Treatment is primarily by medications, but lifestyle changes are also important. The main treatment of excessive daytime sleepiness in narcolepsy is with a group of drugs called central nervous system stimulants. For cataplexy and other REM-sleep symptoms, antidepressant medications and other drugs that suppress REM sleep are prescribed. Caffeine and over-the-counter drugs have not been shown to be effective and are not recommended.

In addition to drug therapy, an important part of treatment is scheduling short naps (10 to 15 minutes) two to three times per day to help control excessive daytime sleepiness and help the person stay as alert as possible. Daytime naps are not a replacement for night-time sleep.

Ongoing communication among the physician, the person with narcolepsy, and family members about the response to treatment is necessary to achieve and maintain the best control.

What Is Being Done to Better Understand Narcolepsy?

Studies supported by the National Institutes of Health (NIH) are trying to increase understanding of what causes narcolepsy and improve physicians' ability to detect and treat the disease. Scientists are studying narcolepsy patients and families, looking for clues to the causes, course, and effective treatment of this sleep disorder. Recent discovery of families of dogs that are naturally afflicted with narcolepsy has been of great help in these studies. Some of the specific questions being addressed in NIH-supported studies are the nature of genetic and environmental factors that might combine to cause narcolepsy and the immunological, biochemical, physiological, and neuromuscular disturbances associated with narcolepsy. Scientists are also working to better understand sleep mechanisms and the physical and psychological effects of sleep deprivation and to develop better ways of measuring sleepiness and cataplexy.

How Can Individuals and Their Families and Friends Cope with Narcolepsy?

Learning as much about narcolepsy as possible and finding a support system can help patients and families deal with the practical and emotional effects of the disease, possible occupational limitations, and situations that might cause injury. A variety of educational and other materials are available from sleep medicine or narcolepsy organizations. Support groups exist to help persons with narcolepsy and their families.

Individuals with narcolepsy, their families, friends, and potential employers should know that:

- Narcolepsy is a life-long condition that requires continuous medication.

- Although there is not a cure for narcolepsy at present, several medications can help reduce its symptoms.

- People with narcolepsy can lead productive lives if they are provided with proper medical care.

- If possible, individuals with narcolepsy should avoid jobs that require driving long distances or handling hazardous equipment or that require alertness for lengthy periods.

- Parents, teachers, spouses, and employers should be aware of the symptoms of narcolepsy. This will help them avoid the mistake of confusing the person's behavior with laziness, hostility, rejection, or lack of interest and motivation. It will also help them provide essential support and cooperation.

- Employers can promote better working opportunities for individuals with narcolepsy by permitting special work schedules and nap breaks.

For More Information

For additional information on sleep and sleep disorders, contact the following offices of the National Heart, Lung, and Blood Institute of the National Institutes of Health:

National Center on Sleep Disorders Research (NCSDR)

The NCSDR supports research, scientist training, dissemination of health information, and other activities on sleep and sleep disorders. The NCSDR also coordinates sleep research activities with other Federal agencies and with public and nonprofit organizations.

National Center on Sleep Disorders Research
Two Rockledge Centre
Suite 7024
6701 Rockledge Drive, MSC 7920
Bethesda, MD 20892-7920
(301) 435-0199
(301) 480-3451 (fax)

National Heart, Lung, and Blood Institute Information Center

The Information Center acquires, analyzes, promotes, maintains, and disseminates programmatic and educational information related to sleep and sleep disorders. Write for a list of available publications or to order additional copies of this fact sheet.

NHLBI Information Center
PO. Box 30105
Bethesda, MD 20824-0105
(301) 251-1222
(301) 251-1223 (fax)

For more information about narcolepsy and patient support groups, contact:

Narcolepsy Network
PO. Box 42460
Cincinnati, OH 45242

Chapter 41

Neurotrauma

At a vacation resort last summer, an 11-month-old child fell a few feet onto a floor. He remained conscious, cried, and was consoled by his parents. A few hours later, he started vomiting and was somewhat lethargic; four hours after the fall, he was seen in a local emergency room, where the medical staff felt he was a little sleepy, but neurologically intact. However, a CT scan they performed showed an epidural hematoma (bleeding between the dura, the tissue covering the brain, and the skull).

When the helicopter arrived to airlift the child to a pediatric neurosurgical center, doctors found that his left pupil had become dilated. This implied that the hematoma was pushing the brain beyond its normal confines on the side of the injury and beginning to press upon the brainstem and the nerve that controls light reflex in the pupil.

The child was placed on a mechanical ventilator and medicines were given to try to draw fluid out of the brain tissue to decrease the pressure. He was immediately loaded into the helicopter. As the aircraft raced against a thunderstorm, also headed for Boston, the child's other pupil dilated and became fixed. The airborne team alerted the hospital of the gravity of the situation and arranged to bring the child directly from the helipad to the operating room, where he would be met by a neurosurgeon.

Madsen, Joseph R. "After Neurotrauma: Brain and Spinal Cord Repair," *The Harvard Mahoney Neuroscience Institute Letter*, Fall 1996, Vol. 5, No. 4; reprinted with permission.

Within nine minutes of touchdown of the helicopter and about one hour from leaving the other hospital, the blood clot was out. The child's pupillary responses returned to normal on the operating table, and he was neurologically intact the following morning.

He returned home with his family six days later.

The Neurotrauma Epidemic

The technical term for the boy's injury is "neurotrauma," traumatic injury to either the brain or spinal cord. Neurotrauma is an epidemic based on accidents and violence. Neurological trauma causes thousands of deaths and devastating irreversible tragedies annually. Because it afflicts many perfectly healthy young people, the productive years lost as a result of its ravages are particularly high. About half of the 150,000 trauma-caused deaths in the United States each year are due to fatal brain injuries.

An additional 10,000 persons sustain spinal cord injuries each year, resulting in loss of motor control, sensation, and bowel and bladder control. An estimated 200,000 survivors of severe central nervous system injuries in the United States live with their neurological disabilities, and often, with little hope.

Rescue: Preventing Delayed Injuries

Human brains and spinal cords tolerate the usual shock of bumps from playground falls, soccer balls, and unexpected low doorways fairly well. Concussion—temporary alteration in neurological function without structural damage—probably results from momentary change in the chemical surroundings of the brain cells. This would include disruptions in release of neurotransmitters, some of which are excitatory (speeding up electrical firing in the neurons they signal) and others inhibitory (slowing firing down).

More severe impacts to the brain can disrupt neurons' fine filaments, called axons, that travel through the brain; such disruption can interrupt communications between cells and shut down the machineries of consciousness and even the life-sustaining control of breathing. Death or a vegetative state may result. Disruption of the integrity of the bony armor of the spinal cord can tear the cables connecting voluntary activity in the brain to the muscles of the limbs, causing paralysis.

The physical impact causing trauma can be over in less than a second, but the damage to central nervous system (CNS) tissue can worsen over hours or days. Some neurons may die at the moment of trauma, but not all; others survive but are weakened by the initial insult plus a lack of nutrients or oxygen, or the presence of toxins produced by the first neurons killed.

Prevention and treatment of the effects of these various delayed insults or "secondary injuries" to the brain and spinal cord at cellular and biochemical levels has added much to the therapeutic armamentarium. The urgency to limit ongoing damage—and its costly long-term consequences—makes trauma one of the most aggressively-managed of neurological diseases.

In the field, the emergency room, and the first hours of treatment, "optimization of the neuronal environment" is the watchword and the motivation for all of the standard goals of resuscitation: maintenance of blood pressure and oxygenation, correction of acid-base balance, normalization of electrolyte status, control of the electrical storms of seizure activity, and optimization of nutritional support. These steps contribute to keeping the sick neurons alive.

One treatable crisis, increased intracranial pressure (ICP), unique to head injury, occurs because the soft tissues of the brain are enclosed in the inelastic skull. Elevated ICP occurs whenever cellular swelling or leakage of fluid through blood vessels overfills the limited capacity of the skull, as it did with the child treated last summer. Traditional neurosurgical treatment, such as removal of blood clots outside of the brain (epidural or subdural hematomas) or within the brain (contusions or parenchymal hemorrhages), aims to decrease intracranial pressure and thereby allows metabolic conditions more favorable to neuronal survival.

A mainstay of neurosurgical treatment has become the insertion of small temporary devices called ICP monitors, which directly measure intracranial pressure, allowing an optimal approach to resuscitative fluid management, respirator settings, and the use of osmotic agents to try to draw fluid out of the brain. The results of unchecked ICP have been known for decades: loss of consciousness, loss of regulated circulation to the brain, and ultimately loss of life.

A recent observation about the death of individual neurons in culture has suggested an additional possibility for intervention to limit damage. Partially-injured neurons become sensitive to normal excitatory neurotransmitters, such as glutamic acid. Some neuronal death after trauma is a result of this phenomenon of excitotoxicity, and specific blockers of the nerve cell receptors for the transmitter can limit this death in the culture dish. So far, this strategy has not reached routine clinical use, but it is part of a larger trend toward highly specific approaches to treatment based on our increasingly sophisticated understanding of the neurobiology of trauma. Another such strategy might take advantage of neurotrophic factors, naturally occurring peptides that keep neurons alive in development. These may also sustain injured neurons and prevent the march toward cell death. It seems virtually inevitable that specific neurotrophins and/or excitotoxicity blockers will one day be used to limit secondary injury.

In a broader sense, however, all non-specific interventions currently used (such as minimizing ICP, maximizing cerebral perfusion, and mechanically stabilizing the spine) ultimately work because they limit secondary damage and cell death.

Repair: Future Strategies

While current efforts are targeted toward the optimal physical and chemical nature of the neuronal milieu, the instantaneous disruption of axons and resulting disability requires its own strategic response, and there is hope that regeneration-promoting biological manipulations will become available. New approaches to improving axonal regeneration in the CNS have generated hope for finding such strategies. Particular interest in this area has involved spinal cord injury, because disruption of the long, cable-like nerve fiber tracts is the major cause of disability. The same biological principles would apply to the brain.

In the peripheral nervous system, and when the central nervous system first develops, nerve cell axons, long threadlike projections through which neurons send their signals, grow out over long distances and form functionally appropriate connections. But once the CNS of higher vertebrates becomes mature, this capability is turned off. Thus, strategies for CNS repair might seek to alter the environment to recapitulate early development stages, or to supply conditions similar to those for peripheral nerves.

Proposed strategies for spinal cord repair include blocking the molecules (called endogenous neurite outgrowth inhibitors) that prevent CNS neurons from regrowing, and using non-CNS tissue to build "bridges" to promote outgrowth of axons. These approaches, which show great promise in animal studies, would be particularly important for survivors of neurotrauma with fixed deficits.

The latest dramatic study was published in the journal, *Science*, in July [1996]. Henrich Cheng, Yihai Cao, and Lars Olson at the Karolinska Institute in Stockholm reported a procedure in which they used multiple peripheral nerve grafts to replace an excised portion of the spinal cord in rats and stabilized the grafts in a protein gel framework laced with a growth factor called acidic fibroblast growth factor.

With this combination, they saw evidence of genuine bridging of long tracks of neurons across a gap, with recovery of function that seems to require all these aspects of the treatment. Promotion of regeneration, using multiple modalities of neurobiological knowledge, seems an imaginable goal.

While Waiting for Regeneration

As a result of neuroscientific research, better physical health after trauma need not await biological implants to promote regeneration. Because some electrical signals to nerves and muscle and some neurotransmitter signals in the damaged brain and cord are understood, computer-driven interim solutions seem reasonable and are being tested in clinical trials. Functional electrical stimulation, for example, attempts to provide electrical impulses to the peripheral nerves to maintain tone and, hopefully, function, in the muscle groups isolated from the functioning CNS by a spinal cord injury. However, the requirements of standing and walking without aid of an intact spinal cord have so far eluded satisfactory computational solutions.

Another computer-assisted approach has hinged on the identification of specific neurotransmitters that help damp down involuntary movement that may result from brain and spinal cord injury. Baclofen, a drug that closely resembles one inhibitory neurotransmitter, GABA, can now be delivered by a programmable, microchip directed pump implanted under the skin. The result is control of potentially severe spasticity and painful spasms, which may plague survivors of CNS injury and cause joint deformity and destruction. Although a far cry from restoration of voluntary function, in certain patients these implantable bionic devices can be a veritable godsend. Although a mere dream a decade ago, they are FDA-approved and available now.

The challenge for basic scientists and clinicians alike is clear: Can the rescue be made robust, and the possibility of repair be made real? Tens of thousands await the answers—some who have had a split-second of neurotrauma, and some who have not.

—by Joseph R. Madsen

Dr. Madsen is a neurosurgeon at Children's Hospital interested in injury, regeneration and operations to improve functional recovery.

Chapter 42

Tourette Syndrome

What Is Tourette Syndrome?

Tourette syndrome (TS) is an inherited, neurological disorder characterized by repeated involuntary movements and uncontrollable vocal (phonic) sounds called tics. In a few cases, such tics can include inappropriate words and phrases.

The disorder is named for Dr. Georges Gilles de la Tourette, the pioneering French neurologist who first described an 86-year-old French noblewoman with the condition in 1885.

The symptoms of TS generally appear before the individual is 18 years old. TS can affect people of all ethnic groups; males are affected 3 to 4 times more often than females. It is estimated that 100,000 Americans have full-blown TS, and that perhaps as many as 1 in 200 show a partial expression of the disorder, such as chronic multiple tics or transient childhood tics.

The natural course of TS varies from patient to patient. Although TS symptoms range from very mild to quite severe, the majority of cases fall in the mild category.

What Are the Symptoms?

The first symptoms of TS are usually facial tics—commonly eye blinking. However, facial tics can also include nose twitching or grimaces.

National Institute of Neurological Disorders and Stroke (NINDS), NIH Pub. No. 95-2163, February 1995.

With time, other motor tics may appear, such as head jerking, neck stretching, foot stamping, or body twisting and bending.

TS patients may utter strange and unacceptable sounds, words, or phrases. It is not uncommon for a person with TS to continuously clear his or her throat, cough, sniff, grunt, yelp, bark, or shout.

People with TS may involuntarily shout obscenities (coprolalia) or constantly repeat the words of other people (echolalia). They may touch other people excessively or repeat actions obsessively and unnecessarily. A few patients with severe TS demonstrate self-harming behaviors such as lip and cheek biting and head banging against hard objects. However, these behaviors are extremely rare.

Tics alternately increase and decrease in severity, and periodically change in number, frequency, type, and location. Symptoms may subside for weeks or months at a time and later recur.

How Are Tics Classified?

There are two categories of tics: simple and complex. Simple tics are sudden, brief movements that involve a limited number of muscle groups. They occur in a single or isolated fashion and are often repetitive. Some of the more common examples of simple tics include eye blinking, shoulder shrugging, facial grimacing, head jerking, yelping, and sniffing. Complex tics are distinct, coordinated patterns of successive movements involving several muscle groups. Complex tics might include jumping, smelling objects, touching the nose, touching other people, coprolalia, echolalia, or self-harming behaviors.

Can People with TS Control Their Tics?

People with TS can sometimes suppress their tics for a short time, but the effort is similar to that of holding back a sneeze. Eventually tension mounts to the point where the tic escapes. Tics worsen in stressful situations; however they improve when the person is relaxed or absorbed in an activity. In most cases tics decrease markedly during sleep.

What Causes TS?

Although the basic cause of TS is unknown, current research suggests that there is an abnormality in the gene(s) affecting the brain's metabolism of neurotransmitters such as dopamine, serotonin, and norepinephrine. Neurotransmitters are chemicals in the brain that carry signals from one nerve cell to another.

What Disorders Are Associated with TS?

Not all people with TS have disorders other than tics. However, many people experience additional problems such as obsessive compulsive disorder, where the person feels that something must be done repeatedly, such as hand washing or checking that a door is locked; attention deficit disorder, where the person has difficulty concentrating and is easily distracted; learning disabilities, which include reading, writing, arithmetic, and perceptual difficulties; problems with impulse control, which can result in overly aggressive behaviors or socially inappropriate acts; or sleep disorders, which include frequent awakenings or talking in one's sleep.

The wide range of behavioral symptoms that can accompany tics may, in fact, be more disabling than the tics themselves. Patients, families, and physicians need to determine which set of symptoms is most disabling so that appropriate medications and therapies can be selected.

How Is TS Diagnosed?

Generally, TS is diagnosed by observing the symptoms and evaluating family history. For a diagnosis of TS to be made, both motor and phonic tics must be present for at least 1 year. Neuroimaging studies, such as magnetic resonance imaging (MRI), computerized tomography (CT), and electroencephalogram (EEG) scans, or certain blood tests may be used to rule out other conditions that might be confused with TS. However, TS is a clinical diagnosis. There are no blood tests or other laboratory tests that definitively diagnose the disorder.

Studies show that correct diagnosis of TS is frequently delayed after the start of symptoms because many physicians may not be familiar with the disorder. The behavioral symptoms and tics are easily misinterpreted, often causing children with TS to be misunderstood at school, at home, and even in the doctor's office. Parents, relatives, and peers who are unfamiliar with the disorder may incorrectly attribute the tics and other symptoms to psychological problems, thereby increasing the social isolation of those with the disorder. And because tics can wax and wane in severity and can also be suppressed, they are often absent during doctor visits, which further complicates making a diagnosis.

In many cases, parents, relatives, friends, or even the patients themselves become aware of the disorder based on information they have heard or read in the popular media.

How Is TS Treated?

Because symptoms do not impair most patients and development usually proceeds normally, the majority of people with TS require no medication. However, medications are available to help when symptoms interfere with functioning.

Unfortunately, there is no one medication that is helpful to all persons with TS, nor does any medication completely eliminate symptoms; in addition, all medications have side effects. Instead, the available TS medications are only able to help reduce specific symptoms.

Some patients who require medication to reduce the frequency and intensity of the tic symptoms may be treated with neuroleptic drugs such as haloperidol and pimozide. These medications are usually given in very small doses that are increased slowly until the best possible balance between symptoms and side effects is achieved.

Recently scientists have discovered that long-term use of neuroleptic drugs may cause an involuntary movement disorder called tardive dyskinesia. However, this condition usually disappears when medication is discontinued. Short-term side effects of haloperidol and pimozide include muscular rigidity, drooling, tremor, lack of facial expression, slow movement, and restlessness. These side effects can be reduced by drugs commonly used to treat Parkinson's disease. Other side effects such as fatigue, depression, anxiety, weight gain, and difficulties in thinking clearly may be more troublesome.

Clonidine, an antihypertensive drug, is also used in the treatment of tics. Studies show that it is more effective in reducing motor tics than reducing vocal tics. Fatigue, dry mouth, irritability, dizziness, headache, and insomnia are common side effects associated with clonidine use. Fluphenazine and clonazepam may also be prescribed to help control tic symptoms.

Medications are also available to treat some of the associated behavioral disorders. Stimulants such as methylphenidate, pemoline, and dextroamphetamine, usually prescribed for attention deficit disorders, although somewhat effective, have also been reported to increase tics; therefore their use is controversial. For obsessive compulsive behaviors that significantly disrupt daily functioning, fluoxetine, clomipramine, sertraline, and paroxetine may be prescribed.

Other types of therapy may also be helpful. Although psychological problems do not cause TS, psychotherapy may help the person better cope with the disorder and deal with the secondary social and emotional problems that sometimes occur. Psychotherapy does not help suppress the patient's tics.

Relaxation techniques and biofeedback may be useful in alleviating stress which can lead to an increase in tic symptoms.

Is TS Inherited?

Evidence from genetic studies suggests that TS is inherited in a dominant mode and the gene(s) involved can cause a variable range of symptoms in different family members. A person with TS has about a 50-50 chance of passing on the gene(s) to one of his or her offspring. However, that genetic predisposition may not necessarily result in full-blown TS; instead, it may express itself as a milder tic disorder or as obsessive compulsive behaviors or possibly attention deficit disorder with few or no tics at all. It is also possible that the gene-carrying offspring will not develop any TS symptoms. A higher than normal incidence of milder tic disorders and obsessive compulsive behaviors has been found in families of individuals with TS.

Gender also plays an important role in TS gene expression. If the gene-carrying offspring of a TS patient is male, then the risk of developing symptoms is 3 to 4 times higher. However, most people who inherit the gene(s) will not develop symptoms severe enough to warrant medical attention. In some cases of TS, inheritance cannot be determined. These cases are called sporadic and their cause is unknown.

What Is the Prognosis?

There is no cure for TS; however, the condition in many individuals improves as they mature. Individuals with TS can expect to live a normal life span. Although the disorder is generally lifelong and chronic, it is not a degenerative condition. TS does not impair intelligence. Tics tend to decrease with age, enabling some patients to discontinue using medication. In a few cases, complete remission occurs after adolescence. Although tic symptoms tend to decrease with age, it is possible that neuropsychiatric disorders such as depression, panic attacks, mood swings, and antisocial behaviors may increase.

What Is the Best Educational Setting for Children with TS?

Although students with TS often function well in the regular classroom, it is estimated that many may have some kind of learning disability. When attention deficit disorder, obsessive compulsive disorder, and frequent tics greatly interfere with academic performance or social adjustment, students should be placed in an educational setting that meets their individual needs. These students may require tutoring, smaller or special classes, and in some cases special schools.

All students with TS need a tolerant and compassionate setting that both encourages them to work to their full potential and is flexible enough to accommodate their special needs. This setting may include a private study area, exams outside the regular classroom, or even oral exams when the child's symptoms interfere with his or her ability to write. Untimed testing reduces stress for students with TS.

What Research Is Being Done?

Within the Federal Government, the leading supporter of research on TS and other neurological disorders is the National Institute of Neurological Disorders and Stroke (NINDS). The NINDS, a part of the National Institutes of Health (NIH), is responsible for supporting and conducting research on the brain and central nervous system.

NINDS sponsors research on TS both in its laboratories at the NIH and through grants to major medical institutions across the country. The National Institute of Mental Health, the National Center for Research Resources, the National Institute of Child Health and Human Development, the National Institute on Drug Abuse, and the National Institute on Deafness and Other Communication Disorders also support research of relevance to TS.

Recent research has led to several notable advances in the understanding of TS. Already scientists have learned that TS is inherited from a dominant gene(s) that causes different symptoms from patient to patient, and that the disorder is more common than was previously thought.

Genetic Studies

Currently, investigators are conducting genetic linkage studies in large multigenerational families affected with TS in an effort to find

404

the chromosomal location of the TS gene(s). Finding a genetic marker (a biochemical abnormality that all TS patients might share) for TS would be a major step toward understanding the genetic risk factors for TS. Once the marker is found, research efforts would then focus on locating the TS gene(s).

Understanding the genetics of TS will directly benefit patients who are concerned about recurrence in their families and will ultimately help to clarify the development of the disorder. Localization of the TS gene will strengthen clinical diagnosis, improve genetic counseling, lead to the clarification of pathophysiology, and provide clues for more effective therapies.

Neurotransmitter Studies

Investigators continue to study certain neurotransmitters to increase our understanding of the syndrome, explore the role they play in the disease process, and provide more effective therapies.

Environmental Studies

Other research projects currently under way include analyzing young unaffected children at high risk for TS in order to identify environmental factors such as life stresses or exposure to certain medications that may influence the expression of the disorder.

Other Studies

Scientists are also conducting neuropsychological tests and neuroimaging studies of brain activity and structure to determine the extent to which specific environmental exposures may affect the emergence of tics and/or obsessive compulsive symptoms.

Where Can I Go for More Information?

For more information about TS or other neurological disorders, or about the NINDS and its research programs, contact:

Office of Scientific and Health Reports
NIH Neurological Institute
P.O. Box 5801
Bethesda, Maryland 20824
(301) 496-5751
(800) 352-9424

The Tourette Syndrome Association, Inc., is a voluntary, nonprofit organization whose members include people with TS, their families and friends, and health care professionals. The Association funds research, provides services to patients and their families, and offers a variety of publications, including a newsletter, brochures, and fact sheets. For further information, contact:

Tourette Syndrome Association, Inc.
42-40 Bell Boulevard
Bayside, New York 11361-2861
(718) 224-2999
(800) 237-0717

Chapter 43

Tuberous Sclerosis

Description

Tuberous sclerosis is a rare genetic, neurological disorder primarily characterized by seizures, mental retardation, and skin and eye lesions. In some cases, neurobehavioral problems may also occur. Individuals with tuberous sclerosis may experience none or all of the symptoms with varying degrees of severity. Tuberous sclerosis is a multi-system disease that can affect the brain, kidneys, heart, eyes, lungs, and other organs. Small benign tumors may grow on the face and eyes, as well as in the brain, kidneys, and other organs. Neuroimaging studies may be able to confirm the diagnosis.

Treatment

There is no specific treatment for tuberous sclerosis. Treatment is symptomatic and may include dermabrasion and laser removal techniques for the skin manifestations; drug therapy for neurobehavioral problems; treatment of high blood pressure caused by the kidney problems; anticonvulsant therapy for seizures; and surgery to remove growing tumors.

Prognosis

The prognosis for individuals with tuberous sclerosis varies depending on the severity of symptoms. There is no cure.

National Institute of Neurological Disorders and Stroke (NINDS), July 1997.

Research

The NINDS supports research on genetic disorders such as tuberous sclerosis aimed at increasing scientific understanding of these disorders and finding ways to prevent, treat, and cure them. These articles, available from a medical library, are sources of in-depth information on tuberous sclerosis:

Bradley, W, *et al* (eds). *Neurology in Clinical Practice: Principles of Diagnosis and Management*, Vol. 11, Butterworth-Heinemann, Boston, pp. 1327-1342 (1991).

Perspective Newsletter, National Tuberous Sclerosis Association, Inc., Landover, MD, Special Edition (Winter 1994).

Provenzale, J, and Deluca, S. "Tuberous Sclerosis," *American Family Physician* 43:2; 470-472 (February 1991).

Roach, E. "Neurocutaneous Syndromes." *Pediatric Clinics of North America*, 36:4; 591-620 (August 1992).

Roach, E, *et al*. "Diagnostic Criteria: Tuberous Sclerosis Complex." *Journal of Child Neurology* 7; 221-224 (April 1992).

Wyngaarden, J, *et al* (eds). *Cecil Textbook of Medicine*, 19th edition, W.B. Saunders Co., Philadelphia, p. 2143 (1992).

Additional information is available from the following organizations:

National Tuberous Sclerosis Association, Inc.
8181 Professional Pl., Suite 110
Landover, MD 20785
(301) 459-9888
(800) 225-6872

Epilepsy Foundation of America
4351 Garden City Drive
Landover, MD 20785
(301) 459-3700
(800) EFA-1000

National Organization for Rare Disorders (NORD)
P.O. Box 8923
New Fairfield, CT 06812-1783
(203) 746-6518
(800) 999-6673

Part Seven

Additional Help and Information

Chapter 44

Brain Terms

A

activities of daily living (ADL): basic daily activities such as eating, grooming, toileting, and dressing.

acoustic: related to sound or hearing.

agraphia: inability to express one's thoughts in writing.

alexia: inability to understand written language.

ambulation: the act of walking.

amyotrophic lateral sclerosis (ALS): a progressive disease of the nervous system in which motor neurons are affected; also called Lou Gehrig's disease.

anaplastic: a term used to describe cancer cells that divide rapidly and bear little or no resemblance to normal cells.

aneurysm: a sac created by expansion of an artery, vein, or the heart.

angiogram: an x-ray of blood vessels. A dye is injected into an artery to outline the blood vessels on the x-ray picture. Also called an arteriogram.

angiography: an imaging technique that provides a picture, called an angiogram, of blood vessels.

This glossary includes terms from NIH Pub. Nos. 93-159, 94-139, 95-0662, 95-1558, and 96-158.

anticonvulsant: medicine to stop, prevent, or control seizures (convulsions).

Apgar score: a numbered score doctors use to assess a baby's physical state at the time of birth.

aphasia: the loss of ability to communicate orally, through signs, or in writing, or the inability to understand such communications; the loss of language usage ability.

apraxia: a disorder of learned movement unexplained by deficits in strength, coordination, sensation, or comprehension.

asphyxia: interference with oxygen delivery to the brain and other vital organs.

assessment: determining the scope, importance, and value of a medical or psychological condition, social or environmental situation, or treatment.

aspiration: the act of inhaling solid or liquid materials into the lungs.

astereognosis: the inability to recognize or characterize objects by touch.

astrocytoma: a type of brain tumor.

ataxia: a disorder in which muscles fail to move in a coordinated fashion.

ataxic gait: awkward, uncoordinated walking.

aura: a symptom of classic migraine headache in which the patient sees flashing lights or zigzag fines, or may temporarily lose vision. In epilepsy: a warning of a coming seizure in which the patient experiences some change in sensation.

B

basilar artery migraine: migraine, occurring primarily in young women and often associated with the menstrual cycle, that involves a disturbance of a major brain artery. Symptoms include vertigo, double vision, and poor muscular coordination.

benign: not cancerous; a benign brain tumor may be life threatening, depending on its size and location.

benign exertional headache: headache brought on by running, lifting, coughing, sneezing, or bending.

biofeedback: a technique in which patients are trained to gain some voluntary control over certain physiological conditions, such as blood pressure and muscle tension, to promote relaxation. Thermal biofeedback helps patients consciously raise hand temperature, which can sometimes reduce the number and intensity of migraines.

bradykinesia: gradual loss of spontaneous movement.

brain stem: the stemlike part of the brain that is connected to the spinal cord.

brain stem glioma: a type of brain tumor.

C

carotid artery: a major artery in the neck that supplies blood to the head and brain.

carotid endarterectomy: surgical removal of deposits in the walls of the carotid artery that, when present, have the effect of narrowing its lumen [the channel inside].

cataplexy: sudden episodes of loss of muscle function ranging from slight weakness to complete body collapse.

central nervous system: the brain and the spinal cord. Also called CNS.

cerebellum: The portion of the brain in the back of the head between the cerebrum and the brain stem.

cerebral: relating to the two hemispheres of the human brain.

cerebral hemispheres: the two halves of the cerebrum.

cerebrospinal fluid: the watery fluid flowing around the brain and spinal cord. Also called CSF.

cerebrum: the main portion of the brain that includes the two cerebral hemispheres; this term is also used to refer to the entire brain.

clinical trials: studies in which new treatments are tested in patients. Each study is designed to answer scientific questions and to find better ways to treat patients.

cluster headaches: intensely painful headaches occurring suddenly and lasting between 30 and 45 minutes; named for their repeated occurrence in groups or clusters. They begin as minor pain around one eye and eventually spread to that side of the face.

cognition/cognitive: the process of knowing, including awareness, perception, reasoning, remembering, and problem solving.

compensation: in stroke rehabilitation, the ability of an individual with disabilities from a stroke to perform a task (or tasks) either using the impaired limb with an adapted (different) approach or using the unaffected limb to perform the task; an approach to rehabilitation in which the patient is taught to adapt to and offset residual disabilities.

computed tomography (CT): an imaging technique that uses X rays and a computer to create a picture of the brain's tissues and structures.

congenital: present at birth.

continence: the ability to control bodily functions, especially urinary bladder and bowel function.

contracture: a condition of fixed, high resistance to passive stretching that results from fibrosis and shortening of tissues that support muscles or joints.

contralateral: the opposite side of the body.

corpus striatum: a part of the brain that helps regulate motor activities.

cryothalamotomy: a surgical procedure in which a supercooled probe is inserted into a part of the brain called the thalamus in order to stop tremors.

craniopharyngioma: a type of brain tumor.

craniotomy: an operation in which an opening is made in the skull so the doctor can reach the brain.

CT (or CAT) scan: An x-ray procedure using a computer to produce detailed pictures of areas inside the body (*see also* **computed tomography**).

cyst: A closed sac or capsule, usually filled with fluid or semisolid material.

D

deep vein thrombosis (DVT): the clotting of blood in the deep veins of the leg or arm.

dementia: a mental disorder characterized by the loss of intellectual abilities and, frequently, personality changes due to deterioration of the brain. Alzheimer's disease is a frequent example.

depression: a mental state marked by feelings of despair, discouragement, and sadness.

diagnosis: determining the exact nature of a specific disease.

dihydroergotamine: a drug that is given by injection to treat cluster headaches. It is a form of the antimigraine drug ergotamine tartrate.

dopamine: a chemical messenger, deficient in the brains of Parkinson's disease patients, that transmits impulses from one nerve cell to another.

dysarthria: problems with speaking caused by difficulty moving or coordinating the muscles needed for speech.

dyskinesias: abnormal involuntary movements that can result from long-term use of high doses of levodopa.

dysphagia: difficulty swallowing.

E

edema: swelling; an abnormal buildup of fluid.

electroencephalogram (EEG): a technique for recording the pattern of electrical currents inside the brain.

electromyography (EMG): a special recording technique that detects electric activity in muscle. Patients are sometimes offered a type of biofeedback called EMG training, in which they learn to control muscle tension in the face, neck, and shoulders.

encapsulated: confined to a specific area; the tumor remains in a compact form.

endorphins: naturally occurring painkilling chemicals. Some scientists theorize that people who suffer from severe headache have lower levels of endorphins than people who are generally pain free.

embolus/embolism: a blood clot of other foreign substance that travels in the bloodstream to occlude an artery or vein.

epilepsy: a family of neurological conditions that cause seizures.

ependymoma: a type of brain tumor.

ergotainine tartrate: a drug that is used to control the painful dilation stage of migraine.

F

failure to thrive: [in infants] a condition characterized by lag in physical growth and development.

febrile seizures: convulsions brought on by a fever in infants or small children.

festination: a symptom characterized by small, quick forward steps.

G

gait symmetry: a normal walking pattern, in which the movements of one leg are mirrored by similar movements of the other leg.

gamma knife: radiation therapy in which high-energy rays are aimed at a tumor from many angles in a single treatment session.

generalized seizure: a seizure in which the entire brain is involved (*see also* **partial seizure**).

germ cell tumors: A type of brain tumor.

germinoma: a type of germ cell tumor.

glioblastoma multiforme: a type of brain tumor.

glioma: a name for brain tumors that begin in the glial cells, or supportive cells, in the brain. "Glia" is the Greek word for glue.

graphesthesia: the sense by which figures or numbers drawn on the skin with a dull point are recognized.

H

hair follicle: a sac from which a hair grows.

hemi-inattention: a disturbance of a person's awareness of space on the side of the body opposite a stroke-causing lesion; often referred to as unilateral neglect.

hemiparesis: muscular weakness or partial paralysis of one side of the body.

hemiplegia: paralysis of one side of the body.

hemiplegic migraine: a type of migraine causing temporary paralysis on one side of the body.

hydrocephalus: the abnormal buildup of cerebrospinal fluid in the ventricles of the brain.

hemorrhage: bleeding from the rupture of a blood vessel.

hemorrhagic stroke: a stroke resulting from the rupture of a blood vessel in the brain.

homonymous hemianopsia: defective vision or blindness affecting the right or left halves of the visual fields of both eyes.

hypoarousal: below normal level of arousal.

hypothalamus: the area of the brain that controls body temperature, hunger, and thirst.

hypoxic-ischemic encephalopathy: brain damage caused by poor blood flow or insufficient oxygen supply to the brain.

I

incontinence: lack of control over excretory functions (urination, bowels).

infarction: death of part of an organ, such as the brain, due to lack of oxygen and other nutrients.

inflammatory headache: a headache that is a symptom of another disorder, such as sinus infection, and is treated by curing the underlying problem.

intracerebral hemorrhage: hemorrhage into the cerebrum.

intrathecal chemotherapy: injection of anticancer drugs into cerebral fluid.

ipsilateral: the same side of the body.

ischemic stroke: a stroke caused by an insufficient supply of blood and oxygen to a part of the brain.

M

magnetic resonance imaging (MRI): an imaging technique which uses radio waves, magnetic fields, and computer analysis to create a picture of body tissues and structures.

malignant: cancerous; life threatening. A malignant brain tumor seriously threatens vital functions.

medulloblastoma: a type of brain tumor.

membrane: a very thin layer of tissue that covers a surface.

meninges: the three membranes that cover the brain and spinal cord.

meningioma: a type of brain tumor.

migraine: a vascular headache believed to be caused by blood flow changes and certain chemical changes in the brain leading to a cascade of events—including constriction of arteries supplying blood to the brain and the release of certain brain chemicals—that result in severe head pain, stomach upset, and visual disturbances.

motor control: ability to control movements of the body.

muscle-contraction headaches: headaches caused primarily by sustained muscle tension or, possibly, by restricted blood flow to the brain. Two forms of muscle-contraction headache are tension headache, induced by stress, and chronic muscle-contraction headache, which can last for extended periods, involves steady pain, and is usually felt on both sides of the head.

myelin: the fatty substance that covers and protects nerves.

myelogram: an x-ray of the spinal cord and the bones of the spine.

N

narcolepsy: a chronic sleep disorder.

neurologist: a doctor who specializes in the diagnosis and treatment of disorders of the nervous system.

neurology: the branch of medicine that focuses on the study of the nervous system.

neuroma: a tumor that arises in nerve cells.

neurosurgeon: a doctor who specializes in surgery on the brain and other parts of the nervous system.

nitrosoureas: a group of anticancer drugs that can cross the blood-brain barrier. Carmustine (BCNU) and lomustine (CCNU) are nitrosoureas.

nociceptors: the endings of pain-sensitive nerves that, when stimulated by stress, muscular tension, dilated blood vessels, or other triggers, send messages up the nerve fibers to nerve ceus in the brain, signaling that a part of the body hurts.

O

occlusion: blockage.

oligodendroglioma: a type of brain tumor.

on-off effect: a change in a Parkinson's disease patient's condition, with sometimes rapid fluctuations between uncontrolled movements and normal movement, usually occurring after long-term use of levodopa and probably caused by changes in the ability to respond to this drug.

ophthalmoplegic migraine: a form of migraine felt around the eye and associated with a droopy eyelid, double vision, and other sight problems.

ophthalmoscope: a lighted instrument used to examine the inside of the eye, including the retina and the optic nerve.

optic nerve: the nerve that carries messages from the retina to the brain.

orthostatic hypotension: lowering of blood pressure with a change of body position from supine to erect.

orthostatic tolerance: the ability to maintain blood pressure while standing upright.

P

pallidotomy: a surgical procedure in which a part of the brain called the globus palfidus is lesioned in order to improve symptoms of tremor, rigidity, and bradykinesia.

papilledema: swelling around the optic nerve, usually due to pressure on the nerve by a tumor.

paralysis: loss of ability to move all or part of the body.

parkinsonism: a term referring to a group of conditions that are characterized by four typical symptoms—tremor, rigidity, postural instability, and bradykinesia.

partial seizure: a seizure in which abnormal electrical activity involves one area of the brain (*see also* **generalized seizure**).

pathologist: a doctor who identifies diseases by studying cells and tissues under a microscope.

perception: conscious mental recognition of a sensory stimulus.

perseveration: involuntary and pathologic persistence of the same verbal response or motor activity regardless of the stimulus or its duration.

pineal gland: a small gland located in the cerebrum.

pineal region tumors: types of brain tumors.

pineoblastoma: a type of brain tumor.

pineocytoma: a type of brain tumor.

pituitary gland: the main endocrine gland; it produces hormones that control other glands and many body functions, especially growth.

positron emission tomography (PET): an imaging technique that shows ongoing metabolic activity in various regions of the brain.

postural instability: impaired balance and coordination, often causing patients to lean forward or backward and to fall easily.

primitive neuroectodermal tumors: a type of brain tumor.

prognosis: the probable outcome or course of a disease.

prophylaxis: treatments aimed at preventing disease.

proprioception: perception of body movements or position.

prostaglandins: naturally occurring pain-producing substances thought to be implicated in migraine attacks. Their release is triggered by the dilation of arteries. Prostaglandins are extremely potent chemicals involved in a diverse group of physiological processes.

R

remediation: approaches to rehabilitation that attempt to reduce the severity of neurological deficits.

retropulsion: the tendency to step backwards if bumped from the front or upon initiating walking, usually seen in patients who tend to lean backwards because of problems with balance.

Rh incompatibility: a blood condition in which antibodies in a pregnant woman's blood can attack fetal blood cells, impairing the fetus's supply of oxygen.

rigidity: a symptom of Parkinson's disease in which muscles feel stiff and display resistance to movement even when another person tries to move the affected part of the body, such as an arm.

risk factor: something that increases a person's chances of getting a disease.

rubella: also known as German measles, rubella is a viral infection that can damage the nervous system in the developing fetus.

S

schwannoma: a type of brain tumor.

seizures: convulsions; sudden, involuntary movements of the muscles.

shunt: a catheter (tube) that carries cerebrospinal fluid from a ventricle in the brain to another area of the body.

serotonin: a key neurotransmitter that acts as a powerful constrictor of arteries, reducing the blood supply to the brain and contributing to the pain of headache.

sinusitis: an infection, either viral or bacterial, of the sinus cavities. The infection leads to inflammation of these cavities, causing pain and sometimes headache.

spastic diplegia: a form of cerebral palsy in which both arms and both legs are affected, the legs being more severely affected.

spastic hemiplegia (or hemiparesis): a form of cerebral palsy in which spasticity affects the arm and leg on one side of the body.

spastic paraplegia (or paraparesis): a form of cerebral palsy in which spasticity affects both legs but the arms are relatively or completely spared.

spastic quadriplegia (or quadriparesis): a form of cerebral palsy in which all four limbs are affected equally.

spasticity: abnormally increased tone in a muscle.

status migrainosus: a rare, sustained, and severe type of migraine, characterized by intense pain and nausea and often leading to hospitalization of the patient.

stenosis: reduction in the size of a vessel or other opening.

stereognosia: difficulty perceiving and identifying objects using the sense of touch.

stereognosis: the ability to perceive the nature and form of objects by the sense of touch.

stereotaxis: use of a computer and scanning devices to create three-dimensional pictures. This method can be used to direct a biopsy, external radiation, or the insertion of radiation implants.

steroids: drugs used to relieve swelling and inflammation.

strabismus: misalignment of the eyes.

stroke: an acute neurological dysfunction of vascular origin with symptoms and signs corresponding to the involvement of focal areas of the brain; alternatively, the rapid onset of a neurological deficit that persists for at least 24 hours and is caused by intracerebral or subarachnoid hemorrhage or blockage of a blood vessel supplying or draining the brain.

subarachnoid hemorrhage: a hemorrhage in the space underneath the subarachnoid membrane that results in pressure on the brain or bleeding into the brain.

substantia nigra: movement-control center in the brain where loss of dopamine-producing nerve cells triggers the symptoms of Parkinson's disease; substantia nigra means "black substance," so called because the cells in this area are dark.

surgery: an operation.

T

temporomandibular joint dysfunction: a disorder of the joint between the temporal bone (above the ear) and the lower jaw bone that can cause muscle-contraction headaches.

thermography: a technique sometimes used for diagnosing headache in which an infrared camera converts skin temperature into a color picture, called a thermogram, with different degrees of heat appearing as different colors.

thromboembolism: an embolus that originates in and breaks away from a clot in one vessel to become lodged in another vessel.

thrombophlebitis: inflammation of a vein that occurs when a blood clot forms.

thrombosis: the clotting of blood within a blood vessel.

tic douloureux: see trigeminal neuralgia

tissue: a group or layer of similar cells that perform a special function.

tonic-clonic seizure: a full convulsion with loss of consciousness and jerking movements of the limbs.

Tourette syndrome: a neurological disorder characterized by repeated involuntary movements and uncontrollable vocal sounds called tics.

traction headaches: headaches caused by pulling or stretching pain-sensitive parts of the head, as, for example, when eye muscles are tensed to compensate for eyestrain.

transient ischemic attack (TIA): the rapid onset of a neurological deficit that clears spontaneously in minutes or a few hours.

tremor: shakiness or trembling, often in a hand, which in Parkinson's disease is usually most apparent when the affected part is at rest.

trigeminal neuralgia: a condition resulting from a disorder of the trigeminal nerve. Symptoms are headache and intense facial pain that comes in short, excruciating jabs.

tuberous sclerosis: a genetic disorder characterized by seizures, mental retardation, and skin and eye lesions.

tumor: an abnormal mass of tissue.

U

ultrasonography: a technique that bounces sound waves off of tissues and structures and uses the pattern of echoes to form an image, called a sonogram.

unilateral neglect: a disturbance of a person's awareness of space on the side of the body opposite a stroke-causing lesion; often referred to as hemi-inattention.

V

vascular headaches: headaches caused by abnormal function of the brain's blood vessels or vascular system. Migraine is a type of vascular headache.

ventricles: four connected cavities (hollow spaces) in the brain.

vital: necessary to maintain life. Breathing is a vital function.

W

wearing-off effect: the tendency, following long-term levodopa treatment, for each dose of the drug to be effective for shorter and shorter periods.

X

X-ray: high-energy radiation. It is used in low doses to diagnose diseases and in high doses to treat cancer.

Chapter 45

Organizational Resources for Patients with Brain Disorders

Alzheimer's Disease

Alzheimer's Association
919 North Michigan Avenue
Suite 1000
Chicago, IL 60611-1676
(312) 335-8700
(800) 272-3900
(312) 335-1110 fax
E-mail: info@alz.org
Website: http://www.alz.org

American Health Assistance Foundation
15825 Shady Grove Road
Rockville, MD 20850
(301) 948-3244
(800) 437-AHAF (-2423)
(301) 258-9454 fax
Website: http://www.ahaf.org

C-Mac Informational Services. Inc./"Caregiver News"
271 Cedar Lane
East Meadow, NY 11554
(516) 481-6682
(516) 486-7829 (fax)

Amyotrophic Lateral Sclerosis (ALS—Lou Gehrig's Disease)

ALS Association
21021 Ventura Boulevard
Suite 321
Woodland Hills, CA 91364
(818) 340-7500
(810) 679-9109 fax
(800) 782-4747
E-mail: alsinfo@als-national.org
Website: www.ALSA.org

This compiled list of resources includes information from the National Institute of Neurological Disorders and Stroke and other sources deemed reliable; all contact information updated and verified in October 1998.

Center for Neurologic Study
9850 Genesee Ave., #320
La Jolla, CA 92037
(619) 455-5463
(619) 455-1713 fax
E-mail: cns@cts.com
Website: www.cnsonline.org

Forbes Norris ALS Research Center
California Pacific Med. Center
2324 Sacramento Street
San Francisco, CA 94115
(415) 923-3604
(415) 673-5184 fax

Les Turner Amyotrophic Lateral Sclerosis Foundation, Ltd.
8142 N. Lawedale Ave.
Skokie, IL 60076
(847) 679-3311
(847) 676-9109 fax
E-mail: info@lesturnerals.org
Website: http://
www.skikienet.org/ltalsfol/

Muscular Dystrophy Association
3300 East Sunrise Drive
Tucson, AZ 85718
(602) 529-2000
(800) 572-1717
Website: http://www.mda.org

Aphasia

National Aphasia Assoc.
156 5th, Ave., Suite707
New York, NY 10010
(212) 255-4329
(800) 922-4NAA (-4622)
E-mail: kline@aphasia.org
Website: www.aphasia.org

Ataxia

National Ataxia Foundation
2600 Fembrook Lane, Suite 119
Plymouth, MN 55447-4752
(612) 553-0020
(612) 553-0167 fax
E-mail: naf@mr.net
Website: http://www.ataxia.org/

Ataxia-Telangiectasia

A-T Children's Project
1 West Camino Real, Suite 212
Boca Raton, FL 33432-5966
(561) 395-2621
(800) 5 HELP-AT (543-5728)
(561) 395-2640 fax
E-mail: rosa@atcp.org
Website: http://
www.med.jhu.edu/ataxia/

A-T Medical Research Foundation
5241 Round Meadow Road
Hidden Hills, CA 91302
(818) 704-8146

A-T Project
3002 Enfield Road
Austin, Texas 78703
(512) 472-3417

Bell's Palsy

Bell's Palsy Research Foundation
9121 E. Tanque Verde
#105-286
Tucson, AZ 85749
(520) 749-4614
E-mail: bellspalsey@aol.com

Brain Tumors

American Brain Tumor Association
2720 River Road, Suite 146
Des Plaines, IL 60016
(847) 827-9910
(847) 827-9918 fax
(800) 886-2282
E-mail: info@abta.org
Website: www.abta.org

American Cancer Society
1599 Clifton Road, NE
Atlanta, GA 30329
(404) 320-333
(404) 325-0230 fax
(800) ACS-2345
Website: http://www.cancer.org

Brain Tumor Foundation for Children, Inc.
1835 Savoy Drive, Suite 316
Atlanta, GA 30341
(770) 458-5554
(770) 458-5467 fax
E-mail: eallman1@juno.com

Brain Tumor Foundation of Canada
650 Waterloo Street, Suite 100
London, ON Canada N6B 2R4
(519) 642-7755
(519) 642-7193
E-mail: btfc@gtn.net
Website: http://www.btfc.org

The Brain Tumor Society
84 Seattle St.
Boston, MA 02134-1245
(617) 783-0340
(617) 783-9712 fax
E-mail: info@tbts.org
Website: http://www.tbts.org

Candlelighters Childhood Cancer Foundation
7910 Woodmont Avenue
Suite 460
Bethesda, MD 20814
(301) 657-8401
(800) 366-CCCF (-2223)
(301) 718-2686 fax
E-mail: info@candlelighters.org
Website: http://
www.candlelighters.org/

Childhood Brain Tumor Foundation
20312 Watkins Meadow Dr
Germantown, MD 20876
(301) 515-2900
E-mail: cbtf@monumental.com
Website: http://
www.monumental.com/cbtf/

Children's Brain Tumor Foundation
274 Madison Avenue
#1301
New York, NY 10016
(212) 448-9494
(212) 448-1022 fax
Website:
www.childrensneuronet.org

National Brain Tumor Foundation
785 Market St., Suite 1600
San Francisco, CA 94103
(415) 284-0208
(415) 284-0209 fax
(800) 934-CURE (-2873)
E-mail: nbtf@braintumor.org
Website: http://
www.braintumor.org/

National Cancer Institute
Building 31, 10A07
9000 Rockville Pike
Bethesda, MD 20892
(800) 4-CANCER
Website:
www.cancernet.nci.nih.gov

Pediatric Brain Tumor Foundation
315 Ridgefield Ct.
Asheville, NC 28806
(704) 665-6891
(704) 665-6894 fax

Pituitary Tumor Network Association
16350 Ventura Blvd., Suite 231
Encino, CA 91436
(805) 499-9973
(800) 642-9211
(805) 499-1523 fax
E-mail: ptna@triax.com
Website: http://www./neurosurgery.
mgh.harvard.edu/ptna/

Cerebral Palsy

United Cerebral Palsy Associations, Inc.
1660 L Street NW, Suite 700
Washington, DC 20036
(800) USA-5UCP (872-5827)
(800) 776-0414 fax
E-mail: ucpnatl@ucpa.org
Website: http://www.ucpa.org/

Pedal with Pete, Inc.
P.O. Box 274
Kent, OH 44240
(800) 304-PETE (-7383)

Comprehensive/General

Administration on Aging
330 Independence Avenue SW
Washington, DC 20201
(800) 677-1116
(202) 401-7575 fax
Website: http://www.aoa.gov

Agency for Health Care Policy and Research (AHCPR)
2101 East Jefferson Street
Rockville, MD 20852
(301) 594-6662
E-mail: info@ahcpr.gov
Website: www.ahcpr.gov

American Academy of Neurology
1080 Montreal Avenue
St. Paul, MN 55116
(612) 692-1940
Website: www.aan.com

Association for the Care of Children's Health
19 Mancua Road
Mt. Royal, NJ 08061
(609) 224-1742
(609) 423-3420 (fax)
E-mail:
amkent@tmg.smarthub.com
Website: http://www.acch.org

Brain Tissue Resource Center
McLean Hospital
115 Mill Street
Belmont, MA 02178
(617) 855-2400
(800) 333-0388
(617) 855-3199 fax

Charles A. Dana Foundation
747 Fifth Avenue, Suite 700
New York, NY 10151
(212) 223-4040
E-mail:
danainfo@danany.dana.org
Website: http://www.dana.org

Family Caregiver Alliance
425 Bush Street, Suite 500
San Francisco, CA 94108
(415) 434-3388
(415) 434-3508 fax
(800) 445-8106 (Toll free in CA)
E-mail: info@caregiver.org
Website: www.caregiver.org

International Radiosurgery Support Assn.
P.O. Box 60950
Harrisburg, PA 17106
(717) 671-1701
(717) 671-1703 fax
E-mail: getinfo@irsa.org
Website: http://www.irsa.org

March of Dimes Birth Defects Foundation
1275 Mamaroneck Avenue
White Plains, NY 10605
(914) 428-7100
Website: http://www.modimes.org

National Center for Education in Maternal and Child Health
2000 15th Street North, Suite 701
Arlington, VA 22201-2617
(703) 524-7802
(703) 524-9335
E-mail: info@ncemch.org
Website: http://www.ncemch.org

National Council on Patient Information and Education
666 11th St. NW, Suite 810
Washington, DC 20001-4542
(202) 347-6711
(202) 638-0773
E-mail: ncpie@erols.com

National Family Caregivers Assn.
10605 Concord St., Suite 501
Kensington, MD 20895
(800) 896-3650
(301) 942-2302 fax
E-mail: info@nfcacares.org
Website: http://
www.nfcacares.org

National Foundation for Brain Research
1250 24th Street NW, Suite 300
Washington, DC 20037
(202) 293-5453
(202) 466-0585
E-mail: hoffheimer@aol.com

National Health Council, Inc.
1730 M Street NW, Suite 500
Washington, DC 20036
(202) 785-3910
(202) 785-5923
E-mail: info@nhcouncil.org

National Health Education Committee, Inc.
865 United Nations Plaza
New York, NY 10017
(212) 421-9010

National Institute of Neurological Disorders and Stroke (NINDS)
P.O. Box 5801
31 Center Drive, MSC 2540
Bethesda, MD 20892-2540
(301) 496-5751
(800) 352-9424
Website: www.ninds.nih.gov

National Organization for Rare Disorders (NORD)
P.O. Box 8923
New Fairfield, CT 06812-8923
(203) 746-6518
(800) 999-6673
(203) 746-6481 fax
E-mail:
orphan@rarediseases.org
Website: http://
www.rarediseases.org/

National Parent to Parent Support and Information System
P.O. Box 907
Blue Ridge, Georgia 30513
(800) 651-1151

Pilot International
244 College St.
P.O. Box 4844
Macon, GA 31208
(912) 743-7403
(912) 743-2173
Website: http://
www.pilotinternational.org

Research!America
908 King Street, Suite 400 E
East Alexandria, Virginia 22314
(703) 739-2577
(800) FON-CURE (366-2873)
E-mail: researcham@aol.com
Website:
www.researchamerica.org

Well Spouse Foundation
P.O. Box 801
New York, NY 10023
(212) 644-1241
(800) 838-0879
(212) 644-1338 fax
E-mail: wellsP.O.use@aol.com
Website: http://www.sky.net/
~dP.O.rter/wellsp.htm

Disability and Rehabilitation

American Occupational Therapy Association
4720 Montgomery Lane
P.O. Box 31220
Bethesda, MD 20814-3425
(301) 652-2682
(301) 652-7711 fax
E-mail: praota@aota.org
Website: http://www.aota.org/
index.html

The Arc of the United States
500 East Border Street
Suite 300
Arlington, TX 76010
(817) 261-6003
(817) 277-0553 fax
E-mail: thearc@metronet.com
Website: http://www.thearc.org/

Disability Resources
Four Glatter Lane
Centerreach, NY 11720-1023
(516) 585-0290

National Easter Seal Society, Inc.
230 W. Monroe Street
Suite 1800
Chicago, IL 60606
(312) 726-6200 (Voice)
(312) 726-4258 (TDD)
(800) 221-6827
E-mail: info@easter-seals.org
Website: http://www.seals.com

National Rehabilitation Information Center (NARIC)
Macro Systems, Suite 935
8455 Colesville Road
Silver Spring, MD 20910-3319
(301) 588-9284
(800) 346-2742
(301) 495-5626 (TT)
(301) 587-1967 fax
E-mail: wendling@macroint.com
Website: www.cais.net/naric

National Information Center for Children & Youth with Disabilities (NICHCY)
P.O. Box 1492
Washington, DC 20013-1492
(202) 884-8200
(800) 695-0285
E-mail: nichcy@aed.org
Website: http://www.nichcy.org/

National Institute on Disability and Rehabilitation Research (NIDRR)
400 Maryland Ave. SW
Washington, DC 20201-2572
(202) 205-8134
Website: http://www.ed.gov/offices/OSERS/NIDRR/

Dizziness and Balance

Ear Foundation
1817 Patterson Street
Nashville, TN 37203
(615) 329-7809
(800) 545-HEAR
(615) 329-7935 fax
E-mail:
earfound@theearfound.org
Website: http://
www.theearfound.com/

Vestibular Disorders Association
P.O. Box 4467
P.O.rtland, OR 97208-4467
(503) 229-7705
(503) 229-8064 fax
E-mail: veda@vestibular.org
Website: http://
www.teleP.O.rt.com/~veda/
index.shtml

Epilepsy

Comprehensive Epilepsy Program
Washington University
Box 8111
660 S. Euclid Avenue
St. Louis, MO 63110
(314) 632-3888
(314) 362-0296 fax
Website: www.neuro.wustl.edu/
epilepsy/

Epilepsy Canada
1470 Peel Street, Suite 745
Montreal, Quebec, Canada
H3A 1T1
(514) 845-7855
(800) 860-5499 (toll free)
(514) 845-7866 fax
E-mail: epilepsy@epilepsy.ca
Website: www.epilepsy.ca

Epilepsy Foundation of America
4351 Garden City Drive
Landover, MD 20785
(301) 459-3700
(301) 577-4941 fax
(800) 332-1000
E-mail: info@efa.org
Website: www.efa.org

Epilepsy Ontario
1 Promenade Circle, Suite 308
Thronhill, ON, Canada L4J 4P8
(416) 229-2291
(905) 764-5099
(800) 463-1119
(905) 764-1231 fax
E-mail:
infor@epilepsyontario.org
Website: http://
epilepsyontario.org/

Epilepsy Research Centers

Department of Neurology
Medical College of Virginia
Virginia Commonwealth University
Box 599, MCV Station
Richmond, VA 23298-0599
(804) 828-9720

University of California, LA
Department of Neurology
Room 1250
710 Westwood Plaza
Los Angeles, Ca 90095-1769
(310) 825-5745

University of Texas Health Science Center
Department of Neurology
6431 Fannin Street
Houston, TX 77030
(713) 500-7125
Website: http://
www.uth.tmc.edu/schools/med/
neurology/

MINCEP Epilepsy Care
5775 Wayzata Blvd.
MinneaP.O.lis, MN 55416
(612) 525-2400
(612) 525-1560

Department of Neurology
Baylor College of Medicine
One Baylor Plaza
Houston, TX 77030
(713) 798-5860
Website: http://
www.bcm.tmc.edu/neurol/
index.html

Department of Neurology
Yale University School of Medicine
333 Cedar Street
New Haven, CT 06520
(203) 785-3938
Website: http://
info.med.yale.edu/medical/

Epilepsy Research Laboratory
Duke University School of
Medicine
P.O. Box 3676
401 Byran Research Building
Durham, NC 27710
(916) 684-4241
E-mail: jmc@neuro.duke.edu
Website: http://
www2mc.duke.edu/som/

UCLA School of Medicine
Department of Pediatric
Neurology
Los Angeles, CA 90095-1752
(310) 825-6196
Website: http://
neurology.medsch.ucla.edu/
seizure.htm#pediatricepilepsy

Neurology and Neurological Services
Stanford University Medical Center
300 Pasteur Drive
Stanford, CA 94305-5300
(650) 723-6469
(650) 498-6326 fax
Website: http://
www.stanford.edu/group/neurology/

Georgetown University
3800 Reservoir Road NW
Washington, DC 20007
(202) 687-1607

Headache

American Council for Headache Education (ACHE)
19 Mantua Road
Mt. Royal, NJ 08061
(609) 423-0258
(609) 423-0082 fax
E-mail:
achehq@achw.smarthub.com
Website: http://www.achenet.org

National Headache Foundation
428 W. St. James Pl., 2nd Floor
Chicago, IL 60614
(773) 388-6399
(800) 843-2256
(773) 525-7357 fax
Website: http://
www.headaches.org

Huntington's Disease

Hereditary Disease Foundation
1427 7th Street, Suite 2
Santa Monica, CA 90401-9990
(310) 458-4183
(310) 458-3937 fax
E-mail: cures@hdfoundation.org
Website: http://
www.hdfoundation.org

Huntington's Disease Society of America (HDSA)
158 West 29th St, 7th Floor
New York, NY 10011-5300
(212) 242-1968
(800) 345-HDSA (-4372)
E-mail: curehd@idt.net
Website: http://neuro-
www2.mgh.harvard.edu/hdsa/
hdsamain.nclk

Hydrocephalus

Guardians of Hydrocephalus Research Foundation
2618 Avenue Z
Brooklyn, NY 11235
(718) 743-4473
(800) 458-8655
(718) 743-1171 fax
E-mail: hwinfo@healthy.net
Website: http://www.healthy.net/
pan/cso/cioi/GHRF.HTM

Hydrocephalus Association
870 Market Street, Suite 955
San Francisco, CA 94102
(415) 776-4713

Hydrocephalus Support Group
P.O. Box 4236
Chesterfield, MO 63006
(314) 532-8228

National Hydrocephalus Foundation
400 North Michigan Ave.
Suite 1102
Chicago, IL 60611-4102
(815) 467-6549

Language Disabilities

American Speech-Language Hearing Association
10801 Rockville Pike
Rockville, MD 20852
(301) 897-5700
(301) 897-0157 TTY
(301) 571-0457 fax
Website: http://www.asha.org

Mental Health

National Institute of Mental Health
Parklawn Building, Room 7C02
5600 Fisher's Lane
Rockville, MD 20857
(310) 443-4515
Website: http://
www.nimh.nih.gov/home.htm

National Mental Health Association
1021 Prince Street
Alexandria, VA 22314
(703) 684-7722
(703) 684-5968 fax
Website: http://www.nmha.org/

Myelin Disorders

Myelin Messenger
7320 N. Stable Lane
Prescott, AZ 86305
(520) 776-7556
E-mail: rutha@bslnet.com
Website: http://www.bslnet.com/
accounts/rutha/www/

Organization for Myelin Disorders Research & Support
3928 Youngman Drive
Cincinnati, OH 45245
(513) 752-6076

Neurotoxicity

Association of Birth Defects Children
827 Irma Avenue
Orlando, Florida 32802
(407) 245-7035
(800) 313-ABCD (-2232)
E-mail: abdc@birthdefects.org
Website: http://
www.birthdefects.org/
MAIN.HTM

Niemann-Pick Disorder

Ara Parseghian Medical Research Foundation
1760 E. River Road, Suite 115
Tucson, Arizona 85718
(520) 577-5106
(520) 577-5212 fax
E-mail: victory@parseghian.org
Website: http://
www.parseghian.org

National Niemann-Pick Foundation
3734 E. Olive Ave.
Gilbert, AZ 85234
(602) 940-8164
E-mail: vohrpahl@idcnet.com
Website: http://www.nnpdf.org

Pain

American Chronic Pain Association
P.O. Box 850
Rocklin, CA 95677
(916) 632-0922
(916) 6332-3208 fax
E-mail: ACPA@pacbell.net
Website: http://www.theacpa.org/

"Chronic Pain Letter"
c/o Fabian Memorial Foundation
P.O. Box 1303 Old Chelsea Station
New York, NY 10011
Website: http://www.chronicpainletter.com

National Chronic Pain Outreach Association
7979 Old Georgetown Road, Suite 100
Bethesda, MD 20814-2429
(301) 652-4948
(301) 907-0745 fax
Website: http://brain.mgh.harvard.edu:100/ncpainoa.htm

Parkinson's Disease

American Parkinson Disease Association
833 N. Orleans
Chicago, IL 60610
(312) 664-3880
(312) 664-3673 fax
Website: http://www.apda.qpg.com/

National Parkinson Foundation, Inc.
1501 NW 9th Ave. (Bob Hope Road)
Miami, FL 33136-1494
(305) 547-6666
(305) 548-4403 fax
(800) 327-4545
E-mail: mailbox@npf.med.miami.edu
Website: http://www.parkinson.org

Parkinson's Action Network
818 College Avenue, Suite C
Santa Rosa, CA 95404
(707) 544-1994
(800) 850-4726
(707) 544-2363 fax
E-mail: pan@sonic.net
Website: http://pages.prodigy.com/VRGS59A/

Parkinson's Disease Foundation
710 West 168th Street
New York, NY 10032-9982
(212) 923-4700
(212) 923-4778 fax
(800) 457-6676
E-mail: pds cpmc@aol.com

Parkinson's Institute
1170 Morse Avenue
Sunnyvale, CA 94089-1605
(408) 734-2800
(800) 786-2978
(800) 655-2273 (in CA)
(408) 734-8522 fax
Website: http://www.parkinsoninstitute.org

United Parkinson Foundation
833 West Washington Blvd.
Chicago, IL 60607
(312) 664-2344
(312) 664-2344 fax

Prader-Willi Syndrome

Prader-Willi Syndrome Association
5700 Midnight Pass Rd.
Sarasota, FL
(941) 312-0400
(800) 926-4797
(941) 312-0142 fax
E-mail: pwsausa@aol.com
Website: http://
www.pwsausa.org/

Reye's Syndrome

National Reye's Syndrome Foundation
426 North Lewis, P. O. Box 829
Bryan, OH 43506
(419) 636-2679
(800) 233-7393
Website: http://www.bright.net/
~reyessyn/

Sleep Disorders

American Sleep Apnea Association
1424 K Street NW
Washington, DC 20005
(202) 293-3650
(202) 293-3656 fax
E-mail: asaa@nicom.com
Website: http://
www.sleepapnea.org/

Narcolepsy Network
277 Fairfield Road, Suite 310B
Fairfield, NJ 07004
(973) 276-0115
(973) 227-8224 fax
E-mail: narnet@aol.com
Website: http://
www.websciences.org/narnet/

National Sleep Foundation
729 15th St. NW, 4th Floor
Washington, DC 20005
Website: http://
www.sleepfoundation.org

Stroke

American Heart Association
7272 Greenville Avenue
Dallas, TX 75231
(214) 373-6300
(800) 242-8721
Website: www.amhrt.org

Brain Aneurysm Foundation, Inc.
66 Canal St.
Boston, MA 02114
(617) 723-3870
(617) 723-8672 fax
Website: http://
neurosurgery.mgh.harvard.edu/
natl-brn.htm

National Heart, Lung, and Blood Institute
Building 31, Room 4A-21
Bethesda, MD 20892-2470
(301) 251-1222
E-mail: NHLBIIC@dgsys.com
Website: http://
quidetohealth.com\lnk/
link6.html

National Institute on Deafness and Other Communication Disorders (NIDC)
National Institutes of Health
Bethesda, MC 20892
(800) 241-1044
(800) 241-1055 (TTY/TDD/TT)
E-mail: nidcd@aerie.com
Website: http://www.nih.gov/
nidcd/homepage.htm

National Stroke Association
96 Inverness Drive East, Suite I
Englewood, CO 80112-5112
(303) 649-9299
(800) STROKES (787-6537)
E-mail: info@stroke.org
Website: www.stroke.org

Stroke Research Centers

Department of Neurology (127)
University of California, San
Francisco
4150 Clement Street
San Francisco, CA 94121
Website: http://itssrv1.ucsf.edu/
brain/

Department of Neurology
Henry Ford Health Science Center
27229 West Grand Boulevard
Detroit, MI 48202
(800) 999-4340
(800) 434-8834 (out of state)
Website: http://
www.henryfordhealth.org/GME/
Neurology.htm

Oregon Stroke Center
Oregon Health Sciences University
3181 SW Sam Jackson Park Road
P.O.rtland, OR 97201-3098
(503) 494-7225
E-mail: roakav@ahsu.edu
Website: http://www.ohsu.edu/
stroke/

Department of Neurology
University of Southern California School of Medicine
1540 San Pablo Street
Suite 268
Los Angeles, CA 90033
(213) 342-5710
(213) 342-5736 fax
Website: http://www.usc.edu/
schools/medicine/neurology

Department of Neurology
University of Miami School of Medicine
P.O. Box 016960
Miami, FL 33101
(305) 243-7610
Website: http://
www.med.miami.edu/crg/
neurology.html

University of Iowa College of Medicine
E 3180I GH
Iowa City, IA 52242
(319) 356-8250
Website: http://
www.medicine.uiowa.edu/

Departments of Neurology and Neurosurgery
Massachusetts General Hospital
Fruit Street
Boston, MA 03225
(617) 726-8442
Website: http://
dem0nmac.mgh.harvard.edu \

Department of Medicine
School of Medicine
University of California, LA
Los Angeles, CA 90095-1361
(310) 825-4321
(310) 825-2833 (TDD)
Website: http://
www.medsch.ucla.edu/

Department of Neurology
University of Maryland School
of Medicine
655 West Baltimore Street
Baltimore, MD 2120-1559
Website: http://
neuroscience.umaryland.edu/

Neurology and Radiation Science
Washington University School of
Medicine
Campus Box 8108
St. Louis, MO 63110
Website: http://
thalamus.wustl.edu/

Department of Neurology
University of Pennsylvania
Medical Center
3 Gates Building
3400 Spruce Street
Philadelphia, PA 19104
(215) 662-2700
Website: http://
www.med.upenn.edu/neuro

Department of Neurology
University of Pittsburgh School
of Medicine
Liliane S. Kaurmann Building
3471 Fifth Avenue, Suite 811
Pittsburgh, PA 15213
(412) 692-4622
Website: http://
www.neurology.pitt.edu/

Department of Anesthesiology
The Johns Hopkins University
600 North Wolfe Street
Blalock 1412
Baltimore, MD 21287-4963
(410) 955-7609
(410) 955-5607 fax
Website: http://
www.med.jhu.edu/anesthesiology/

Department of Neurology
Bowman Gray School of Medicine
Medical Center Boulevard
Winston-Salem, NC 27157-1078
(919) 716-3429

*Department of Health Sciences
Research*
Mayo Clinic Foundation
Rochester, MN 55901
(507) 284-1101
Website: http://www.mayo.edu/

Division of Hematology / Oncology
University of Texas Health Science Center
P.O. Box 20036
Houston, TX 77225
(713) 500-4472
E-mail:
ifried@admin4.hsc.uth.tmc.edu
Website: http://
www.uth.tmc.edu/

Department of Neurosciences
School of Medicine
Univ. of California, San Diego
9500 Gilman Drive
La Jolla, CA 92093-0624
(619) 534-4606
(619) 534-5748 fax
Website: http://
medicine.ucsd.edu/
somdepts.ntm#neuro

Sturge-Weber Syndrome

Sturge-Weber Foundation
P.O. Box 418
Mt. Freedom, NJ 07970
(973) 895-4445
(800) 627-5482
Website: http://
www.avenza.com/~swf/new/

Tay-Sachs Disease

National Tay-Sachs and Allied Diseases Assoc., Inc.
2001 Beacon Street, Suite 204
Brighton, MA 02135
(800) 906-8723
(617) 277-0134
E-mail: NTSAD-
Boston@worldnet.att.net
Website: http://mcrcr2med.nyu.
edu/murphp01/taysachs.htm

Late Onset Tay-Sachs Foundation
1303 Paper Mill Road
Erdenheim, PA 19038
(215) 836-9426
(800) 672-2022
Website: http://
www.webknx.com/LOTSF/

Tourette Syndrome

Tourette Syndrome Association
42-40 Bell Boulevard
Bayside, NY 11361-2820
(718) 224-2999
(718) 279-9596 fax
E-mail: tourette@ix.netcom.com
Website: http://neuro-
www2.mgh.harvard.edu/tsa/
tsamain.nclk

Tourette Syndrome Foundation of Canada
9559 Highway #7
Halifax, NS B0J 1T0
Website: http://
www.cfn.cs.dal.ca/Libraries/
HCRL/CommunityDB/
TSFC.html

Trauma

American Paralysis Association
500 Morris Avenue
Springfield, NJ 07081
(973) 379-2690
(800) 225-0292
Website: http://
www.apacure.com/Default.htm

Brain Injury Association, Inc.
105 N. Alfred St.
Alexandria, VA 22314
(703) 236-6000
(703) 236-6001 fax
Website: http://www.biausa.org/

Aitken Brain Trauma Foundation
523 E. 72nd St., 8th Floor
New York, NY 10021
(212) 772-0608
(212) 772-0357 fax
E-mail: info@aitken.org
Website: http://www.aitken.org/

California Brain Injury Association
P.O. Box 160786
Sacramento, CA 95816
(916) 442-1710
(800) 457-2443
(916) 442-7305
E-mail: biac@juno.com
Website: http://freeyellow.com/
members/BIAC/index.html

Coma Recovery Association, Inc.
100 East Old Country Road, Suite 9
Mineola, NY 11501
(516) 746-7714
(516) 746-7706 fax
E-mail: office@comarecovery.org
Website: http://
www.comarecovery.org

Head Injury Association of Niagara
183 King Street, Suite 101
St. Catharines, ON Canada L2R 3J5
(905) 984-5058
(905) 984-5354 fax
Website: http://
www.niagara.com/hian/

San Diego Head Injury Foundation, Inc.
P.O. Box 84601
San Diego, CA 92138
(619) 294-6541

Think First Foundation
22 South Washington Street
Park Ridge, IL 60068
(847) 692-2740
(800) THINK-56
(847) 692-2394 fax
E-mail: thinkfirst@aans.org
Website: http://
ww.thinkfirst.org/home.htm

Tuberous Sclerosis

National Tuberous Sclerosis Association
8181 Professional Place, Suite 110
Landover, MD 20785-2226
(800) 225-6872
(301) 459-0394 fax
E-mail: ntsa@ntsa.org
Website: http://www.ntsa.org/

Von Hippel-Lindau Disease

Von Hippel-Lindau Family Alliance
171 Clinton Road
Brookline, MA 02445-5815
(617) 232-5946
(800) 767-4VHL (4845)
(617) 734-8233 fax
E-mail: info@vhl.org
Website: http://ww.vhl.org/

Williams Syndrome

Williams Syndrome Association

P.O. Box 297
Clawson, MI 48017-0297
(248) 541-3630
(248) 541-3631 fax
E-mail: TMonkaba@aol.com
Website: http://www.williams-syndrome.org/

Chapter 46

Further Reading on Brain Disorders

The following list provides suggestions for additional sources of information on a wide variety of topics related to brain disorders. These suggestions are intended to serve as a starting place for research; the list is not comprehensive. Inclusion here does not constitute endorsement; omission does not constitute judgement. For easy identification, documents are classified by topic and alphabetized by title.

This list includes books, brochures, journal articles, web pages, and other sources of written information. Some items may be available at public or medical libraries or local bookstores. Others may be obtained directly from the publisher. Please verify availability and prices before ordering.

Amyotrophic Lateral Sclerosis (ALS)

ALS Demands Diligent Nursing Care (1995)
by Theresa Shellenbarger and John Stover
RN, March 1995, vol. 58, no. 3., p. 30(5).

Amyotrophic Lateral Sclerosis (unknown)
Muscular Dystrophy Association, 3300 East Sunrise Drive, Tucson, AZ 85718; (800) 572-1717.

The listings in this chapter were compiled in 1998 from documents reviewed by the editor and from other various sources deemed reliable.

Amyotrophic Lateral Sclerosis: A Comprehensive Guide to Management (unknown)
edited by Hiroshi Mitsumoto, MD and Forbes H. Norris, Jr. MD
Demos Publications, 386 Park Avenue W., Suite 201, New York, NY 10016; $39.95 plus $4.00 shipping and handling.

Amyotrophic Lateral Sclerosis (ALS) (1997)
National Institute of Neurological Disorders and Stroke (NINDS), P.O. Box 5801, 31 Center Drive, MSC 2540, Bethesda, MD 20892-2540; (800) 352-9424.

Communication and Swallowing Solutions for the ALS/MND Community (unknown)
by Marta S. Kazandjian
CINI, 250 Marcer, Street, Suite B1608, New York, NY 10012; (516) 874-8354; $7.95 plus $1.50 shipping and handling.

Fact Sheet: Amyotrophic Lateral Sclerosis (undated)
Family Caregiver Alliance, 425 Bush Street, Suite 500, San Francisco, CA 94108; (415) 434-3388. Available on the internet at www.care giver.org.

Heredity and ALS (undated)
The ALS Association, 21021 Ventura Blvd., Suite 321, Woodland Hills, CA 91364; (800) 782-4747.

It Helps to Talk about It: Living, Not Dying, with Lou Gehrig's Disease (unknown)
by Bob MacLean
The ALS Association, 21021 Ventura Blvd., Suite 321, Woodland Hills, CA 91364; (800) 782-4747; $18.00.

Living with ALS: A Series of Manuals (various)
The ALS Association, 21021 Ventura Blvd., Suite 321, Woodland Hills, CA 91364; (800) 782-4747; prices vary.

Patients with Amyotrophic Lateral Sclerosis Receiving Long-Term Mechanical Ventilation: Advance Care Planning and Outcomes (1996)
by Alvin H. Moss, Edward Anthony Oppenheimer, Patricia Casey, Pamela A. Cazzolli, Raymond P. Roos, Carol B. Stocking, and Mark Siegler
Chest, July 1996, vol. 110, no. 1, p. 249(7).

Brain Tumors

Brain Tumors: A Guide (1994)
National Brain Tumor Foundation, 785 Market St., Suite 1600, San Francisco, CA 94103; (800) 934-CURE (-2873).

Brain Tumor: Understanding Your Disease. How to Choose a Doctor and Hospital for Your Treatment (1995)
The Cleveland Clinic Foundation, 9500 Euclid Avenue, Cleveland, OH 44195; (216) 444-2200.

Dictionary for Brain Tumor Patients (1993)
American Brain Tumor Association, 2720 River Road, Suite 146, Des Plaines, IL 60016; (800) 886-2282. Also available on the internet at www.abta.org.

The Importance of Brain Tumor Support Groups (undated)
The Brain Tumor Society, 84 Seattle St., Boston, MA 02134-1245; (617) 783-0340. Also available on the internet at www.tbts.org.

A Primer of Brain Tumors: A Patient's Reference Manual (1996)
American Brain Tumor Association, 2720 River Road, Suite 146, Des Plaines, IL 60016; (800) 886-2282.

Support Groups for Brain Tumor Patients and Families in North America (1998)
National Brain Tumor Foundation, 785 Market St., Suite 1600, San Francisco, CA 94103; (800) 934-CURE (-2873).

Caregiving and General Information

Avoiding the Medicaid Trap: How Every American Can Beat the Catastrophic Costs of Nursing Home Care (unknown)
by Armond D. Budish
Avon Books, 1350 Avenue of the Americas, New York, NY 10019; (800) 238-0658; $15.00 plus shipping and handing.

Caring and Coping When a Loved One is Seriously Ill (unknown)
by Earl A. Grollman
Beacon Press, Order Department, 25 Street, Boston, MA 02108; (800) 706-2220; $10.00 plus shipping and handling.

Everything You Need to Know about Medical Tests (1996)
Springhouse Corporation, 111 Bethlehem Pike, Springhouse PA,
19444; (215) 646-8700.

Family Caregiver's Guide (unknown)
by Joan Ellen Foyder
The Futuro Company, 5801 Marimont Avenue, Cincinnati, OH 45227;
(513) 271-3782; $14.95 plus $2.50 shipping and handing.

Home Health Care (unknown)
by JoAnn Friedman
W.W. Norton and Company, Ltd., 550 Fifth Avenue, New York, NY
10010; $22.50 plus shipping and handling.

Neuroanatomy and Physiology
by Jesse Huang, MD
Beth Israel Medical Center, 170 East End Avenue at 87th Street, New
York, NY 10018. Available on the internet at www.bethisraelny.org/
inn.anatomy/anatomy.html.

*Questions and Answers about Pain Control: A Guide for People with
Cancer and Their Families* (1992)
by the American Cancer Society and the National Cancer Institute
National Cancer Institute, Building 31, 10A07, 9000 Rockville Pike,
Bethesda, MD 20892; (800) 4-CANCER.

Share the Care (unknown)
by Cappy Capossela and Shiela Warnock
Simon and Schuster, Fireside, 1230 Avenue of the Americas, New York,
NY 10020: $13.00 plus shipping and handling.

What Cancer Survivors Need to Know about Health Insurance (1993)
by I. C. Card
National Coalition for Cancer Survivorship, 1010 Wayne Avenue,
Suite 505, Silver Spring, MD 20910; (301) 650-8868.

We are Not Alone—Learning to Live with Chronic Illness (unknown)
by Sefra Korbin Pitzel
Workman Publishing, 708 Broadway, New York, NY 10013; (212) 254-
5900; $10.95 plus $3.00 shipping and handling.

Epilepsy

Brainstorms: Epilepsy in Our Words (1993) and *The Brainstorms Companion: Epilepsy in Our View* (1994)
by Stephen C. Schachter
Raven Press, 1185 Avenue of the Americas, New York, NY 10036.

Current View of Advances in Epilepsy (1997)
by Pat Phillips
JAMA, Journal of the American Medical Association, September 17, 1997 vol. 278, no. 11, p. 883(4).

Epilspy (1998)
National Institute of Neurological Disorders and Stroke (NINDS), P.O. Box 5801
31 Center Drive, MSC 2540, Bethesda, MD 20892-2540, (800) 352-9424. Available on the internet at www.ninds.nih.gov.

Epilepsy: You and Your Treatment (1994)
Epilepsy Foundation of America, 4351 Garden City Drive, Landover, MD 20785; (800) 332-1000.

How Should Febrile Seizures Be Evaluated and Treated? (1997?)
by Susan T. Arnold MD
Comprehensive Epilepsy Program, Washington University, Box 8111, 660 S. Euclid Avenue, St. Louis, MO 63110, (314) 632-3888. Available on the internet at www.neuro.wustl.edu/epilepsy.

Living Well with Epilepsy (1990)
by Robert J. Gumnit
Demos Publications, 386 Park Avenue W., Suite 201, New York, NY 10016.

Medicines for Epilepsy (1990)
Epilepsy Foundation of America, 4351 Garden City Drive, Landover, MD 20785; (800) 332-1000.

Recognizing the Hidden Signs of Childhood Seizures (1996)
Epilepsy Foundation of America, 4351 Garden City Drive, Landover, MD 20785; (800) 332-1000.

Safety and Seizures (1996)
Epilepsy Foundation of America, 4351 Garden City Drive, Landover, MD 20785; (800) 332-1000.

Seizures and Epilepsy in Childhood: A Guide for Parents (1990)
edited by John M. Freeman, Eileen P. G. Vining, and Diana J. Pillas
The Johns Hopkins University Press, 701 West 40ᵗʰ Street, Baltimore, MD 21211.

Seizures and Epilepsy in the Elderly (1997)
by Robert J. Thomas
Archives of Internal Medicine, March 24, 1997, vol. 157, no. 6, p. 605(13).

Seizure Recognition and First Aid (1996)
Epilepsy Foundation of America, 4351 Garden City Drive, Landover, MD 20785; (800) 332-1000.

Treatment of Medically Refractory Epilepsy (undated)
by Orrin Devinsky MD and Rick Abbott MD
Beth Israel Medical Center, 170 East End Avenue at 87th Street, New York, NY 10018. Available on the internet at www.bethisraelny.org/inn/epilep/epilep.txt.

Parkinson's Disease

Parkinson's Disease (1997)
American Academy of Neurology, 1080 Montreal Avenue, St. Paul, MN 55116; (612) 692-1940. Available on the internet at www.aan.com.

Parkinson's Disease: Quality of Life Issues (1993?)
by Barbara Fitzsimmons, RN, MS and Lissette K. Bunting, RN, MScN
Center for Neurologic Study, 9850 Genesee Ave., #320, La Jolla, CA 92037; (619) 455-5463. Available on the internet at www.cnsonline.org.

The Parkinson Patient at Home (undated)
by Robert S. Schwab, MD and Lewis J. Doshay, MD
Center for Neurologic Study, 9850 Genesee Ave., #320, La Jolla, CA 92037; (619) 455-5463. Available on the internet at www.cnsonline.org.

PD 'n' Me (1997)
American Parkinson Disease Association, 833 N. Orleans, Chicago, IL 60610; (312) 664-3880.

Stroke

Aneurysm Answers (undated)
National Stroke Association, 96 Inverness Drive East, Suite I, Englewood, CO 80112, (800) STROKES (787-6537). Available on the internet at www.stroke.org.

First Hours: Emergency Evaluation and Treatment (1996?)
National Stroke Association, 96 Inverness Drive East, Suite I, Englewood, CO 80112, (800) STROKES (787-6537). Available on the internet at www.stroke.org.

Intracranial Aneurysm (1998)
American Association of Neurological Surgeons/Congress of Neurological Surgeons, available on the internet at www.aans.org.

National Stroke Association Releases Stroke Prevention Guidelines
National Stroke Association, 96 Inverness Drive East, Suite I, Englewood, CO 80112, (800) STROKES (787-6537). Available on the internet at www.stroke.org.

Post-Stroke Rehabilitation: Assessment, Referral, and Patient Management (1995)
Agency for Health Care Policy and Research (AHCPR), 2101 East Jefferson Street, Rockville, MD 20852; (301) 594-6662.

Preventing Stroke (1994)
NIH Neurological Institute; P.O. Box 5801, Bethesda, MD 20824; (301) 496-5751 or (800) 352-9242.

Save Your Life: Understand Stroke (1998)
American Medical Association
AMA Health Insight, available on the internet at www.ama-assn.org/insight.

Sex after Stroke (1995)
American Heart Association, 7272 Greenville Avenue, Dallas, TX 75231; (800) 242-8721.

Stroke: A NARIC Resource Guide for Stroke Survivors and Their Families (1994)
National Rehabilitation Information Center (NARIC), 8455 Colesville Road, Suite 935, Silver Spring MD 20910-3319; (800) 347-2742 or (301) 588-9284.

Stroke Update (1998)
American Association of Neurological Surgeons/Congress of Neurological Surgeons, available on the internet at www.aans.org.

Tourette Syndrome

Facts You Should Know about the Genetics of Tourette Syndrome (1991)
Tourette Syndrome Association, 42-40 Bell Boulevard, Bayside, NY 11361; (718) 224-2999.

Tourette's Syndrome (1997)
American Academy of Neurology, 1080 Montreal Avenue, St. Paul, MN 55116; (612) 692-1940. Available on the internet at www.aan.com.

Index

Index

C

461

Contagious & Non-Contagious Infectious Diseases Sourcebook

Basic Information about Contagious Diseases like Measles, Polio, Hepatitis B, and Infectious Mononucleosis, and Non-Contagious Infectious Diseases like Tetanus and Toxic Shock Syndrome, and Diseases Occurring as Secondary Infections Such as Shingles and Reye Syndrome, Along with Vaccination, Prevention, and Treatment Information, and a Section Describing Emerging Infectious Disease Threats

Edited by Karen Bellenir and Peter D. Dresser. 566 pages. 1996. 0-7808-0075-3. $78.

Death & Dying Sourcebook

Basic Information for the Layperson about End-of-Life Care and Related Ethical and Legal Issues, Including Chief Causes of Death, Autopsies, Pain Management for the Terminally Ill, Life Support Systems, Coma, Euthanasia, Assisted Suicide, Hospice Programs, Living Wills, Near-Death Experiences, Counseling, Mourning, Organ Donation, Cryogenics and Physician Training and Liability, Along with Statistical Data, a Glossary, and Listings of Sources for Additional Help and Information

Edited by Annemarie Muth. 600 pages. 1999. 0-7808-0230-6. $78.

Diabetes Sourcebook, 1st Edition

Basic Information about Insulin-Dependent and Noninsulin-Dependent Diabetes Mellitus, Gestational Diabetes, and Diabetic Complications, Symptoms, Treatment, and Research Results, Including Statistics on Prevalence, Morbidity, and Mortality, Along with Source Listings for Further Help and Information

Edited by Karen Bellenir and Peter D. Dresser. 827 pages. 1994. 1-55888-751-2. $78.

"...very informative and understandable for the layperson without being simplistic. It provides a comprehensive overview for laypersons who want a general understanding of the disease or who want to focus on various aspects of the disease." — *Bulletin of the MLA, Jan '96*

Diabetes Sourcebook, 2nd Edition

Basic Consumer Health Information about Type 1 Diabetes (Insulin-Dependent or Juvenile-Onset Diabetes), Type 2 (Noninsulin-Dependent or Adult-Onset Diabetes), Gestational Diabetes, and Related Disorders, Including Diabetes Prevalence Data, Management Issues, the Role of Diet and Exercise in Controlling Diabetes, Insulin and Other Diabetes Medicines, and Complications of Diabetes Such as Eye Diseases, Periodontal Disease, Amputation, and End-Stage Renal Disease; Along with Reports on Current Research Initiatives, a Glossary, and Resource Listings for Further Help and Information

Edited by Karen Bellenir. 725 pages. 1998. 0-7808-0224-1. $78.

Diet & Nutrition Sourcebook, 1st Edition

Basic Information about Nutrition, Including the Dietary Guidelines for Americans, the Food Guide Pyramid, and Their Applications in Daily Diet, Nutritional Advice for Specific Age Groups, Current Nutritional Issues and Controversies, the New Food Label and How to Use It to Promote Healthy Eating, and Recent Developments in Nutritional Research

Edited by Dan R. Harris. 662 pages. 1996. 0-7808-0084-2. $78.

"Useful reference as a food and nutrition sourcebook for the general consumer."
— *Booklist Health Sciences Supplement, Oct '97*

"Recommended for public libraries and medical libraries that receive general information requests on nutrition. It is readable and will appeal to those interested in learning more about healthy dietary practices."
— *Medical Reference Services Quarterly, Fall '97*

"With dozens of questionable diet books on the market, it is so refreshing to find a reliable and factual reference book. Recommended to aspiring professionals, librarians, and others seeking and giving reliable dietary advice. An excellent compilation." — *Choice, Feb '97*

Diet & Nutrition Sourcebook, 2nd Edition

Basic Consumer Health Information about Dietary Guidelines, Recommended Daily Intake Values, Vitamins, Minerals, Fiber, Fat, Weight Control, Dietary Supplements, and Food Additives; Along with Special Sections on Nutrition Needs throughout Life and Nutrition for People with Such Specific Medical Concerns as Allergies, High Blood Cholesterol, Hypertension, Diabetes, Celiac Disease, Seizure Disorders, Phenylketonuria (PKU), Cancer, and Eating Disorders, and Including Reports on Current Nutrition Research and Source Listings for Additional Help and Information

Edited by Karen Bellenir. 600 pages. 1999. 0-7808-0228-4. $78.

Domestic Violence Sourcebook

Basic Information about the Physical, Emotional and Sexual Abuse of Partners, Children, and Elders, Including Information about Hotlines, Safe Houses, Safety Plans, Resources for Support and Assistance, Community Initiatives, and Reports on Current Directions in Research and Treatment; Along with a Glossary, Sources for Further Reading, and Listings of Governmental and Non-Governmental Organizations

Edited by Helene Henderson. 600 pages. 1999. 0-7808-0235-7. $78.

Ear, Nose & Throat Disorders Sourcebook

Basic Information about Disorders of the Ears, Nose, Sinus Cavities, Pharynx, and Larynx, Including Ear Infections, Tinnitus, Vestibular Disorders, Allergic and Non-Allergic Rhinitis, Sore Throats, Tonsillitis, and Cancers That Affect the Ears, Nose, Sinuses, and Throat, Along with Reports on Current Research Initiatives, a Glossary of Related Medical Terms, and a Directory of Sources for Further Help and Information

Edited by Karen Bellenir and Linda M. Shin. 592 pages. 1998. 0-7808-0206-3. $78.

Endocrine & Metabolic Disorders Sourcebook

Basic Information for the Layperson about Pancreatic and Insulin-Related Disorders Such as Pancreatitis, Diabetes, and Hypoglycemia; Adrenal Gland Disorders Such as Cushing's Syndrome, Addison's Disease, and Congenital Adrenal Hyperplasia; Pituitary Gland Disorders Such as Growth Hormone Deficiency, Acromegaly, and Pituitary Tumors; Thyroid Disorders Such as Hypothyroidism, Graves' Disease, Hashimoto's Disease, and Goiter; Hyperparathyroidism; and Other Diseases and Syndromes of Hormone Imbalance or Metabolic Dysfunction, Along with Reports on Current Research Initiatives

Edited by Linda M. Shin. 632 pages. 1998. 0-7808-0207-1. $78.

Environmentally Induced Disorders Sourcebook

Basic Information about Diseases and Syndromes Linked to Exposure to Pollutants and Other Substances in Outdoor and Indoor Environments Such as Lead, Asbestos, Formaldehyde, Mercury, Emissions, Noise, and More

Edited by Allan R. Cook. 620 pages. 1997. 0-7808-0083-4. $78.

". . . a good survey of numerous environmentally induced physical disorders . . . a useful addition to anyone's library."
— Doody's Health Science Book Reviews, Jan '98

". . . provide[s] introductory information from the best authorities around. Since this volume covers topics that potentially affect everyone, it will surely be one of the most frequently consulted volumes in the *Health Reference Series*." — Rettig on Reference, Nov '97

"Recommended reference source."
— Booklist, Oct '97

Ethical Issues in Medicine Sourcebook

Basic Information about Controversial Treatment Issues, Genetic Research, Reproductive Technologies, and End-of-Life Decisions, Including Topics Such as Cloning, Abortion, Fertility Management, Organ Transplantation, Health Care Rationing, Advance Directives, Living Wills, Physician-Assisted Suicide, Euthanasia, and More; Along with a Glossary and Resources for Additional Information

Edited by Helene Henderson. 600 pages. 1999. 0-7808-0237-3. $78.

Fitness & Exercise Sourcebook

Basic Information on Fitness and Exercise, Including Fitness Activities for Specific Age Groups, Exercise for People with Specific Medical Conditions, How to Begin a Fitness Program in Running, Walking, Swimming, Cycling, and Other Athletic Activities, and Recent Research in Fitness and Exercise

Edited by Dan R. Harris. 663 pages. 1996. 0-7808-0186-5. $78.

"A good resource for general readers."
— Choice, Nov '97

"The perennial popularity of the topic . . . make this an appealing selection for public libraries."
— Rettig on Reference, Jun/Jul '97

Food & Animal Borne Diseases Sourcebook

Basic Information about Diseases That Can Be Spread to Humans through the Ingestion of Contaminated Food or Water or by Contact with Infected Animals and Insects, Such as Botulism, E. Coli, Hepatitis A, Trichinosis, Lyme Disease, and Rabies, Along with Information Regarding Prevention and Treatment Methods, and a Special Section for International Travelers Describing Diseases Such as Cholera, Malaria, Travelers' Diarrhea, and Yellow Fever, and Offering Recommendations for Avoiding Illness

Edited by Karen Bellenir and Peter D. Dresser. 535 pages. 1995. 0-7808-0033-8. $78.

"Targeting general readers and providing them with a single, comprehensive source of information on selected topics, this book continues, with the excellent caliber of its predecessors, to catalog topical information on health matters of general interest. Readable and thorough, this valuable resource is highly recommended for all libraries."
— Academic Library Book Review, Summer '96

"A comprehensive collection of authoritative information." — Emergency Medical Services, Oct '95

Continues next page

Gastrointestinal Diseases & Disorders Sourcebook

Basic Information about Gastroesophageal Reflux Disease (Heartburn), Ulcers, Diverticulosis, Irritable Bowel Syndrome, Crohn's Disease, Ulcerative Colitis, Diarrhea, Constipation, Lactose Intolerance, Hemorrhoids, Hepatitis, Cirrhosis, and Other Digestive Problems, Featuring Statistics, Descriptions of Symptoms, and Current Treatment Methods of Interest for Persons Living with Upper and Lower Gastrointestinal Maladies

Edited by Linda M. Ross. 413 pages. 1996. 0-7808-0078-8. $78.

". . . very readable form. The successful editorial work that brought this material together into a useful and understandable reference makes accessible to all readers information that can help them more effectively understand and obtain help for digestive tract problems." — *Choice, Feb '97*

Genetic Disorders Sourcebook

Basic Information about Heritable Diseases and Disorders Such as Down Syndrome, PKU, Hemophilia, Von Willebrand Disease, Gaucher Disease, Tay-Sachs Disease, and Sickle-Cell Disease, Along with Information about Genetic Screening, Gene Therapy, Home Care, and Including Source Listings for Further Help and Information on More Than 300 Disorders

Edited by Karen Bellenir. 642 pages. 1996. 0-7808-0034-6. $78.

"Provides essential medical information to both the general public and those diagnosed with a serious or fatal genetic disease or disorder." — *Choice, Jan '97*

"Geared toward the lay public. It would be well placed in all public libraries and in those hospital and medical libraries in which access to genetic references is limited." — *Doody's Health Sciences Book Review, Oct '96*

Head Trauma Sourcebook

Basic Information for the Layperson about Open-Head and Closed-Head Injuries, Treatment Advances, Recovery, and Rehabilitation, Along with Reports on Current Research Initiatives

Edited by Karen Bellenir. 414 pages. 1997. 0-7808-0208-X. $78.

Health Insurance Sourcebook

Basic Information about Managed Care Organizations, Traditional Fee-for-Service Insurance, Insurance Portability and Pre-Existing Conditions Clauses, Medicare, Medicaid, Social Security, and Military Health Care, Along with Information about Insurance Fraud

Edited by Wendy Wilcox. 530 pages. 1997. 0-7808-0222-5. $78.

"The layout of the book is particularly helpful as it provides easy access to reference material. A most useful addition to the vast amount of information about health insurance. The use of data from U.S. government agencies is most commendable. Useful in a library or learning center for healthcare professional students." — *Doody's Health Sciences Book Reviews, Nov '97*

Healthy Aging Sourcebook

Basic Consumer Health Information about Maintaining Health through the Aging Process, Including Advice on Nutrition, Exercise, and Sleep, Along with Help in Making Decisions about Midlife Issues and Retirement, Practical and Informed Choices in Health Consumerism, and Data Concerning the Theories of Aging, Aging Now, and Aging in the Future, Including a Glossary and Practical Resource Directory

Edited by Jenifer Swanson. 500 pages. 1999. 0-7808-0390-6. $78.

Immune System Disorders Sourcebook

Basic Information about Lupus, Multiple Sclerosis, Guillain-Barré Syndrome, Chronic Granulomatous Disease, and More, Along with Statistical and Demographic Data and Reports on Current Research Initiatives

Edited by Allan R. Cook. 608 pages. 1997. 0-7808-0209-8. $78.

Kidney & Urinary Tract Diseases & Disorders Sourcebook

Basic Information about Kidney Stones, Urinary Incontinence, Bladder Disease, End Stage Renal Disease, Dialysis, and More, Along with Statistical and Demographic Data and Reports on Current Research Initiatives

Edited by Linda M. Ross. 602 pages. 1997. 0-7808-0079-6. $78.

Learning Disabilities Sourcebook

Basic Information about Disorders Such as Dyslexia, Visual and Auditory Processing Deficits, Attention Deficit/Hyperactivity Disorder, and Autism, Along with Statistical and Demographic Data, Reports on Current Research Initiatives, an Explanation of the Assessment Process, and a Special Section for Adults with Learning Disabilities

Edited by Linda M. Shin. 579 pages. 1998. 0-7808-0210-1. $78.

Medical Tests Sourcebook

Basic Consumer Health Information about Medical Tests, Including Periodic Health Exams, General Screening Tests, X-ray and Radiology Tests, Electrical Tests, Tests of Body Fluids and Tissues, Scope Tests, Lung Tests, Gene Tests, Pregnancy Tests, Newborn Screening Tests, Sexually Transmitted Disease Tests, and Computer Aided Diagnoses; Along with a Section on Paying for Medical Tests, a Glossary, and Resource Listings

Edited by Joyce B. Shannon. 600 pages. 1999. 0-7808-0243-8. $78.

Men's Health Concerns Sourcebook

Basic Information about Health Issues That Affect Men, Featuring Facts about the Top Causes of Death in Men, Including Heart Disease, Stroke, Cancers, Prostate Disorders, Chronic Obstructive Pulmonary Disease, Pneumonia and Influenza, Human Immuno-deficiency Virus and Acquired Immune Deficiency Syndrome, Diabetes Mellitus, Stress, Suicide, Accidents and Homicides; and Facts about Common Concerns for Men, Including Impotence, Contraception, Circumcision, Sleep Disorders, Snoring, Hair Loss, Diet, Nutrition, Exercise, Kidney and Urological Disorders, and Backaches

Edited by Allan R. Cook. 760 pages. 1998. 0-7808-0212-8. $78.

Mental Health Disorders Sourcebook

Basic Information about Schizophrenia, Depression, Bipolar Disorder, Panic Disorder, Obsessive-Compulsive Disorder, Phobias and Other Anxiety Disorders, Paranoia and Other Personality Disorders, Eating Disorders, and Sleep Disorders, Along with Information about Treatment and Therapies

Edited by Karen Bellenir. 548 pages. 1995. 0-7808-0040-0. $78.

"This is an excellent new book . . . written in easy-to-understand language."
— Booklist Health Science Supplement, Oct '97

". . . useful for public and academic libraries and consumer health collections."
— Medical Reference Services Quarterly, Spring '97

"The great strengths of the book are its readability and its inclusion of places to find more information. Especially recommended."   — RQ, Winter '96

". . . a good resource for a consumer health library."
— Bulletin of the MLA, Oct '96

"The information is data-based and couched in brief, concise language that avoids jargon. . . . a useful reference source."
— Readings, Sept '96

"The text is well organized and adequately written for its target audience."   — Choice, Jun '96

". . . provides information on a wide range of mental disorders, presented in nontechnical language."
— Exceptional Child Education Resources, Spring '96

"Recommended for public and academic libraries."
— Reference Book Review, '96

Ophthalmic Disorders Sourcebook

Basic Information about Glaucoma, Cataracts, Macular Degeneration, Strabismus, Refractive Disorders, and More, Along with Statistical and Demographic Data and Reports on Current Research Initiatives

Edited by Linda M. Ross. 631 pages. 1996. 0-7808-0081-8. $78.

Oral Health Sourcebook

Basic Information about Diseases and Conditions Affecting Oral Health, Including Cavities, Gum Disease, Dry Mouth, Oral Cancers, Fever Blisters, Canker Sores, Oral Thrush, Bad Breath, Temporomandibular Disorders, and other Craniofacial Syndromes, Along with Statistical Data on the Oral Health of Americans, Oral Hygiene, Emergency First Aid, Information on Treatment Procedures and Methods of Replacing Lost Teeth

Edited by Allan R. Cook. 558 pages. 1997. 0-7808-0082-6. $78.

"Recommended reference source." — Booklist, Dec '97

Pain Sourcebook

Basic Information about Specific Forms of Acute and Chronic Pain, Including Headaches, Back Pain, Muscular Pain, Neuralgia, Surgical Pain, and Cancer Pain, Along with Pain Relief Options Such as Analgesics, Narcotics, Nerve Blocks, Transcutaneous Nerve Stimulation, and Alternative Forms of Pain Control, Including Biofeedback, Imaging, Behavior Modification, and Relaxation Techniques

Edited by Allan R. Cook. 667 pages. 1997. 0-7808-0213-6. $78.

"The information is basic in terms of scholarship and is appropriate for general readers. Written in journalistic style . . . intended for non-professionals. Quite thorough in its coverage of different pain conditions and summarizes the latest clinical information regarding pain treatment."   — Choice, Jun '98

"Recommended reference source."
— Booklist, Mar '98

Continues next page

Physical & Mental Issues in Aging Sourcebook

Basic Consumer Health Information on Physical and Mental Disorders Associated with the Aging Process, Including Concerns about Cardiovascular Disease, Pulmonary Disease, Oral Health, Digestive Disorders, Musculoskeletal and Skin Disorders, Metabolic Changes, Sexual and Reproductive Issues, and Changes in Vision, Hearing, and Other Senses; Along with Data about Longevity and Causes of Death, Information on Acute and Chronic Pain, Descriptions of Mental Concerns, a Glossary of Terms, and Resource Listings for Additional Help

Edited by Heather E. Aldred. 625 pages. 1999. 0-7808-0233-0. $78.

Pregnancy & Birth Sourcebook

Basic Information about Planning for Pregnancy, Maternal Health, Fetal Growth and Development, Labor and Delivery, Postpartum and Perinatal Care, Pregnancy in Mothers with Special Concerns, and Disorders of Pregnancy, Including Genetic Counseling, Nutrition and Exercise, Obstetrical Tests, Pregnancy Discomfort, Multiple Births, Cesarean Sections, Medical Testing of Newborns, Breastfeeding, Gestational Diabetes, and Ectopic Pregnancy

Edited by Heather E. Aldred. 737 pages. 1997. 0-7808-0216-0. $78.

". . . for the layperson. A well-organized handbook. Recommended for college libraries . . . general readers."
— Choice, Apr '98

"Recommended reference source."
— Booklist, Mar '98

"This resource is recommended for public libraries to have on hand."
— American Reference Books Annual, '98

Public Health Sourcebook

Basic Information about Government Health Agencies, Including National Health Statistics and Trends, Healthy People 2000 Program Goals and Objectives, the Centers for Disease Control and Prevention, the Food and Drug Administration, and the National Institutes of Health, Along with Full Contact Information for Each Agency

Edited by Wendy Wilcox. 698 pages. 1998. 0-7808-0220-9. $78.

Rehabilitation Sourcebook

Basic Information for the Layperson about Physical Medicine (Physiatry) and Rehabilitative Therapies, Including Physical, Occupational, Recreational, Speech, and Vocational Therapy; Along with Descriptions of Devices and Equipment Such as Orthotics, Gait Aids, Prostheses, and Adaptive Systems Used during Rehabilitation and for Activities of Daily Living, and Featuring a Glossary and Source Listings for Further Help and Information

Edited by Theresa K. Murray. 600 pages. 1999. 0-7808-0236-5. $78.

Respiratory Diseases & Disorders Sourcebook

Basic Information about Respiratory Diseases and Disorders, Including Asthma, Cystic Fibrosis, Pneumonia, the Common Cold, Influenza, and Others, Featuring Facts about the Respiratory System, Statistical and Demographic Data, Treatments, Self-Help Management Suggestions, and Current Research Initiatives

Edited by Allan R. Cook and Peter D. Dresser. 771 pages. 1995. 0-7808-0037-0. $78.

"Designed for the layperson and for patients and their families coping with respiratory illness. . . . an extensive array of information on diagnosis, treatment, management, and prevention of respiratory illnesses for the general reader."
— Choice, Jun '96

"A highly recommended text for all collections. It is a comforting reminder of the power of knowledge that good books carry between their covers."
— Academic Library Book Review, Spring '96

"This sourcebook offers a comprehensive collection of authoritative information presented in a nontechnical, humanitarian style for patients, families, and caregivers."
— Association of Operating Room Nurses, Sept/Oct '95

Sexually Transmitted Diseases Sourcebook

Basic Information about Herpes, Chlamydia, Gonorrhea, Hepatitis, Nongonoccocal Urethritis, Pelvic Inflammatory Disease, Syphilis, AIDS, and More, Along with Current Data on Treatments and Preventions

Edited by Linda M. Ross. 550 pages. 1997. 0-7808-0217-9. $78.